Perspectives in Neural Computing

Springer

London
Berlin
Heidelberg
New York
Barcelona
Budapest
Hong Kong
Milan
Paris
Santa Clara
Singapore
Tokyo

John A. Bullinaria, David W. Glasspool and
George Houghton (Eds)

4th Neural Computation and Psychology Workshop, London, 9-11 April 1997

Connectionist Representations

Springer

NCPW4

London 1997

John A. Bullinaria, BSc, MSc, PhD
Centre for Speech and Language, Department of Psychology,
Birkbeck College, University of London, Malet Street,
London WC1E 7HX, UK

David W. Glasspool, BSc, Msc
George Houghton, BA, MSc, PhD
Department of Psychology, University College London,
Gower Street, London WC1E 6BT, UK

Series Editor

J.G. Taylor, BA, BSc, MA, PhD, FInstP
Centre for Neural Networks,
Department of Mathematics, Kings College,
Strand, London WC2R 2LS, UK

ISBN 978-3-540-76208-9   ISBN 978-1-4471-1546-5 (eBook)
DOI 10.1007/978-1-4471-1546-5

British Library Cataloguing in Publication Data
A catalogue record for this book is available from the British Library

Library of Congress Cataloging-in-Publication Data
Neural Computation and Psychology Workshop(4th : 1997 : London. England)
   4th Neural Computation and Psychology Workshop : London, 9-11 April 1997 /
   John A. Bullinaria, David W. Glasspool, and George Houghton (Eds.)
      p. cm. – (Perspectives in neural computing)
      Includes bibliographical references.
      ISBN 978-3-540-76208-9 (pbk. : alk. paper)
      1. Neural networks (Computer science) – Psychological aspects – Congresses.
   I. Bullinaria, John A. (John Andrew), 1959–.   II. Glasspool, David W. (David William),
   1965–.   III. Houghton, George, 1957–.   IV. Series
   QA76.87.N4731997   97-33526
   006.3'2- -dc21   CIP

Typesetting: Camera ready by editors

34/3830-543210 Printed on acid-free paper

Preface

This volume collects together refereed versions of twenty-five papers presented at the 4th Neural Computation and Psychology Workshop, held at University College London in April 1997. The "NCPW" workshop series is now well established as a lively forum which brings together researchers from such diverse disciplines as artificial intelligence, mathematics, cognitive science, computer science, neurobiology, philosophy and psychology to discuss their work on connectionist modelling in psychology.

The general theme of this fourth workshop in the series was "Connectionist Representations", a topic which not only attracted participants from all these fields, but from all over the world as well. From the point of view of the conference organisers focusing on representational issues had the advantage that it immediately involved researchers from all branches of neural computation. Being so central both to psychology and to connectionist modelling, it is one area about which everyone in the field has their own strong views, and the diversity and quality of the presentations and, just as importantly, the discussion which followed them, certainly attested to this.

As editors of this volume, the breadth of the workshop's theme has become even more apparent to us, as papers from quite different areas of psychological modelling relate to each other in many different ways. While this leads to some fascinating and unexpected common threads running through different groups of papers, it does of course also make it difficult to separate the papers into coherent sections. We have attempted to divide them into five broad areas, but there is inevitably much overlap between them, and many papers would be equally at home in more than one of these categories. The first section covers general representational issues central to many connectionist models. This is followed by four more specific sections addressing representation in the areas of vision and audition, working memory and attention, lexical/semantic processing, and serial order.

The first few papers of the first section, on *Representational Issues for Connectionist Psychological Models*, explore the ground between representational schemes which are "distributed" on the one hand and those which are "localist" on the other, and thus address themselves straight away to an issue which is at the very heart of representation in connectionist models, and is central to much of the controversy both surrounding and within the field in recent years. Our first paper, by Mike Page, sets the scene for the rest of the section by discussing the distinction between localist and distributed representations and coming to the conclusion that localist representations show more promise than fully distributed approaches for the development of realistic connectionist psychological-level and brain-level models. Neil Middleton then looks at representation in Radial Basis Function (RBF) networks, and shows that it is possible for these networks to develop hybrid localist/distributed representations, demonstrating the continuum of possibilities between the two extremes which can combine the properties of both. This continuum is again addressed by Tulay Yildirim and John Marsland in their paper, where they develop a framework which subsumes both the predominantly localist RBF network and the predominantly distributed Multi-Layer Perceptron (MLP). Their network is able to combine the two approaches and thus position itself on the localist/distributed continuum according to task demands.

Chris Thornton deals with a related continuum in the way automatic learning methods operate – between those which employ boundaries of various sorts to separate meaningful regions in the input data and those which go beyond this to exploit more abstract relationships between input and output. He shows how the concept of geometric separability allows learning problems to be conceptualised along this axis. Elena Pérez-Miñana then shows us how Computational Geometry can be used to guarantee the correct design of an MLP network by making use of the structural knowledge of the input domain. This section ends with a paper by Morten Christiansen that offers support for the idea that learning and generalisation can be improved by forcing a network to learn several related functions. He illustrates the general ideas with a connectionist model of speech segmentation and discusses the implications for language acquisition.

Our next paper, by Geoff Goodhill and Terrence Sejnowski, deals with the comparison and optimisation of topographic mappings. This work could equally well sit in the first section, but since topographic representations are so common in the visual system it provides a useful link into our second section on Representation in Vision and Audition. Peter Hancock, Vicki Bruce and Mike Burton look at principal component representations of faces and investigate the psychological plausibility of these representations by looking at correlations with human perceptions of memorability and similarity. Glyn Humphreys and Dietmar Heinke also consider representations of visual space, and model the neuropsychological syndrome of unilateral neglect. Finally, we move on to auditory representations with a paper by Leslie Smith on the use of auditory modelling techniques to extract features from the short-term time structure of cochlear filtered sound.

Our third section covers the broad area of *Representation in Working Memory and Attention*. Raju Bapi and Michael Denham begin this section with a model of the acquisition of attentional set. The model addresses both the Set-Shifting Paradigm and the Wisconsin Card Sorting Test (WCST), and leads to a specific hypothesised role for Prefrontal Cortex in both the acquisition and the shifting of attentional set. The second paper in this section, by Oury Monchi and John Taylor, again addresses the WCST, this time along with Delayed Response Tasks. Their model is particularly concerned with the establishment of working memories in an architecture heavily constrained by the connectivity of brain areas known to be involved in the tasks. Jacques Sougné and Bob French then present another neurobiologically inspired model, this time of working memory based on neuronal synchrony and rythmicity. Their model makes predictions that have been tested experimentally, with results that seem to challenge modular models of memory. John Taylor then goes on to discuss how neural activity of relatively long temporal duration can come about through the creation of "bubbles" of activity sustained by recurrent connections in a uniform field of neurons, and relates the properties of these bubbles to those which may be required for the emergence of consciousness. The final paper in this section, by Bob French, discusses pseudo-recurrent networks based on the separation of fast learning in the hippocampus and its gradual consolidation in the neocortex. He shows how these models can provide insights into the selective memory loss in aphasic patients of natural semantic categories compared to artificial categories.

This work provides the link into our fourth section on more general *Lexical/Semantic Representations*. Malti Patel, John Bullinaria and Joe Levy begin by arguing that more realistic semantic representations are needed for connectionist models and show how they can be extracted from the word co-occurrence statistics of large text corpora. They also discuss the evaluation of these representations and find that there is more variation across the extraction procedures and evaluation criteria than is commonly assumed. John Bullinaria and Chris Huckle then discuss how such semantic representations can be used in a reasonably realistic connectionist model of a psychological task, namely a model of lexical decision with semantic and associative reaction time priming. Will Lowe then goes on to show how self-organising maps and corpus based representations can be used together to form topographic representations of semantics. These two dimensional representations are intended to correspond to the dimensions of the cortex and can also provide an account of lexical decision semantic priming. Having considered the mono-lingual lexicon, we move on to a study of the bilingual lexicon by Michael Thomas. He explores the possibility of storing representations of words in two languages in a single connectionist network and presents such a model which simulates evidence that is normally taken to indicate independent lexical representations. Finally, Matt Davis, Gareth Gaskell and William Marslen-Wilson consider how it is that one gets from continuous speech into a lexical/semantic representation. They present a connectionist model of lexical segmentation and word recognition that can do this well, including notoriously difficult cases such as onset-embedded words.

Our final section is on various aspects of *The Representation of Serial Order*. The first four papers in this section all relate to models which take a rather similar general approach to the problem of representing serial order in connectionist systems. David Glasspool and George Houghton look at the problem of representing generic constraints on sequential behaviour, such as the constraints on which erroneous outputs may be produced by the speech system and which may not in the light of general rules about phoneme or word order in a particular language. They conclude that the general approach to sequential behaviour taken by these four papers lends itself naturally to the inclusion of such constraints, and identify two basic ways in which they might be implemented. The differences between the models described in these four papers indicate a healthy level of debate in the community, and there is much evidence that this modelling work has reached a level of detail where it is starting to drive experimental work in an attempt to distinguish between alternative possibilities. Rik Henson and Neil Burgess look in some detail at alternative means of representing serial order in connectionist models, and discuss a model which implements the one variant of the one approach which appears viable in the field of short-term memory (STM) in the light of recent data. Janet Vousden and Gordon Brown again look at a variation in this type of model which affects the fit with experimental data - the degree of suppression following the production of a response in a sequence. In this case they show that variation in this parameter in accordance with the demands of two different sequential tasks - speech production and STM - can explain the differences in error patterns between the tasks. In the last paper of this group of four, Dennis Norris and Mike Page describe a connectionist implementation of their established model of short-term memory. In doing so they argue for yet another variation in the representation of order in the same general class of models of serial behaviour, and show how their model dovetails with current connectionist approaches to speech production. We end this section, and this volume, with a paper by Roman Pozarlik which takes a contrasting approach to causal representations and serial operation. He addresses the important problem of representing and processing symbolic information in connectionist systems.

To conclude, we would like to thank all the participants who made the 4th Neural Computation and Psychology Workshop such an exciting and rewarding meeting. We particularly thank all the contributors to this volume for the effort they have put into meeting our very demanding production timescale. We are also appreciative of the work of the peer review panel which consisted of the editors plus Raju Bapi, Gordon Brown, Tony Browne, Morten Christiansen, Matt Davis, Peter Hancock, Samantha Hartley, Tom Hartley, Rik Henson, Joe Levy, Will Lowe, John Marsland, Neil Middleton, Oury Monchi, Mike Page, Malti Patel, Elena Pérez-Miñana, Stuart Rosen, Leslie Smith, John Taylor, Michael Thomas and Janet Vousden. Finally, this volume would not have been possible without the help of John Taylor, the editor of the *Perspectives in Neural Computing* series, and Rosie Kemp, the editor at Springer-Verlag London.

John A. Bullinaria and David W. Glasspool
London, August 1997

Contents

List of Contributors

Raju S. Bapi, Neural & Adaptive Systems Group, School of Computing, University of Plymouth, Plymouth, PL4 8AA, UK. rajubapi@soc.plym.ac.uk

Gordon D. A. Brown, Psychology Department, University of Warwick, Coventry, CV4 7AL, UK. g.d.a.brown@warwick.ac.uk

Viki Bruce, Department of Psychology, University of Stirling, Stirling, FK9 4LA, UK. vb1@forth.stir.ac.uk

John A. Bullinaria, Centre for Speech and Language, Psychology Department, Birkbeck College, Malet Street, London, WC1E 7HX, UK. j.bullinaria@ed.ac.uk

Neil Burgess, Department of Anatomy and Developmental Biology, University College London, Gower Street, London, WC1E 6BT, UK. ucganlb@ucl.ac.uk

Mike Burton, Department of Psychology, University of Glasgow, Glasgow, G12 8RT, UK. mike@psy.gla.ac.uk

Morten H. Christiansen, Program in Neural, Informational and Behavioral Sciences, University of Southern California, Los Angeles, CA 90089-2520, USA. morten@gizmo.usc.edu

Matt H. Davis, Centre for Speech and Language, Psychology Department, Birkbeck College, Malet Street, London, WC1E 7HX, UK. m.davis@psychology.bbk.ac.uk

Michael J. Denham, Neural & Adaptive Systems Group, School of Computing, University of Plymouth, Plymouth, PL4 8AA, UK. mike@soc.plym.ac.uk

Robert M. French, Psychology Department (B32), University of Liege, 4000 Liege, Belgium. rfrench@ulg.ac.be

Gareth Gaskell, Centre for Speech and Language, Psychology Department, Birkbeck College, Malet Street, London, WC1E 7HX, UK. g.gaskell@psychology.bbk.ac.uk

David W. Glasspool, Department of Psychology, University College London, Gower Street, London, WC1E 6BT, UK. d.glasspool@psychol.ucl.ac.uk

Geoffrey J. Goodhill, Georgetown Institute for Cognitive and Computational Sciences Research Building, Georgetown University Medical Center, 3970 Reservoir Road, Washington DC 20007, USA. geoff@salk.edu

Peter Hancock, Department of Psychology, University of Stirling Stirling, FK9 4LA, UK. p.j.b.hancock@psych.stir.ac.uk

Dietmar Heinke, Department of Neuroinformatics, University of Illmenau, Illmenau, Germany.

Rik Henson, Department of Psychology, University College London, Gower Street, London, WC1E 6BT, UK. r.henson@psychol.ucl. ac.uk

George Houghton, Department of Psychology, University College London, Gower Street, London, WC1E 6BT, UK. g.houghton@psychol.ucl.ac.uk

Christopher C. Huckle, Department of Psychology, Edinburgh University, 7 George Square, Edinburgh, EH8 9JZ, UK. c.huckle@ed.ac.uk

Glyn W. Humphreys, Cognitive Science Research Centre, School of Psychology, University of Birmingham, Edgbaston, Birmingham, B15 2TT, UK. g.w.humphreys@bham.ac.uk

Joseph P. Levy, Psychology Department, Birkbeck College, Malet Street, London, WC1E 7HX, UK. j.levy@psyc.bbk.ac.uk

Will Lowe, Centre for Cognitive Science, Edinburgh University, 2 Buccleauch Place, Edinburgh, EH8 9LW, UK. will@cogsci.ed.ac.uk

John S. Marsland, Department of Electrical Engineering and Electronics, The University of Liverpool, Liverpool, L69 3BX, UK. marsland@liverpool.ac.uk

William Marslen-Wilson, MRC Applied Psychology Unit, 15 Chaucer Road, Cambridge, CB2 2EF, UK. william.marslen-wilson@mrc-apu.cam.ac.uk

Neil Middleton, Department of Computer Science, Brunel University, Uxbridge, Middlesex, UB8 3PH, UK. neil.middleton@brunel.ac.uk

Oury Monchi, Centre for Neural Networks, King's College London, Strand, London, WC2R 2LS, UK. omonchi@mth.kcl.ac.uk

Dennis Norris, MRC Applied Psychology Unit, 15 Chaucer Road, Cambridge, CB2 2EF, UK. dennis.norris@mrc-apu.cam.ac.uk

Mike Page, MRC Applied Psychology Unit, 15 Chaucer Road, Cambridge, CB2 2EF, UK. mike.page@mrc-apu.cam.ac.uk

Malti Patel, Department of Computer Science, Macquarie University, Sydney, NSW 2109, Australia. malti@mpce.mq.edu.au

Elena Pérez-Miñana, Department of Artifical Intelligence, University of Edinburgh, 80 Southbridge, Edinburgh, EH1 1HN, UK. elenapm@dai.ed.ac.uk

Roman Pozarlik, Technical University of Wroclaw, Institute of Engineering Cybernetics, Janiszewskiego Str. 11-17, PL 50-370 Wroclaw, Poland. rpoz@pwr.wroc.pl

Terrence J. Sejnowski, The Howard Hughes Medical Institute, The Salk Institute, 0010 North Torrey Pines Road, La Jolla, CA 92037, USA & Department of Biology, University of California San Diego, La Jolla, CA 92037, USA. terry@edu.salk

Leslie S. Smith, Department of Computing Science and Mathematics, University of Stirling, Stirling, FK9 4LA, UK. lss@cs.stir.ac.uk

Jacques Sougne, Department of Psychology (B32), University of Liege, 4000 Liege, Belgium. j.sougne@ulg.ac.be

John G. Taylor, Department of Mathematics, King's College, Strand, London, WC2R 2LS, UK & Institut fur Medizin, Forschungszentrum-Juelich, Juelich, D-52425, Germany. taylor@medicom03.ime.kfa-juelich.de

Chris J. Thornton, Cognitive and Computing Sciences, University of Sussex, Falmer, Brighton, BN1 9QH, UK. christ@cogs.susx.ac.uk

Michael S.C. Thomas, Department of Experimental Psychology, South Parks Road, Oxford, OX1 3UD, UK. michael.thomas@linacre.oxford.ac.uk

Janet I. Vousden, Psychology Department, University of Warwick, Coventry, CV4 7AL, UK. psran@csv.warwick.ac.uk

Tulay Yildirim, Department of Electrical Engineering and Electronics, The University of Liverpool, Liverpool, L69 3BX, UK. t.yildirim@liv.ac.uk

Representational Issues for Connectionist Psychological Models

Some Advantages of Localist over Distributed Representations

Mike Page

Medical Research Council Applied Psychology Unit

Cambridge, U.K.

Abstract

In this paper, I suggest that localist models in psychology have commonly been underestimated relative to their fully-distributed counterparts. I make a clear distinction between the two types of model and address some of the reasons for this popular bias. I conclude that, contrary to conventional wisdom, a localist approach shows more promise than a fully-distributed approach with regard to the development of both psychological-level and brain-level models.

1   Introduction

Over the last decade much connectionist modelling in psychology has employed so-called "distributed models", that is, models in which localist representations play no part. Perhaps as a result of this emphasis, the power and plausibility of localist models have been underestimated. My aim in this paper is to clarify some of the issues over which localists and distributionists have traditionally disagreed and to offer some reasons why I believe the localist approach to be the more promising.

2   Localist and Distributed Representations

A vital first step is to define what is meant by the terms "localist" and "distributed" in the context of connectionist modelling. In doing so I will assume that basic connectionist terms such as "nodes", "activations", "weights" etc. are well known and uncontroversial, their use being common to both types of modelling.

The following definitions, drawn from recent literature, largely capture the difference between localist and distributed representations. First, distributed representations:

> "many neurons participate in the representation of each memory and different representations share neurons" ([1])

To illustrate the point, suppose we wished to represent the four entities "John", "Paul", "George" and "Ringo" with the distributed representations 1100, 0110,

0011, 1001 respectively. Each representation involves a pattern of activation across four nodes and, importantly, there is overlap between the representations. For instance, the first node is active in the patterns representing both John and Ringo, the second node is active in the patterns representing both John and Paul, and so on. The identity of the entity that is currently represented cannot be unambiguously determined by inspecting the state of any single node.

Now consider the contrast with localist representations

> "...with a local representation, activity in individual units can be interpreted directly... with distributed coding individual units cannot be interpreted without knowing the state of other units in the network" ([44]).

As an example of a localist representation of our four entities we might employ the activation patterns 1000, 0100, 0010, 0001. In such representations, a distinct node (or in general a distinct set of nodes) is active for each entity. As as result, activity at a given unit can unambiguously identify the currently represented entity.

While the definitions here are illustrated using binary nodes, the basic distinction extends to circumstances in which nodes can have continuously varying activations. One way in which this might be characterized was suggested by Barlow ([2]):

> "the frequency of neural impulses codes subjective certainty: a high impulse frequency in a given neuron corresponds to a high degree of confidence that the cause of the percept is present in the external world" ([2])

It may be that the significance of activation of a given node is assessed in relation to a threshold value, such that only super-threshold activations are capable of indicating nonzero confidence. Put another way, the function relating activation to "degree of confidence" would not necessarily be linear, or even continuously differentiable, in spite of being monotonic nondecreasing.

2.1 Grandmother Cells

In a discussion of localist and distributed representations it is hard to avoid the subject of "grandmother cells", a modification of a term coined by Jerome Lettvin in 1969 (see Lettvin's appendix to [3]). The term has been used extensively in discussions of neural representation and refers to the assumption that there is a cell in ones brain that responds uniquely to, for instance, your grandmother. Such a notion is, in my experience, deemed by some to be almost comically absurd, thereby demonstrating, without further argument, the folly of the localist approach. Needless to say, I reject such a conclusion for at least two reasons. Firstly, I simply do not find the grandmother cell proposition, even as baldly stated here, obviously absurd. Secondly, while all grandmother cells are necessarily localist representations, not all localist representations are necessarily grandmother cells. For instance, a localist representation of one's grandmother might respond partially, but subthreshold, to a similar entity, thus violating one interpretation of the "unique response" criterion that most often forms part of the grandmother-cell definition.

On a related point, the problem of "yellow Volkswagen cells" raised by Harris ([15]), who feared combinatorial explosion of cell numbers in the case where all possible combinations of adjectives and nouns were to require their own localist representation, is more apparent than real. The problem is finessed if one restricts the number of cells to those required to represent all encountered combinations, or better all combinations "worth remembering", rather than all *possible* combinations.

2.2 Featural Representations

The discussion above, regarding yellow VWs, illustrates the issue of *featural representations*. A featural representation is essentially an array of localist nodes in appropriate states. Thus featural representations of Tony Blair, Glenda Jackson, Anthony Hopkins and Queen Elizabeth II, might be 010, 111, 001, 100, where the relevant features are "is-a-woman", "is-a-politician" and "is/was-a-film-actor". Clearly, the representations of these four entities are distributed, in the sense that the identity of the currently present entity cannot be discerned by examining the activity of any individual node. Nonetheless, the features themselves are locally represented. Whether or not a politician is currently present can be decided by examining the activity of a single node.

Some researchers otherwise committed to the use of fully-distributed networks have been happy to employ such featural representations — localist at one level, distributed at another. For instance, Farah, O'Reilly and Vecera ([10]), in a model of face-to-semantic mapping state:

> "The information encoded by a given unit will be some 'microfeature'. . . that may or may not correspond to an easily labeled feature (such as eye color in the case of faces). The only units for which we have assigned an interpretation are the 'occupation units' within the semantic pool. One of them represents the semantic microfeature 'actor' and the other represents the semantic microfeature 'politician'." ([10])

Such usage rather undermines any in-principle objection to the use of localist representations. If "is-an-actor" is a legitimate "microfeature", then why is "is-Tony-Blair" or "is-my-Grandmother" not? And how are such microfeatures learned prior to the learning of the associative mapping in which they take part?

Whether or not we choose to define featural representations as a subclass of distributed representations, has little to do with the core of the localist/distributed debate. No localist has ever denied the existence of distributed representations, especially, but not exclusively, if these are taken to include featural representations. The key tenet of the localist position is that, on occasion, localist representations of entities in the world (e.g. words, names, people, etc.) allow distributed/featural patterns to be classified and/or associated.

In the remainder of this paper I will show that many of the common criticisms of localist models are without justification, and that fully-distributed models might not be as useful as is generally believed.

3 Generalized Localist Models

In this section I shall describe, in general terms, a localist approach to both the unsupervised learning of representations and to the supervised learning of pattern associations. I will not give details of a particular model since such models have been described in detail elsewhere, including in a companion paper ([32]). In characterizing a localist approach I have sought to generalize from a number of different models (e.g. [6, 8, 7, 28, 30, 37]), which while differing in their details, are similar in structure.

The localist approach is essentially one of hierarchical feature extraction. For example, let us suppose that the image of an old lady falls on the retina — how can we recognize that it is our grandmother? The localist proposes that the highly distributed pattern on the retina is subject to feature extraction at multiple hierarchically structured levels until at some stage there exists a layer of nodes, each of which represents a distinct person and each of which activates to the extent that the constituent features of that person are currently active. There are various options for continued processing. We might assume that at this layer of identity nodes, there is a functional threshold in operation, such that only nodes with super-threshold activation can forward activation on to later layers. Such a threshold might be able to be varied over time so as to accomplish different tasks. For instance, the threshold might be set sufficiently high that only a single identity node will have superthreshold activation, this node thus signalling the presumed identity of the current percept. We can insure that only a single node reaches the recognition threshold by setting the threshold very high at the start of processing, lowering it thereafter until the it is first exceeded by a node activation. Alternatively we can allow the identity nodes to race towards a fixed criterion level of activation, driven by the perceptual evidence for their referents, with the first node to arrive signalling recognition. Once a single node has been activated superthreshold it can proceed to pass activation on to further associated areas, such as those for generating, for instance, semantic or name information about the recognized object.

A number of authors have described mechanisms by which networks can learn to perform the hierarchical processing described above. Many of these have at their basis a two-layer module which is capable of pattern classification. For instance, suppose we have two layers of nodes, such that each node in the upper layer is connected to each node in the lower layer by weighted connections, whose weights are initially small and random. When the activations of the lower-layer nodes are clamped to some activation pattern, the upper-layer nodes will activate to the extent that their incoming weight-vectors match the current input-pattern-vector. Various activation rules are possible but the most usual involves a normalized dot product between the activation and weight vectors. If none of the upper-layer nodes acquires an activation that exceeds a given threshold (as will be the case at the start of learning when no upper-layer nodes have learned to represent anything) then an "uncommitted" upper-layer node will have its weight vector set to the current lower-level activation vector and will thus become "committed". In the case where the activation of an upper layer node exceeds the current threshold, the pattern at the lower-layer will be considered as falling into the pattern class signalled by the identity of that node. In this case the weight-vector of the relevant upper-layer node might be updated so as to move nearer to the current activation vector.

This learning process, by which pattern classes can be constructed from the presentation of individual pattern instances, can be self-organizing and unsupervised. The nature of the pattern-classes formed will be determined by the way in which the threshold varies during training. A high threshold regime will result in more pattern classes than will a low-threshold regime. In the extreme, a high enough threshold will result in each lower-level pattern's being classified by its own upper-level node (i.e. an exemplar model). The operation of such a network is very similar to the ART2A network ([9]).

If supervised learning is required, so that, for instance, a pattern representing a name, and another pattern representing a face, can be enduringly associated, the networks described above can be simply extended. All that is necessary is for two classification networks to be connected "back-to-back". One of the networks classifies the face, resulting in the activation of a single, high-level, face node; the other classifies the name resulting in a single, high-level, name node. The association is then simply learned by strengthening a link between these two nodes (perhaps via some intermediate, modality-nonspecific node). Supervised learning of this type has a number of desirable features: it solves the stability-plasticity dilemma (see [14]), that is, it avoids the catastrophic interference that plagues most, if not all, fully distributed models; it is a self-organizing, "on-line" process; it can be performed under fast learning or slow learning conditions; and it permits piecemeal knowledge acquisition. None of these features is achieved at the expense of being able to learn nonlinearly-separable mappings, such as the XOR mapping.

Contrary to popular belief, networks such as those described above are capable of robust generalization. In the two-layer network, for instance, on presentation of a novel pattern of activation at the lower layer, the activations of the committed upper-layer nodes, whose incoming weights encode patterns of activation encountered in previous experiences, will reflect, in a graded fashion, the degree of similarity that the current input shares with each of those learned patterns. If the current pattern is not sufficiently similar to any learned pattern to evoke super-threshold input, then no generalization will be possible, but to the extent that similarities exist, the network can choose a classification/response on the basis developed above. If no L_2 node receives super-threshold input, yet generalization is required, the threshold can simply be dropped until input is forthcoming.

In a companion paper ([32]), I show how similar localist networks can be shown to be practically equivalent to classical models of stimulus generalization, such as that developed in most detail by Nosofsky (e.g. [31]). Usher and McClelland ([45]) have also shown how similar networks can be used to model the time-course of perceptual choice and in [32] I show how this approach can be extended so as to account for speed-up with practice. Localist networks are also capable ([32]) of modelling the "attractor behaviour" often considered the preserve of more fully distributed models, "categorical perception" ([38, 20]), and effects of age of acquisition (e.g. [26]).

4 Localist Models in Psychology

In spite of the popularity of the fully-distributed modelling approach there are, in fact, numerous, successful models in psychology that are either localist connectionist models, or which can be readily implemented as such. I list some of these in [32] in an attempt to convince the reader that any assertion to the effect that localist models are somehow less powerful as psychological-level models than their fully-distributed counterparts will likely prove unsupportable. Indeed, in cases where localist and fully distributed approaches have been directly compared with reference to their ability to explain data, the localist models have often proved superior (e.g. [41]).

So why are there not more localist connectionist models in psychology? In what follows I cover many of the issues raised by Thorpe ([44]) in relation to common arguments used against localist models.

5 Why Are Localist Models Not More Widely Used

5.1 "They don't generalize"

The fact that fully distributed networks can generalize is sometimes taken to imply that localist networks cannot. As noted above, and in more detail in [32], this is not the case.

5.2 "They are not efficient"

It is certainly true, as observed by Hinton, McClelland and Rumelhart ([16]), that certain associative mappings can be achieved, using fully distributed networks, with far fewer hidden units than are used by the corresponding localist network. In this restricted sense the distributed networks are more efficient. Nevertheless, it is very questionable whether this type of efficiency is worth having if the process by which the mapping must be learned is not only grossly inefficient but also rather implausible — this point relates to the later discussion of catastrophic interference.

5.3 "They do not degrade gracefully"

Fully distributed networks are often said to degrade gracefully, in that they continue to perform well after damage, usually considered as loss of nodes. Since even localist networks employ distributed/featural representations at their "lower" levels, they inherit most of this ability to degrade gracefully. Even at the levels at which representation is local there is nothing in the localist approach that precludes some redundancy in the representation of a given entity. For instance, a given entity might be represented by a number of localist nodes (N.B. this does not make the representation distributed) such that the loss of any one of these representations will not be of critical importance.

5.4 "There are not enough neurons in the brain and/or they are too noisy"

Most estimates put the number of cells in the brain at around 10^{11}. Mountcastle ([27]) estimates the number of cells in the neocortex alone as being approximately 3×10^{10}. Even if one considers the number of cortical minicolumns rather than cells, the number is in the region of 10^8. Similarly, Rolls ([36]) cites a figure of 6×10^6 cells in area CA1 of the hippocampus, an area he proposes is responsible for the storage of episodic memories. (Allowing 10 cells per episode, this number represents a capacity equivalent to one memorable episode every 5 waking minutes for about 9 years.) These are large numbers and I suggest they place the burden of proof on those who wish to claim that they are not large enough to enable successful local coding.

With regard to "neural noise", I follow [44] in citing Newsome, Britten and Movshon ([29]) and, hence, Britten, Shadlen, Newsome and Movshon ([4]), who measured the activity of relevant MT cortex neurons while a monkey performed a psychophysical discrimination task. They found that the "performance" of certain individual neurons, assessed by placing a discriminant threshold on their activity, was just as good as the performance of the monkey. In other words the monkey possessed no more information than could be derived from the activity of single cells.

5.5 "No one has ever found a grandmother cell"

This common objection is written here as usually phrased, although given the discussion earlier it should be clear that the nonexistence in the brain of grandmother cells, as most strictly defined, would not necessarily imply the nonexistence of localist representations. Whether or not grandmother cells have been found is a moot point. For instance, Young and Yamane ([46]) measured activity from a cell that responded uniquely to one of the 27 face stimuli that they presented. The cell was the only one of 850 tested cells to behave in such a stimulus-specific manner. Nonetheless, when one considers the small stimulus set, and the huge number of cells out of which the 850 were chosen, the probability of locating even a single stimulus-specific cell is likely to be very small. The finding of localist representations, or at least of data consistent with their existence, is more common. Many studies have found fields of cells each of which responds with a different strength to different stimuli from a common domain. This pattern of results has often been considered evidence for a "population coding", though it is perfectly consistent with the localist models described earlier. Miyashita and colleagues (e.g. [17, 25, 39, 40]) have gone furthest in investigating the responses to complex visual patterns of cells from primate IT cortex. They have located cells in inferotemporal cortex whose response peaks on presentation of one of a set of recently learned, visually-presented geometric patterns - small parametric variations of the learned patterns always elicit a weaker response. Moreover, they have located other cells which respond selectively to both patterns in an associated pair. Their data offer convincing evidence in favour of the localist hypothesis.

6 Why Not Use Distributed Representations Throughout?

Having offered a number of reasons why localist models might be more effective than is often assumed, I now turn briefly to a number of reasons why fully distributed networks might be less effective than is often assumed. I shall use as an example of a fully distributed network the 3-layer perceptron trained by backpropagation of error (BP).

6.1 The Stability-Plasticity Dilemma a.k.a. Catastrophic Interference

Grossberg ([14]) has proposed in principle reasons why BP networks exhibit unstable learning. McCloskey and Cohen ([22]) identified the same problem in a simulation of association learning and coined the term "catastrophic interference". Essentially the same phenomenon was noted by Ratcliff ([35]). There has been a good deal of work on the subject since (e.g. [12, 13, 19, 24, 28, 42, 43]), but a general solution to the problem has remained elusive. One proposal advanced by McClelland, McNaughton and O'Reilly ([21]), seeks to mitigate the effects of catastrophic interference on learning in vivo by suggesting a dual-store, fast/slow system which they identify with the hippocampal/neocortical brain systems. In [32], I have identified potential problems with the particular solution proposed, which detract from its plausibility as a brain mechanism.

6.2 Implausibility of the Learning Rules

The learning rules associated with fully distributed networks are often implausible as models of brain function. In the case of the BP algorithm this is often freely admitted even by its proponents. This has not stopped the network from being applied to the modelling of data from patients with brain lesions etc. One is perhaps entitled to ask why a network that has been trained with a nonbrain-like learning rule is a fitting subject for a brain-like lesion. The usual response is that the precise nature of the learning rule is largely irrelevant to investigations of the effects of damage to the learned network. This response is rarely justified, however. One might have thought that the localist/distributed debate itself argued against such a response, by illustrating how the choice of learning rule can have a profound effects on the structure of the learned network, and thus, presumably, on the effects of subsequent damage.

6.3 Problems of Interpretation

Fully distributed networks are very much more difficult to interpret than their localist counterparts — it is often very difficult to explain how a distributed network performs a given mapping task. This is a distinct problem for such models qua explanatory theories. For excellent discussions of this point see [23, 18, 11, 34].

6.4 Problems of Manipulation

It sometimes proves difficult to manipulate distributed representations in the same way as one can manipulate localist representations. As an example, in most models of immediate serial recall (e.g. [5, 33]) it proves necessary to suppress the recall of items that have already been recalled. If the items are locally represented then such suppression can easily be achieved by suppressing the activation of the relevant node. If, however, the items are represented in a distributed fashion, such that the representations of different items overlap, it is difficult to suppress one item without partially suppressing others.

7 Conclusion

In this article I have sought to identify the crucial difference between localist and fully-distributed modelling. I have briefly described a class of localist models and have detailed some of their properties. I have offered counterarguments to some commonly voiced objections to localist modelling and, in turn, have reviewed some objections to fully distributed models, most of which remain unanswered. I conclude that localist models ought to be taken seriously as models of psychological and brain function.

Author Notes

I would like to thank Dennis Norris, Rik Henson, John Duncan, Ian Nimmo-Smith and Andy Young for their invaluable assistance in the work described here. I would also like to thank two anonymous reviewers and John Bullinaria for their comments on an earlier draft.

All correspondence and requests for reprints should be sent to Mike Page, M.R.C. Applied Psychology Unit, 15, Chaucer Rd., Cambridge, CB2 2EF, U.K. (mike.page@mrc-apu.cam.ac.uk)

References

[1] Amit D. J. The Hebbian paradigm reintegrated: Local reverberations as internal representations. Behavioural and Brain Sciences, 1995, 18:617–657.

[2] Barlow H. Single units and sensation: A neuron doctrine for perceptual psychology. Perception, 1972, 1:371–394.

[3] Barlow H. The neuron doctrine in perception. In Gazzaniga M. S., editor, The Cognitive Neurosciences, 1995, pages 415–434. MIT Press, Cambridge, MA.

[4] Britten K. H., Shadlen M. N., Newsome W. T., and Movshon J. A. The analysis of visual motion: A comparison of neuronal and psychophysical performance. The Journal of Neuroscience, 1992, 12(12):4745–4765.

[5] Burgess N. and Hitch G. J. Towards a network model of the articulatory loop. Journal of Memory and Language, 1992, 31:429–460.

[6] Burton A. M. Learning new faces in an interactive activation and competition model. Visual Cognition, 1994, 1(2/3):313–348.

[7] Carpenter G. A. and Grossberg S. ART2: Stable self-organizationof pattern recognition codes for analog input patterns. Applied Optics, 1987, 26:4919–4930.

[8] Carpenter G. A. and Grossberg S. A massively parallel architecture for a self-organizing neural pattern recognition machine. Computer Vision, Graphics and Image Processing, 1987, 37:54–115.

[9] Carpenter G. A., Grossberg S., and Rosen D. B. ART 2-A: An adaptive resonance algorithm for rapid category learning and recognition. Neural Networks, 1991, 4(4):493–504.

[10] Farah M. J., O'Reilly R. C., and Vecera S. P. Dissociated overt and covert recognition as an emergent property of a lesioned neural network. Psychological Review, 1993, 100(4):571–588.

[11] Forster K. I. Computational modeling and elementary process analysis in visual word recognition. Journal of Experimental Psychology: Human Perception and Performance, 1994, 20(6):1292–1310.

[12] French R. M. Using semi-distributed representations to overcome catastrophic interference in connectionist networks. In Proceedings of the Thirteenth Annual Conference of the Cognitive Science Society, 1991, pages 173–178, Hillsdale, NJ. Lawrence Erlbaum.

[13] French R. M. Dynamically constraining connectionist networks to produce orthogonal, distributed representations to reduce catastrophic interference. In Proceedings of the Sixteenth Annual Conference of the Cognitive Science Society, 1994, pages 335–340, Hillsdale, NJ. Lawrence Erlbaum.

[14] Grossberg S. Competitive learning: from interactive activation to adaptive resonance. Cognitive Science, 1987, 11:23–63.

[15] Harris C. S. Insight or out of sight: Two examples of perceptual plasticity in the human adult. In Harris C. S., editor, Visual Coding and Adaptability, 1980, pages 95–149. Erlbaum Associates, Hillsdale, NJ.

[16] Hinton G. E., McClelland J. L., and Rumelhart D. E. Distributed representations. In Rumelhart D. E., McClelland J. L., and PDP Research Group, editors, Parallel Distributed Processing: Explorations in the Microstructure of Cognition, 1986, volume 1. Foundations, pages 77–109. MIT Press, Cambridge, MA.

[17] Hoguchi S.-I. and Miyashita Y. Formation of mnemonic neural responses to visual paired ssociates in inferotemporal cortex is impaired by perirhinal and entorhinal lesions. Proceedings of the National Academy of Sciences, 1996, 93:739–743.

[18] Jacobs A. M. and Grainger J. Models of visual word recognition—sampling the state of the art. Journal of Experimental Psychology: Human Perception and Performance, 1994, 20(6):1311–1334.

[19] Lewandowsky S. Gradual unlearning and catastrophic interference: A comparison of distributed architectures. In Hockley W. E. and Lewandowsky S., editors, Relating Theory and Data: Essays on Human Memory on Honor of Bennet B. Murdock, 1991. Lawrence Erlbaum Associates, Hillsdale, NJ.

[20] Massaro D. W. Categorical partition: A fuzzy logical model of categorization behavior. In Harnad S., editor, Categorical Perception: The Groundwork of Cognition, 1987, pages 254–283. Cambridge University Press, New York.

[21] McClelland J. L., McNaughton B. L., and O'Reilly R. C. Why are there compementary learning systems in the hippocampus and neocortex: Insights from the successes and failures of connectionist models of learning and memory. Psychological Review, 1995, 102(3):419–457.

[22] McCloskey M. and Cohen N. J. Catastrophic interference in connectionist networks: The sequential learning problem. In Bower G., editor, The Psychology of Learning and Motivation, 1989, volume 24, pages 109–165. Academic Press, New York.

[23] McCloskey M. Networks and theories. Psychological Science, 1991, 2(6):387–395.

[24] McLaren I. P. L. Catastrophic interference is eliminated in pretrained networks. In Proceedings of the Fifteenth Annual Conference of the Cognitive Science Society, 1993, pages 723–728, Hillsdale, NJ. Erlbaum.

[25] Miyashita Y. Inferior temporal cortex: Where visual perception meets memory. Annual Review of Neuroscience, 1993, 16:245–263.

[26] Morrison C. M. and Ellis A. W. Roles of word frequency and age of acquisition in word naming and lexical decision. Journal of Experimental Psychology: Learning, Memory and Cognition, 1995, 21(1):116–133.

[27] Mountcastle V. B. The columnar organization of the neocortex. Brain, 1997, 120:701–722.

[28] Murre J. M. J. Learning and Categorization in Modular Neural Networks, 1992. Harvester Wheatsheaf, Hertfordshire, UK.

[29] Newsome W. T., Britten K. H., and Movshon J. A. Neuronal correlates of a perceptual decision. Nature, 1989, 341:52–54.

[30] Nigrin A. L. Neural Networks for Pattern Recognition, 1993. MIT Press, Cambridge, MA.

[31] Nosofsky R. M. Attention, similarity and the identification-categorization relationship. Journal of Experimental Psychology: Learning, Memory and Cognition, 1986, 115(1):39–57.

[32] Page M. P. A. Connectionist modelling in psychology: A localist manifesto. submitted to Behavioral and Brain Sciences, 1997.

[33] Page M. P. A. and Norris D. The primacy model: A new model of immediate serial recall. submitted to Psychological Review, 1995.

[34] Ramsey W. Do connectionist representations earn their explanatory keep. Mind and Language, 1997, 12(1):34–66.

[35] Ratcliff R. Connectionist models of recognition memory: Constraints imposed by learning and forgetting functions. Psychological Review, 1990, 97:285–308.

[36] Rolls E. T. Parallel distributed processing in the brain: Implications of the functional architecture of neuronal networks in the hippocampus. In Morris R. G. M., editor, Parallel Distributed Processing: Implications for Psychology and Neurobiology, 1989. Oxford University Press, Oxford, UK.

[37] Rumelhart D. E. and Zipser D. Feature discovery by competitive learning. In Rumelhart D. E., L.McClelland J., and the PDP Research Group, editors, Parallel Distributed Processing: Explorations in the Microstructure of Cognition, 1986, volume 1. Foundations, pages 151–193. MIT Press, Cambridge, MA.

[38] S. Harnad (Ed.). Categorical Perception: The Groundwork of Cognition, 1987. Cambridge University Press, New York.

[39] Sakai K. and Miyashita Y. Neural organization for the long-term memory of paired associates. Nature, 1991, 354:152–155.

[40] Sakai K., Naya Y., and Miyashita Y. Neuronal tuning and associative mechanisms in form representation. Learning and Memory, 1994, 1:83–105.

[41] Shanks D. R. and Darby R. J. Connectionist models of categorization and generalization. In Dienes Z., editor, Connectionism and Human Learning, in press. Oxford University Press, Oxford.

[42] Sharkey N. E. and Sharkey A. J. C. An analysis of catastrophic interference. Connection Science, 1995, 7(3/4):301–329.

[43] Sloman S. A. and Rumelhart D. E. Reducing interference in distributed memories through episodic gating. In Healy A. S., Kosslyn S., and Shiffrin R., editors, From Learning Theory to Cognitive Processes: Essays in Honor of William K. Estes, 1992. Lawrence Erlbaum Associates, Hillsdale, NJ.

[44] Thorpe S. Localized versus distributed representations. In Arbib M. A., editor, The Handbook of Brain Theory and Neural Networks, 1995, pages 549–552. MIT Press, Cambridge, MA.

[45] Usher M. and McClelland J. L. On the time course of perceptual choice: A model based on principles of neural computation. Technical Report PDP.CNS.95.5, Dept. of Psychology, Carnegie Mellon University, December 1995.

[46] Young M. P. and Yamane S. Sparse population coding of faces in the inferotemporal cortex. Science, May 1992, 256:1327–1331.

Distributed Representations in Radial Basis Function Networks

Neil Middleton
Brunel University

Abstract

This chapter locates Gaussian radial basis function (RBF) networks within the school of connectionist modelling that has successfully exploited the properties of multi layer perceptrons (MLPs). In particular, the highly regarded use of distributed representations in MLPs is established in RBF networks. RBF networks have been used to learn a categorization task, and the way in which the networks have learned the task is interpreted in terms of localist and distributed representations. The problem of catastrophic forgetting as a psychologically implausible feature of MLPs, and an undesirable property of neural network engineering systems, is also reconsidered.

1 Introduction

MLPs have been successfully used to model aspects of psychology [1][2]. RBF networks are functionally equivalent with MLPs and have the same universal approximation properties [3]. So RBF networks are able to learn whatever an MLP can learn, in theory at least. Given that both networks can learn a particular task, the way in which the networks learn the task can be compared for psychological plausibility.

RBF networks have been used as exemplar models of molar level human categorization performance [4], and as multiple view models of visual object recognition [5]. RBF networks have two major advantages over MLPs for modelling psychology. They are able to pay attention to input dimensions, and are less prone to catastrophic forgetting than are MLPs. The first property is due to the use of a diagonal inverse RBF covariance matrix; and the second property is due to the closed nature of the decision boundaries formed by RBF hidden units. These properties are described in section 2.

This chapter first describes RBF networks, picking out those properties described above that are of importance for connectionist modelling. Following this, experimental results are presented in which RBF networks learn a simple categorization task from distorted prototypes. The networks are found to exhibit the ubiquitous prototype effects that are a minimal requirement for psychological plausibility. Finally, the way in which the networks learn the task is interpreted in terms of localist and distributed representations.

2 Radial Basis Function Networks

RBF networks are functionally equivalent to MLPs as both are feed-forward networks, usually having a single hidden layer. Typically, a hidden unit in an MLP computes the sigmoid function of the dot product of the input vector and the weight vector to that hidden unit, while an RBF hidden unit computes the Gaussian of the Euclidean distance between the input vector and the centre vector of that unit.

The RBF network architecture is shown in Figure 1. The centre vector **c** can be interpreted as the weight vector to a hidden unit. The output layer activation function is chosen according to the network task [6].

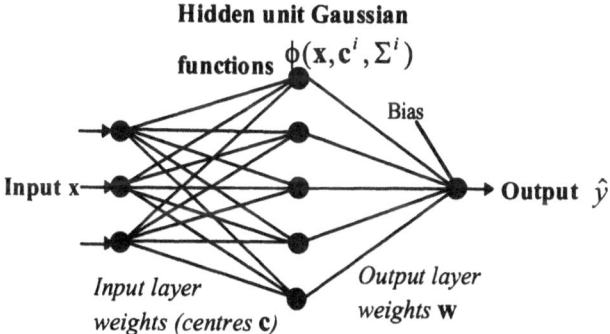

Figure 1. Radial basis function network architecture.

The centre vector together with the covariance matrix Σ determine the position and shape of a Gaussian RBF's receptive field. A one-dimensional Gaussian is shown in Figure 2.

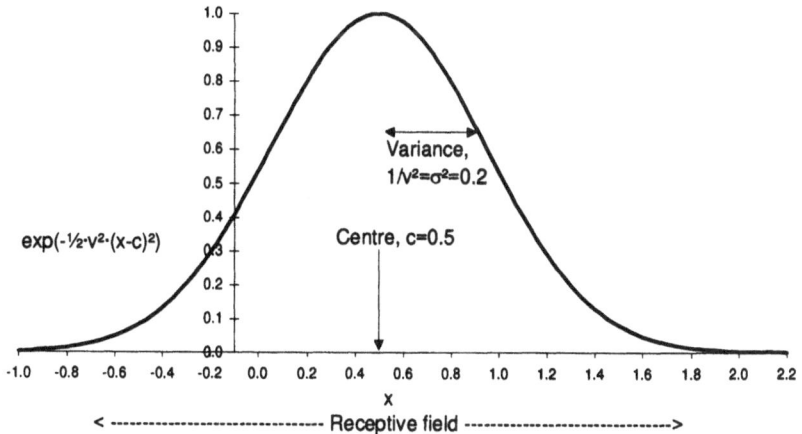

Figure 2. The Gaussian receptive field.

If the inverse covariance matrix is approximated by its main diagonal then it can be decomposed as the square of a diagonal norm weighting matrix

$$\Sigma^{i^{-1}} = diag(\mathbf{v}^i)^T diag(\mathbf{v}^i) \tag{1}$$

where $\mathbf{v}$ is the vector of the diagonal elements of the norm weighting matrix. The elements of $\mathbf{v}$ are referred to as the norm weights. The square of a norm weight is the reciprocal of the variance along that dimension, as shown in Figure 2.

The network output is given by

$$\hat{y}(\mathbf{x}) = \sum_{i=1}^{N} w_i \exp\left[-\tfrac{1}{2} \sum_{j=1}^{P} v_j^{i\,2}(x_j - c_j^i)^2 \right] \tag{2}$$

where there are P inputs and N hidden units.

If a norm weight is zero then the corresponding input line is ignored. A nonzero norm weight indicates the attention strength along the corresponding input. With a diagonal covariance matrix the network is only able to pay attention to individual orthogonal dimensions.

The output of the Gaussian function is greatest when its argument is zero. A Gaussian RBF unit therefore has maximal output of one when the input matches the centre vector. If the input pattern differs from the centre then the output is one only if the norm weights along the differing dimensions are zero.

2.1 Standard and Generalized RBF Networks

In the original form RBF networks had one hidden unit to store each example training pattern [7]. The norm weights are computed so as to avoid overlap of RBF receptive fields. In this case, with fixed centres and norm weights, learning a mapping between the inputs and outputs involves linear optimization of the weights on connections to the output layer. Such networks behave much like a look-up table, and can be called localist networks because each hidden unit can be interpreted as standing for a training pattern. When an input pattern matches a training pattern, a single hidden unit has maximum output.

If the norm weight along each dimension is decreased at some RBFs, the receptive fields will overlap, and the network will form a distributed representation by employing an extended, and possibly superposed representation on its hidden layer. In this case the network retains its localist status by representing training patterns at the RBF centre vectors, but now represents the mapping in a distributed fashion.

In the generalized form an RBF network has fewer RBF hidden units than there are training patterns [8]. In order to learn the training patterns all of the network parameters have to be adapted thus changing the position and shape of the RBF receptive fields. Given fewer resources, the network may be better able to generalize as it is forced to model the underlying function that generated the training data, rather than modelling the individual training examples.

Optimization of network parameters requires a tradeoff between the bias and the variance of the model. The model is biased if it does not fit the training data closely enough. The variance of the model is high if the network overfits the data, or models noise in the data. The bias and variance tradeoff in generalized RBF networks is determined by placing the centres so as to be close to large numbers of training inputs, while the norm weights should ensure that the relevant part of the input space is covered. If the norm weights are large, the model fits the data points closely, but if the norm weights are too small the model becomes over-biased.

Avoiding significant overlap of RBF receptive fields prevents interference between patterns. This interference is one cause of catastrophic forgetting in MLPs in which the learning of a single new pattern can cause the network to forget all previously learned patterns. The problem of catastrophic forgetting is therefore closely related to the tradeoff between the bias and the variance, and to the shape of decision surfaces, as illustrated in the following section.

2.2 Decision Surfaces

The most significant and interesting difference between RBF networks and MLPs is the nature of the decision surfaces in each of the networks. The decision surfaces are determined by the receptive field characteristics, which in turn indicate the source of the problem of catastrophic forgetting.

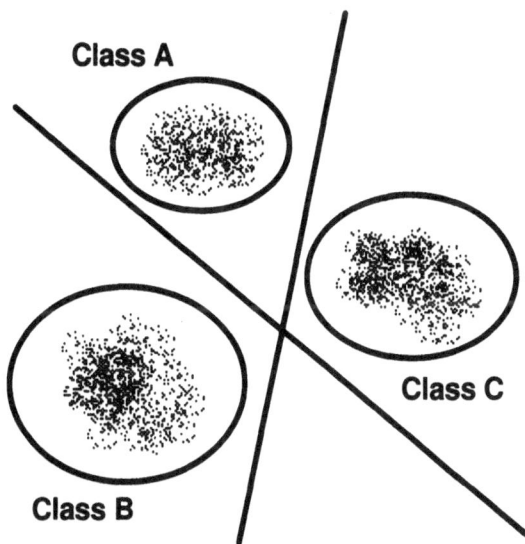

Figure 3. Network decision surfaces.

Figure 3 shows three natural classes of input data in an input space. An RBF network can model the data using one RBF to fit each cluster, and the decision boundaries are the ellipses in the figure. If an input is inside one of the closed decision boundaries, then the corresponding RBF is on. If the variance along each input dimension, for all RBFs, is sufficiently small then only one RBF will have a significant output[1] in response to an input. In this case the decision boundaries can be chosen so as not to overlap.

---

[1] Gaussian functions have infinite support but the residual output is ignored here.

MLPs model the boundaries between classes, shown as two straight lines in Figure 3. In general, each MLP hidden unit has a hyperplanar decision surface, and that hidden unit is on if the pattern is one side of the hyperplane, and off otherwise. Each hidden unit can have a significant response to patterns from two clusters. An MLP is therefore likely to form distributed representations on its hidden layer.

The RBF network is less likely to suffer from catastrophic forgetting precisely because the network resources used to learn one contiguous cluster of patterns are not required for learning another.

3 Dynamics of Learning in RBF Networks

With pattern-update gradient descent supervised training, RBF network dynamics are such that each element of the centre and norm weighting matrix at hidden unit i is updated according to the following equations.

$$\frac{dc_j^i}{dt} = -\mu_2 \left(x_j - c_j^i\right) v_j^{i^2} \phi_i \frac{\partial E}{\partial a} w_i \tag{3}$$

$$\frac{dv_j^i}{dt} = \mu_3 \left(x_j - c_j^i\right)^2 v_j^i \phi_i \frac{\partial E}{\partial a} w_i \tag{4}$$

E is a suitable error function, and a is the argument of the output unit activation function. The μs are learning rates, and the presentation of a single pattern represents a time step.

The stable points with respect to time are at zero norm weights, and at the mean of input vectors within the receptive field of the unit, where over the training set

$$\left(x_j - c_j^i\right) = 0 \tag{5}$$

A hidden unit learns to ignore patterns that are too far away from its centre, and to pay attention to features of the input by ignoring dimensions.

For a fixed input vector the centres and norm weights are coupled since (ignoring the superscript i)

$$\frac{1}{\mu_2} \frac{d\left(x_j - c_j\right)^2}{dt} = \frac{1}{\mu_3} \frac{d(v_j)^2}{dt} \tag{6}$$

This says that with appropriate learning rates the network does indeed compute the covariance matrix with respect to the centre at each RBF. Each RBF is independent, so network initialization must ensure that the RBFs do not converge to the global mean and covariances.

In some of the experiments that follow, the centre vectors have been initialized with small random values to break network symmetry. Also, some parameters remain fixed by using zero learning rates. The network dynamics are potentially analysable in terms of equation (6), although this analysis is not reported here.

4 A Categorization Task

An RBF network was trained on distorted versions of three binary prototype patterns as shown in Figure 4. Connectionist modelling of human performance on this sort of task has a long history [9], and this task has been used to illustrate the properties of RBF networks rather than to advance human categorization theory.

In Figure 4 the black filled cells represent one and white represent zero. For each of the three prototypes, each bit was flipped (0→1, or 1→0) resulting in nine distorted, or noisy, patterns from each prototype, and 27 training patterns in total.

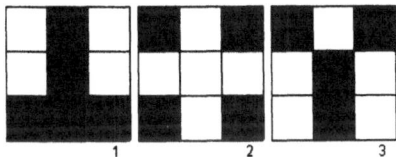

Figure 4. Prototype patterns.

An initial analysis of the prototypes revealed that they are linearly separable, as are the distorted patterns. Also, input 2 is one only in response to prototype 1, thus providing definitive information, or a cue, for classification of prototype 1. The initial hypothesis was that the network would learn to pay attention to definitive information, and also learn to ignore the constant inputs 4 and 6.

4.1 Localist Representations

A network was constructed as a standard RBF network with 27 hidden units, each with a centre as one of the training patterns. The norm weights for each of the nine inputs were set to various values so that the receptive fields had varying amounts of overlap. The network was then trained to assign each training pattern to the correct class using a 1-of-3 softmax output layer activation function. Network training involved adapting the weights to the output layer using gradient descent with momentum. As expected, the network learns the distorted patterns, and generalizes to treat the undistorted patterns correctly.

Figure 5 shows the percentage of training and test patterns correctly classified after a fixed amount of training, for various fixed norm weights. As the norm weight increases the network overfits the training patterns. In this case all of the training patterns are classified correctly but none of the test patterns is correctly classified. With a small norm weight all of the RBFs have large receptive fields and therefore a significant response to all of the training and test patterns. The third of patterns correctly classified is determined by the random placement of the bias to the output units.

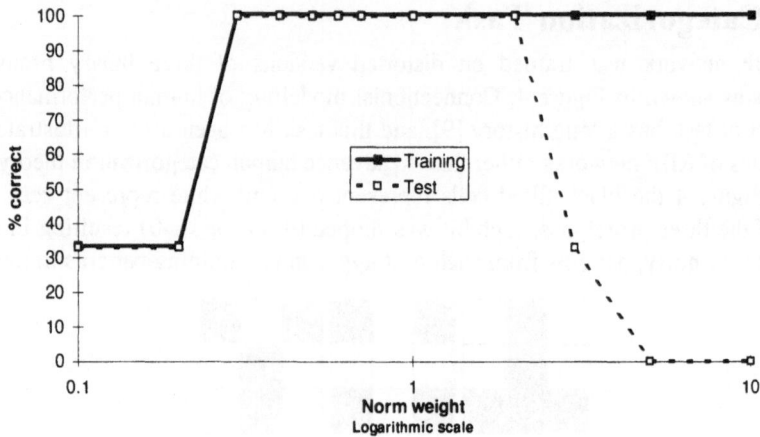

Figure 5. Overfitting in standard RBF networks.

4.2 Distributed Representations

A generalized RBF network was constructed with two RBFs. The centres were initialized with small random values, uniformly distributed between 0 and 0.01. The diagonal elements of the norm weighting matrix were initialized at 1.0 as this produced good performance in the standard RBF network.

The network could not learn the task with fixed centres and norm weights, so firstly the norm weights were adapted using gradient descent with momentum. Following training to 100% correct performance on the training and test data, the network had the following norm weights, Figure 6.

In the following diagrams of norm weights, the network has nine inputs, and these are arranged as a 3 x 3 grid, indexed by column, then row so that the top left element is 1, and the bottom right is 9. The area of the grid cell shaded black is proportional to the magnitude of the norm weight divided by the largest norm weight over all RBFs. Negative norm weights are cross hatched.

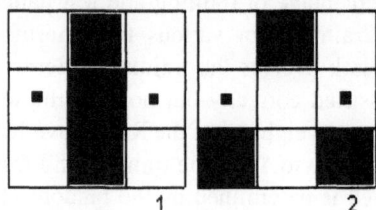

Figure 6. Norm weights (maximum was 1.340).

The norm weights show how the RBFs pay attention to 3-bit features in the input space. The network did not pay attention to definitive information about prototype 1, but did ignore constant inputs (4 and 6).

Next, a network was initialized as above, but the centre vectors were adapted while the norm weights remained fixed at 1.0. After training to 100% correct performance the network had the following centres, Figure 7. Negative values are hatched.

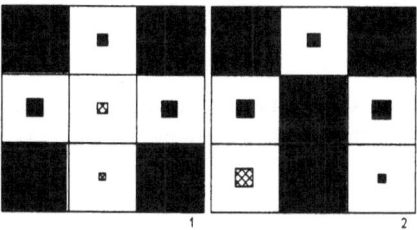

Figure 7. Centre vectors (maximum 1.000).

The network has extracted two of the prototypes as centres. Since the norm weights were fixed at 1.0, each RBF pays attention to all input dimensions, and the network therefore performs template matching.

Finally, the centres and the norm weights were all adapted as were the weights and the network learned the following structure, Figure 8.

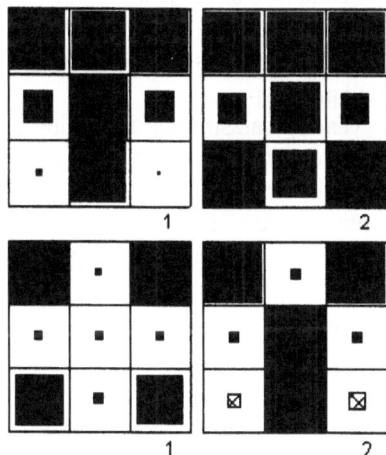

Figure 8. Norms (top, maximum 1.140) and centres (maximum 1.030).

The network has again extracted two of the prototypes as centre vectors, but now ignores some of the inputs. In particular, two of the inputs (7 and 9) in centre 1 are ignored so that this RBF acts as a feature detector rather than a template matcher.

5 Localist and Distributed Representations Together?

RBF networks pay attention to areas of input space determined by their centre vectors. They also pay attention to individual dimensions in the input space determined by their norm weights. The RBF network is therefore able to model both template or exemplar based accounts of categorization, and feature based accounts.

What sort of representations did the networks learn?

A representation can be described as localist if there is a set of network parameters that can be interpreted as representing an object, at a suitable level of analysis. If a single hidden unit responds to each prototype and its distortions, then with the hidden unit as the unit of analysis the network mapping is a localist representation.

Within a range of norm weights (determined by the Euclidean distance between patterns) it was shown how the standard RBF network behaves as a localist network at the hidden unit level.

Van Gelder presents a definition of distributed representations in terms of distributing transformations [10]. A connectionist representation is distributed if the activation of any hidden unit varies as a function of the activation of every input unit. The output of each RBF hidden unit is indeed a function of each input unit, as required for distributed representations. However, if a hidden unit ignores an input line, the resulting representation can be described as partially distributed.

The network in which all parameters were adapted extracted prototypes, but also ignored part of those prototypes. The network can be said to learn a hybrid localist and distributed representation of the mapping between the input and output patterns. The representation is distributed since the output of each of the hidden units is a function of all of the input units, but localist because the centres can be interpreted as the undistorted prototypes.

Finally, one way of preventing catastrophic forgetting in MLPs is to make the hidden layer representations less distributed [11]. It has been shown how RBF networks' hidden layer representations can be made more distributed by increasing the overlap of RBF receptive fields. This can improve generalization, as the network is better able to interpolate between training patterns. The closed nature of RBF receptive fields restricts the resources used to represent the patterns, and therefore prevents excessive interference.

6 Conclusion

It has been shown how RBF networks form the distributed representations that are highly regarded in MLPs [12]. Furthermore, the way in which the networks ignore areas of input space and individual dimensions of that space has implications for modelling human categorization processes.

Further work is required to establish that the results are not dependent on the particular set of prototype patterns that were used here.

Acknowledgement

This work was supported by the Engineering and Physical Sciences Research Council, UK.

References

1. Rumelhart DE, McClelland JL: On learning the past tenses of English verbs. In Parallel Distributed Processing: Explorations in the Microstructure of Cognition, Vol. 2, Rumelhart DE, McClelland JL (Eds). MIT Press, Cambridge, Mass, 1986, pp 216-271

2. Plunkett K, Marchman V: U-shaped learning and frequency effects in a multi-layered perceptron: Implications for child development. Cognition 1991, 38: 1-60

3. Park J, Sandberg PK. Universal approximation using radial-basis-function networks. Neural Computation 1991, 3: 246-257

4. Kruschke JK. ALCOVE: an exemplar-based connectionist model of category learning. Psychological Review 1992, 99: 22-44

5. Poggio T, Edelman S. A network that learns to recognize three dimensional objects. Nature (London) 1990, 343: 263-266

6. Bishop CM. Neural networks for pattern recognition. Clarendon Press, Oxford, 1995

7. Moody JE, Darken CJ. Fast learning in networks of locally tuned processing units. Neural Computation 1989, 1: 281-294

8. Poggio T, Girosi F. Networks for approximation and learning. Proceedings of the IEEE 1990, 78: 1481-1497

9. Knapp AG, Anderson JA. Theory of categorization based on distributed memory storage. Journal of Experimental Psychology: Learning, Memory and Cognition 1984, 10: 616-637

10. Van Gelder T. Defining 'distributed representation'. Connection Science 1992, 4(3 & 4): 175-191

11. French RM. Using semi-distributed representations to overcome catastrophic forgetting in connectionist networks. CRCC TR 51-1991, 1991

12. Clark A. Associative Engines: Connectionism, Concepts, and Representational Change. MIT Press, Cambridge, Mass, 1993

A unified framework for connectionist models

T.Yıldırım

Yıldız Technical University

Türkiye

J.S.Marsland

University of Liverpool

UK

Abstract

A novel connectionist neural network model based on a propagation rule which contains Multilayer Perceptron (MLP) and Radial Basis Function (RBF) parts is introduced in this paper. The network using this propagation rule is known as a Conic Section Function Network (CSFN). Two different strategies have been used for training the network. The contact lens fitting problem has been considered to demonstrate the performance of the training algorithms. The performances of a standard MLP trained by back propagation, a fast back propagation with adapted learning rates, a standard RBFN using Matlab Neural Network software toolbox, and the proposed algorithm are compared for this particular problem.

1 Introduction

Artificial neural networks may be categorized in many different ways and for some purposes such as classification and neurocontrol the differentiation between local and global representation is useful. Network representation is global if one or more of the network weights can affect the network output for any and every point in the input space whereas local representation occurs in networks for which only a few weights affect the network output response for points within a local region of the input space. MLPs are examples of globally representing networks and global representation results in problems of slow learning and network wide learning interference. RBF networks are examples of localized ones. [1]

Classification with neural networks can often be conveniently described in geometric terms. If the inputs presented from two classes are separable, that is if they lie on opposite sides of some hyperplane, then the perceptron convergence procedure will be successful and positions the decision hyperplane between those two classes. Some hyperplane decision boundaries in weight space are shown in Fig.1(a). MLPs with one or more hidden layers are used to classify non-separable classes. Another type of decision region is the localized one such as bounded hyperspherical (e.g. circular) decision regions. Differing from hyperplanar (open) decision regions which cover an infinite portion of the input space, the receptive field of each unit is local and restricted to only a small region in input space. Fig.1(b) illustrates hyperspherical (closed) decision regions.

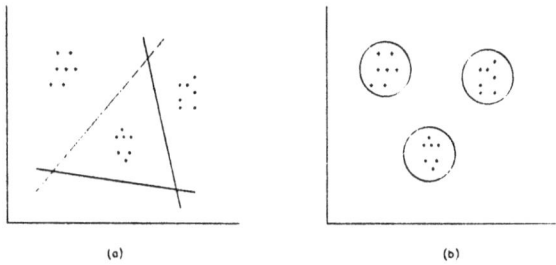

Figure 1: (a)Hyperplanar and (b) hyperspherical decision regions

The conic section function network (CSFN), first described by Dorffner [2], is a novel neural network model based on the observation that both hyperplane and hypersphere are special cases of conic section functions. These are the decision boundaries of MLP and RBF, respectively. There would be intermediate types of decision boundaries such as ellipses, hyperbolas or parabolas in between those two cases which are also valid for decision regions. The main idea of the use of CSFN is to generalize the function of a unit to include all these decision regions in one network, providing a relationship between an MLP and an RBF unit. The CSFN is capable of making automatic decisions with respect to open (hyperplane) and closed (hypersphere) decision regions and can use these regions wherever appropriate, depending on the data distribution of a given application.

There are many advantages arising from the conic section function network training algorithm presented here. It combines the error-minimization of back propagation with speed of hyperspherical networks so that learning is faster than MLP. It is more efficient than standard RBF for problems with higher dimensional inputs. The number of RBF hidden nodes increases exponentially with the input space dimensionality so that RBF is time-consuming if the number of inputs is large. In this case, MLP is preferred to RBF but CSFN is better than either alternative.

2   Conic sections

Conic sections are the shapes obtained when a right circular cone, which has its vertex above the centre of its base, is cut along a plane at various angles to the cone's axes. In other words, the conic sections are formed from the intersection between a cone and a plane. Mathematically, conic sections are all variations of one basic shape.

The possible sections of a right circular cone with a plane are illustrated in Fig.2, which gives the intersection curves, forming ellipses, parabolas, and hyperbolas respectively. There are also circles, which can be considered as a special case of ellipses where the cutting plane is perpendicular to the axis of cone shown in Fig.2.

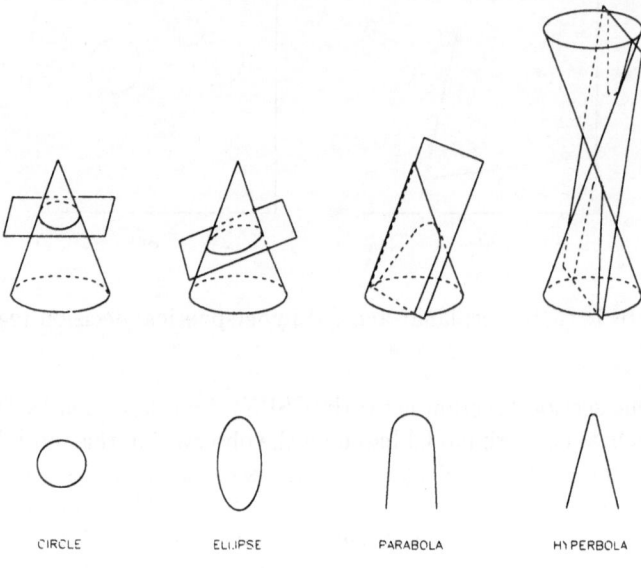

Figure 2: Plane sections of a cone

More formally, conic sections are the loci of points in a plane where the ratio of the distance from a fixed point (the focus) to a fixed line (the directrix) is a constant. The shape of the curve is determined by this ratio, which is called the eccentricity and is denoted by e. If $0 < e < 1$, the conic section is an ellipse. If e=1, it is a parabola and if $e > 1$, it is a hyperbola. Fig.3 shows the conic sections with variable eccentricity.

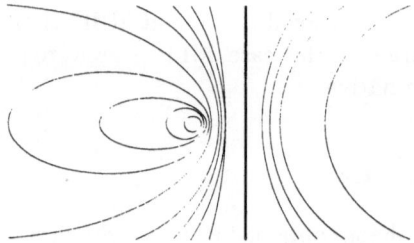

Figure 3: Conic sections with variable eccentricity

The definition of the curves can also be expressed by angles. Let α be the angle between the axis of a right circular cone and its element (the generating lines) and θ be the (smaller) angle formed by the axis of the cone and the cutting plane, and let d be the distance from the vertex of the cone to the cutting plane. The relation of α and θ defines the shape of the curve. d affects the scaling or size of the curve, except when d=0 (degenerate conics case). The magnitude of d is proportional to the size of the curve. The following cases are formed:

If $\theta < \alpha$, hyperbola; and if d = 0, two non-parallel lines.

If $\theta = \alpha$, parabola; and if d = 0, a line.

If $\theta > \alpha$, ellipse; and if d = 0, a point.

3 Conic Section Function Network

The idea of the conic section function neural network is to provide a unification between RBF and MLP networks. The new propagation rule (which will consist of RBF and MLP propagation rules) can be derived using analytical equations for a cone. Let x be any point on the surface of the right circular cone. ω can be any value in the range $[-\pi/2, \pi/2]$, v vertex of the cone and a the unity vector defining the axis of the cone. Thus the equation of the circular cone is

$$(\vec{x} - \vec{v})\vec{a} = cos\omega \parallel \vec{x} - \vec{v} \parallel \tag{1}$$

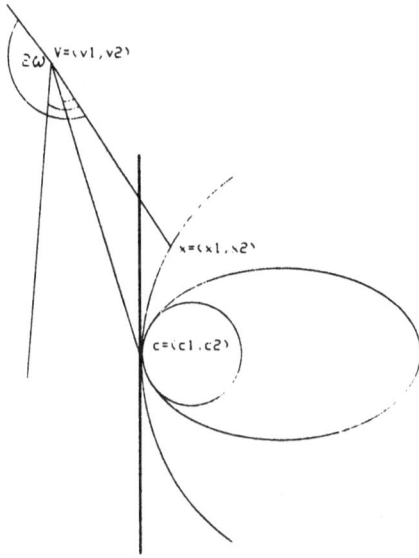

Figure 4: Three different cones with vertex V and opening angle 2ω intersecting by an input plane forming variable decision boundaries - a circle, an ellipse, a parabola, and a straight line.

Fig.4 shows a three-dimensional cone with vertex v and opening angle 2ω intersected by a plane forming a circle, an ellipse, a parabola, and a straight line by varying the opening angle 2ω in two-dimensional space. The angle changes depending on how high the vertex is. In this figure, straight line (hyperplane) and circle (hypersphere) represent the decision borders for MLP and RBF, respectively. Other type of decision borders, such as ellipses and parabolas, represent the intermediate functions. If the coordinates of the points and vectors are defined by x=(x1,x2), v=(v1,v2) and a=(a1,a2) for two dimensional space, Eq.1 can be written as below

$$(x_1 - v_1)a_1 + (x_2 - v_2)a_2 = cos\omega\sqrt{(x_1 - v_1)^2 + (x_2 - v_2)^2} \qquad (2)$$

The propagation rule of the conic section function network is described using Eq.2. First of all, the following form is obtained for n-dimensional input space.

$$\sum_{i=1}^{n+1}(x_i - v_i)a_i = cos\omega\sqrt{\sum_{i=1}^{n+1}(x_i - v_i)^2} \qquad (3)$$

This form gives the equation for the intersection between the cone and the input space if the coordinate system is set such that n dimensions are identical to the n dimensions of the input space by setting $x_{n+1} \equiv 0$. The centre coordinate of the circle c can be used instead of the coordinate of vertex v since the distance between the x point and the vertex v equals to the radius of the circle when the opening angle, 2ω, is 90 degrees. Subtracting the right hand side from the left hand side, the propagation rule of the CSFN is obtained as

$$y_j = \sum_{i=1}^{n+1}(x_i - c_{ij})a_{ij} - cos\omega_j\sqrt{\sum_{i=1}^{n+1}(x_i - c_{ij})^2} \qquad (4)$$

where a_{ij} refers to the weights (w_{ij}) for each connection between the input and hidden layer units in an MLP network, and c_{ij} refers to the centre coordinates in an RBF network, i and j are the indices referring to the units in the input and hidden layer, respectively, and y_j are the activation values of the CSFN neurons. As can be seen easily, this equation consists of two major parts analogous to the MLP and the RBF. The equation simply turns into the propagation rule of an MLP network, which is the dot product (weighted sum) when the ω is $\pi/2$. The second part of the equation gives the Euclidean distance between the inputs and the centres for an RBF network. Fig.5 illustrates the structure of a Conic Section Function Network.

4 Conic Section Function Neural Network Training

The main learning process involves the determination of the centres and updating weights, centres, and the vertex angle of cone, ω, appropriately.

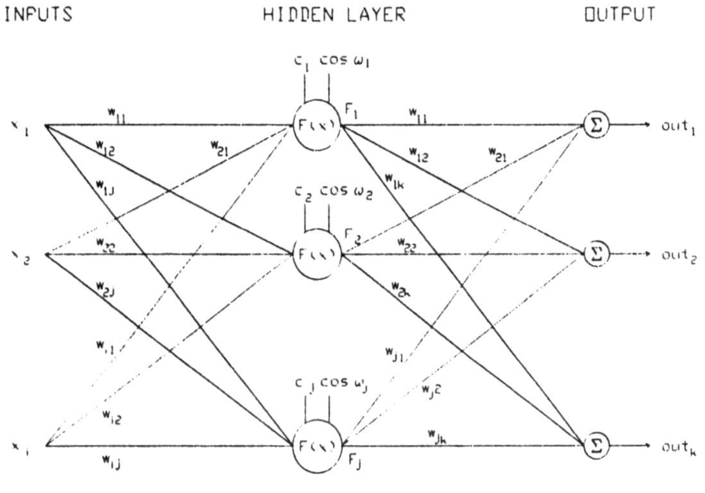

INPUTS   HIDDEN LAYER   OUTPUT

Figure 5: Conic Section Function Network

The centres are determined using the orthogonal least squares (OLS) learning algorithm [3] which is based on choosing radial basis function centres one by one in a rational way until an adequate network has been constructed. The OLS method is a recursive algorithm for selecting a suitable subset of data points as radial basis function centres. The OLS algorithm is used for selecting and optimally locating a minimal number of hidden neurons to avoid oversize problems which occur frequently when the centres are randomly selected. The problem of how to select a suitable set of RBF centres from the data set can be regarded as an example of how to select a subset of significant regressors from a given candidate set. The training starts with no hidden units. New hidden units are added to the network at each step of the procedure until the desired error level is reached [3], [5] or in this work, until the required number of hidden units is reached. The weights from input layer to hidden layer are set to 0. The weights from hidden layer to output layer are initially produced using the output of the hidden layer and the training data by applying a linear function. The vertex angle is chosen in such a way that the network would start as RBF. Then, the weights, centres and angle values are updated using error back propagation so that the network converges quickly. The terms and the connections used in the training algorithm are basically shown in Fig.6.

4.1   Optimisation of The Parameters

Activation function of the Conic Section Function Network (CSFN) can be expressed as follows

$$y_{pj} = \sum_{i=1}^{n+1}(a_{pi} - c_{ij})w_{ij} - cos\omega_j\sqrt{\sum_{i=1}^{n+1}(a_{pi} - c_{ij})^2} \qquad (5)$$

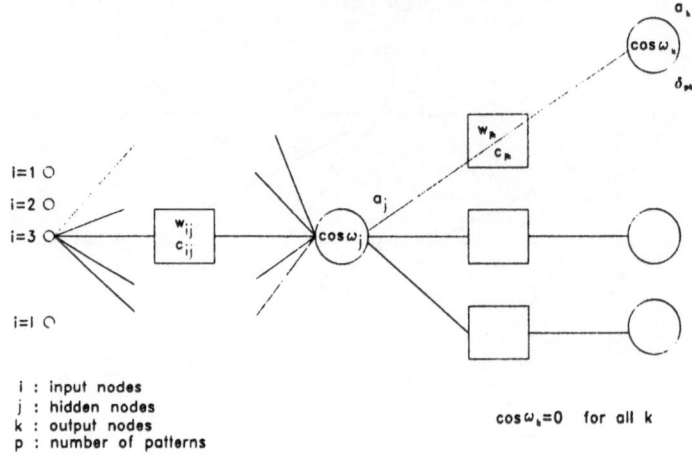

i : input nodes
j : hidden nodes
k : output nodes
p : number of patterns

$\cos \omega_k = 0$ for all k

Figure 6: Block diagram of CSFN for training

where $a_{pi} = x_{pi}$ if unit i is an input unit, c_{ij} are the centres for the RBF network, w_{ij} are the weights in an MLP, ω is the half opening angle, which can be any value in the range $[-\pi/2, \pi/2]$ and determines the different forms of the decision borders, i and j are the indices referring to units in the input and the hidden layer and p refers to the number of the patterns. In the work presented here the output layer has weights only and no RBF contribution. The general formula for delta learning weight adjustment for a single layer network and the chain rule is applied [4]. Assuming a unipolar activation function, the weight update is expressed for hidden layer units as follows

$$\Delta_p w_{ij} = \eta a_{pj}(1 - a_{pj}).A.(a_{pi} - c_{ij}) \tag{6}$$

where η is the learning rate and for the output units as:

$$\Delta_p w_{ij} = \eta \delta_{pj}(a_{pi} - c_{ij}) = \eta a_{pj}(1 - a_{pj})(d_{pj} - apj)(a_{pi} - c_{ij}) \tag{7}$$

where

$$\sum_k \frac{\partial E_p}{\partial y_{pk}} \cdot \frac{\partial y_{pk}}{\partial a_{pj}} = -\sum_k \delta_{pk}[w_{ik} - cos\omega.\frac{a_i - c_i}{\| a - c_j \|}] = A \tag{8}$$

The same procedure as in adapting weights is applied for updating the centres.

$$\Delta_p c_{ij} \propto -\frac{\partial E_p}{\partial c_{ij}} \tag{9}$$

The centre update for hidden layer units can be written as

$$\Delta_p c_{ij} \propto -a_{pj}.A.(w_{ik} + cos\omega.\frac{a_i - c_i}{\| a_p - c_j \|}) \tag{10}$$

The centres in the output layer are not adapted since cos = 0 for all k, output nodes. The rule to update the opening angle is described by

$$\Delta_p \omega_j \propto -\frac{\partial E_p}{\partial \omega_j} \tag{11}$$

The angle update is given for the hidden layer units by

$$\Delta_p \omega_j \propto a_{pj}(1 - a_{pj}).A.sin\omega_j \parallel a_p - c_j \parallel \tag{12}$$

4.2 Summary of The Basic Training Algorithm

The training algorithm has two phases: 1) a network initialization phase with centre placement (Phase A) and 2) an error back propagation phase (Phase B or C).

Phase A (network initialization and centre placement phase):

Step A1: The number of centres and Sum-Squared Error (SSE) chosen. First layer weights are set to zero and the opening angle, ω is started from $\pi/4$, which initializes the network as an RBF.

Step A2 : Training step starts here. A new centre is determined from the input set using orthogonal least squares algorithm. The output of the hidden layer is computed and used with the training set to initialize the output layer weights. The output of the second layer is computed.

Step A3 : Sum-Squared Error is calculated.

Step A4 : Steps A2 and A3 are repeated for the required number of centres.

Phase B (error back propagation phase):

Step B1 : The error signal vectors δ , of both layers are calculated.

Step B2 : Output layer weights are adjusted by the back propagation algorithm.

Step B3 : Hidden layer weights, centres and opening angle ω are updated.

Step B4 : The outputs of the layers are calculated.

Step B5 : New SSE is computed. If this is larger than the error goal, go to step B1, otherwise, terminate the training session.

4.3 Methods For Training

Two different algorithms for training the CSFN are proposed in this work. The first algorithm is based on updating the weights, the centres, and the opening angle in the same epoch as described above. The second algorithm uses the same Phase A (network initialization and placement of centres) but differs in the second phase as follows:

Phase C (error back propagation for the second algorithm):

Step C1 : A predetermined number of training epochs (i.e. Phase B) is executed but only weights are updated; centres and angles are not changed.

Step C2 : One training epoch is executed where only the opening angles are adjusted; weights and centres remain same.

Step C3 : Another training epoch is performed to update the centres; weights and angles are not changed.

The Sum-Squared Error is computed after every training epoch. If the network output reaches the error goal, then training is stopped, otherwise, the algorithm is repeated from first step.

5 Lens Fitting Problem

The database for fitting contact lenses [6] has been used as an application to test the training algorithm for conic section function network. The data set contains three classes where each class refers to the type of contact lenses with which the patient should be fitted. A training set and a test set were formed using 24 samples. The training set contains 16 patterns, 3 from first two classes, and 10 from third class. The remaining 8 patterns have been used to test the training algorithm. The target vectors were (0.9, 0.1, 0.1), (0.1, 0.9, 0.1) and (0.1, 0.1, 0.9).

The first algorithm with no centre update needs 76 training epochs to reach the error goal of 1 for 6 centres. It needs 87 training epochs with centre update to reach the same error goal for the same number of centres.

Fig.7 and 8 show the results for 4 and 7 centres with different learning rates. The results are dependent on the learning rate. The number of training epochs decreases by the increment of learning rate, and the network has an unstable behaviour for 7 centres with learning rate = 0.09.

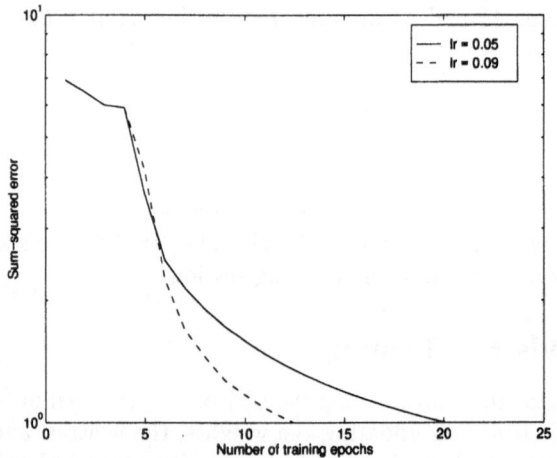

Figure 7: Results for 4 centres (first 4 epochs are OLS)

Fig.9 shows the effect of the learning rate for 5 centres. Fig.10 illustrates how the number of centres affects the training time. The learning rate was 0.05. The network has best convergence for 5 centres.

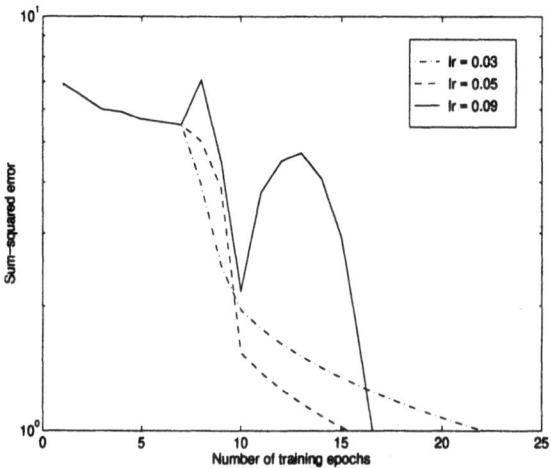

Figure 8: Results for 7 centres (first 7 epochs are OLS)

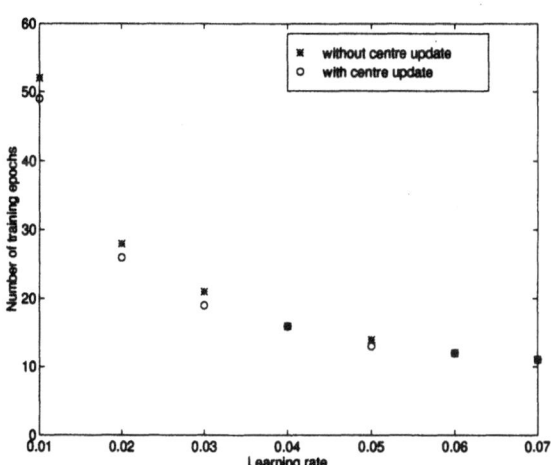

Figure 9: The effect of the learning rate (for 5 centres)

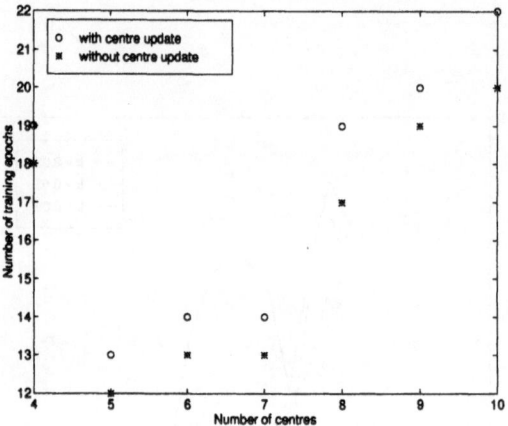

Figure 10: The effect of the number of centres (lr=0.05)

5.1 The effect of the width

The effect of the width in RBF part of the algorithm was also investigated for the lens fitting problem. Fig.11 shows the results when the width is equal to 1 with learning rates, 0.05 and 0.02. Fig.12 illustrates the effect of the width on the training time. 5 centres have been used to obtain the results and the learning rate is 0.5 for Fig.12. The network converges quicker when the width is smaller, but it is not very stable. It converges slowly but smoothly for the larger value of the width.

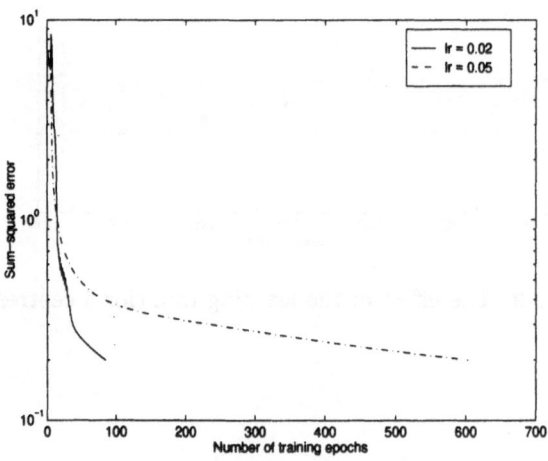

Figure 11: Results for width=1 with 5 centres

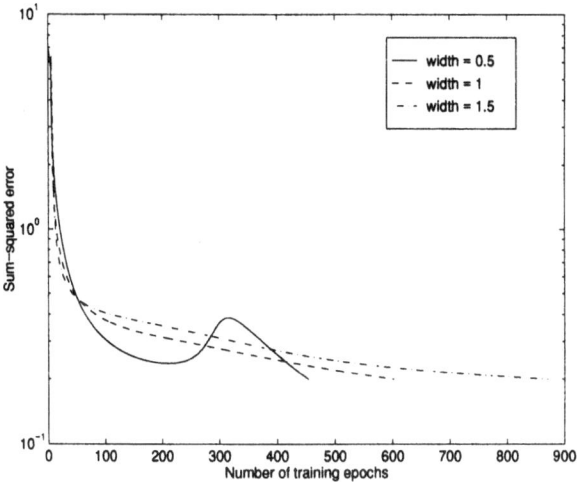

Figure 12: The effects of the width (lr=0.05)

5.2 Back propagation and fast back propagation algorithms results

Back propagation and fast back propagation algorithms are applied to the lens fitting problem to compare the results. Fig.13 shows back propagation results for 5 and 7 hidden nodes.

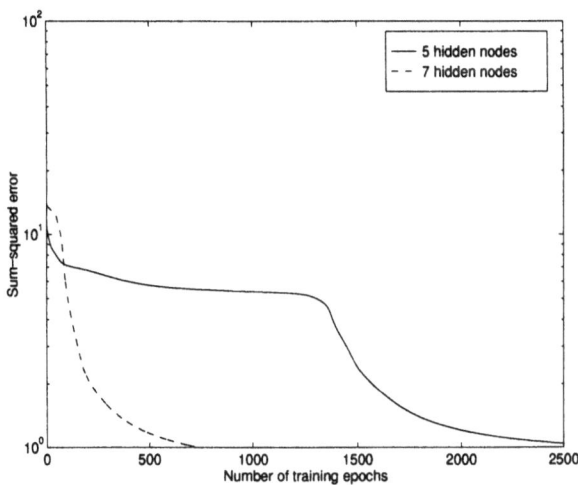

Figure 13: Back propagation results for 5 and 7 hidden nodes (lr=0.05)

Fig.14 shows the results for the back propagation algorithm with 7 hidden nodes with learning rates, 0.05 and 0.09.

The performance of the back propagation and fast back propagation algo-

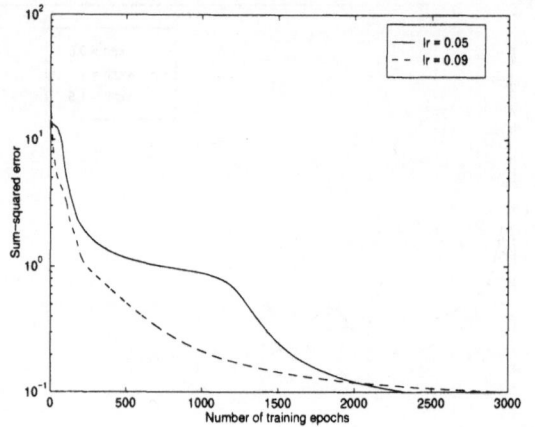

Figure 14: Back propagation results with different learning rates for 7 hidden nodes

rithm are strongly dependent on the random initialization. There was sometimes no separation between the classes even though the same error goal has been reached. For example the fast back propagation algorithm was trained to an error goal of 1 with three different random initializations. The learning rate was 0.05 and there were 5 hidden nodes. The first of these three trials could only classify five of the eight test patterns correctly. The second trial classified seven correctly; the eight output vector was (0.38, 0.46, 0.22) for a target of (0.1, 0.9, 0.1). The third trial was completely successful.

5.3 RBF result

The lens fitting problem was applied to the standard RBF algorithm in MATLAB. The training procedure requires 6 centres to be placed when the error goal is 1 and 10 centres for the error goal, 0.1, whereas, the CSFN algorithm will train successfully with as few as 4 centres for an error goal of 1.

6 Discussion

This work was concerned with the use of conic section functions which contain RBF and MLP parts to improve the back propagation training algorithm which is one of the standard methods used for the training of multilayer neural networks. It reduces the number of centres needed for an RBF (4 rather than 6) and the hidden nodes for an MLP (4 rather than 5 or more). Furthermore, it converges to a determined error goal at lower training epochs than an MLP (less than 22 rather than 700 or more). The results show that the introduced algorithm here is much better than the others in most cases, in terms of not only training epochs but also the number of hidden units and centres since the decision boundaries can match the real data more closely. This algorithm is much faster and more stable than a standard MLP trained with back propagation or adaptive back propagation which can be unstable due to random initialization. It also needs less centres than standard RBF.

References

[1] Warwick K, Irwin GW, and Hunt KJ, Neural networks for control and systems, Peter Peregrinus Ltd., London, UK, 1992.

[2] Dorffner G, Unified framework for MLPs and RBFNs: Introducing conic section function networks, Cybernetics and Systems, 1994, Vol.25 pp.511-554.

[3] Chen S, Cowan CFN, Grant PM, Orthogonal least squares learning algorithm for radial basis function networks, IEEE Transactions on Neural Networks, March 1991, Vol.2, No.2, pp.302-309.

[4] Rumelhart DE, Hinton GE, Williams RJ, Learning internal representations by error propagation, in Parallel Distributed Processing, ed. D.E.Rumelhart and J.L.McClelland, Cambridge, MA:MIT Press, 1987, Vol.1, pp.318-362.

[5] Haykin S, Neural Networks: A comprehensive foundation, Macmillan College Publishing, New York, 1994.

[6] Cendrowska J, PRISM: An algorithm for inaucing modular rules, International Journal of Man-Machine Studies, 1987, Vol.27, pp.349-370.

Separability is a Learner's Best Friend

Chris Thornton

Cognitive and Computing Sciences

University of Sussex

Brighton

BN1 9QH

UK

Abstract

Geometric separability is a generalisation of linear separability, familiar to many from Minsky and Papert's analysis of the Perceptron learning method. The concept forms a novel dimension along which to conceptualise learning methods. The present paper shows how geometric separability can be defined and demonstrates that it accurately predicts the performance of a at least one empirical learning method.

1 Separability

Given the 'spatial' way in which we tend to conceptualise the process of learning, it is not surprising to discover that many learning methods operate on a distinctively 'geometric' basis. Implicitly or explicitly, their aim is to divide the input-space up into regions such that all the points in a given region map onto the same output-space point. We expect this approach to achieve good generalisation since, once a region has been identified in which all the known points map onto the same output, it seems safe to assume that *most* points in that region will map onto the same output. We also expect it to achieve good storage performance since, once we have identified the regions and associated output-points we can throw away the original data.

But these region- or boundary-oriented methods all make a rather strong assumption about the input data and the underlying task. They assume, in effect, that the function is 'smooth' [1] and that input points with the same target output will therefore tend to cluster together in the same region of the input space. Unfortunately, this assumption turns out to be valid only in certain situations. In other situations, it is totally invalid.

The general idea that **boundary methods** have severe limitations is familiar to the Cognitive Science community via the work of Minsky and Papert

[2, 3] on the Perceptron learning method. The Perceptron is a neural-network method which, in its simplest manifestation, attempts to acquire a target function using the simplest boundary method of all. Making the assumption that there are just two points in the output space, it tries to find a single, *linear* boundary which separates all the input points associated with one of the outputs from points associated with the other. The primitive nature of the operation paves the way for excellent performance. But it also imposes dire limitations. Only in certain types of task will we find the points mapping onto one output neatly separated by a line boundary from the points mapping onto the other. In other tasks the points will be dispersed in a more complex fashion. Thus the Perceptron method is only effective in certain cases.

Minsky and Papert described tasks which could be handled using the Perceptron method as 'linearly separable.' They pointed out that many tasks which we might consider to be straightforward, such as deciding on whether two binary values are the same — the so-called 'parity' task — do not fall into the linearly separable category. This led many researchers to turn their backs on the perceptron method and on neural network methods in general. In hindsight, however, we can see that there is no reason to 'take it out' on the Perceptron. The Perceptron method is a special-purpose member in a special-purpose class of methods. First and foremost, it is a boundary method and therefore assumes that the input/output function is smooth (points with similar outputs cluster together). Second, it is a method which assumes that just one linear boundary will do the trick. It makes a particularly strong assumption about the data. But when that assumption is valid it operates in a very efficient way.

Minsky and Papert focussed primarily on the Perceptron and related architectures. But their separability result is easily generalised to other learning methods. All boundary methods operate on the assumption that the target function is smooth and that the target function can therefore be acquired by placing boundaries around regions of uniform[1] input points. Thus these methods effectively assume that the data exhibit 'regional' or *geometric* separability and are only effective when that particularly type of separability actually exists within the relevant data.

But this concept of *geometric separability* differs from that of linear separability in an important way. Linear separability is a boolean property. A particular task either *is* or *is not* linearly separable. Geometric separability, on the other hand, is a continuous property. Provided we are allowed to make regions arbitrarily small — small enough to enclose a single input point — then *all* tasks are geometrically separable in the limit, since we can represent any function in terms of some set of point-sized, regions. Thus the issue is not whether a task exhibits geometric separability but the degree to which it does so, i.e., the degree to which regions of uniform input points can be identified.

Geometric separability, then, is a measure of the degree to which inputs associated with the same output cluster together. As this property increases,

---

[1]Uniform in the sense of having the same target output.

we see an increase in the frequency with which nearest-neighbours in the input space share the same output, and vice versa. Thus a convenient way of measuring geometric separability — and one which does not necessitate making any restrictive assumptions about the 'shape' of the regions that will be utilised — is in terms of the proportion of nearest-neighbour inputs in the function which share the same output.

We therefore define the *Geometric Separability Index* or *GSI* for a given task f to be the proportion of nearest neighbour inputs which share the same output:

$$GSI(f) = \frac{\sum_{i=1}^{n} f(x_i) + f(x_i') + 1 \bmod 2}{n}$$

Here, f is a binary target function, x is the data set, x_i' is the nearest neighbour of x_i and n is the total number of data. The nearest neighbour function is assumed to utilise a suitable metric, e.g., a Manhalobis metric for symbolic data or a Euclidean metric for spatial data.

The GSI generalises Minsky and Papert's linear-separability concept to the general case of boundary methods. Although it is not a boolean measure (i.e., a predicate) it can be viewed, like the linear-separability concept, as differentiating tasks which are appropriate for a particular learning strategy. The strategy in this case is boundary-making. If the GSI for a particular task is high, boundary-making methods are effective. If it is low, they are not.

2 Geometric separability of common tasks

A satisfying property of the GSI is the fact that it is zero for all parity problems such as the notorious 'XOR' problem which featured prominently in Minsky and Papert's analysis. In a parity problem, a single increment or decrement of any input variable flips the output (classification) from positive to negative, or vice versa. Thus, in the input space, points associated with one output always appear next to points with the opposite output. Nearest neighbours always have opposite outputs and the geometric separability of a parity problem is necessarily zero.

This is, of course, exactly what we would expect. Minsky and Papert showed that Perceptrons could not learn parity functions. The Perceptron is a simple boundary method. Boundary methods produce poor performance when geometric separability is low. The geometric separability of any parity problem is zero. Thus, Perceptron's should not be able to learn parity problems. In fact, any boundary method tends to produce poor performance on parity problems [4].

But what about other common learning problems? Do frequently used learning problems such as those which reside in the UCI repository[2], tend to have high, low, or indifferent geometric separability? To investigate this issue,

---

[2]http://www.ics.uci.edu/&learn/MLRepository.html

the geometric separability of all 16 'frequently used datasets' (as featured in the Holte [5] study) was tested. The results are shown in Table 1.

Dataset	BC	CH	GL	G2	HD	HE	HO	HY
GSI	0.67	0.91	0.73	0.82	0.76	0.62	0.77	0.98
C4.5	0.72	0.99	0.63	0.74	0.74	0.81	0.84	0.99
Dataset	IR	LA	LY	MU	SE	SO	VO	V1
GSI	0.94	0.95	0.77	1.00	0.93	1.00	0.93	0.88
C4.5	0.94	0.77	0.77	1.00	0.98	0.98	0.96	0.89

Table 1: Comparison of GSIs with C4.5 generalisation rate on Holte datasets.

The GSI for each dataset is shown in the first cell of each column. The second cell shows the error rate on the same dataset as reported by Holte for the C4.5 decision tree learner, one of the best performing of all empirical learning methods. A striking feature of the results is that the GSI for half of these datasets (CH, MY, IR, LA, MU, SE, SO, VO,) is extremely high, i.e., greater than 0.9. The implication is that these datasets are rich in geometric separability and thus highly suitable for processing by boundary methods. A second striking feature is the fact that the GSI turns out to predict the performance of C4.5 reasonably well. The average difference between the GSI for a dataset and the corresponding mean generalisation rate reported by Holte is 0.056, i.e., slightly under 6 percentage points. The correspondence between GSI and C4.5 generalisation rates is illustrated graphically in Figure 1.

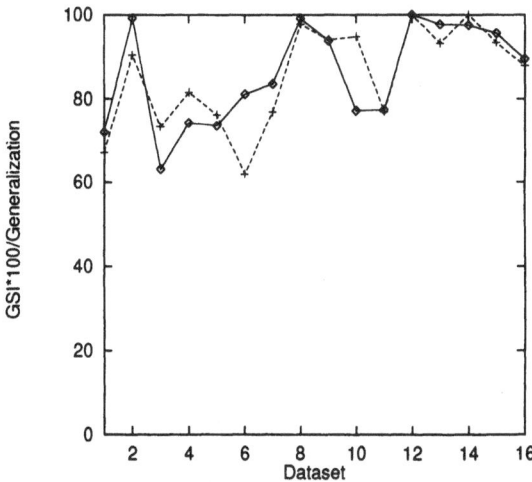

Figure 1: Graphical comparison of GSIs and C4.5 generalisation.

The broad correspondence between C4.5 generalisation rates and GSIs is, again, as per expectation. C4.5 operates by constructing hyper-rectangular boundaries in the input space and is thus unambiguously a boundary method. We therefore expect that its performance on a particular task will be predicted by the GSI for that task.

Interestingly, GSI values can be viewed as identifying the *expected* performance of a 1-nearest-neighbour classifier. The generalisation performance of a 1-nearest-neighbour classifier depends on the degree to which inputs in the testing sample have nearest-neighbours in the training sample with identical target outputs.[3] Clearly, the proportion of nearest neighbours in the dataset which share the same output is identical to the expected proportion of such cases in a randomly selected testing set. Thus, on average, the 1-nearest-neighbour classifier will produce a level of generalisation which is identical to the GSI. We note in passing the interesting fact that though the 1-nearest-neighbour classifier is a somewhat primitive boundary method, it produces performance (on average) which in over half of the 16 cases is either equal to or greater than that of the state-of-the-art method C4.5.[4]

3 The relational origins of geometric inseparability

The empirical tests on the UCI datasets show that most of the 16 frequently used datasets tasks exhibit high geometric separability. Typical boundary methods such as C4.5 and backpropagation produce the expected levels of high performance on such problems. Is this due cause for celebration? Can we safely assume that these results suggest that learning problems are geometrically separable *in general*?

We have already seen that one important class of tasks — the parity problems — all exhibit a zero GSI. But the parity problem turns out to be just the tip of an iceberg. By reasoning backwards from what we know about geometric separability, we can demonstrate that any task which involves the recognition or testing of a *relationship* will typically exhibit negligable geometric separability.

In a task exhibiting high geometric separability, inputs with identical outputs tend to cluster together in the input space. But this clustering effect requires that inputs with identical outputs exhibit similar 'coordinates' or values. But if they do so, we know that absolute values (or continuous ranges of values) must be significant in the determination of the output. We can then deduce counter-factually that problems in which absolute component values are known to have *no* significance in the determination of output *must* exhibit low geometric separability.

---

[3] We assume that the same metric is used for the nearest-neighbour classifier as was used in computing the GSI.

[4] Of course, C4.5 and its near relation ID3 have been shown on numerous occasions to produce performance which is comparable to that of many other empirical learning methods, e.g., the connectionist MLP method [6]

Such problems are termed *relational* and parity is the extreme case. In a parity problem, absolute variables values have no significance whatsoever in the determination of output: it is only the relationships which count. This is nicely reflected in the fact that the GSI value for parity problems is always zero.

In other seemingly relational problems (e.g., the greater-than relationship between two numbers), absolute values may have some significance in the determination of output: zero for example cannot be greater-than any other non-negative integer. So a zero might constitute evidence that the value of the greater-than relationship is false. In such cases the GSI of the task will be non-zero but still low. The general rule is that the more characteristically relational a problem is, the less significant are absolute values and the lower the geometric separability of the task is likely to be. Boundary methods tend to perform poorly on all relational problems. But the more characteristically relational they are (i.e., the less significant absolute values are in the determination of output) the lower the GSI and the poorer the expected performance. Widespread (if often implicit) recognition of this fact has meant that characteristically relational problems are typically addressed using special-purpose relational learning methods (e.g., ILP methods [7]). In those rare cases where a boundary method is tested on a relational task the performance tends to be poor [4].

Interestingly, the argument which allows us to deduce that low geometric separability is associated with relational problems can be turned around to demonstrate that problems with high geometric separability are always efficiently processed using boundary methods. If a problem is non-relational, the absolute variable values (or continuous ranges of same) must be significant in the determination of output. If this is the case, inputs sharing the same output will tend to share coordinates and will therefore tend to cluster together in the input space. Thus boundary methods must be appropriate for all non-relational problems.

The situation comes into focus, therefore, as a *dichotomy*. On the one hand we have learning tasks exhibiting high geometric separability. These are characteristically non-relational and are efficiently processed by boundary methods. On the other hand we have learning tasks exhibiting low geometric separability. These are characteristically relational and are not efficiently processed by boundary methods. One implication of this is that we could, if we like, make the separability distinction in terms of the difference between relational and non-relational tasks. This was in fact the approach taken in the earlier paper, Trading Spaces. That paper distinguished relational tasks from non-relational or 'statistical' tasks.[5]

Of course in saying that geometrically separable tasks are well processed by boundary methods, we are making a broad generalisation. There are a large number of boundary methods originating in superficially distinct fields of investigation (connectionism, machine learning, genetic algorithms, pattern recognition, case-based learning etc.). Each one tends to make boundaries

---

[5] The terms type-1 and type-2 were also used to label the non-relational and relational cases respectively.

and thus identify regions in a slightly different way. The Perceptron favours extreme simplicity: it uses a single linear boundary. ID3 and its near relation C4.5 constructs hyper-rectangular, axis-aligned regions. The MLP, in its vanilla form employing one layer of hidden units, uses multiple linear boundaries (cf. Lipmann figure) to identify more or less arbitrarily-shaped regions. The crossover-based genetic algorithm can be viewed as manipulating hyperplanes [8].

4 Concluding comments

The concept of geometric separability gets to the heart of what empirical learning is really all about. As we have seen, empirical learning *is* the exploitation of geometric separability. The success of any attempted empirical learning is thus inextricably bound up with the degree of geometric separability inherent in the relevant data. In those cases where we know that geometric separability is negligable (e.g., relational problems) we need to move beyond utilisation of familiar, statistically-oriented learning methods into the domain of relational methods. The fact that such methods are not easily implemented as neural networks presents an interesting challenge for future work.

References

[1] Rendell, L. and Seshu, R. (1990). Learning hard concepts through constructive induction. *Computational Intelligence, 6* (pp. 247-270).

[2] Minsky, M. and Papert, S. (1969). *Perceptrons.* Cambridge, Mass.: MIT Press.

[3] Minsky, M. and Papert, S. (1988). *Perceptrons: An Introduction to Computational Geometry* (expanded edn). Cambridge, Mass.: MIT Press.

[4] Thornton, C. (1996). Parity: the problem that won't go away. In G. McCalla (Ed.), *Proceeding of AI-96* (Toronto, Canada) (pp. 362-374). Springer.

[5] Holte, R. (1993). Very simple classification rules perform well on most commonly used datasets. *Machine learning, 3* (pp. 63-91).

[6] Fisher, D. and McKusick, K. (1989). An empirical comparison of ID3 and back-propagation. *Proceedings of the Eleventh International Joint Conference on Artificial Intelligence* (pp. 788-793). Morgan Kaufmann.

[7] Muggleton, S. (Ed.) (1992). *Inductive Logic Programming.* Academic Press.

[8] Holland, J. (1975). *Adaptation in Natural and Artificial Systems.* Ann Arbor: University of Michigan Press.

A Generative Learning Algorithm that uses Structural Knowledge of the Input Domain yields a better Multi-layer Perceptron

Elena Pérez-Miñana

Department of Artificial Intelligence, University of Edinburgh
Edinburgh, Scotland

Abstract

Many classifier applications have been developed using the Multi-layer perceptron (MLP) model as representation form. The main difficulty found in designing an architecture based on the model has been, for the most part, induced by a lack of understanding of what each of an MLP's network components embodies. Expressing the input domain to a classification task in terms of a subspace in R^N, the problem to solve consists of computing an appropriate segmentation of the domain so that every input point will be assigned to a region of the space into which only points of the same class have fallen. This can be achieved with an MLP network if every weight vector is computed as the normal to each of the surfaces in the input domain that will induce the same sort of partitioning that is engendered by the classification criteria associated to the problem for which the network has been built. As the Delaunay Triangulation (DT) of a set of points is a geometric structure in which everything one would ever want to know about the proximity of the points from which it was derived is recorded, it provides an ideal source of information for computing the number and form of those weight vectors, enabling the possibility of building an initial **maximal** network architecture for a particular problem.

1 Introduction

The Multi-layer perceptron (MLP) model, at the present time, is one of the tools most commonly employed for building classifier systems. The main difficulty found in designing architectures based on it has been, for the most part, induced by a lack of understanding of what each of an MLP's network components, i.e. weighted connections and hidden units, embodies.

Of all the types of networks engendered by the different, valid combinations of the values that the MLP model's parameters can take, the one that offers the most powerful representation form corresponds to the MLP with at most two hidden layers of units with **sigmoid** activation function. There is no need to consider architectures allowing a higher number of layers, because Cybenko [4] proved that with this particular network model it is possible to represent any function. Therefore, even though a greater number of hidden layers facilitate the representation of more complex mappings with an MLP network, given

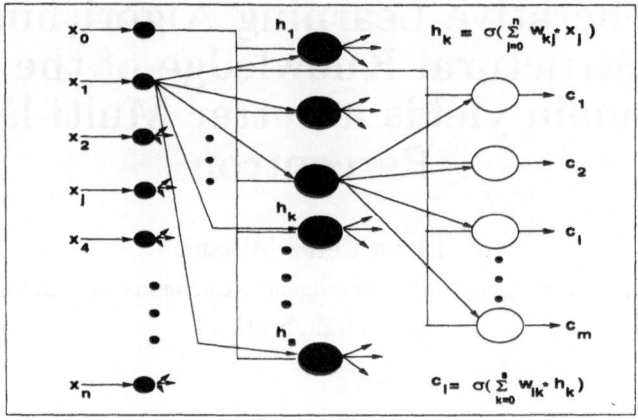

Figure 1: Network model of interest

the difficulty there is in computing the **best** number of layers, nothing much is gained in a network design process involving an elaborate decision step to decide on this issue. Furthermore as a series of empirical results, some of which are described in [8], have shown that for problems requiring more than one hidden layer there are more adequate knowledge representation forms, it was deemed sufficient to restrict the definition of the geometric interpretation under discussion to the one-hidden layer MLP shown in Figure 1. The main features of this particular model are:

(a) The input set is comprised of a number of N-dimension vectors $X^p \in R^n$,

$$(\mathbf{X^P})^t = (x_1^p, x_2^p, \cdots, x_n^p),$$
(1)

where p indexes the occurrence of $\mathbf{X}$ in a training set;

(b) the mathematical definition of the **one-hidden** layer network that has to be created for recognising all its members has the following form:

$$\mathbf{c_i} = \sigma(\sum_{j=o}^{l}(w_{ik} h_k))$$
(2)

where

$$\mathbf{h_k} = \sigma(\sum_{j=0}^{n}(w_{kj} x_j^p))$$
(3)

corresponds to the output of a generic hidden unit h_k of the architecture; σ represents the activation function employed, which subsequently will be considered to be the **sigmoid** unless otherwise stated;

(c) the network produces as output a class index $\mathbf{C} = (c_1, \cdots, c_j, \cdots, c_m)$, $c_i \in \{0, 1\}$ and $\mathbf{C} \in \zeta$. Every class index, is represented in the set of possible outputs, ζ, with a binary pattern $(0, 0, \cdots, 1, \cdots, 0, 0)$, in which only one of the components has a unitary value. $c_i = 1$ in the pattern, indicates that the binary label is associated to class i. It should be remarked that it is possible to define ζ in this manner because the multi-layer perceptron is being designed for a classification task.

For the type of task mentioned, the MLP network that will provide the solution required is one in which each of the regions comprising the partitioning engendered by its weight vectors contains only input points belonging to one of the problem's classes.

The Delaunay Triangulation (DT) of a set of points is a geometric structure in which everything one would ever want to know about proximity of the points from which it was derived is recorded [7]. By building the DT of the elements comprising the problem domain of the classification task of interest, it is possible to determine the number of hidden units the appropriate perceptron network will need. Furthermore, it is possible to compute the form of the associated weight vectors. This can be achieved by exploiting the proximity information imbued in the components of the relevant DT.

Details of this approach are subsequently provided through an example of a classification task in a 2-dimension space since, in this case, it can be graphically illustrated. Nevertheless, it should be noted that the results described are easily extended to higher dimensions because all the pertinent geometric principles are also applicable in N-dimension spaces, $N > 2$. This is evidenced by the information included in the tables presented in section 4. It corresponds to a summary of the results achieved with the networks designed for the high dimension input domains of certain well known problems.

Section 2 provides a summary of the main geometric concepts employed in the geometric interpretation designed. Section 3 describes the domain of a classification task in R^2 and the manner in which the geometric information can help in designing the MLP that is needed. Section 4 discusses the networks built by exploiting the same type of geometric information in certain high-dimension domains. The concluding remarks on the convenience, or otherwise, of this interpretation are included in Section 5.

2 Delaunay Triangulations, Voronoi Diagrams

In Computational Geometry the formal definition of the Delaunay Triangulation (DT) of a set of points belonging to an N-dimension space is usually stated in terms of its dual association with another important geometric form, the Voronoi Diagram (VD). The two constructs are a type of tessellation [2] whose main distinguishing property is that both are totally derived from the data. The VD generated from a set of M points, $\{P_1, P_2, ..., P_k, ..., P_M\}$ in N-dimension space, called sites, corresponds to a partition of the space into

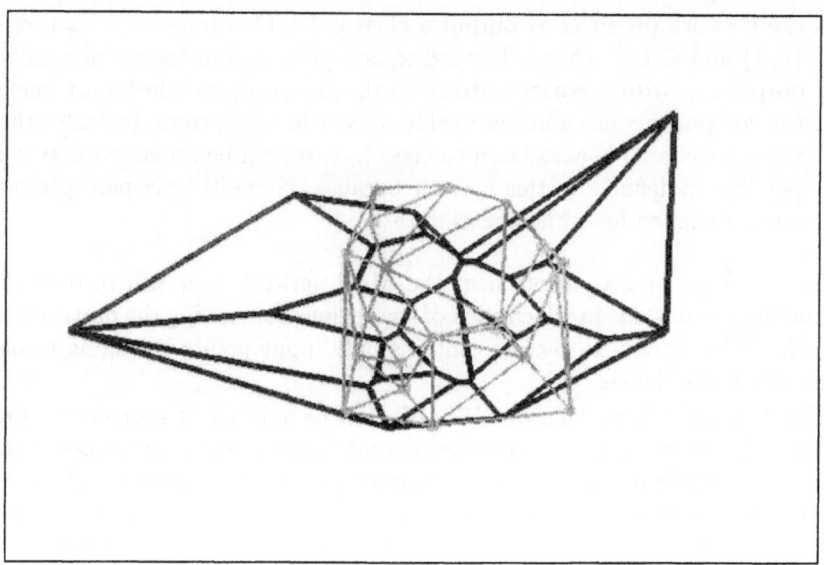

Figure 2: Voronoi Diagram, Delaunay Triangulation of the input domain

convex regions, called Voronoi cells. Each cell represents a "region of influence" surrounding each site. In two dimensions the Voronoi cells are convex polygons whose edges agree with the perpendicular bisectors of the Delaunay triangle edges joining neighbouring sites. The triangulation results from connecting each pair of data sites that share a common Voronoi region boundary. Extending the concept to higher dimensions a Voronoi cell is an N-dimension polytope which can be defined as the intersection of a finite number of closed half-spaces and is, therefore, supported by a finite number of hyperplanes. For a set of N-dimension points its dual, the DT, can be obtained from the projection of the "lower" hull of these same points transformed into an (N+1)-dimension space.

The DT and VD of a T_s provide a very detailed description of the degree of existing proximity of the points included therein given the conditions each must satisfy. An extensive analysis of the properties and applications of these geometric constructs is not the main objective of this publication and can be found in [6], therefore an outline of the general definition of the main underlying concept should be sufficient, at least for obtaining a clearer understanding of the manner in which this theory can be used in the context of the MLP model.

As was previously mentioned the VD is comprised of a number of "Voronoi regions" (VR_i, $i \in [1, M]$) one for each of the elements (sites) in the set from which it is being derived . The Voronoi region VR_i associated to the site P_i is given by:

$$VR_i = \{P/\|P - P_i\| <= \|P - P_j\|\}$$
$$for \ j \neq i; \ i, j \in [1, M]$$

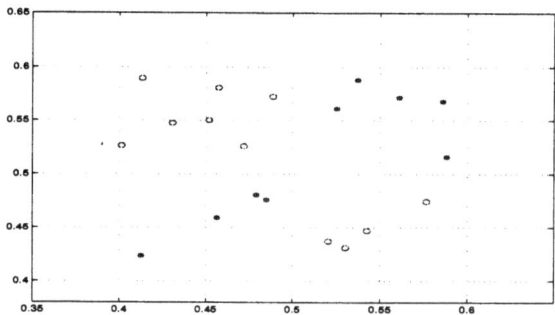

Figure 3: Structure of the input domain

where $||P - P_i||$ is the Euclidean distance between the points P and P_i. The above means that each VR_i is conformed by all those points in the N-dimension space whose closest site of the input set is P_i. The boundaries of a region VR_i correspond to ridges, eg. edges in the plane, and include those points which are equally close to the sites sharing the ridge. The geometric constructs shown in Figure 2, correspond to the VD and DT derived from the points that comprise the training set T_s exhibited in Figure 3. The solid black lines in Figure 2 form the Voronoi Diagram, the lighter edges constitute the Delaunay Triangulation. It is worth pointing out that the geometric constructs shown in this publication might not comply totally with its mathematical definition. This is due to precision problems in the software used to generate them.

Knowing which sites of a VD share boundaries allows one to infer information concerning their proximity which can be successfully exploited in the network design process. Given that the DT is the dual of the VD, it provides the same information but, as it is organised in a different manner it opens the possibility of applying it in other ways.

Bose and Garga in [1] describe a method for designing a MLP that exploits the VD of a training set for deciding on the number of hidden units, layers and on the values of the weights. The outcome is an adequate architecture that requires no further training or adjustment but, because each layer of the network model has a very specific function and most problems require, to a certain degree, the integration of all of them, the resulting architectures will usually be more complex than what is really needed and much too tailored to the peculiarities of the T_s. A set of experiments performed in our research, [8], proved this to be the case. It supplied enough reasons for exploiting the geometric information that can be derived from the VD but, only for building an appropriate initial MLP architecture.

Additionally, as the edges of the DT connect the different sites, it is easier to appreciate the degree of intersection that exists between the points of the different classes comprising the T_s. This provides information that helps in

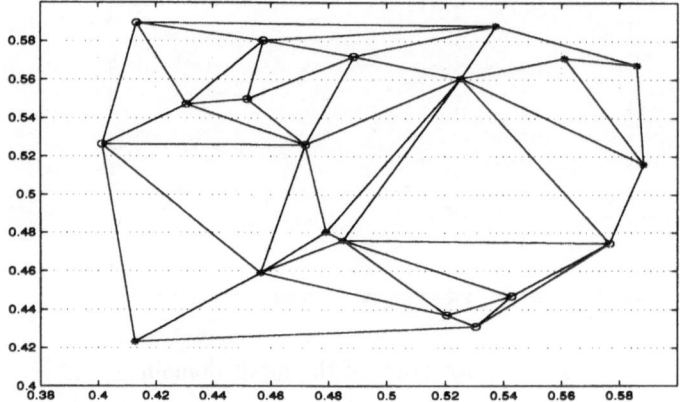

Figure 4: Delaunay Triangulation of the input domain

assessing the practicality of using the MLP as a knowledge representation tool.

3 Designing the appropriate MLP Classifier

The problem domain used to describe the applicability of the geometric concepts specified in the previous section is an instance of the 2-dimension continuous parity problem. The distribution of the points contained therein is shown in Figure 3. The circles correspond to elements of class one, the stars denote the members of the other class. It is clear from the plot that the MLP network designed to correctly classify these points must include a layer of hidden units since it is a non-linearly separable space.

The DT of this T_s consists of a set of triangles which are organised in the manner shown in Figure 4. The endpoints of each of them have been connected because they lie closer to each other than to any of the other inputs complying with the conditions that must be satisfied by the DT, VD of a set of points. Furthermore, they are organised in a closed structure accounting for all the elements provided as input. Selecting the edges that connect points belonging to different classes, an appropriate set of weight vectors for the network required to solve this particular problem can be computed. It corresponds to their bisectors, *i.e.* the edges of the relevant VD.

This means, that the VD provides information for computing the initial number of hidden units required and the values of the weight vectors associated to the input-hidden layer connections. These can be computed by selecting those edges of the VD that separate points belonging to different classes and calculating the direction cosines of the lines associated to each of these edges. The initial set of weight vectors obtained might be reduced by clustering those which are sufficiently aligned and taking one of them as cluster exemplar.

Since the geometric data is only used for the first layer of connections, the architecture still requires further tuning with a training process which will not

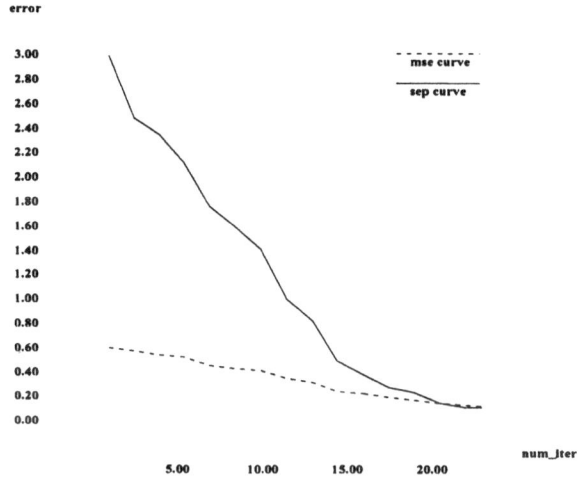

Figure 5: Error evolution during training: x-axis iterations, y-axis error

take too many iterations given the kind of network on which it is initially operating. It will be using a number of hidden units directly proportional to the number of "hard" cases and at least one layer of connections, ie. input-hidden, will be initialised in accordance to the disposition of the points in the input space. The connections of the other layer are set to random values as is the usual policy in many network developing processes.

The plot shown in figure 5 contains the curves of two types of error measure registered at different intervals during the network's training process. The broken line corresponds to the mean square error (*MSE*), the continuous line is associated to the square error percentage (*SEP*), a performance measure described in detail in [9] which allows for a better evaluation of the evolution of a network training process. It is clear from the plot that only a few number of iterations were required to achieve complete recognition of all the elements in T_s, providing empirical proof substantiating the reliability of the geometric information employed for building the initial network.

The final architecture computed with the training process can be considered "maximal" for the following reasons: (a) all the set of points comprising the T_s will be accounted for given the number of hidden units and initial location of certain of its weight vectors, (b) performing a Principal Component Analysis (*PCA*) on the output of its hidden units brings to light the existence of "superfluous" units, (c) the network obtained by subtracting the ones labeled as such generally shows itself to be a better generaliser.

problem	attributes				**Proben1**	**GROPING**	classes	
	b	c	n	tot	inputs	inputs	b	size
cancer	0	9	0	9	9	9	2	699
gene	0	0	60	60	120	60	3	3175
glass	0	9	0	9	9	9	6	214
soybean	16	6	13	35	82	35	19	683

Table 1: Attribute structure of data in the classification tasks considered

4 Networks for high dimension domains obtained with Geometry

Prechelt in [9] describes a set of benchmarks and benchmarking rules for MLP learning algorithms. The most important characteristic is that all the classification problems considered therein have high dimension input spaces which means it constitutes an appropriate source of results against which to compare those obtained from designing networks using instead the geometric information described in the previous sections.

The relevant properties of the domains of the selected problems are outlined in table 1. There is one line for each of them. The first column of the table contains the name of the problem. Columns two through to five indicate the number of binary, continuous, and nominal attributes present in the input vectors of the original space. The numbers in columns six and seven correspond, respectively, to the final number of inputs used by each of the learning methods that are being compared since it is possible to organise the data in various ways. The number of classes and total number of instances comprising each data set is the information presented in the final two columns of table 1.

All the input spaces are associated to classification tasks which are described in detail in [8], [9]. The learning methods under scrutiny are: (a) the one used by Prechelt [9] to build the **Proben1** benchmark, (b) **GROPING** the learning method described in [8] which uses the geometric information discussed previously as its main source for designing the network required to solve a particular problem.

The values presented in table 2 correspond to various errors registered at the time of building the networks for each of the classification tasks being considered. Those under the **GROPING** heading were compiled at the end of the network's training process. They correspond to the *SEP*, *MSE* computed on the training set (sep_tr, merr_tr) and the test set (sep_ts, merr_ts).

Since the strategy followed in **Proben1** consisted in initialising the same architecture with different randomly generated sets of weights the results described in [9] all represent averages over these initialisations. For this reason, the set of values presented in table 2 under the **Proben1** heading correspond to the mean (avr_sep_tr, avr_sep_ts) and standard deviations (std_sep_tr, std_sep_ts) of the *SEP* computed on the network when processing the same training and test sets as the ones used in **GROPING**. The total number of iterations re-

Final Errors computed with GROPING Networks					
problem	iterations	sep_tr	sep_ts	merr_tr	merr_ts
cancer	43	0.0038	3.0743	0.0014	0.0399
gene	16	1.3780	6.7345	0.0579	0.1237
glass	101	0.0126	2.1223	0.0029	0.0302
soybean	26	0.0144	0.7225	0.0010	0.0096
Average Errors computed with Proben1 Networks					
problem	avr_iter	avr_sep_tr	std_sep_tr	avr_sep_ts	std_sep_ts
cancer	93	2.08	0.35	3.40	0.33
gene	46	6.45	0.42	10.72	0.31
glass	66	7.56	0.98	10.91	0.48
soybean	759	0.40	0.07	1.05	0.09

Table 2: Results for well-known classification tasks in high dimension spaces

quired to achieve a successful classifier network also constitute an average value since the training process for each random initialisation was completed in a particular amount of time.

Comparing the values registered with **Proben1**'s networks against those computed with **GROPING**'s final architectures, it is possible to arrive at the following conclusions:

(a) the initial set of weights used in **GROPING** allowed for faster training because fewer iterations were required in most cases.

(b) the final *SEP* error computed on the training sets with the **GROPING** networks is much smaller than the averages computed with the networks built applying **Proben1**. The column of the *MSE* measure was included as part of the results in **GROPING** because it is a more commonly used type of error. This means a wider audience will better understand the effectiveness of applying this type of algorithm.

(c) the information contained in table 3 describes the number of input-hidden-output units, layers and connections of all the networks used to compute the error values included in table 2. Although certain of them have fewer connections in **Proben1**, the fact that there are more layers allows to conclude that **GROPING** is more effective in producing simpler architectures.

(d) the most important result showing the convenience of using Computational Geometry to initialise classifier networks refers to the error calculated with the test set. Since it is much smaller in the final **GROPING** networks for all the classification tasks evaluated, better generalisers are built by applying it.

Network architectures				
	Proben1		**GROPING**	
problem	architecture	num_connect	architecture	num_connect
cancer	9-4-2-2	100	9-15-2	165
gene	120-4-2-3	1115	60-216-2	7751
glass	9-16-8-6	572	9-32-6	518
soybean	82-16-8-19	4153	35-28-19	1559

Table 3: Network architectures in **Proben1** and **GROPING**

5 Conclusions

The geometric method described clearly constitutes an appropriate means for performing a reliable design of the multi-layer perceptron required for a particular application, considering that it complies vary well with the different network components. It constitutes a sound theoretical framework on which to base the analysis of the model's functionality. Apart from the experiments conducted for this study, the analysis completed by other researchers, [5], [1], provided additional proof on the convenience of pursuing this kind of solution.

Even though it is possible to completely compute the architecture that is necessary to correctly classify all the elements of the T_s of an application, doing so results in a poor generaliser. This is caused by the fact that the network components are too finely tuned to the peculiarities of the T_s.

A sensible approach to surmount the difficulties induced by a poor generaliser and, at the same time profit from the new source of information is to use it just in the creation of an initial architecture. Since this architecture can be confidently labeled a "maximal" solution for the pertinent T_s, it is a good starting point for a subsequent network pruning process designed to build a good generaliser. This is the philosophy underlying **GROPING**, the learning method used for building the networks described in section 4. All these architectures can be labeled appropriate generalisers given the results contained in table 2.

The results discussed in this work are all related to classifier networks which happens to be the type of task for which the MLP model is particularly well suited. The convenience of applying the type of learning method described in other contexts, *eg.* applications with continuous outputs, depends on the possibility of building a MLP network for problems with that type of output domain. The theoretical results described in [4] indicate that it is possible. Furthermore, since the outputs of any network built with **GROPING** are continuous valued, initially it appears that it should be equally effective for building MLPs for problems with such outputs. What will require further investigation is the mechanism for selecting the hyperplanes that are used to compute the weight vectors. In the context of a classification task it is easy to decide on whether a surface is necessary or not because the issue is resolved by comparing if the connected points belong to the same class but, for continuous-valued output domains, what should be the selection criteria?

The possibility of reproducing with this learning system the kind of representations induced by the brain depends on how easy it is to interpret the neural representations in terms of a classification task since this is the type of application best reproduced with an MLP network.

The experiments and analysis realised during the definition of **GROPING** allowed us to conclude that an appropriate way of determining whether the MLP model is the most adequate representation form for building an application is by measuring the difficulty of expressing it in terms of a classification task, one in which the domains involved are reasonably well known.

References

[1] N.K. Bose, A.K. Garga, Neural Network Design using Voronoi Diagrams, IEEE Transactions on Neural Networks 1993; 4, 5: 778-787.

[2] A. Bowyer, J. Woodwark, Introduction to Computing with Geometry, Winchester: Information Geometers 1993.

[3] N. Burgess, S. Di Zenzo, M. Notturno Granieri, The Generalisation of a Constructive Algorithm in Pattern Classification Problems, International Journal of Neural Systems 1992; 3:1-6.

[4] G. Cybenko, Continuous valued neural networks with two hidden layers are sufficient, technical report, Department of Computer Science, Tufts University, USA 1988.

[5] J. Hertz, A. Krogh, R. Palmer, Introduction to the Theory of Neural Computation, Addison-Wesley 1991.

[6] A. Okabe, B. Boots, K. Sugihara, Spatial Tessellations: Concepts and Applications of Voronoi Diagrams, Wiley series in Probability and Statistics, John Wiley & Sons 1992.

[7] J. O'Rourke, Computational Geometry in C, Cambridge University Press 1994.

[8] E. Pérez-Miñana, Learning Nature of the Feedforward Neural Networks, PhD thesis, Department of Artificial Intelligence, University of Edinburgh 1997.

[9] L. Prechelt, **Proben1**: A Set of Benchmarks and Benchmarking Rules for Neural Network Training Algorithms, Fakultät für Informatik Universität Karlsruhe 1994.

Improving Learning and Generalization in Neural Networks through the Acquisition of Multiple Related Functions

Morten H. Christiansen

Program in Neural, Informational and Behavioral Sciences
University of Southern California
Los Angeles, CA 90089-2520, U.S.A.

Abstract

This paper presents evidence from connectionist simulations providing support for the idea that forcing neural networks to learn several related functions together results in both improved learning and better generalization. More specifically, if a neural network employing gradient descent learning is forced to capture the regularities of many semi-correlated sources of information within the same representational substrate, it then becomes necessary for it to only represent hypotheses that are consistent with all the cues provided. When the different sources of information are sufficiently correlated the number of candidate solutions will be reduced through the development of more efficient representations. To illustrate this, the paper draws briefly on research in the neural network engineering literature, while focusing on recent work on the segmentation of speech using connectionist networks. Finally, some implications for language acquisition of the present approach are discussed.

1   Introduction

Systems that learn from examples are likely to run into the problem of induction —that is, given any finite set of examples, there will always be a considerable number of different hypotheses consistent with the example set. However, many of these hypotheses may not lead to correct generalization. The problem of induction is pervasive in the domain of cognitive behavior—especially within the field of language acquisition where it has promoted the influential idea that a child must bring a substantial amount of innate linguistic knowledge to the acquisition process in order to avoid false generalizations (e.g., [7]). However, this conclusion may be premature because it is based on a simplistic view of computational mechanisms. Recent developments within connectionist modeling have revealed that neural networks embody a number of computational properties that may help constrain learning processes in appropriate ways.

This paper focuses on one such property, presenting evidence from connectionist simulations that provides support for the idea that forcing neural networks to learn several related functions together results in better learning and generalization. First, learning with hints as applied in the neural network engineering literature will be discussed. The following section addresses the problem of learning multiple related functions within cognitive domains, using word segmentation as an example. Next, an analysis of how learning multiple functions may help constrain the hypothesis space that a learning system has to negotiate. The conclusion suggests that the integration of multiple partially informative cues may help develop the kind of representations necessary to account for acquisition data which have previously formed the basis for poverty of stimulus arguments against connectionist and other learning-based models of language acquisition.

2 Learning using hints

One way in which the problem of induction may be reduced for a system learning from examples is if it is possible to furnish the learning mechanism with additional information which can constrain the learning process. In the neural network engineering literature, this has come to be known as learning with hints. Hints are ways in which additional information not present in the example set may be incorporated into the learning process [1, 21], thus potentially helping the learning mechanism overcome the problem of induction.

There are numerous ways in which hints may be implemented, two of which are relevant for the purposes of the present paper: (a) The *insertion* of explicit rules into networks via the pre-setting of weights [16]; and (b) the addition of extra *"catalyst"* units encoding additional related functions [20, 21]. The idea behind providing hints in the form of rule insertion is to place the network in a certain part of weight space deemed by prior analysis to be the locus of the most optimal solutions to the training task. The rules used for this purpose typically encode information estimated by prior analysis to capture important aspects of the target function. If the right rules are inserted, it will reduce the number of possible weight configurations that the network has to search through during learning. Catalyst hints are also introduced to reduce the overall weight configuration space that a network has to negotiate, but this reduction is accomplished by forcing the network to acquire one or more additional related functions encoded over extra output units. These units are often ignored after they have served their purpose during training (hence the name "catalyst" hint). The learning process is facilitated by catalyst hints because fewer weight configurations can accommodate both the original target function as well as the additional catalyst function(s) (as will be explained in more detail below). As a consequence of reducing the weight space, both types of hints have been shown to constrain the induction problem, promoting faster learning and better generalization.

Mathematical analyses in terms of the Vapnik-Chervonenkis (VC) dimension [2] and vector field analysis [21] have shown that learning with hints may reduce the number of hypotheses a learning system has to entertain. The VC dimension establishes an upper bound for the number of examples needed by a learning process that starts with a set of hypotheses about the task solution. A hint may lead to a reduction in the VC dimension by weeding out bad hypotheses and reduce the number of examples needed to learn the solution. Vector field analysis uses a measure of "functional" entropy to estimate the overall probability for correct rule extraction from a trained network. The introduction of a hint may reduce the functional entropy, improving the probability of rule extraction. The results from this approach demonstrate that hints may constrain the number of possible hypotheses to entertain, and thus lead to faster convergence.

In sum, these mathematical analyses have revealed that the potential advantage of using hints in neural network training is twofold: First, hints may reduce learning time by reducing the number of steps necessary to find an appropriate implementation of the target function. Second, hints may reduce the number of candidate functions for the target function being learned, thus potentially ensuring better generalization. As mentioned above, in neural networks this amounts to reducing the number of possible weight configurations that the learning algorithm has to choose between[1]. However, it should be noted that there is no guarantee that a particular hint will improve performance. Nevertheless, in practice this does not appear to pose a major problem because hints are typically carefully chosen to reflect important and informative aspects of the original target function.

From the perspective of language acquisition we can construe rule-insertion hints as analogous to the kind of innate knowledge prescribed by theories of Universal Grammar (e.g., [7]). Although this way of implementing a Universal Grammar is an interesting topic in itself (see [17] for a discussion) and may potentially provide insights into whether this approach could be implemented in the brain, the remainder of this paper will focus on learning with catalyst hints because this approach may provide learning-based solutions to certain language acquisition puzzles. In particular, this conception of learning allows for the possibility that the simultaneous learning of related functions may pose significant constraints on the acquisition process by reducing the number of possible candidate solutions.

Having thus established the potential advantages of learning with hints in neural networks, we can now apply the idea of learning using catalyst units to the domain of language acquisition—exemplified by the task of learning to segment the speech stream.

3   Learning multiple related functions in language acquisition

The input to the language acquisition process—often referred to as motherese—comprises a complex combination of multiple sources of information. Clusters of such information sources appear to inform the learning of various linguistic

---

[1] It should be noted that the results of the mathematical analyses apply independently of whether the extra catalyst units are discarded after training (as is typical in the engineering literature) or remain a part of the network as in the simulations presented below.

tasks (see contributions in [15]). Individually, each source of information, which will be referred to as a *cue*, is only partially reliable with respect to the task in question. Consider the task of locating words in fluent speech.

Speech segmentation is a difficult problem because there are no direct cues to word boundaries comparable to the white spaces between words in written text. Instead the speech input contains numerous sources of information, each of which is probabilistic in nature. Here I discuss three such cues which have been hypothesized to provide useful information with respect to locating word boundaries: (a) phonotactics in the form of phonological regularities [18], (b) utterance boundary information [4, 5], and (c) lexical stress [11]. As an example consider the two unsegmented utterances:

Therearenospacesbetweenwordsinfluentspeech#
Yeteachchildseemstograspthebasicsquickly#

(a) The sequential regularities found in the phonology (here represented as orthography) can be used to determine where words may begin or end. For example, the consonant cluster *sp* can be found both at word beginnings (*sp*aces and *sp*eech) and at word endings (gra*sp*). However, a language learner cannot rely solely on such information to detect possible word boundaries, as evident when considering that the *sp* consonant cluster also can straddle a word boundary, as in cat*sp*ajamas, and occur word internally as in re*sp*ect.

(b) The pauses at the end of utterances (indicated above by #) also provide useful information for the segmentation task. If children realize that sound sequences occurring at the end of an utterance must also be the end of a word, then they can use information about utterance final phonological sequences to postulate word boundaries whenever these sequences occur inside an utterance. Thus, in the example above knowledge of the rhyme *eech#* from the first utterance can be used to postulate a word boundary after the similar sounding sequence *each* in the second utterance. As with phonology, utterance boundary information cannot be used as the only source of information about word boundaries because some words, such as the determiner *the*, rarely, if ever, occur at the end of an utterance.

(c) Lexical stress is another useful cue to word boundaries. Among the disyllabic words in English, most take a trochaic stress pattern with a strongly stressed syllable followed by a weakly stressed syllable. The two utterances above include four such words: *spaces, fluent, basics,* and *quickly*. Word boundaries can thus be postulated following a weak syllable, but, once again, this source of segmentation information is only partially reliable because in the above example there is also a disyllabic word with the opposite iambic stress pattern: *between*.

Returning to the notion of learning with hints, we can usefully construe word segmentation in terms of two simultaneous learning tasks [9]. For children acquiring their native language, the goal is presumably to comprehend the utterances to which they are exposed for the purpose of achieving specific outcomes. In the service of this goal the child pays attention to the linguistic input. Recent studies [18, 19] have shown that adults, children and 9-month old

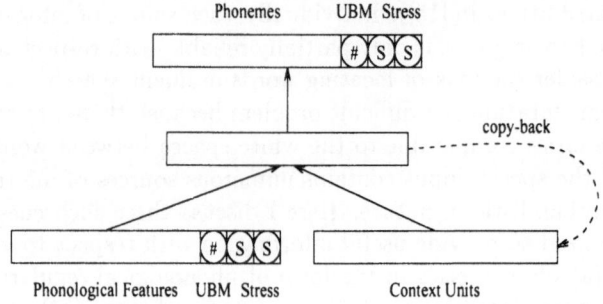

Figure 1: Illustration of the SRN used in [9]. Arrows with solid lines indicate trainable weights, whereas the arrow with the dashed line denotes the copy-back weights (which are always 1). The SRN had 14 input units, 36 output units and 80 hidden/context units.

infants cannot help but incidentally encode the statistical regularities in the input. This task of encoding statistical regularities governing the individual cues will be referred to as the *immediate* task. In the case of word segmentation, phonology, utterance boundary information, and lexical stress would be some of the more obvious cues to attend to. On the basis of the acquired representations of these regularities the learning system may derive knowledge about aspects of the language for which there is no single reliable cue in the input. This means that the individual cues may be integrated and serve as hints towards the *derived* task of detecting word boundaries in the input. In other words, the hints represent a set of related functions which together may help solve the derived task.

This is illustrated by the account of early word segmentation developed in [9]. A Simple Recurrent Network [12] was trained on a single pass through a corpus consisting of 8181 utterances of child directed speech. These utterances were extracted from the Korman corpus [13] (a part of the CHILDES database [14]) consisting of speech directed at pre-verbal infants aged 6–16 weeks. The training corpus consisted of 24,648 words distributed over 814 types (type-token ratio = .03) and had an average utterance length of 3.0 words (see [9] for further details). A separate corpus consisting of 927 utterances and with the same statistical properties as the training corpus was used for testing. Each word in the utterances was transformed from its orthographic format into a phonological form and lexical stress assigned using a dictionary compiled from the MRC Psycholinguistic Database available from the Oxford Text Archive[2].

As input the network was provided with different combinations of three cues dependent on the training condition. The cues were (a) phonology represented in terms of 11 features on the input and 36 phonemes on the output[3], (b) ut-

---

[2]Note that these phonological *citation forms* are unreduced (i.e., they do not include the reduced vowel *schwa*). The stress cue therefore provides additional information not available in the phonological input.

[3]Phonemes were used as output in order to facilitate subsequent analyses of how much knowledge of phonotactics the net had acquired.

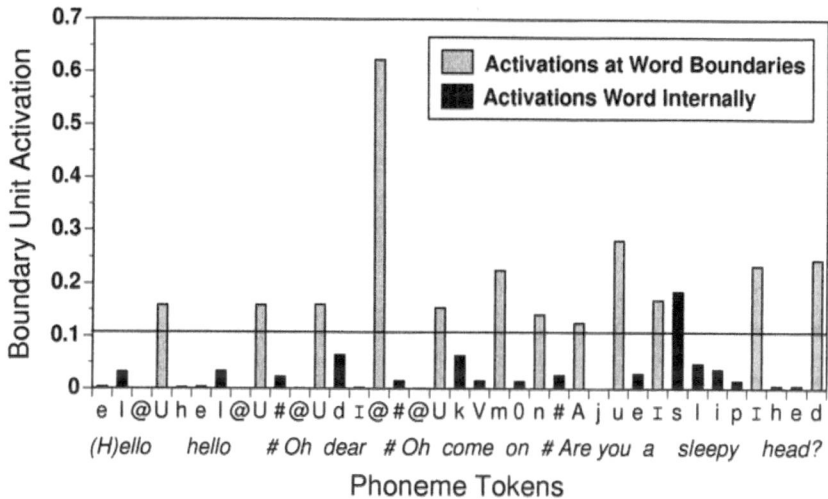

Figure 2: The activation of the boundary unit during the processing of the first 37 phoneme tokens in the training corpus. A gloss of the input utterances is found beneath the input phoneme tokens.

terance boundary information represented as an extra feature (UBM) marking utterance endings, and (c) lexical stress coded over two units as either no stress, secondary or primary stress. Figure 1 provides an illustration of the network.

The network was trained on the *immediate task* of predicting the next phoneme in a sequence as well as the appropriate values for the utterance boundary and stress units. In learning to perform this task it was expected that the network would also learn to integrate the cues such that it could carry out the *derived task* of segmenting the input into words. On the reasonable assumption that phonology is the basic cue to word segmentation, the utterance boundary and lexical stress cues can then be considered as extra *catalyst units*, providing hints towards the derived task.

With respect to the network, the logic behind the derived task is that the end of an utterance is also the end of a word. If the network is able to integrate the provided cues in order to activate the boundary unit at the ends of words occurring at the end of an utterance, it should also be able to generalize this knowledge so as to activate the boundary unit at the ends of words which occur *inside* an utterance [4]. Figure 2 shows a snapshot of SRN segmentation performance on the first 37 phoneme tokens in the training corpus. Activation of the boundary unit at a particular position corresponds to the network's hypothesis that a boundary follows this phoneme. Grey bars indicate the activation at lexical boundaries, whereas the black bars correspond to activation at word internal positions. Activations above the mean (horizontal line) are interpreted as the postulation of a word boundary. As can be seen from the figure, the SRN performed well on this part of the training set, correctly segmenting out all of the 12 words save one (/slipI/ = *sleepy*).

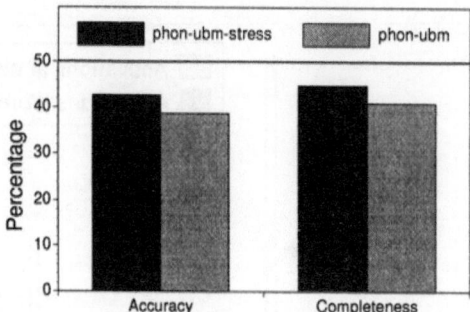

Figure 3: Word accuracy and completeness for the net trained with three cues (phon-ubm-stress – black bars) and the net trained with two cues (phon-ubm – grey bars).

In order to provide a more quantitative measure of performance, accuracy and completeness scores [5] were calculated for the separate test corpus consisting of utterances not seen during training:

$$\text{Accuracy} = \frac{\text{Hits}}{\text{Hits} + \text{False Alarms}}$$

$$\text{Completeness} = \frac{\text{Hits}}{\text{Hits} + \text{Misses}}$$

Accuracy provides a measure of how many of the words that the network postulated were actual words, whereas completeness provides a measure of how many of the actual words that the net discovered. Consider the following hypothetical example:

$$\# \, t \, h \, e \, \# \, d \, o \, g \, \# \, s \, \# \, c \, h \, a \, s \, e \, \# \, t \, h \, e \, c \, \# \, a \, t \, \#$$

where $\#$ corresponds to a predicted word boundary. Here the hypothetical learner correctly segmented out two words, *the* and *chase*, but also falsely segmented out *dog*, *s*, *thec*, and *at*, thus missing the words *dogs*, *the*, and *cat*. This results in an accuracy of $\frac{2}{2+4} = 33.3\%$ and a completeness of $\frac{2}{2+3} = 40.0\%$.

With these measures in hand, we compare the performance of nets trained using phonology and utterance boundary information—with or without the lexical stress cue—to illustrate the advantage of getting an extra hint. Figure 3 shows the accuracy and completeness scores for the networks forced to integrate two or three cues during training. The phon-ubm-stress network was significantly more accurate (42.71% vs. 38.67%: $\chi^2 = 18.27, p < .001$) and had a significantly higher completeness score (44.87% vs. 40.97%: $\chi^2 = 11.51, p < .001$) than the phon-ubm network. These results thus demonstrate that having to integrate the additional stress cue with the phonology and utterance boundary cues during learning provides for better performance.

To test the generalization abilities of the networks, segmentation performance was recorded on the task of correctly segmenting novel words. Figure 4 shows the performance of the two networks on this task. The three cue net was

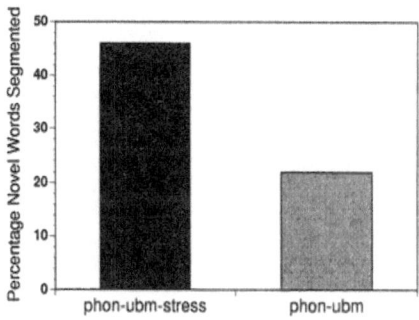

Figure 4: Percentage of novel words correctly segmented (word completeness) for the net trained with three cues (phon-ubm-stress – black bar) and the net trained with two cues (phon-ubm – grey bar).

able to segment 23 of the 50 novel words, whereas the two cue network only was able to segment 11 novel words. Thus, the phon-ubm-stress network achieved a word completeness of 46% which was significantly better ($\chi^2 = 4.23, p < .05$) than the 22% completeness obtained by the phon-ubm net. These results therefore supports the supposition that the integration of three cues promotes better generalization than the integration of two cues.

Overall, these simulation results from [9] show that the integration of probabilistic cues forces the networks to develop representations that allow them to perform quite reliably on the task of detecting word boundaries in the speech stream[4]. The comparisons between the nets provided with one and two additional related cues in the form of catalyst units, demonstrate that the availability of the extra cue results in the better learning and generalization. This result is encouraging given that the segmentation task shares many properties with other language acquisition problems which have been taken to require innate linguistic knowledge for their solution, and yet it seems clear that discovering the words of one's native language must be an acquired skill.

4 Constraining the hypothesis space

The integration of the additional cues provided by the catalyst units significantly improved network performance on the derived task of word segmentation. We can get insight into why such hints may help the SRN by considering one of its basic architectural limitations, originally discovered in [10]; namely that SRNs tend only to encode information about previous subsequences if this information is locally relevant for making subsequent predictions. This means that the SRN has problems learning sequences in which the local dependencies are essentially arbitrary. For example, results in [6] show that the SRN performs poorly on the task of learning to be a delay-line; that is, outputting the

---

[4]These results were replicated across different initial weight configurations and with different input/output representations.

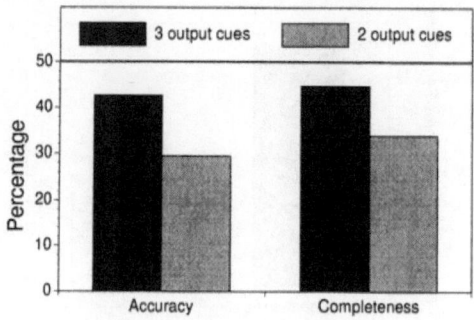

Figure 5: Word accuracy and completeness for the net trained with three output cues (phon-ubm-stress – black bars) and the net trained with two output cues (phon-ubm – grey bars). Both nets received three cues as input.

current input after a delay of N time-steps.

However, this architectural limitation can be alleviated to some degree if the set of training items has a nonuniform probability distribution. This forces the SRN to encode sequences further back in time in order to minimize the error on subsequent predictions. Interestingly, many aspects of natural language are characterized by nonuniform probability distributions; for example, approximately 70-80% of the disyllabic words in English speech directed at infants have a trochaic stress pattern (e.g., 77.3% of the disyllabic words in the training corpus used in [9] had a strong-weak stress pattern).

What the integration of cues buys the network is that it forces it to encode more previous information than it would otherwise. For example, analyses of the simplified model of word segmentation in [3] showed that if an SRN only had to predict the next phoneme, then it could get away with encoding only relatively short sequences. However, the addition of another cue in the form of a catalyst unit representing utterance boundary information forced the net to represent longer sequences of previous input tokens. Encoding longer sequences is necessary in order to reduce the error on the task of predicting both the next phoneme and the on-off status of the utterance boundary unit. The network can thus reduce its error by keeping track of the range of previous sequences which are likely to lead to the utterance boundary unit being activated. A similar story appears to hold with respect to the stress cue in [9].

These analyses suggest how cue integration may force the SRN to acquire more efficient internal representations in order to make correct predictions, focusing on the benefit of having extra catalyst units in the output layer. However, given that the above phon-ubm-stress SRN received three cues both as target output and as input, it is conceivable that it is the *extra input* that is causing the improved performance over the two cue net, rather than the *extra output* cue. In other words, perhaps it is the availability of the extra information on the input which underlies the performance improvement. To investigate this possibility, additional simulations were run. In these simulations, an SRN received three cues as input (i.e., phonology, utterance boundary, and stress

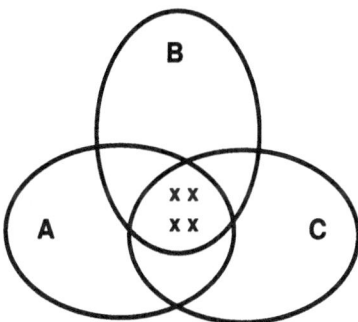

Figure 6: An abstract illustration of the reduction in weight configuration space which follows as a product of accommodating several partially overlapping cues within the same representational substrate.

information), but was only required to make predictions for two of these cues; that is, for the phonology and utterance boundary cues. All other simulation details were identical to [9].

Figure 5 provides a comparison between the network provided with three input/two output cues and the earlier presented phon-ubm-stress network which received three input/output cues. The latter network was both significantly more accurate (42.71% vs. 29.44%: $\chi^2 = 118.81, p < .001$) and had a significantly higher completeness score (44.87% vs. 33.95%: $\chi^2 = 70.46, p < .001$). These additional results demonstrate that it is indeed the integration of the extra stress cue with respect to the prediction task, rather than the availability of this cue in the input, which is driving the process of successful integration of cues. Cue integration via catalyst units thus seems to be able to constrain the set of hypotheses that the SRN can successfully entertain.

4.1 Reducing weight space search

We can conceptualize the effect that the cue integration process has on learning by considering the following illustration. In Figure 6, each ellipse designates for a particular cue the set of weight configurations which will enable a network to learn the function denoted by that cue. For example, the ellipse marked A designates the set of weight configurations which allow for the learning of the function A described by the A cue. With respect to the simulation reported above, A, B and C can be construed as the phonology, utterance boundary, and lexical stress cues, respectively.

If a gradient descent network was only required to learn the regularities underlying, say, the A cue, it could settle on any of the weight configurations in the A set. However, if the net was also required to learn the regularities underlying cue B, it would have to find a weight configuration which would accommodate the regularities of both cues. The net would therefore have to settle on a set of weights from the intersection between A and B in order to minimize its error. This constrains the overall set of weight configurations that the net has to choose between—unless the cues are entirely overlapping (in which case there would not be any added benefit from learning this cue) or are disjoint (in which case the net would not be able to find an appropriate weight configuration). If the net furthermore had to learn the regularities associated with the third cue C, the available set of weight configurations would be constrained even further.

Thus, the introduction of cues via catalyst units may reduce the size of the weight space that a network has to search for an appropriate set of weights. And since the cues designate functions which correlate with respect to the derived task, the reduction in weight space is also likely to provide a better representational basis for solving this task and lead to better learning and generalization.

5 Conclusion

This paper has presented evidence in support of the idea that the integration of multiple sufficiently correlated, partially informative cues may constrain learning and over-generalization. In this connection, results from an SRN model of word segmentation was presented which was able to achieve a high level of performance on a derived task for which there is no single reliable cue. This SRN model has also recently been shown to be able to successfully deal with variations in the speech input in terms of coarticulation and high degrees of segmental variation [8].

The approach presented here may have ramifications outside the domain of speech segmentation insofar as children readily learn aspects of their language for which traditional theories suggest that there is insufficient evidence (e.g., [7]). The traditional answer to this poverty of the stimulus problem is that knowledge of such aspects of language is specified by an innate Universal Grammar. A more compelling solution may lie in the integration of cues as exemplified in the word segmentation model. Since recent research has revealed that higher level language phenomena also appear to involve a variety of probabilistic cues [15], the integration of such cues may provide a sufficient representational basis for the acquisition of other kinds of linguistic structure through derived tasks.

Acknowledgments

Many thanks to Joe Allen, Jim Hoeffner, Mark Seidenberg, and two anonymous reviewers for their helpful comments on an earlier version of this paper.

References

[1] Y.S. Abu-Mostafa, Learning from hints in neural networks, *Journal of Complexity*, 6, 192–198, 1990.

[2] Y.S. Abu-Mostafa, Hints and the VC Dimension, *Neural Computation*, 5, 278–288, 1993.

[3] J. Allen & M.H. Christiansen, Integrating multiple cues in word segmentation: A connectionist model using hints, in *Proceedings of the Eighteenth Annual Cognitive Science Society Conference*, pp. 370–375. Mahwah, NJ: Lawrence Erlbaum Associates, 1996.

[4] R.N. Aslin, J.Z. Woodward, N.P. LaMendola & T.G. Bever, Models of word segmentation in fluent maternal speech to infants, in J.L. Morgan & K. Demuth (Eds.), *Signal to Syntax*, pp. 117–134, Mahwah, NJ, Lawrence Erlbaum Associates, 1996.

[5] M.R. Brent & T.A. Cartwright, Distributional regularity and phonotactic constraints are useful for segmentation, *Cognition*, 61, 93–125, 1996.

[6] N. Chater & P. Conkey, Finding linguistic structure with recurrent neural networks, in *Proceedings of the Fourteenth Annual Meeting of the Cognitive Science Society*, pp. 402–407, Hillsdale, NJ: Lawrence Erlbaum Associates, 1992.

[7] N. Chomsky, *Knowledge of Language*, New York: Praeger, 1986.

[8] M.H. Christiansen & J. Allen, Coping with variation in speech segmentation, in submission.

[9] M.H. Christiansen, J. Allen & M.S. Seidenberg, Learning to segment speech using multiple cues: A connectionist model, *Language and Cognitive Processes*, in press.

[10] A. Cleeremans, *Mechanisms of implicit learning: Connectionist models of sequence processing*, Cambridge, Mass: MIT Press, 1993.

[11] A. Cutler & J. Mehler, The periodicity bias, *Journal of Phonetics*, 21, 103–108, 1993.

[12] J.L. Elman, Finding structure in time. *Cognitive Science*, 14, 179–211, 1990.

[13] M. Korman, Adaptive aspects of maternal vocalizations in differing contexts at ten weeks, *First Language*, 5, 44–45, 1984.

[14] B. MacWhinney, *The CHILDES Project*, Hillsdale, NJ: Lawrence Erlbaum Associates, 1991.

[15] J. Morgan & K. Demuth (Eds), *From Signal to Syntax*, Mahwah, NJ: Lawrence Erlbaum Associates, 1996.

[16] C. Omlin & C. Giles, Training second-order recurrent neural networks using hints, in *Proceedings of the Ninth International Conference on Machine Learning* (D. Sleeman & P. Edwards, Eds.), pp. 363–368, San Mateo, CA, Morgan Kaufmann Publishers, 1992.

[17] W. Ramsey & S. Stich, Connectionism and three levels of nativism, in W. Ramsey, S. Stich & D. Rumelhart (Eds.), *Philosophy and Connectionist Theory*, Hillsdale, NJ: Lawrence Erlbaum Associates, pp. 287–310, 1991.

[18] J.R Saffran, R.N. Aslin & E.L. Newport, Statistical learning by 8-month-old infants, *Science*, 274, 1926–1928, 1996.

[19] J.R Saffran, E.L. Newport, R.N. Aslin, R.A. Tunick & S. Barruego, Incidental language learning - listening (and learning) out of the corner of your ear, *Psychological Science*, 8, 101–105, 1997.

[20] S.C. Suddarth & A.D.C. Holden, Symbolic-neural systems and the use of hints for developing complex systems, *International Journal of Man-Machine Studies*, 35, 291–311, 1991.

[21] S.C. Suddarth & Y.L.Kergosien, Rule-injection hints as a means of improving network performance and learning time, in *Proceedings of the Networks/EURIP Workshop 1990* (L.B. Almeida & C.J. Wellekens, Eds.), (Lecture Notes in Computer Science, Vol. 412), pp. 120–129, Berlin, Springer-Verlag, 1991.

Representation in Vision and Audition

Objective Functions for Topography: A Comparison of Optimal Maps

Geoffrey J. Goodhill

Georgetown Institute for Cognitive and Computational Sciences
Georgetown University Medical Center
Washington DC 20007, USA

Terrence J. Sejnowski

The Salk Institute for Biological Studies
La Jolla, CA 92037, USA

Abstract

Topographic mappings are important in several contexts, including data visualization, connectionist representation, and cortical structure. Many different ways of quantifying the degree of topography of a mapping have been proposed. In order to investigate the consequences of the varying assumptions that these different approaches embody, we have optimized the mapping with respect to a number of different measures for a very simple problem - the mapping from a square to a line. The principal results are that (1) different objective functions can produce very different maps, (2) only a small number of these functions produce mappings which match common intuitions as to what a topographic mapping "should" actually look like for this problem, (3) the objective functions can be put into certain broad categories based on the overall form of the maps, and (4) certain categories of objective functions may be more appropriate for particular types of problem than other categories.

1   Introduction

Problems of mapping occur frequently in understanding biological processes, in designing connectionist representations, and in formulating abstract methods of data analysis. An important concept in all these domains is that of a "neighbourhood preserving" map, also sometimes referred to as a topographic, topological, topology-preserving, orderly, or systematic map. Intuitively speaking, such maps take points in one space to points in another space such that nearby points map to nearby points (and sometimes in addition far-away points map to far-away points). Such maps are useful in data analysis and data visualization, where a common goal is to represent data from a high-dimensional space in a low-dimensional space so as to preserve as far as possible the "internal structure" of the data in the high dimensional space (see e.g. [11]). In psychology, topographic mappings have been used to understand mental representations: for instance the idea that similar features of the world are represented close together in some internal semantic space [18]. In neurobiology there are many examples of neighbourhood-preserving mappings, for instance between the retina and more central structures [20]. Another type of neighbourhood-preserving mapping in the brain is that, for instance, from the visual world to cells in the primary visual cortex which represent a small line segment at a particular position and orientation in the visual scene [8]. A possible goal of such biological maps is to represent nearby points in some sensory "feature space" by nearby points in the cortex [4]. This could be desirable since sensory inputs are often locally redundant: for instance in a visual scene pixel intensities are highly predictable from those of their neighbours. In order to perform "redundancy reduction" [1], it is necessary to make comparisons between the output of cells in the cortex that represent redundant inputs. Two ways this could be achieved are either by making a direct connection between these cells, or by constructing a suitable higher-order receptive field at the next level of processing. In both cases, the total length of wire required can be made short when nearby points in the feature space map to nearby points in the cortex (see [3, 4, 16, 14] for further discussion).

A number of different objective functions have been proposed to measure the degree of topography of a particular mapping (for reviews see [6, 7]). Given the wide variety of quantification choices available, it is important to understand what impact these choices have on the form of the maps that each measure best favors. This gives insight into which measures are most appropriate for particular types of applications. This paper addresses this question for a very simple problem: the mapping of 10×10 points in a square array to 1×100 points in a linear array (see figure 1). Our approach is to explicitly optimize several different objective functions from the topographic mapping literature for this case, and thus gain insight into the type of representation that each measure forms.

2 Objective functions

The objective functions investigated are as follows (for more details see [6]). Define the similarities in the input space (square) as $F(i, j)$, and in the output space (line) as $G(p, q)$ (figure 1), where i and j are points in the input space and p and q are points in the output space. Let there be N points in total, and M be a 1-1 mapping from points in the input space to points in the output space. For the first three of the measures considered, both F and G are taken to be euclidean distances in the two spaces, with distance between neighbouring points in each space taken as unity.

- **Metric Multidimensional Scaling** [19]: minimize

$$\sum_{i=1}^{N} \sum_{j<i} (F(i,j) - G(M(i), M(j)))^2$$

- **Sammon measure** [17]: minimize

$$\frac{1}{\sum_{i=1}^{N} \sum_{j<i} F(i,j)} \sum_{i=1}^{N} \sum_{j<i} \frac{(F(i,j) - G(M(i), M(j)))^2}{F(i,j)}$$

- **Spearman coefficient** [2]: maximize

$$\frac{\sum_i (R_i - \overline{R})(S_i - \overline{S})}{\sqrt{\sum_i (R_i - \overline{R})^2}\sqrt{\sum_i (S_i - \overline{S})^2}}$$

where R_i and S_i are the corresponding rankings in the ordered lists of the F's and and G's.

For the other four measures we consider, similarities are nonlinear functions of euclidean distance. They are all cases of the C measure [5, 7]:

$$C = \sum_{i=1}^{N} \sum_{j<i} F(i,j)G(M(i), M(j)),$$

for different choices of similarity function.

- **Minimal path length** [4]: $F(i,j) =$ euclidean distance, $G(p,q) = 1$ if p, q are neighbouring on the line and 0 otherwise.

- **Minimal wiring** [4]: $G(p,q) =$ euclidean distance, $F(i,j) = 1$ if i, j are neighbouring in the square and 0 otherwise.

- **Minimal distortion** [13]: $F(i,j) =$ squared euclidean distance, $G(p,q) = e^{-d^2/\sigma^2}$, where $d =$ euclidean distance between p and q, and σ is the length scale in the output space over which nearby output points should represent similar input points. This is related to the minimal path length measure, but with a broader neighbourhood function in the output space.

- **Inverted minimal distortion** [15]: $G(p,q) =$ squared euclidean distance, $F(i,j) = e^{-d^2/\sigma^2}$, where $d =$ euclidean distance between i and j, and σ is now the equivalent length scale in the input space. This is related to the minimal wiring measure, but with a broader neighbourhood function in the input space.

3 Minimization procedure

There are of the order of 100! possible mappings for this problem, and thus optimization by exhaustive search is clearly impractical. Instead we used simulated annealing, a heuristic optimization method [9]. This performs gradient descent (or ascent, as appropriate) in the objective function, but allows occasional steps in the wrong direction so that the solution is less likely to get stuck in a local optimum. The probability of taking a step in the wrong direction is controlled by a "temperature" parameter that is gradually reduced. The parameters used were as follows [12]. The initial map between points in the square and points on the line was random. At each step, a candidate move consisted of interchanging a random pair of points in the map. This move was accepted with 100%

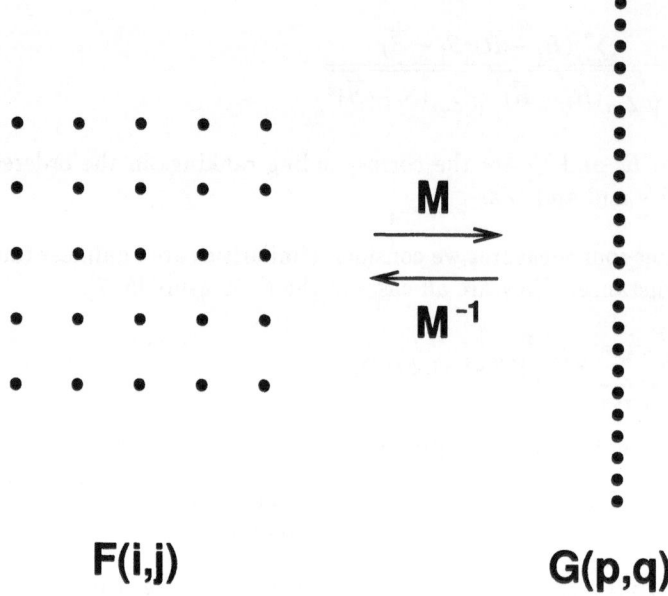

$$F(i,j) \qquad\qquad G(p,q)$$

Figure 1: The example mapping problem (only 25 points are shown). The matrix $F(i,j)$ defines similarities in the input space (square), the matrix $G(p,q)$ defines similarities in the output space (line), and M is the 1-1 map between the two spaces.

probability if it improved the value of the objective function, or with a probability determined by the temperature if it did not. Once the sooner of 10,000 candidate moves had been generated or 1000 moves accepted, the temperature was multiplied by 0.998. The procedure was terminated when no moves were accepted out of 10,000 candidates at the same temperature. Empirically, these values were found to produce close to optimal solutions for cases where the optimal solution is explicitly known (see figure 2).

4   Results

Figure 3 shows the maps found for the metric MDS, Sammon and Spearman measures. The illusion of multiple ends to the line is due to the map frequently doubling back on itself. For instance, consider the fifth column of the square for the optimal Sammon map (figure 3(b)). Initially the line meets this column at the point (5,1), counting from the bottom left corner of the square. However, the next point in the map is actually (5,10), followed by (5, 6), (5, 8), (5, 7), (5,4), (5,9), (5,5), (5,3), and (5,2), where the line then proceeds on to the sixth column. This strong local discontinuity is the result of the more global optimization concerns that dominate these measures.

Figure 4 shows minimal distortion solutions for varying σ. For small σ,

(a)   (b)

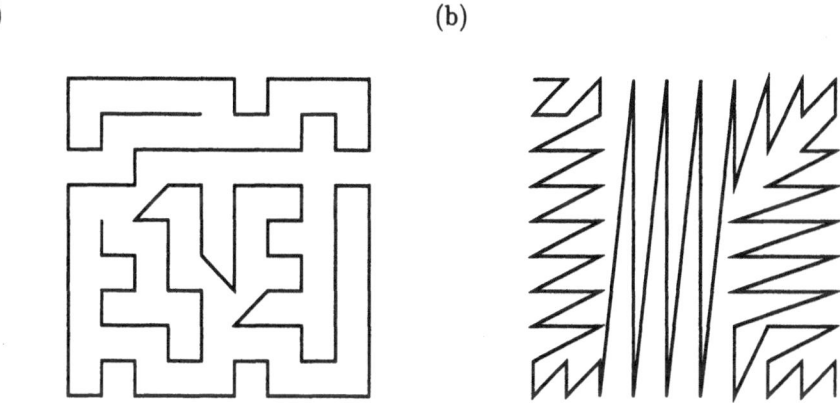

Figure 2: Testing the minimization algorithm for cases where the optima are explicitly known. (a) Mininal path length solution, length = 100.243, 1.3% longer than the optimal of 99.0. (b) Minimal wiring solution, length = 917.0, 0.3% longer than the optimal of 914.0 [4]. An optimal minimal path length solution was found when the cooling rate was increased to 0.9999 and the upper bound increased to 100,000; however it was computationally impractical to run all the simulations this slowly.

the solution resembles the minimal path optimum of figure 2(a), since the contribution from more distant neighbours than nearest neighbours is negligible. However, as σ increases the map changes form. Local continuity becomes less important compared to continuity at the scale of σ, the map becomes more spiky, and the number of large-scale folds in the map gradually decreases until at $\sigma = 20$ there is just one. This last map also shows some of the frequent doubling back behaviour seen in figure 3.

Figure 5 shows analogous results for reversed minimal distortion. For small σ the map somewhat resembles the minimal wiring map of figure 2(b), as expected. However, as σ increases, the map rapidly takes on a form reminiscent of figure 3.

In terms of general appearance, the optimal maps we have calculated can be placed into four classes.

1: Metric MDS, Sammon, reversed minimal distortion for $\sigma = 4.0$ (figs 3(a), 3(b), 5(d)). These maps are very locally discontinuous but have a characteristic overall form. This is because they all take into account neighbourhood preservation *at all scales*. Thus local continuity is not privileged over global continuity, and global concerns dominate.

2: Minimal distortion for $\sigma \leq 4.0$ (fig 4(a-c)). Only local neighbourhoods on the line are of interest. For $\sigma \sim 1$ this means in effect only nearest neighbours, and so the line meanders randomly through the square. As σ increases, the line

(a)   (b)

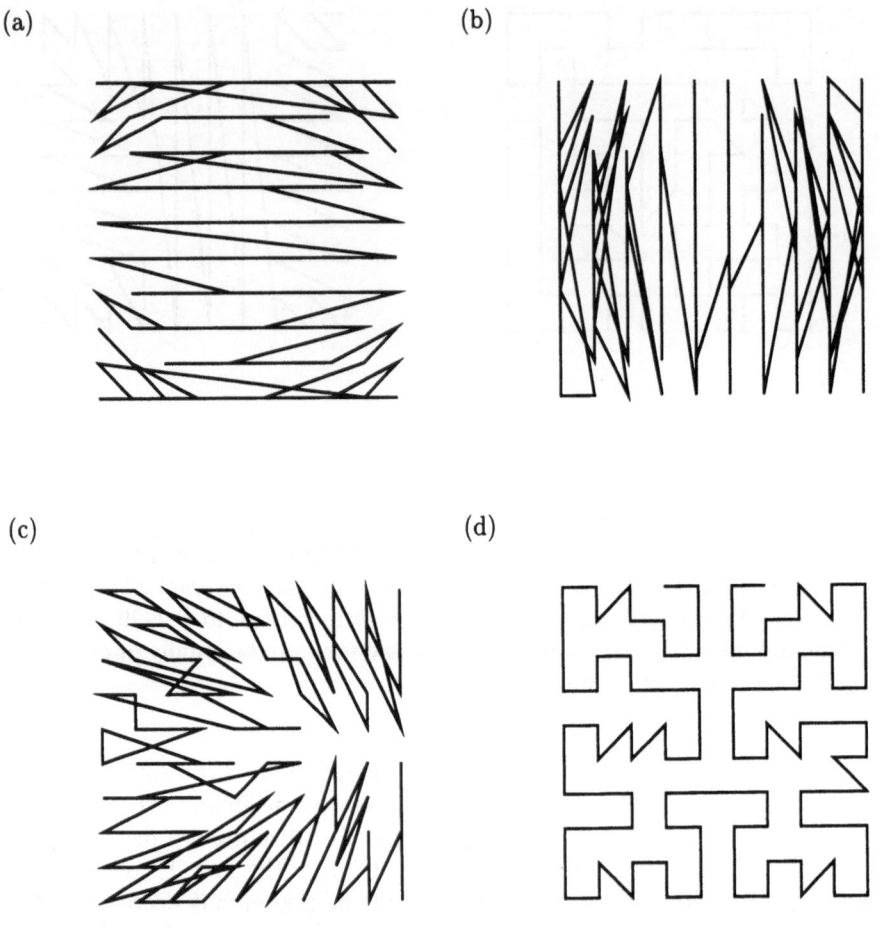

(c)   (d)

Figure 3: Solutions found by simulated annealing for the square to line problem.
(a) Metric MDS measure, cost = 9570087.8 (b) Sammon measure, cost = 38.5.
(c) Spearman measure, cost = 0.698. For these measures, global topography
dominates local topography. (d) For comparison, a map found by the elastic
net algorithm [4]. This is less optimal than any of the maps shown in this paper
with respect to the objective functions for which they were optimized.

(a)   (b)

(c)   (d)

Figure 4: Minimal distortion solutions found by simulated annealing for the square to line problem. (a) $\sigma = 1.0$, cost = 43.3. (b) $\sigma = 2.0$, cost = 214.7. (c) $\sigma = 4.0$, cost = 833.2. (d) $\sigma = 20.0$, cost = 18467.1. Note how the scale of the folding of the map changes with σ.

(a) (b)

(c) (d)

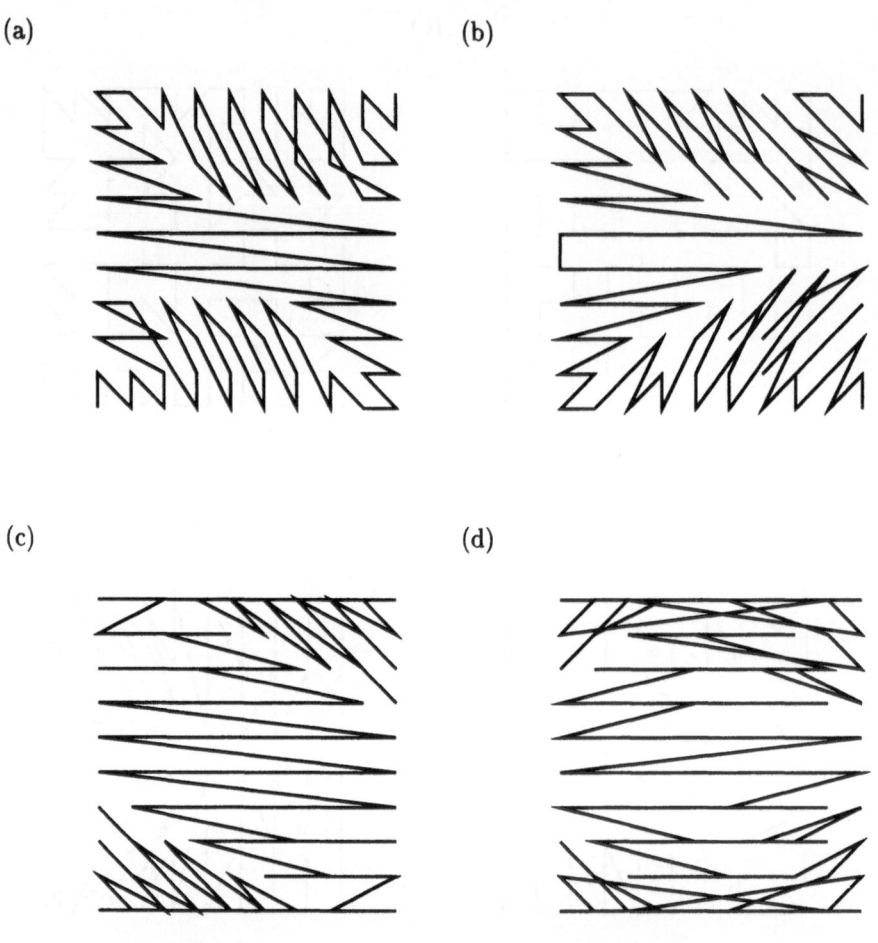

Figure 5: Reversed minimal distortion solutions found by simulated annealing for the square to line problem. (a) $\sigma = 1.0$, cost = 6250.2. (b) $\sigma = 2.0$, cost = 86469.1. (c) $\sigma = 3.0$, cost = 349926.5. (d) $\sigma = 4.0$, cost = 851763.4.

is encouraged to fold to try to keep more distant neighbours close: the scale of the folding depends on σ.

3: Spearman, minimal distortion for $\sigma = 20$ (figs 3(c), 4(d)). Although these share with class 1 the property of having very global concerns, they both have a characteristic horseshoe shape.

4: Reversed minimal distortion with $\sigma \leq 3.0$ (fig 5(a-c)). These have long stretches in the middle, with rapid zig-zags at the edge.

5 Discussion

Of the measures we have considered, only minimal distortion produces intuitively appealing maps for this problem. An interesting point is that the minimal distortion measure is almost an objective function for the SOFM algorithm [10], with σ determining the size of the neighbourhood function [13]. In the SOFM algorithm however σ decreases with time, making it hard to draw direct analogies. It could be that the intuitive appeal of the maps produced by minimal distortion is precisely because of wide familiarity with the behaviour of the SOFM, rather than for any reason more firmly rooted in the mathematics of neighbourhood preservation.

What do these results tell us about which measures are appropriate for different problems? If it is desired that generally nearby points should always map to generally nearby points as much as possible in both directions, and one is not concerned about very local continuity, then measures in class 1 are useful. This may be appropriate for some data visualization applications where the overall structure of the map is more important than its fine detail. If, on the other hand, one wants a smooth progression through the output space to imply a smooth progression through the input space, one should choose from class 2. This may be important for data visualization where it is believed the data actually lies on a lower-dimensional manifold in the high-dimensional space. However, an important weakness for this representation is that some neighbourhood relationships between points in the input space may be completely lost in the resulting representation. For understanding the structure of cortical mappings, self-organizing algorithms that optimize objectives in class 2 have proved useful [4]. Very few other objectives have been applied to this problem though, so it is still an open question which are most appropriate. Classes 3 and 4 represent pathologies that have been hitherto unappreciated. There may be some applications for which they are worthwhile, but for brain maps they are unsuitable.

6 Conclusions

This paper has attempted to impose some order on the space of popular measures of neighbourhood preservation, in order to better understand topographic mapping methods in data analysis, connectionism and neurobiology. We considered a mapping problem that represents an extremely simple example of a mismatch between the dimensions of the input space and the output space. By examining the maps given by optimizing each measure, we tried to group together different types of optimal maps and thus the measures that generated them. The main conclusions are as follows.

1. The optimal maps span a surprisingly broad subspace of possible maps, and include maps lacking local continuity.

2. This subspace is much larger than the space of maps that are often referred to as topographic. This suggests that great caution should be used in relying on visual inspection to judge degrees of topography.

3. The subspace of optimal maps, and thus the measures that generated them, can be divided into four main classes based on the general form of the maps produced.

4. The structure of this subspace can provide guidance in choosing the most appropriate mapping measure to apply to more complex mapping problems. For instance, finding a highly curved manifold in a high dimensional space requires preservation of local but not global topography, whereas forming a low dimensional representation of the relationships between clusters in a high dimensional space (ignoring structure within a cluster) requires preservation of global but not local topography. In general, the sensible use of topographic mapping techniques requires a good understanding of the nature of the particular application.

References

[1] Barlow, H.B. (1989). Unsupervised learning. *Neural Computation*, **1**, 295-311.

[2] Bezdek, J.C. & Pal, N.R. (1995). An index of topological preservation for feature extraction. *Pattern Recognition*, **28**, 381-391.

[3] Cowey, A. (1979). Cortical maps and visual perception. *Qua. Jou. Exper. Psychol.*, **31**, 1-17.

[4] Durbin, R. & Mitchison, G. (1990). A dimension reduction framework for understanding cortical maps. *Nature*, **343**, 644-647.

[5] Goodhill, G. J., Finch, S. & Sejnowski, T. J. (1995). Quantifying neighbourhood preservation in topographic mappings. Institute for Neural Computation Technical Report Series, No. INC-9505, November 1995. Available from http://www.giccs.georgetown.edu/~geoff

[6] Goodhill, G.J. & Sejnowski, T.J. (1996) Quantifying neighbourhood preservation in topographic mappings. In: "Proceedings of the 3rd Joint Symposium on Neural Computation", University of California, San Diego and California Institute of Technology, Vol. 6, Pasadena, CA: California Institute of Technology, 61-82. Available from http://www.giccs.georgetown.edu/~geoff

[7] Goodhill, G.J. & Sejnowski, T.J. (1997). A unifying objective function for topographic mappings. *Neural Computation*, **9**, 1291-1304.

[8] Hubel, D.H. & Wiesel, T.N. (1977). Functional architecture of the macaque monkey visual cortex. *Proc. R. Soc. Lond. B*, **198**, 1-59.

[9] Kirkpatrick, S., Gelatt, C.D. & Vecchi, M.P. (1983). Optimization by simulated annealing. *Science*, **220**, 671-680.

[10] Kohonen, T. (1982). Self-organized formation of topologically correct feature maps. *Biol. Cybern.*, **43**, 59-69.

[11] Krzanowski, W.J. (1988). Principles of multivariate analysis: a user's perspective. Oxford statistical science series; v. 3. Oxford University Press.

[12] van Laarhoven, P.J.M. & Aarts, E.H.L. (1987). Simulated annealing: theory and applications. Reidel, Dordrecht, Holland.

[13] Luttrell, S.P. (1990). Derivation of a class of training algorithms. *IEEE Trans. Neural Networks*, **1**, 229-232.

[14] Mitchison, G. (1991). Neuronal branching patterns and the economy of cortical wiring. *Proc. Roy. Soc. B.*, **245**, 151-158.

[15] Mitchison, G. (1995). A type of duality between self-organizing maps and minimal wiring. *Neural Computation.*, **7**, 25-35.

[16] Nelson, M.E. & Bower, J.M. (1990). Brain maps and parallel computers. *Trends Neurosci.*, **13**, 403-408.

[17] Sammon, J.W. (1969). A nonlinear mapping for data structure analysis. *IEEE Trans. Comput.*, **18**, 401-409.

[18] Shepard, R.N. (1980). Multidimensional scaling, tree-fitting and clustering. *Science*, **210**, 390-398.

[19] Torgerson, W.S. (1952). Multidimensional Scaling, I: theory and method. *Psychometrika*, **17**, 401-419.

[20] Udin, S.B. & Fawcett, J.W. (1988). Formation of topographic maps. *Ann. Rev. Neurosci.*, **11**, 289-327.

Testing Principal Component Representations for Faces

Peter J.B. Hancock, Vicki Bruce
Department of Psychology
University of Stirling, UK

A. Mike Burton
Department of Psychology
University of Glasgow, UK

Abstract

A variety of experimental results indicate that the human visual system processes faces at least to some extent holistically, rather than by analysing individual features such as nose and eyes. Principal Components Analysis (PCA) of face images, which is widely used in engineering approaches to face identification, produces an inherently global representation. We investigate the psychological plausibility of this representation, looking at correlations with human perceptions of memorability and similarity. We show that transformation of faces to an average shape prior to PCA improves correlations with human ratings

1 Introduction

Humans are quite good at recognising faces, given how similar most of them are. Attempts to emulate the feat using computer systems indicate how difficult the task is, with variations in the appearance of an individual caused by changes of expression, lighting or pose vastly exceeding the variations between individuals by most simple measures. Although humans are also adversely affected by changes of lighting and pose, we are evidently able to extract some kind of relatively invariant features, but it is still not clear what these might be.

A number of results suggest that we do not rely on measurements of internal features. For example, line drawings retain such information, but are significantly worse than photographs for identification [4]. Photographic negatives also retain all the information required for feature location, but again are significantly harder to recognise [7]. Inverting a face also makes it harder to recognise, for reasons hinted at by Figure 1. The mutilation of the right hand image is barely perceptible when the face is upside down. Inversion affects our ability to integrate the features into a whole face and it seems that this kind of holistic processing, based on relatively low-level image-features, may underlie our recognition system.

Principal component analysis (PCA) has been proposed as an engineering solution to face recognition [14]. The representations it forms cover the whole face but are based on statistical properties of the lowest possible image-feature, namely individual pixels. Although we do not use neural networks to perform PCA here, for efficiency reasons, there are many network algorithms that would do the job, e.g. Sanger's [12]. Although simple PCA is implausible as a model of what the visual system is doing. it has been shown to have some surprising matches with some aspects of human vision [1]. Here we investigate the psychological plausibility of this form of coding further, by comparing it with

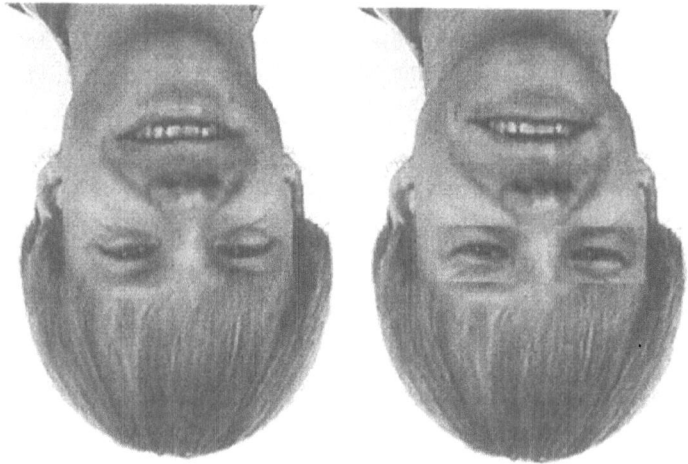

Figure 1: The "Thatcher illusion" [13]. This way up, the modifications to the right hand image are hardly noticeable.

human judgements of a common set of faces. We obtain distinctiveness ratings for each face, and subsequently test how memorable each actually is. We also obtain similarity ratings by asking participants to sort the faces into piles of those that are similar. The following section explains PCA of faces in more detail. The gathering of human data, and comparison with PCA, is described in section 3 for similarity judgements and in section 4 for distinctiveness and memorability. We then describe the effects of horizontal bandpass filtering of the face images prior to PCA.

1.1 Face sets

Experiments reported here use two distinct sets of faces. The first has one image each of 174 individuals [9]. The second has only 50 individuals, but multiple examples [8]. A neutral expression example of each was used as a target set, and 2 or 3 images showing one of happiness, disgust and surprise for a total of 136 in the test set.

2 PCA of faces

PCA is a standard statistical technique for reducing the dimensionality of data while attempting to preserve as much of the information, in the form of variance, as possible. Given an elliptical cloud of data in two dimensions, PCA will return the long axis of the ellipse as the first component, since the position on this axis will say most about where a datapoint is in the cloud. If the data on the x and y axes were the height and weight of a group of children, then the first component returned might usefully be given the label "size". The second component would be at right angles to the first, and might be given the label "obesity". Turk and Pentland [14] applied PCA to images of faces, producing ghostly "eigenfaces" such as those illustrated in the top row of Figure 2. These components correspond to new axes in the pixel space just as size and obesity do in the space of height and weight, but it is much harder to give meaningful labels to them. Several of those shown in Figure 2 seem to code something to do with hair length or style. However, the principle is the same, so the position of a face on the axis defined by the first component will say as much as it is possible to about that face's appearance, given only one dimension. More precisely, it says as much as possible about the values of the pixels in the image of the face: whether this corresponds in a useful way to what we think of as appearance is precisely what we wish to determine.

PCA on a set of n faces can produce up to n components, each accounting for a decreasing amount of variance. Each face may be coded as a vector in the space defined by the components. If all n components are used, the representation is perfect, and the original face images may be recovered by multiplying through the coding vector with the eigenfaces, just as height and weight could be recovered from a knowledge of size and obesity. PCA simply redescribes the data in a way that may be more useful. Typically, fewer eigenfaces will be stored, perhaps 50 from a set of 200 faces, which might account for 90% of the variance. In this case there will be some loss of information, but recreated faces are typically quite accurate, subjectively.

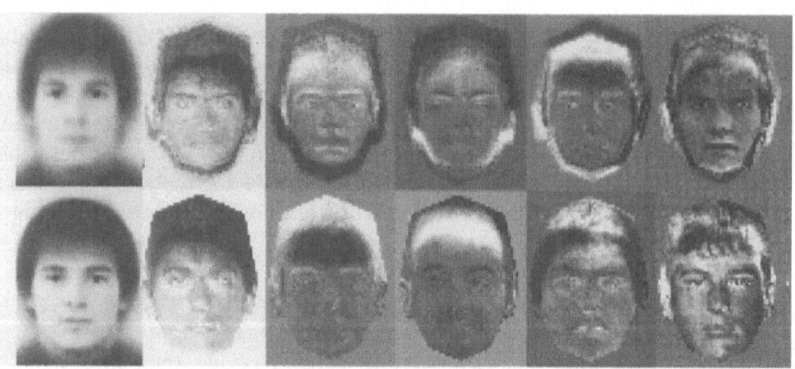

Figure 2: Full image (top row) and "shape-free" eigenfaces. The left-hand image in each row is the average face, followed by the first four and the tenth eigenfaces.

In order for PCA to extract something sensible from face images, they need to be aligned, typically by scaling and translating to bring the two eyes to the same x,y location in each image. Because of the variability in faces, this will mean that other features such as nose and mouth are in different locations, which will have to be accommodated by the eigenfaces. Craw and Cameron [5] proposed morphing the faces to an average shape prior to PCA. Key features around the face are located (in our case by hand, though automatic systems are increasingly successful), see Figure 3. We defined 38 points on each face. An average face shape is computed from the positions marked on all the faces, and then each face is morphed to that shape. PCA now produces much more sharply-defined eigenfaces, see the bottom row of Figure 2. Craw and Cameron showed that this procedure improved identification rates for a computer-based system. One reason for this is that it removes some of the variability due to changes of expression, and even some due to variations in pose.

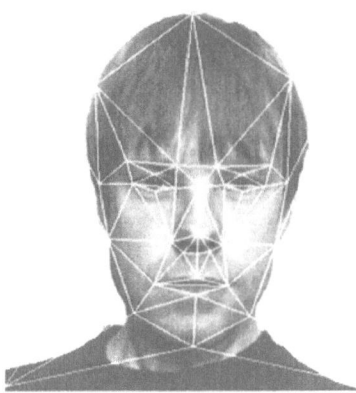

Figure 3: The location of points around the face used for shape averaging.

This procedure also gives us shape information about each face, in the form of a vector of x,y locations. We may perform PCA on these vectors also, to give us the principal modes of shape variation between faces. Figure 4 illustrates the first six of these components, extracted from the second set of faces. The images are generated by moving the points for the average face one and two steps in each direction, as specified by the shape components. The first component turns out to code nodding of the head. Although our participants were asked to look directly at the camera, they evidently differ enough in the angle at which they hold their heads for this to be the major component of variation. The second component codes variation in head size. That this is only the second component is probably because of the normalising effect of adjusting all the images to have their eyes in the same location. This is also responsible for some of the rather strange looking deformations caused by later components, since everything moves with respect to the fixed eyes.

The third component appears to code something about the relative vertical position of the eyes in the face. The fourth and fifth code the two remaining rotational degrees of freedom: shaking from side to side and tilting. The sixth codes face width. Higher components (not shown), then code increasingly subtle variations in face shape.

We calculated 20 shape components, but omitted the first, fourth and fifth from further calculations as we considered that variations in head angle, except in extreme cases, were unlikely to have much bearing on human perceptions of the faces. Initial investigations showed that later components showed rather little correlation with human ratings and we typically used only 7 or 10.

Having separated shape from the finer image detail prior to PCA, we may recombine them again afterwards, typically taking 10 image and 10 shape components (13 image and 7 shape for the multiple correlation results of section 4.1). Some form of normalisation is required, since one set is in the scale of pixel grey-levels, while the other is in x,y pixel locations, so the two sets of components were adjusted to have the same total variance. We therefore have four types of PCA data for comparison with human perceptions: unaltered full im-

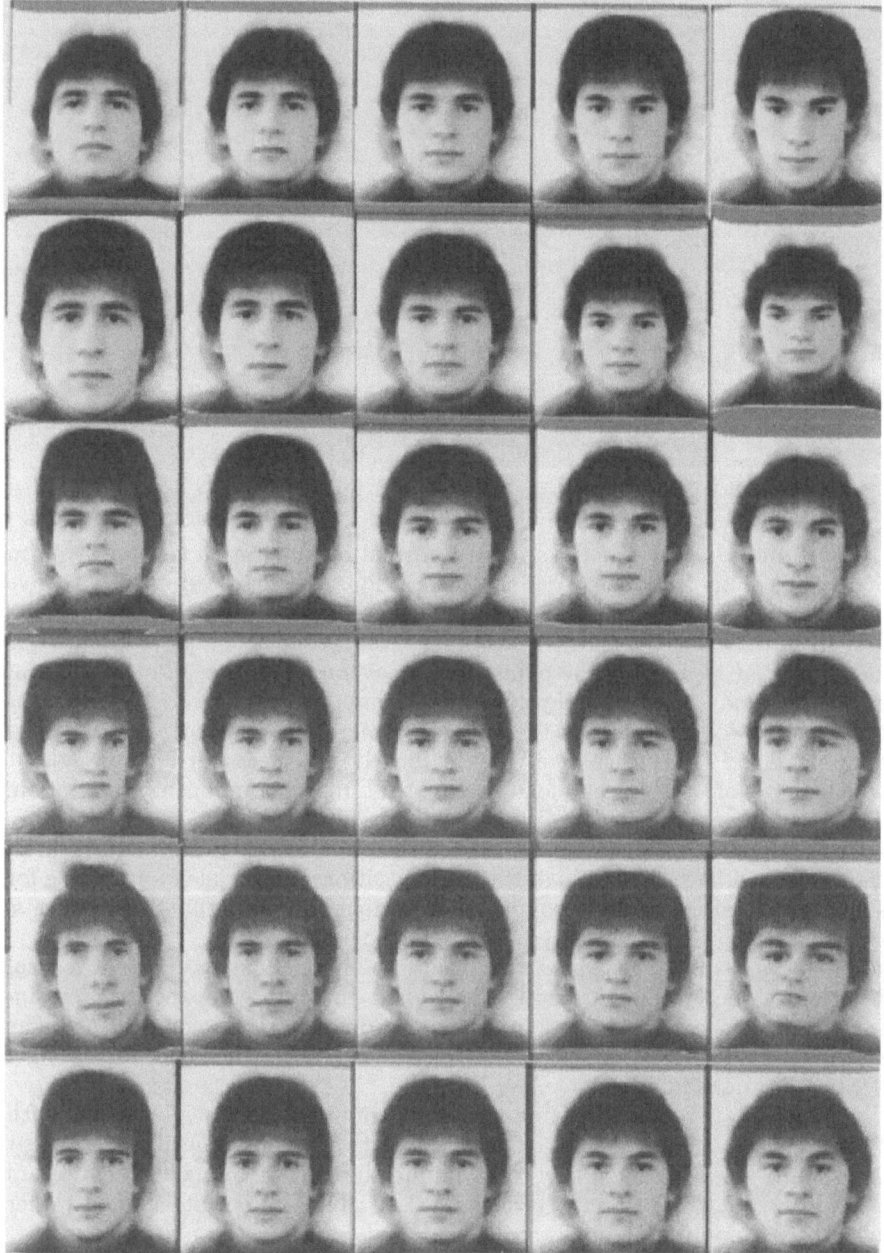

Figure 4: Principal components of face shape. The average shape-free face (centre column) is distorted by adding or subtracting shape components to its control points, and morphing the image to the new shape. The effects of the first 6 shape components are shown, one per row. First component codes head nodding, second head size, third the relative position of the eyes, fourth head rotation, fifth head angle (tilt) and sixth face width.

ages, shape-free images, shape vectors and shape vector and shape-free image recombined.

2.1 PCA measures

There are a variety of possible measures derived from PCA that can be compared with human data. The three considered here are individual component values; the error of reconstruction; and the matching error on identification.

The simplest is the individual value of each component. Suppose that some of our components really do mimic in some way the representations used inside our heads. For a face to be called distinctive implies that it is atypical, or a long way from the mean in some dimension. A face that appears distinctive to us might then be expected to have a large value on one or more of the components. However, since atypical might be in either direction from the mean, it is a large absolute value that might be expected. We may therefore perform multiple correlations between our component values for a face and the human rated distinctiveness or memorability values. In practice we found correlations between both raw and absolute component values and so included both in our correlations, reported in section 4.1.

If the complete set of PCs are used to reconstruct a face, there will be no error. If a subset is used, then there will be inaccuracies. Hancock et al [9] showed that if few components are used, then distinctive faces show a high error of reconstruction, since the early components code that which is common to many faces, leaving unusual faces poorly represented. However, as the number of components rises, there is a reversal, and distinctive faces become relatively well coded, because the best way to reduce the remaining variance is to code the outlying faces. Interpretation of correlations with reconstruction error therefore requires some care and no such results are reported here.

The third measure is the matching error on identification. If a new image of one of the faces is processed by the same set of eigenfaces, it will produce a PC vector, which ideally will be close to the vector produced by the original sample of the same face. We use simple Euclidean distance in the PC space: the test face is declared to match the target face to which it is closest. If several target faces are of similar distance, then our confidence in the match is low. We define a confidence measure as the ratio of the distance to the correct target to the average of the distance to all the others. A face that is distinctive to humans literally stands out from the crowd, and so should have a high confidence measure in the PCA system.

3 Similarity

Some faces are inherently confusable: those of identical twins being an obvious example. However, "s/he looks like..." is a common expression, and is often used as a means to enable identification to be made. Our premise in this section is that if PCA has any kind of psychological plausibility, it ought to find the same faces similar that people do. We therefore gathered similarity ratings from human participants to see whether they correlate with the similarity metrics produced by PCA [8].

40 participants were asked to sort the (second) set of 50 neutral faces into piles that appeared similar to them. They were free to make as many piles as they wished and ranged between 2 and 29, with an average of 11.5. To get similarity ratings for a pair of faces, we simply counted the number of occasions they were put in the same pile: this varied from 0 to 20.

These similarity measures were compared with the matching errors on identification from PCA. Faces that appear similar to humans ought to be close together in PCA space and produce a lower match error than faces that appear dissimilar. For each face, we computed the distance to all the other target faces and then performed a Kendall rank correlation between the PCA distance measures and the human similarity scores. This gave us a set of 50 correlation values, average values for which are shown in Figure 5. Since the correlations are relatively small we treat them as normally distributed and apply t-tests, which indicate that all differ significantly from zero, so the PCA system does capture something of the notion of similarity that humans use. Figure 5 indicates that the transformation to shape-free images improves the correlation, and that while the correlation with shape alone is low, the combination of shape and shape-free gives the highest figure.

Note that while these correlations are significant, they are quite low. We are investigating the reason for this: it may simply be that our method for gathering human similarity data is too noisy - there is a tendency for piles to "drift" with matches being made to the face on the top of the pile, rather than to some average for that pile. Alternative ways of assessing similarity, such as confusability on rapid presentation of two faces, may provide more reliable results [3].

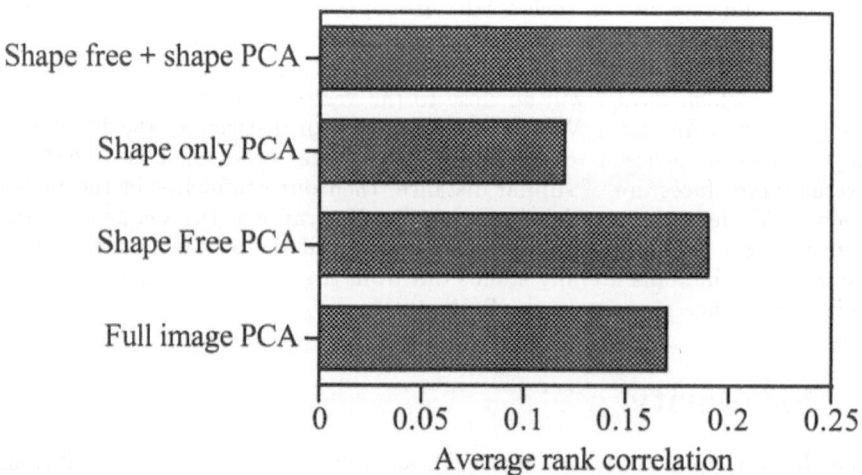

Figure 5: Average Kendall rank correlation values between human similarity ratings and matching errors for the four different sets of PCA data.

4 Distinctiveness and memorability

Participants were asked to rate each face for distinctiveness on a scale of 1-10, in response to the question "How easy would it be to pick this person out at a railway station?" Images were presented via computer, with no time limit for response. The two sets of faces were each divided in half, with participants being asked to rate only one half: 87 faces for the first set, 25 for the second. There were a total of 34 participants for the first set of faces, 20 for the second [9, 8].

After a gap of 10-15 minutes doing other unrelated experiments, participants were shown the complete set of faces (174 or 50, respectively) and asked to rate on the same scale of 1-10 whether they had seen each face in the previous part of the experiment. This gives hit scores for faces that had been seen and false positive scores for those that had not. Participants' scores were combined to give average values of all three measures for each face.

The three measures show a rather odd pattern of correlation. We would expect distinctive faces to be well-remembered and well-rejected. This is indeed generally the case, with significant correlations between distinctiveness and hit score of 0.49 and between distinctiveness and false positive of -0.40 for the first set of faces. However, the correlation between hit score and false positive is not significant ($r = -0.08, p > 0.05$), implying that the faces that are well-remembered are not necessarily the same as those that are well-rejected. The second set of faces display a similar pattern. The cause of this pattern, first observed by Vokey and Read [15] is still unclear. It may be that hit and false positive scores are simply an unreliable indicator of underlying memorability, that actually correlates well with distinctiveness, or it may be that there really are different underlying causes that mediate recognition and rejection.

4.1 PCA multiple regression

We investigated whether there was any correlation between individual component values and the human ratings for the first set of images (a more detailed account of the analysis appears in [9]). Table 1 shows multiple-r values for the correlation between the human ratings and the first 20 principal component outputs, and their absolute values (see section 2.1). Multiple regression was performed using SPSS with stepwise addition of components. Typically about 5 component values were entered into the equation. The figures in Table 1 are the average of 100 results, produced by randomly splitting the set of faces in half. Two things are of note. Firstly, that the transformation to shape-free makes a big difference to the correlation with false positive scores. It seems that the shape vector alone has no significant correlation with false positive responses, since it does not exceed the random multiple correlation for this many variables of 0.33. Secondly, that the combination of shape and shape-free again fares best.

To give some indication of whether individual components correlate with the human data, Figure 6 shows the number of times each component was used in the 100 multiple correlation equations for shape + shape-free coding from Table 1. Of note is the heavy usage of the first component for false positive, with rather little contribution from shape components, as might be expected from the results in Table 1. Distinctiveness and hit score show similar patterns

Type	Distinctiveness	Hit	False positive
Full image	0.51	0.42	0.42
Shape-free	0.48	0.40	0.49
Shape only	0.48	0.37	0.30
Shape-free + shape	0.52	0.43	0.48

Table 1: Multiple correlation between PCs and subject ratings, averaged over 100 random half splits of the set of 184 faces

Type	Distinctiveness	Hit	False positive
Full image	0.21	0.30	-0.16
Shape-free	0.32	0.42	-0.36
Shape only	0.29	0.2	-0.09
Shape-free + shape	0.34	0.41	-0.34

Table 2: Correlation between the PCA match confidence on recognition and the human ratings for the second set of faces. r_{crit} for $p < 0.005$ is 0.24

of results, with a heavy loading on the second image component and much more on the shape components. For the complete set of these images, the first shape component codes size and the fourth codes face shape (long and thin vs. short and fat), while the second and third code nodding and shaking of the head (cf. the results of Figure 4, which come from the second set of faces). As might be expected, the second and third components show rather low usage. It is possible that on at least some of the occasions that they are used, the components appear in a different order due to the particular nature of the images in the random partition, whereupon the second component might, for example, code face size. Because of this uncertainty, we did not attempt to eliminate the components that code head angle from this analysis.

4.2 PCA match confidence

For the second set of faces, we were able to test the recognition performance of the PCA system, by attempting to identify the 136 extra images of the target faces. The correct recognition rate rises from 95% (129/136) for the full images to 100% for the shape-free images. The ratio of the distance to the correct target to the average distance to all the targets produces a confidence measure, that might correlate with distinctiveness. The correlations with the human ratings are shown in Table 2. Again there is a marked increase in correlation accompanying the transformation from full to shape-free images. The shape vector now shows a significant correlation with distinctiveness while, again, the combination of shape and shape-free seems to combine the best of both.

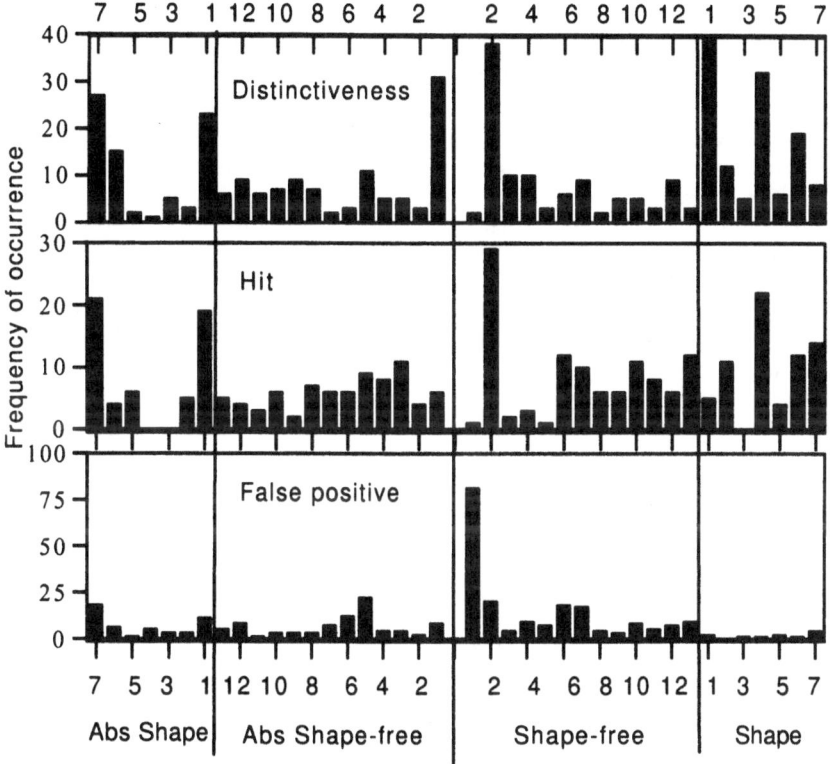

Figure 6: Usage of components in the multiple regression equations for shape + shape-free, for 100 different permutations of the image set. Raw components are shown to the right, absolute values to the left. Note the different vertical scales.

4.3 Discussion

Craw and Cameron [5] showed that the shape-free transformation improved recognition rates, a finding echoed here in section 4.2. The results presented here indicate that the increase in recognition performance is accompanied by an increase in correlation with human perceptions of the same faces. It might however be rather rash to conclude that this is evidence that the human visual system performs some similar separation of shape information. Image PCA performs better when gross shape is removed because the image space becomes more linear - it is possible to add two faces together and produce something that still looks face-like. Putting the shape data back in after PCA might reasonably be expected to give better correlations, since it adds to the information about the face. A misshapen face would be regarded as distinctive, so there ought to be correlations present, which there are, e.g. Figure 2.

The pattern of correlations shown with human false positive data is rather intriguing. It has a particularly marked increase when shape information is removed from the images, and very little correlation with the shape vector alone. Furthermore, the results in Figure refusage-fig indicate that much of the correlation comes from the first image component. Why this should be so is not obvious. A high false positive score means people are likely to think they have seen a face before when they haven't - it just seems "familiar". This could be because it genuinely does resemble someone in the fist set, but such chance occurrences seem unlikely to show the kind of correlations with shape observed here. So is there something about some faces that makes them seem familiar? Adding the first component to the average face, Figure 7, does not give much insight as to what is going on: the faces certainly look different, but it isn't immediately obvious that one looks more "familiar" than the other. This figure was generated by taking the average shape-free face, bottom left of Figure 2, and either adding or subtracting the first image component, next to the average face in Figure 2. Further experimentation is called for.

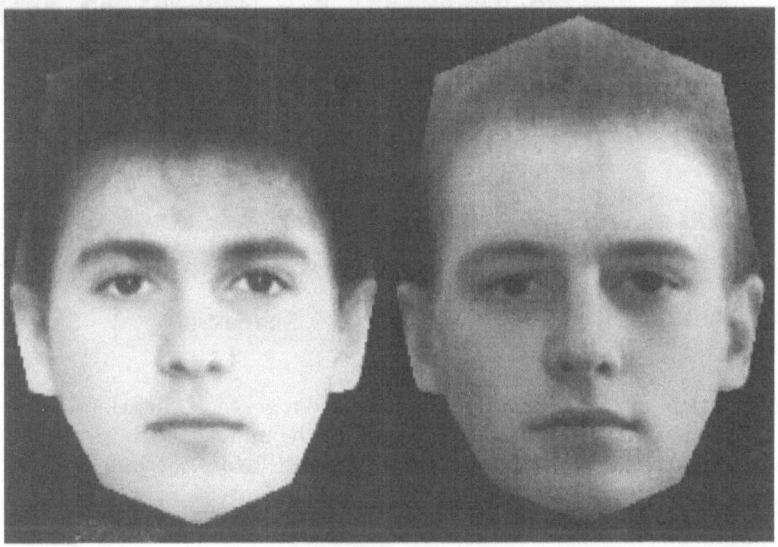

Figure 7: The effects of adding (left) and subtracting the first image eigenface from the average shape-free face. Does one look more "familiar" than the other?

5 Filtered images

One obvious criticism of the approach used here is that the PCA is conducted on raw image pixel values. Even if something like PCA is operating in humans, it will not be performed on anything approaching raw pixels: there is much pre-processing carried out in the retina and early visual cortex. As a preliminary step towards remedying this, we have bandpass filtered our face images prior to PCA. We use horizontally-aligned difference of Gaussian filters, found by Moses et al [11] to reduce variations due to illumination directions and also used by Dakin [6] and Watt [16] to extract experimentally interesting "bar-codes" from faces. We used the first set of faces, and performed multiple regression between the PC outputs and the human rating data as in section 4.1. The results are shown in Figure 8 and show a remarkable crossover between distinctiveness and false positive. Correlation with distinctiveness is greatest at coarse spatial scales, consistent with the notion that rather gross structural deviations from the norm are regarded as distinctive. It is also likely that hair style is regarded as distinctive, and this will also show up at coarse scales. False positives, on the other hand, show almost no correlation at coarse scales, but high correlation at fine scales - the value of 0.51 is somewhat higher than any of the unfiltered results in Table 1. The fall-off at coarse scales is consistent with the lack of information about false positives in the shape vector, as only the general impression of shape survives the filtering. The high correlation at fine scales is harder to understand: why should fine details in a face make you think you've seen them before?

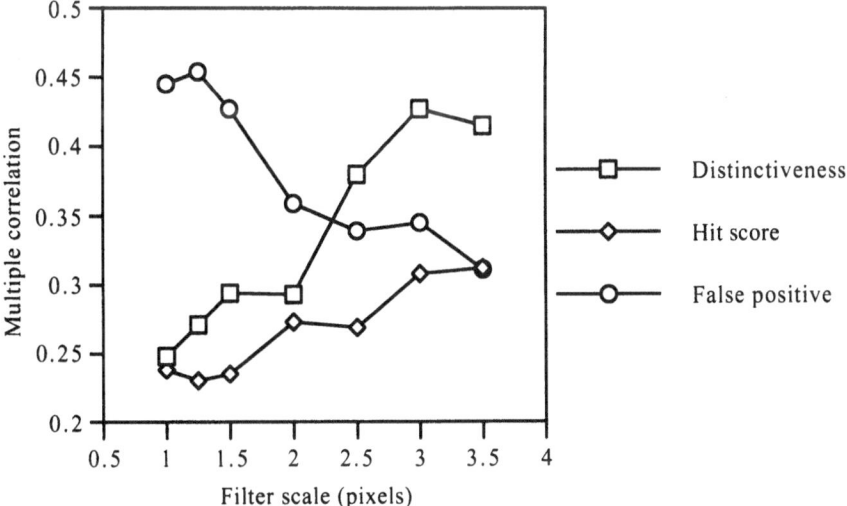

Figure 8: Multiple regression values between the three human ratings and the component values when the images have been bandpass filtered prior to PCA.

6 Future work

PCA is only one of a number of successful engineering approaches to face identification. We have compared the results from the second set of images here with another successful engineering system developed at Ruhr-Univerität Bochum by von der Malsburg's group [10]: this system appears to be rather better at capturing human perceptions than PCA [8]. We are now investigating independent component analysis [2]. This has so far been applied only to full face images: it will be interesting to see what effect separating shape information has on this as well. The false positive results are still something of a puzzle. The results of section 5 suggest that there may be more insight to be gained from experiments with pre-processing: even if PCA has nothing to do with the way we actually process faces, the correlations may yield insights into just what it is that makes a face memorable, or liable to false recognition.

Acknowledgements

This work was funded by grant no. GRH 93828 from the UK Science and Engineering Research Council and R000 236688 from the Economic and Social Research Council. Derek Carson and Kiran Chitta ran the human experiments, Ian Craw and Nick Costen provided the first set of images.

References

[1] Baddeley RJ and Hancock PJB, A statistical analysis of natural images matches psychophysically derived orientation tuning curves. Proceedings of the Royal Society B 1991, 246:219–223

[2] Bartlett MS and Sejnowski TJ, Independent component analysis of face images: a representation for face recognition. Proceedings of the 4th Annual Joint Symposium on Neural Computation, Pasadena, CA. La Jolla, CA: Institute for Neural Computation 1997.

[3] Biederman, I, Neural and psychophysical analysis of object and face recognition, Talk at NATO ASI: Face recognition, from theory to application, Stirling, July 1997.

[4] Bruce V, Hanna E, Dench N, Healy P and Burton AM, The importance of 'mass' in line drawings of faces, Applied Cognitive Psychology 1992, 6:619–628

[5] Craw I and Cameron P, Parameterising images for recognition and reconstruction In Mowforth P, editor, Proceedings of the British Machine Vision Conference, London: Springer Verlag, 1991 pages 367–370

[6] Dakin SC, The visual representation of texture, PhD thesis, Department of Psychology, University of Stirling, 1994.

[7] Galper RE and Hochberg J, Repetition memory for photographs of faces, American Journal of Psychology 1971, 84:351–354

[8] Hancock PJB, Bruce V and Burton AM, A comparison of two computer-based face identification systems with human perceptions of faces, Submitted to Vision Research 1997.

[9] Hancock PJB, Burton AM, and Bruce V, Face processing: human perception and principal components analysis, Memory and Cognition 1996, 24:26–40

[10] Lades M, Vorbrüggen JC, Buhman J, Lage J, von der Malsburg C, Würtz RP and Konen W, Distortion invariant object recognition in the dynamic link architecture, IEEE Transactions on Computers 1993, 42:300–311

[11] Moses Y, Adini Y and Ullman S, Face recognition: the problem of compensating for changes in illumination direction, Proceedings of ECCV-94, Stockholm, 2-6 May 1994, Berlin: Springer-Verlag, 1994, pages 286–296.

[12] Sanger TD, Optimal unsupervised learning in a single-layer linear feedforward neural network, Neural Networks 1989, 2:459–473

[13] Thompson P, Magaret Thatcher: A new illusion, Perception 1980, 9:483–484

[14] Turk M and Pentland A, Eigenfaces for recognition, Journal of Cognitive Neuroscience 1991 3:71–86

[15] Vokey JR and Read JD, Familiarity, memorability and the effect of typicality on the recognition of faces. Memory and Cognition 1992, 20:291–302

[16] Watt RJ, A computational examination of image segmentation and the initial stages of human vision, Perception 1994, 23:383–398

Selection for Object Identification: Modelling Emergent Attentional Processes in Normality and Pathology

Glyn W. Humphreys and Dietmar Heinke
University of Birmingham, UK

Abstract

We report a model of translation-invariant object recognition: SAIM (for Selective Attention for Identification Model). In SAIM, objects compete in a "selection network" to achieve a mapping from their location on the retina to a translation-invariant "focus of attention". We investigated spatially selective lesions affecting either the mapping from one side of the retina into the selection network, or the mapping from the selection network to one side of the attentional window. Lesions into the selection network produced a pattern of retinotopic neglect, with processing biased against stimuli on the affected side of the retina. Lesions out of the selection network produced a form of neglect that was tied to one side of an object irrespective of where the object fell on the retina. These different forms of neglect match patterns reported in brain lesioned human patients. We propose that forms of selection in vision emerge as a consequence of procedures for achieving viewpoint-independent object recognition.

1 Selection for object identification

Visual scenes typically contain many objects, yet actions may only be addressed to a few; consequently, there needs to be some form of selection so that only representations of behaviourally relevant objects are made available to response systems (cf. [1]). Selection is also likely to be a necessary part of successful visual object identification. For example, when multiple objects are present there may be problems in binding their parts together without incorrect (illusory) bindings being formed [2, 3]; a solution to this is spatial selection: select only one object or one spatial area at a time for binding, so that the parts of irrelevant object do not compete in the binding process. Physiological evidence also suggests a need for selection in object identification. It is widely accepted that object identification is dependent on neurons in the inferotemporal cortex that respond to complex properties of objects (e.g., [4]). Such neurons typically have large receptive fields covering wide regions on the retina [5]. These neurons, being tuned to particular stimuli, are activated sub-optimally when multiple objects are present (due to pooling of information within the receptive field). However firing is enhanced if a preferred object can be selected so that only it activates the target neuron (cf. [6, 7]).

Psychological models have typically held that visual selection is spatially-based, assuming (for instance) that selection involves some form of internal spotlight or zoom lens that activates attended locations (e.g., [8, 9, 10]). Strong evidence for spatial selection comes from studies of cueing which show that detection of a target is enhanced when it is preceded by a spatially valid pre-cue [9]. Other work, though, demonstrates that selection is influenced by grouping between the parts of objects, with all the parts of objects being selected together even when parts of irrelevant objects are overlapping or are spatially more proximal (e.g., see [11] for one summary). To accommodate such results, theorists have suggested that object recognition processes can operate in a top-down manner to activate relevant areas of visual field [12, 13] or that recognition procedures can recover parts of objects even when some are processed sub-optimally [14].

Neuropsychological evidence for both spatial and object-based constraints on selection comes from the syndrome of unilateral visual neglect (see [15, 16] for recent summaries). Following brain damage to the dorsal visual system, patients may often fail to respond to stimuli presented on the side of space opposite to their lesion. Performance can be affected by the position of an object relative to the patient's body (e.g., [17, 18]), but also by the positions of parts relative to an object. For example, in neglect dyslexia the impaired identification of letters on the contralesional side of a word can occur even when the word is presented in the ipsilesional visual field [19], suggesting that neglect is then determined by the positions of the letters in the word. There can also be neglect of the contralesional parts of objects when objects are rotated so that these parts appear in the ipsilesional visual field [20]. Neglect tied to the positions of parts in objects can be doubly dissociated from neglect tied to the positions of stimuli in the visual field [21], suggesting that the disorders reflect functionally separable lesions. Neglect has been interpreted as a disorder of visual selection because the performance of neglect patients is improved by cueing their attention to the affected side [22, 18] and because it can be exacerbated under conditions of double simultaneous stimulation [23]. Patients may be able to detect a single stimulus presented contralesionally, but fail to detect it when a second stimulus is presented ipsilesionally at the same time: the phenomenon of extinction. In extinction, the contralesional stimulus appears to lose in competition for selection with the ipsilesional one [24]. Neglect of stimuli presented in the contralesional visual field can be understood as a disorder of spatial attention, in which attentional orienting is biased to the ipsilesional side (and so, for example, cannot disengage from ipsilesional stimuli [22]). Models of spatial attention can also explain neglect of the contralesional sides of ipsilesional stimuli if there is a graded deficit across space (with the orienting bias being strongest to the most ipsilesional positions and weakest to the most contralesional); in this case, there will be a bias against the contralesional side of objects even when they fall in the ipsilesional field (e.g., [25]). It should be noted, however, that neglect has also been interpreted in terms of a loss or a distortion of representations for the contralesional side of space [26, 27, 28] rather than an impairment of an attentional selection mechanism. We will return to this distinction later, after presenting a connectionist model of object identification, SAIM (Selective Attention for Identification Model).

The metaphors of a mental spotlight or zoom lens carry with them the implication that there is a specific module in the brain that focuses attention on a relevant spatial region. Damage to this module may produce neglect. An alternative view, however, is that there is no distinct attentional module in the brain but rather that competition for selection between stimuli is simply an inherent part of the processes that mediate tasks such as object identification [24, 29]. Neglect, then, may arise when the system is lesioned to produce spatial biases in the competition for selection; also such biases may exist at different levels, some of which are tied to the positions of the stimulus in the field and some to its position within an object. This approach to understanding selection in vision is exemplified by the SAIM model. The computational goal of the model is to achieve translation-invariant object identification, but in doing this it embodies spatially-selective processes and it can be shown to simulate aspects of both normal and impaired visual selection (in patients with neglect).

2 SAIM

The aim of SAIM is to achieve translation-invariant object identification. This is done by mapping input from across the retina through to a smaller "attentional" window, the Focus of Attention (FOA), which covers a limited spatial region. The input to the object recognition system comprises activation only from units in the FOA (see [30, 31, 32] for similar approaches). Identification is translation- invariant because the same units in the FOA are activated irrespective of the retinal locations of stimuli.

However, when multiple objects are in the visual field the activation in the FOA will provide ambiguous input, because it will contain the features of each object present. This creates a binding problem, where it is unclear which features belong with which object. This binding problem may be overcome if visual selection operates so that only one of the objects is mapped into the FOA at a time. SAIM embodies this process of selection for identification by means of constraints that determine the mapping of information from the retina into the FOA.

Figure 1 illustrates the architecture of SAIM. Two networks, the "contents" and the "selection" networks, govern how input from the retina is mapped through to the FOA. The contents network utilises "sigma-pi" units [33] which multiply activation from retinal units with that from units in the selection network to generate activation values for units in the FOA. Thus for every unit in the FOA there is one unit in the contents network. The selection network is much larger and governs which retinal locations have activation values transmitted to the FOA (via the contents network). The selection network contains separate "control layers" of units, with one unit in each control layer linked to one location on the retina, and, for each retinal location, there are as many control layers in the network as there are FOA units (1 layer for each mapping). The multiple control layers represent all the possible mappings between each retinal location and each location in the FOA.

To determine which retinal locations are mapped through to the FOA, we used a process of mutual constraint satisfaction between units in the selection network that may be reminiscent of the approach used in Marr and Poggio's model of stereopsis [34]. The constraints were as follows:

(i)   there was competition within each control layer, such that only one location in each layer was allowed to be maximally active; units in each layer inhibited one another in a "winner takes all" fashion. The activation in each control layer was transmitted to the content unit determining access to one FOA unit, so that each FOA unit was determined by just one mapping;

(ii)   there was competition between units that were in separate control layers but that were projecting to a common FOA unit. This ensured that each FOA unit was controlled by just one unit in one control layer.

(iii) control layers did not need to contain any active units (e.g., when one control layer fails to control the mapping through to any unit in the FOA, a situatiuon which arises because the FOA is smaller than the retina).

(iv)   there was inhibition across control layers between units encoding the same retinal location.

(v)   proximity relations between occupied retinal locations were supported by a gaussian spread of activation from one unit in a control layer to units in other control layers representing neighbouring regions.

Details of the activation functions that realise these constraints are given in [21]. Figure 2 shows some of the inter-connections between the units in the selection network for just one dimension of retinal input and one dimension in the FOA, and how these connections implement constraints (iv) and (v). To cover the second dimension of the retina and the FOA, more layers must be added to the selection network (not shown here).

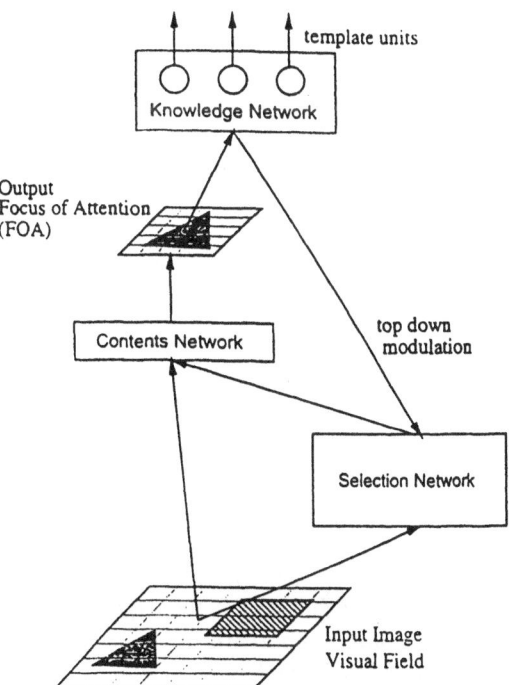

Figure 1. The architecture of SAIM.

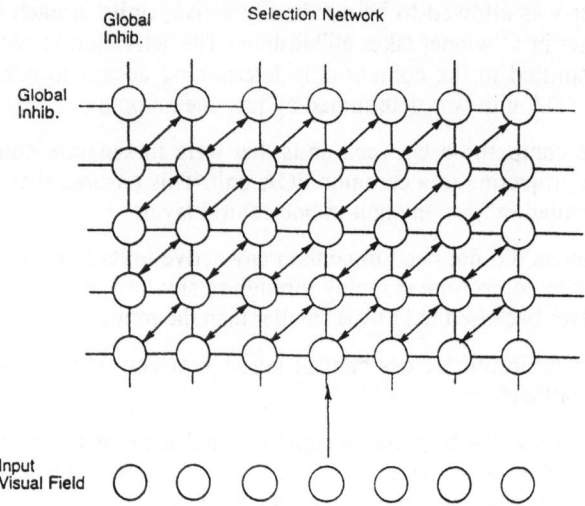

Figure 2. Illustration of the selection network in SAIM. Each row of the network stands for a control layer. Vertical and horizontal connections are inhibitory, in order to prevent respectively (i) more than one dominant connection from the visual field to the selection network (vertical connections) and (ii) more than one dominant connection from the selection network to the FOA (horizontal connections). The arrows between neighbouring units in adjacent layers show excitatory connections that generate grouping by proximity.

Processing in SAIM operates across a time course reflecting the number of network iterations required to map first from the retina through to the FOA, and then from the FOA to stored "templates" representing patterns known by the network. Pixels that fall at the centre of gravity in objects tend to be mapped through to the centre of the FOA. These pixels will be strongly supported by occupied neighbouring locations and so are both maximally active and enjoy the greatest spread of activation. Knowledge about particular patterns is represented by sets of weights connecting locations in the FOA to template units. Note that the same weights are activated irrespective of the position of the object in the visual field, since the object is mapped through to the translation-invariant FOA. Recognition is based on where the parts fall with respect to the centre of gravity of objects, coded in retinal co-ordinates.

In order to achieve a mapping from the retina to the FOA, SAIM instantiates a form of visual selection based on competition within the selection network when units from the same control layer, or from different control layers, attempt to "win" a common unit in the FOA. When two objects are present the outcome of the competition is determined by the object that creates the strongest activation in the selection network. If the objects differ in size, the larger object wins the competition since it gains more mutual support through proximity grouping. When presentations times are limited, only the larger object is identified.

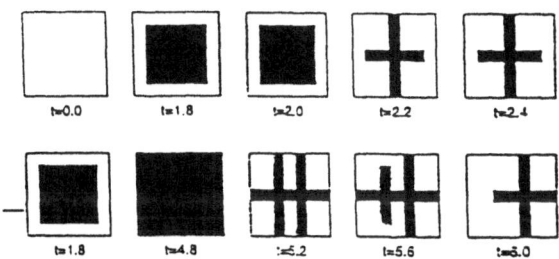

Figure 3. Effects of spatial cueing in the unlesioned model. Each window shows activation within the FOA, as a function of network iterations. Initially a square was presented at one retinal location for 1.3 cycles, and it was followed by a cross either at the same location or at a location on the opposite side of the retina. In the top windows the cue was valid (in the same location as the cross); in the bottom windows the cue was invalid (in the opposite visual field to the cross). It took longer to complete the mapping of the cross into the FOA when the cue was invalid.

Attentional switching, from a first to a second object in the visual field, was accomplished by inhibiting associated template units and units in the selection network linked to the first identified object, once identification has taken place. In this way activation from an initial 'loser' can subsequently win the competition to control the mapping into the FOA; attention is switched from first to second object.

3 Simulations

3.1 Unlesioned model

Although SAIM is ostensibly a model of translation-invariant object recognition, its behavioural properties simulate data normally taken as evidence for a spatial attentional mechanism. For example, the time taken to map a stimulus into the FOA can be facilitated by presenting a pre-cue at the target's location (e.g., if an input is presented for a few iterations at the location of a following target which is 'clamped' onto the retina until recognition takes place). Similarly mapping into the FOA is retarded if the pre-cue is presented at a location other than that of the target (with short intervals between cue and target, there is competition between them for selection) (see Figure 3). This mimics the effects of spatial cueing found in studies of normal human observers [9].

SAIM also shows evidence of "object-based" selection. When two objects are presented simultaneously, competition within the selection network leads to only one being recognised at a time. Nevertheless, all the parts of the object first selected activate stored memory representations together; the parts of the second object are also selected together, but only after inhibition of the first object (see Figure 4). This captures data on both temporal limitations in multiple target identification and on the selection of parts belonging to one rather than two objects [35].

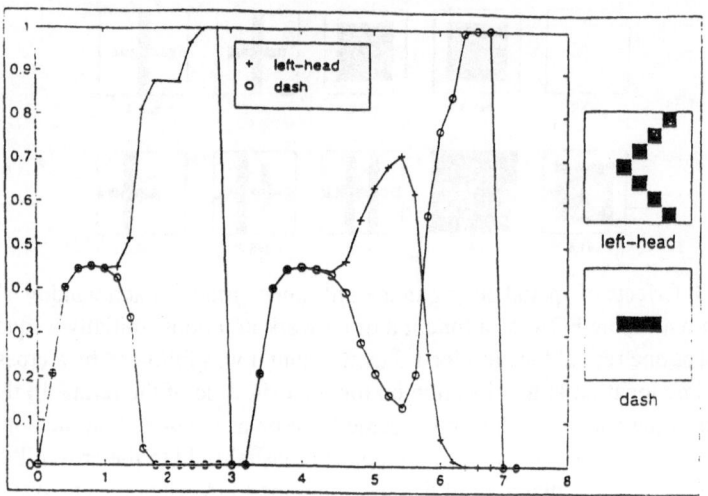

Figure 4. The selection of multiple targets in SAIM. The figure shows activation values in template units corresponding to a bar (-) and an arrow-head (<) (the arrow-head appearing to the left of the bar). First the template for the arrow-head reaches threshold (the template is then re-set); as processing continues the dash then wins the competition for the FOA and its template reaches threshold.

3.2 Lesioned model

We have "lesioned" SAIM in several ways. To simulate unilateral neglect, spatially selective lesions were introduced affecting: (a) input into the selection network from one side of the retina; (b) connections within part of the selection network that receives input from one side of the retina; and (c) connections within the selection network that project out to units on one side of the FOA. For illustrative purposes we can term damage as described in (b) as a "vertical" lesion and damage as described in (c) as a "horizontal" lesion. The terms "vertical" and "horizontal" lesion can be understand by reference to Figure 5. The units in vertical columns in the selection network receive input from one dimension of the visual field, with the columns on the left side of the network receiving input from units on the left of the retina and those on the right side of the network receiving input from the right side of the retina. A "vertical" lesion which, for example, affects the left-most columns in the network, will impair units that respond to stimuli on the left of the retina. Imagine now that the units in the horizontal layers of the selection network feed into one dimension of the FOA; the lowest horizontal layers link to the left side of the FOA and the upper-most layers to the right side. A "horizontal" lesion affecting the lowest rows in the selection network impairs the activation of units on the left of the FOA. These selective lesions, for example affecting only left side units into the selection network or into the FOA, could occur in a real neural system in which neurons responding to the left visual field and the left side of object-centred

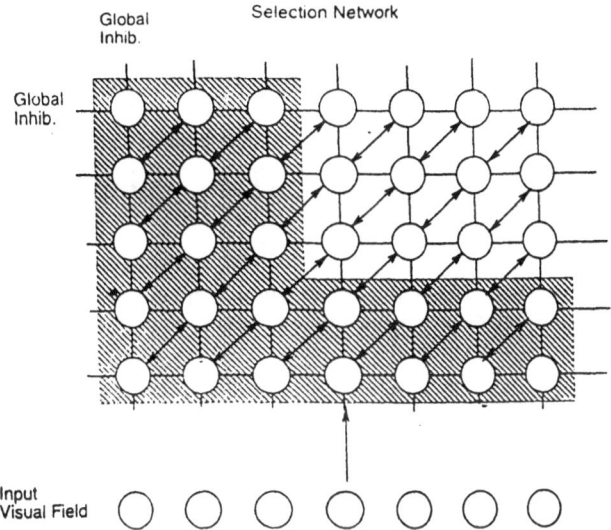

Figure 5. Lesioning of the selection network. The 'vertical' lesion disrupted connections between those units in the network linking to the left side of the retina; the 'horizontal' lesion disrupted connections between units linking to the left side of the FOA.

representations were located selectively in the right hemisphere.

Examples of how the "vertical" and "horizontal" lesions affect the mapping through to the FOA are shown in Figures 6 and 7. For these examples a single cross stimulus was presented. With the model in an unlesioned state, this cross should appear with its centre of gravity at the centre of the FOA. A "vertical" lesion that both (i) disrupted input from the left of the retina and (ii) damaged the intrinsic connections between units in the selection network receiving the damaged retinal projections, produced a field-dependent form of neglect. When presented on the far

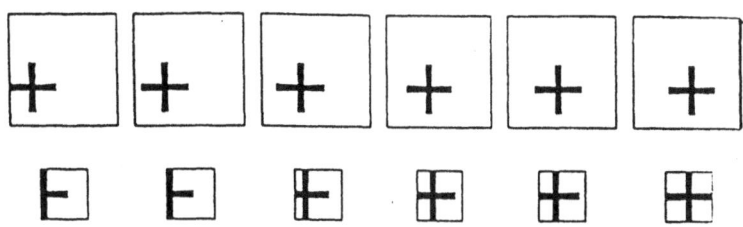

Figure 6. The mapping of activity through to the FOA after a "vertical" lesion. The top windows illustrate the positions of the cross as it is moved from the left to the right side of the retina. The bottom windows show activity in the FOA for each spatial position. When the cross is in the left visual field there is neglect of its left arm; this resolves as the cross is moved to the right.

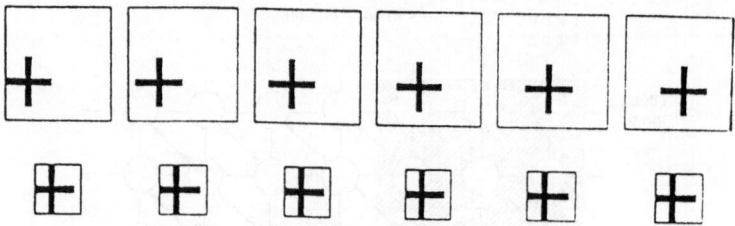

Figure 7. The mapping of activity to the FOA after a "horizontal" lesion. The left arm of the cross is neglected irrespective of where it appears in the field (there is a failure to represent the left-most pixels in the FOA).

left of the retina, only the right-side of the cross was mapped through to the FOA. Due to the lesion there was under-activity on the (lesioned) left side of the selection network so only the right-side of the cross was transmitted to the FOA; also, due to a spread of activation in the selection network to the right but not the left of the cross, the computed centre of gravity was altered so that the cross was projected towards the left of the FOA. However, moving the cross into the centre or right of the visual field allowed it to fall onto unlesioned parts of the selection network, and the neglect resolved.

In contrast to the effect of a "vertical" lesion, a "horizontal" lesion (affecting the connections between units projecting to the left side of the FOA) produced a form of "object-based" neglect: the same pattern of activation occurred in the FOA irrespective of the lateral position of the cross on the retina. As with the "vertical" lesion (and for much the same reason), the cross was projected too far to the left of the FOA. With the "horizontal" lesion, though, the affected units projected into one side of the FOA and were involved independent of the lateral position of the stimulus in the field; consequently there was consistent neglect of the left-side of the object across different lateral presentation conditions.

4   Implications

4.1   Forms of representation.

The results show that contrasting forms of neglect arise from damage to different sites in the model, which is consistent with distinct forms of neglect being associated with separate lesion sites in humans [21]. It is also of some interest that one form of neglect occurs independent of the lateral retinal position of the object, though SAIM uses a retinal rather than an object-centred co-ordinate system for object recognition. Neglect that is independent of the lateral position of the stimulus does not necessarily indicate the existence of object-centred co-ordinate systems.

Although SAIM does account for translation-invariant neglect, it does not readily accommodate those additional cases of apparently true "viewpoint independent" neglect, where the impairment remains on one side of the object even when it is

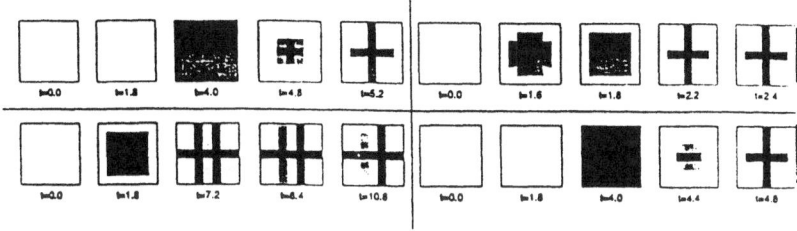

Figure 8. Effects of spatial cueing on a lesioned version of the model (following a "vertical" lesion). The conditions were the same as for the cueing experiment with the unlesioned model (Figure 3). Top left quadrant: a valid cue with the target in the impaired field; bottom left quadrant: an invalid cue with the target in the impaired field; top right quadrant: a valid cue with the target in the unimpaired field; bottom right quadrant: an invalid cue with the target in the unimpaired field. There is a large effect of invalid cueing when the target is in the impaired visual field (note that the cross used was smaller than that in Figures 6 and 7, so showed less neglect).

rotated so that the affected side falls in the ipsilesional field (cf. [36, 37]).

However, it is possible that neglect in such cases is linked to the patients' use of a mental transformation strategy [38], in which rotated objects are aligned with the standard upright and recognised *de novo*. Neglect remains on the contralesional side, but this applies to the transformed rather than retinal space. In the future we aim to assess whether SAIM can capture such rotation effects if top-down activation is fed-back to provide a strong influence on the selection network so that (for example) a left side of an object is mapped into the left side of the FOA even when the object is rotated onto its side.

In other models neglect has been simulated by lesioning a module devoted to attention-based activation of space (e.g., [25]). These simulations capture deficits on the contralesional side of objects presented in ipsilesional space by introducing a graded lesion across the visual field. However for such models it is difficult to explain how some patients can show worse detection of (for example) the left side of a stimulus in the right visual field than the right side of a stimulus in the left visual field, when the stimuli are presented simultaneously in the field. This is because the gradient producing left neglect will always impair the left-most of two stimuli. Nevertheless such a pattern is observable in human patients [21]. SAIM can mimic such a result when lesioning affects mapping into the left side of the FOA. In this case there will be left-side neglect for each object selected into the FOA, irrespective of the relative lateral locations of the objects in the field; performance on the (affected) left of the right object can be worse than that on the (unaffected) right of the left object.

4.2 Attention and representation

As noted in section 1, "attentional" accounts of unilateral neglect are frequently

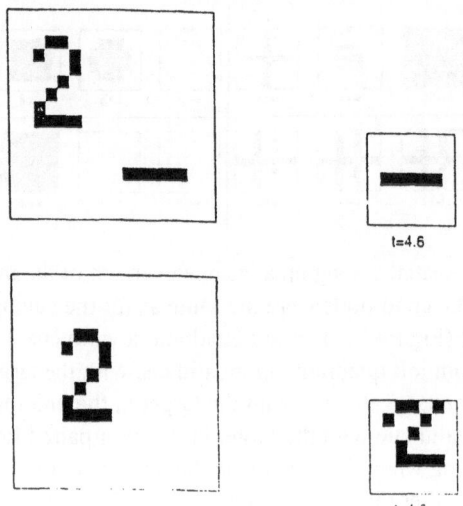

Figure 9. Extinction after a "vertical" lesion and a limited presentation time for the stimuli. With a bar in the unimpaired field and a 2 in the impaired field, there is extinction of the 2 in favour of the bar (even though the bar is the smaller stimulus and would normally lose the competition for mapping into the FOA ; here it wins because of the spatial bias due to lesioning). When just the 2 is present alone in the impaired field, it is mapped into the FOA within the same time period (though here with some degree of spatial distortion).

contrasted with "representational" accounts of the syndrome (compare [26] with [39, 40]). After lesioning, SAIM manifests both facilitatory effects of cueing to the neglected side and extinction, two phenomena that can be interpreted as indicating attentional involvement in neglect. If a spatial pre-cue is presented (e.g., by activating pixels briefly on the affected or unaffected side of space prior to the occurrence of a target on the affected side), there is improved detection of the target on the cued side whilst detection following an ipsilesional cue can be very poor (see Figure 8). Also, though a single stimulus on the affected side may be detected, detection is disrupted when a second stimulus occurs simultaneously on the unaffected side (Figure 9). With brief stimulus presentations, the affected stimulus will not be mapped into the FOA at all; that is there is extinction.

These effects occur in SAIM despite the model having no explicit module for visual attention. Cueing and extinction effects emerge here because the lesion biases the competition to 'win' the mapping from the selection network to the FOA. In this SAIM is similar to other recent simulations in which neglect is caused by lesions unbalancing the competitive interactions between units on the left and right sides of space [41, 42]. However in SAIM the attentional and representational accounts of neglect converge, as 'attentional' operations are implemented through interactions within a spatial mapping process during which different spatial representations of objects are computed.

4.3   Limits of SAIM

SAIM is able to capture aspects of both normal and disordered attentional performance in humans by means of its use of competitive mapping processes to achieve translation-invariant object recognition. It is also true that the model suffers serious limitations. One such limitation is that, apart from simple coding of proximity, the model does not employ any procedures for bottom-up grouping of information. With more complex scenes, where multiple stimuli spatially overlap and occlude one another, additional procedures for bottom-up grouping will be useful, for example enabling parts to be linked and selected together. In addition, the selection network is computationally expensive, using one unit to represent each possible mapping between the retina and the FOA. In a system that is biologically more realistic, the size of the selection network may be made more manageable by using multi-scale representations [31]. For the present simulations local one-to-one mappings were used from retinal units to units in the selection network and the FOA, to facilitate the analysis of network performance. The utility of multi-scale representations is a topic for future exploration.

5   Conclusions

We have shown that different forms of spatial representation and selection can emerge in a computational model, SAIM, in which translation-invariant object recognition operates by selectively mapping input from across the retina into a single focus of attention (FOA). The model simulates aspects of both normal and disordered attentional processes even though it does not employ a distinct module for orienting visual attention. In particular, different forms of 'neglect' can be shown by the model when spatially selective lesions affect either (a) units in the selection network that receive input from one side of the retina, or (b) units projecting from the selection network to one side of the FOA. In this case, lesioning demonstrates the functional specialisation within the different parts of the network. The model also collapses the distinction between 'attentional' and 'representational' accounts of neglect. In the model 'attentional' operations reflect competition within the network to achieve the mappings necessary for translation-invariant identification; the different spatial representations are determined by this mapping process. We conclude that many aspects of selection in vision do not reflect special-purpose attentional modules, but rather competitive processes that are inherent in object representation and recognition.

Acknowledgements

This work was supported by a grant from the DAAD, Germany, to the second author, and by grants from the MRC and the BBSRC (UK) to the first author.

References

[1] Allport DA. Selection for action: Some behavioural and neurophysiological considerations of attention and action. In Perspectives on Perception and Action, Heuer H & Sanders AF (eds) Hillsdale, N.J.: Erlbaum. 1987.

[2] Feldman JA & Ballard DH. Connectionist models and their properties. Cognitive Science, 1982, 6, 205-254.

[3] Hummel J & Biederman I. Dynamic binding in a neural network for shape recognition. Psychological Review, 1992, 99, 480-517.

[4] Tanaka K, Saito HA, Fukada Y & Moriya M. Coding visual images of objects in the infero-temporal cortex of the macaque monkey. Journal of Neurophysiology, 1991, 66, 170-189.

[5] Gross CG, Rocha-Miranda CE & Bender DB. Visual properties of neurons in inferotemporal cortex of the macaque. Journal of Neurophysiology, 1972, 35, 96-111.

[6] Chelazzi L, Miller EK, Duncan J & Desimone R. A neural basis for visual search in inferior temporal cortex. Nature, 1993, 363, 345-347.

[7] Moran J & Desimone R. Selective attention gates visual processing in the extrastriate cortex. Science, 1985, 229, 782-784.

[8] Eriksen, CW & Yeh YY. Allocation of attention in the visual field. Journal of Experimental Psychology: Human Perception and Performance 11, 1985, 583-597.

[9] Posner MI. Orienting of attention. Quarterly Journal of Experimental Psychology, 1980, 32, 3-25.

[10] Treisman A. Features and objects: The fourteenth Bartlett Memorial Lecture. Quarterly Journal of Experimental Psychology, 1988, 40A, 201-237.

[11] Humphreys GW & Bruce V. Visual Cognition. London: Erlbaum. 1989.

[12] Farah MJ. Visual Agnosia Cambridge, Mass.: MIT Press. 1990.

[13] Humphreys GW & Riddoch MJ. Interactions between object and space vision revealed through neuropsychology. In Attention and Performance XIV, Meyer DE & Kornblum S (eds) Hillsdale, N.J.: Erlbaum. 1993.

[14] Mozer MC. The Perception of Multiple Objects: A Connectionist Approach. Cambridge, Mass.: MIT Press. 1991.

[15] Robertson I & Marshall JC (eds) Unilateral neglect: Clinical and experimental studies. London: Erlbaum. 1993.

[16] Walker R. Spatial and object-based neglect. Neurocase, 1995, 1, 371-383.

[17] Karnath HO, Schenkel P & Fischer B. Trunk orientation as the determining factor of the 'contralateral' deficit in the neglect syndrome and as the physical anchor of the internal representation of body orientation in space. Brain, 1991, 114, 1997-2014.

[18] Riddoch MJ & Humphreys GW. The effect of cueing on unilateral neglect. Neuropsychologia, 1983, 21, 589-599.

[19] Young AW, Newcombe F & Ellis AW. Different impairments contribute to neglect dyslexia. Cognitive Neuropsychology, 1991, 8, 177-191.

[20] Driver J & Halligan PW. Can visual neglect operate in object-centred co-

ordinates? An affirmative single-case study. Cognitive Neuropsychology, 1991, 8, 475-496.

[21] Humphreys GW. & Heinke D. Spatial representation and selection in the brain: Neuropsychological and computational constraints. Visual Cognition. In press.

[22] Posner MI, Walker JA, Friedrich FJ & Rafal RD. Effects of parietal lobe injury on covert orienting of visual attention. Journal of Neuroscience, 1984, 4, 1863-1874.

[23] Karnath HO. Deficits of attention in acute and recovered visual hemi-neglect. Neuropsychologia, 1988, 26, 27-43.

[24] Duncan J, Humphreys GW & Ward R. Integrated mechanisms of selective attention. Current Opinion in Biology. In press.

[25] Mozer MC, Halligan PW & Marshall JC. The end of the line for a brain-damaged model of unilateral neglect. Journal of Cognitive Neuroscience, 1997, 9, 171-190.

[26] Bisiach E & Luzzatti C. Unilateral neglect of representational space. Cortex, 1978, 14, 129-13.

[27] Halligan PW & Marshall JC. Toward a principled explanation of unilateral neglect. Cognitive Neuropsychology, 1994, 11, 167-206.

[28] Milner AD, Harvey M, Roberts RC & Forster SV. Line bisection errors in visual neglect: Misguided action or size distortion? Neuropsychologia, 1993, 31, 39-49.

[29] Duncan J. Cooperating brain systems in selective perception and action. In Attention and Performance XVI. Inui T & McClelland JL (eds) Cambridge, Mass.: MIT Press. 1996. pp. 549-578.

[30] Olshausen BA, Andersen CH & Van Essen DC. A neurobiological model of visual attention and invariant pattern recognition based on dynamic routing of information. The Journal of Neuroscience, 1993, 13, 4700-4719.

[31] Olshausen BA, Andersen CH & Van Essen DC. A multiscale dynamic routing circuit for forming size- and position-invariant object representations. Journal of Computational Neuroscience, 1995, 2, 45-62.

[32] Postma EO. SCAN: A neural model of covert attention. PhD thesis, Computer Science Department, University of Limburg, Maastricht, The Netherlands. 1994.

[33] Rumelhart DE, Hinton GE & McClelland JL. A general framework for parallel distributed processing. In Parallel distributed processing: Explorations in the microstructure of cognition. Vol. 1. Rumelhart DE & McClelland JL (eds), Cambridge, Mass.: MIT Press. 1986.

[34] Marr D & Poggio T. Cooperative computation of stereo disparity. Science, 1976, 194, 283-287.

[35] Duncan J. Selective attention and the organisation of visual information. Journal of Experimental Psychology: General, 1984, 113, 501-517.

[36] Caramazza A & Hillis AE. Levels of representation, co-ordinate frames and unilateral neglect. Cognitive Neuropsychology, 1990, 7, 391-445.

[37] Tipper SP & Behrmann M. Object-centred not scene-based visual neglect. Journal of Experimental Psychology: Human Perception and Performance, 1996,

22, 1261- 1278.

[38] Buxbaum LJ, Coslett HB, Montgomery MW & Farah MJ. Mental rotation may underlie apparent object-based neglect. Neuropsychologia, 1996, 14, 113-126.

[39] Riddoch MJ & Humphreys GW. Perceptual and action systems in unilateral visual neglect. In Neurophysiological and neuropsychological aspects of spatial neglect. Jeannerod M (ed), Amsterdam: Elsevier Science. 1987.

[40] Riddoch MJ & Humphreys GW. Towards an understanding of neglect. In Cognitive neuropsychology and cognitive rehabilitation Riddoch MJ & Humphreys GW (eds) London: Erlbaum UK. 1994.

[41] Cohen JD, Romero RD, Servan-Schreiber D & Farah MJ. Mechanisms of spatial attention: The relation of macrostructure to microstructure in parietal neglect. Journal of Cognitive Neuroscience, 1994, 6, 377-387.

[42] Humphreys GW, Olson A, Romani C & Riddoch MJ. Competitive mechanisms of selection by space and object: A neuropsychological approach. In Converging operations in the study of visual selective attention, Kramer AF, Coles MGH & Logan GD (eds)Washington: American Psychological Association. 1996.

Extracting Features from the Short-term Time Structure of Cochlear Filtered Sound

Leslie S. Smith

CCCN, Dept. of Computing Science and Mathematics, University of Stirling
Stirling FK9 4LA, Scotland.

Abstract

Auditory modelling uses the architecture of the auditory system to guide early sound processing. The advantage of this approach is (i) time-resolution is better and (ii) many bandpassed channels are available and can be processed in parallel. Good time-resolution allows sophisticated across-time processing to be applied to each channel, resulting in the discovery of features in each channel. Logically each channel can be processed simultaneously. The features discovered can be correlated across channels. We present some early results for processing sound at three different levels of short-term time structure.

1 Auditory Modelling and Spectral Analysis

From the time of Helmholtz, it has been known that the cochlea, the main component of the inner ear, performs a frequency analysis on the pressure wave that we perceive as sound. This has led workers in speech and sound interpretation to perform a similar analysis as a first step in sound interpretation. Much of the work has used a Fourier transform based approach. Such spectral analysis is usually carried out on short sections of sound (perhaps 40ms long), supplying the Fourier transform with a sound pressure/time vector and resulting in a power/frequency vector of the sound during that section. (The phase information is generally discarded.) This produces a representation consisting of an N-element vector (where N is the order of the Fourier transform) per analysis. An alternative technique, the one used in this work, is to use auditory modelling, in which the sound signal is filtered into bands, following what is known of the response of the cochlea. This produces a representation consisting of M channels, each with the same time-resolution as the original signal. Noting that the sections to which the Fourier transform is applied may overlap, it becomes clear that both techniques give rise to representations larger than the original signal. Downstream representations are strongly influenced by the structure of this initial representation.

Table 1 summarises the advantages and disadvantages of each approach. We should point out that Fourier transform based methods can be used to perform auditory modelling by applying the transform to overlapping segments of sound, (e.g. to a new 40ms segment every 1ms), and then regrouping the power vectors to give an appropriate power/frequency distribution. In this way, both accurate time resolution and frequency resolution can be achieved, though at the cost of considerable computation.

Auditory modelling	Spectral analysis
Good time resolution	Poor time resolution
Poor frequency resolution	Good frequency resolution
Near-logarithmic channel distribution	Linear energy/frequency spectrum
Computationally intensive due to presence of multiple channels	Computationally intensive due to initial transform
aVLSI or DSP solutions are possible	dVLSI or DSP solutions are possible

Table 1: Comparison of auditory modelling and spectral analysis techniques

Which approach is preferable depends on what one is trying to achieve. Current commercial systems aim to achieve direct interpretation of a clean incoming sound, and use spectral analysis. However, if one needs to stream the sound to accentuate the source of interest, then we contend that auditory modelling is the better approach because it can permit segregation of features from differing sources prior to any attempt at interpretation. Generally, interpretation of sound (specifically speech) processed using spectral analysis techniques is performed directly, using hidden Markov models or neural networks which constrain the likely interpretation of some input vector sequence using the statistics of the target (phonemic) vocabulary. Auditory modelling based approaches can use the short-term structure of the signal in different channels to define features: signals from a single source tend to share short-term structure, and this can be used to group the features, thus allowing signals from other sources to be ignored. Streaming techniques based on applying correlogram processing to auditory model processed sounds have been used in [15, 26, 5].

In the current work the features used are onsets, offsets, and amplitude modulation pulses: other features are certainly possible [4]. We do not use correlogram based processing, partly because this technique results in even larger volumes of data, and partly for the reasons outlined in section 2.3. The auditory modelling approach to streaming can take advantage of the general characteristics of sound sources, but does not generally use so much high-level information as is used in direct interpretation. Nonetheless, such information can be used later in the interpretation process.

In the rest of this paper, we consider three levels of the short–term time structure of sound, illustrating them graphically and discussing how each of them can be used.

2 Three levels of short-term structure

We discuss three levels of short-term structure, summarised in table 2. Each level corresponds to a different level of the time structure of speech. These are similar to the envelope, periodicity and fine-structure levels discussed in [22], and resemble the three forms of modulation discussed in [21]. Each level corresponds to a different type of activity in the early auditory system, namely firing of onset cells in the cochlear nucleus (CN), firing of chopper cells in the

Timescale	Timing	Application
Coarse	20–50ms Order of movement of vocal tract articulators in animals	Detecting rhythm and basic sound elements (syllables, phonemes) Monaural streaming
Medium	3–10ms Movement period of glottal folds	Detecting voicing Speaker identification Intonation (from fundamental frequency) Monaural streaming Pitch estimation
Fine	0.35-2 ms Order of period of sound in sensitive area of human hearing Auditory nerve spikes	Speech articulation place and vowel quality Direction detection Binaural streaming Pitch estimation

Table 2: Three levels of short-term time structure of sound

CN, and firing of neurons in the auditory nerve [17]. These levels could be extended to longer times as well, as suggested in [30].

2.1 Across-channel processing

Although the features found in each channel can be used independently, it is the ability to correlate features across channels that makes the auditory modelling approach particularly powerful. Signals in different channels which change in similar ways at the same time usually come from the same source. Indeed, human subjects tend to group together signals in different parts of the audible spectrum if they change in similar ways at the same time [3]. We make use of this by concentrating on those features which are supported by similar features in adjacent channels at about the same time. We have applied this technique to the coarse and medium short-term structure of sound, and used this correlation across features to identify features even in the presence of considerable noise. However, we have not been able to use this grouping for the fine scale short term features.

For all of the examples that follow, the Gammatone cochlear filterbank [19] provides the initial bandpass filtering.

2.2 Coarse short-term time structure

The output of the cochlear filterbank was processed channel by channel. It was first rectified, then bandpass filtered to emphasise changes in the envelope of each signal in the 20-50ms window, using a neurally plausible bandpass filter. This corresponds to across-time processing preceding the across-frequency correlation [1]. The across-frequency integration took the form of applying the signals to a one-dimensional network of leaky integrate-and-fire neurons [8].

We used two networks. In both networks, each neuron receives excitatory input from one channel, and excites the neurons in adjacent channels when it fires. In one network, the neural input corresponded to increases in smoothed envelope (onsets), and in the other network to decreases in the smoothed input (offsets). In both networks the result was that when one neuron fired, nearby neurons which were close to threshold fired almost immediately. This results in temporal and tonotopic clustering, giving a volley of spikes across a number of channels in response to an increase (decrease) in signal power. The technique is described in detail in [28]. The onset cell network is loosely modelled on the onset cells of the cochlear nucleus.

The end result is the detection of features corresponding to the start and end of bursts of energy of between 20 and 50 ms duration in the sound. These bursts are characteristic of speech, occurring in plosives, in voiced sounds, even in sibilances, and can be used to endpoint speech elements even in the presence of considerable noise, as can be seen in figure 1. An analogue VLSI implementation of the neural part is under construction [10].

2.3   Medium short-term time structure

There are a number of possible methods for extracting medium short-term time structure. The autocorrelation function (ACF) was suggested originally by Licklider [13], and has been used by many others (e.g.[26, 14, 15]). This provides detailed information of the signal's periodicity, channel by channel, and this information can be combined across channels to produce a summary ACF [14]. We have chosen to use a different technique, one based on amplitude modulation. We do so (i) because of the amplification and classification of amplitude modulated signals which occurs in the cochlear nucleus [12, 17, 11] and (ii) because the only neurobiological evidence for neurobiological ACF computation occurs in very specialised tasks such as echolocation (e.g. [7]) or localisation [6].

Initial processing was as for the coarse time structure, except that the bandpass filter accentuated envelope changes which were in the 3-10ms range. Low frequency bands were ignored, as their envelope cannot change on this timescale. We were particularly interested in sounds generated by the combination of many harmonics of a low-frequency excitation. Voiced speech is one example of this type of sound.

The major source of amplitude modulation is unresolved harmonics. The organ of Corti in the cochlea performs a frequency analysis, but the bands are relatively wideband, with a minimum equivalent rectangular bandwidth (ERB)

$$ERB = F_c/Q + 24.7Hz$$

where F_c is the centre frequency and Q is the sharpness of the filter in the cochlear model used [19]. Auditory nerve response is complex: at middle and high frequencies, for a constant intensity tone, it consists of a gradual increase as the tone frequency increases, followed by a sharp peak at F_c, followed by a rapid decline [20]. For the cochlear model used, this is best characterised by $Q = 9.265$ [9]. However, this value of Q is for pure tones at low sound pressure level (SPL), and the selectivity broadens (i.e. Q decreases) for higher SPLs, particularly once low–threshold auditory nerve fibres are driven into saturation, and for wideband sounds [16, 24, 23]. The lower value of Q allows unresolved

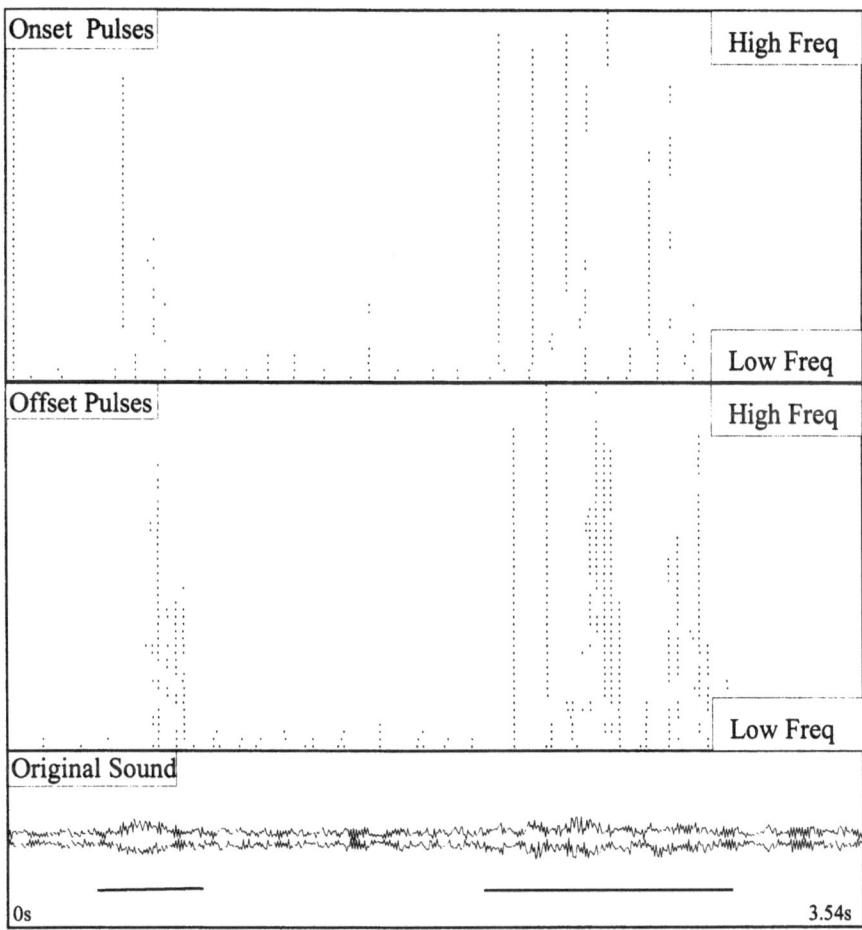

Figure 1: Utterance "Say, that's a nice bike" in motor-bike noise: horizontal lines mark the utterance itself. The clustered onsets and offsets can be seen clearly. even although the SNR is poor, as can be seen from the overall envelope of the sound. The leftmost onset volley marks the start of the wideband motorbike noise.

harmonics to start at a lower F_c. The system is modelled functionally on the chopper cells of the cochlear nucleus. which have been shown to be particularly responsive to AM signals near their best frequency and best AM frequency [17].

Two techniques have been used to combine the channels: the first technique consisted of simply adding up all bandpassed envelopes across the channels. and then detecting amplitude modulation pulses. This requires that the signals in the different bands are accurately time-aligned. To achieve this. it was necessary to compensate for the variations in delay introduced by the filter. This addition loses all information about where in the spectrum the amplitude modulation occurred. so that although the technique can be used to detect voiced sound. it is not useful for streaming. nor for more detailed feature detection. It does. however. provide a technique for detecting voicing which ignores low frequency sound altogether. and can thus achieve good results in the presence of interfering low frequency noise. This is described in detail in [27]. The problem with this technique is that it assumes that the amplitude modulation in different channels is synchronised: this is unlikely to be the case in a real environment.

The second technique maintains channel information. delaying the across channel processing. Each channel is processed to find amplitude modulation pulses. and then pulses which do not conform to the AM expected (i.e. those with AM frequency too high or too low) are discarded. The combination technique used was to retain only pulses "supported" by other pulses: that is. only if there had been a sufficient number of pulses on adjacent channels within a certain length of time. Details are in [29].

The effect of this processing is shown in figure 2. The AM pulses discovered do show the voicing structure of the signal. This is clear both with and without noise (figure 2B-D): retaining only those pulses corresponding to AM between 80 and 140Hz improves the situation (figure 2E-G) for this speaker. The AM detecting technique renders the formant structure of the voiced sections visible: this can be seen both in the absence of noise and when noise was added . Using a simple form of across-frequency processing in which pulses are retained only if supported by sufficient earlier pulses is effective only if the AM extends across many channels. In this case. some of the background noise can be removed. while retaining much of the structure (figure 2F): but if there is much interfering noise. much of the AM structure of the signal may be lost (not shown). In particular. the formant structure is lost.

We can select which pulses should be retained. channel by channel. keeping only those corresponding to some small range of AM frequencies. Figure 3 shows that the frequency of the AM. and hence of the fundamental excitation. F_0. changes in a reasonably smooth way. Detection of amplitude modulation allows the movement of F_0 to be tracked: one can use the inter-pulse interval in each channel as an estimate of the F_0 period. and use the median of these values. thus not requiring the very fine comb-filters which would be needed to find the precise harmonics present.

The example here is of a male speaker. with a relatively low F_0. Female speakers have a higher F_0. so that with the Q used here. unresolved harmonics do not occur until considerably higher F_c. We believe that the wideband nature of speech is such that for normal SPL. the Q will be decreased due to high spontaneous-rate AN fibers becoming saturated [23]. and to changes in the action of the outer hair cells. The effect of this would be to reduce the Q of

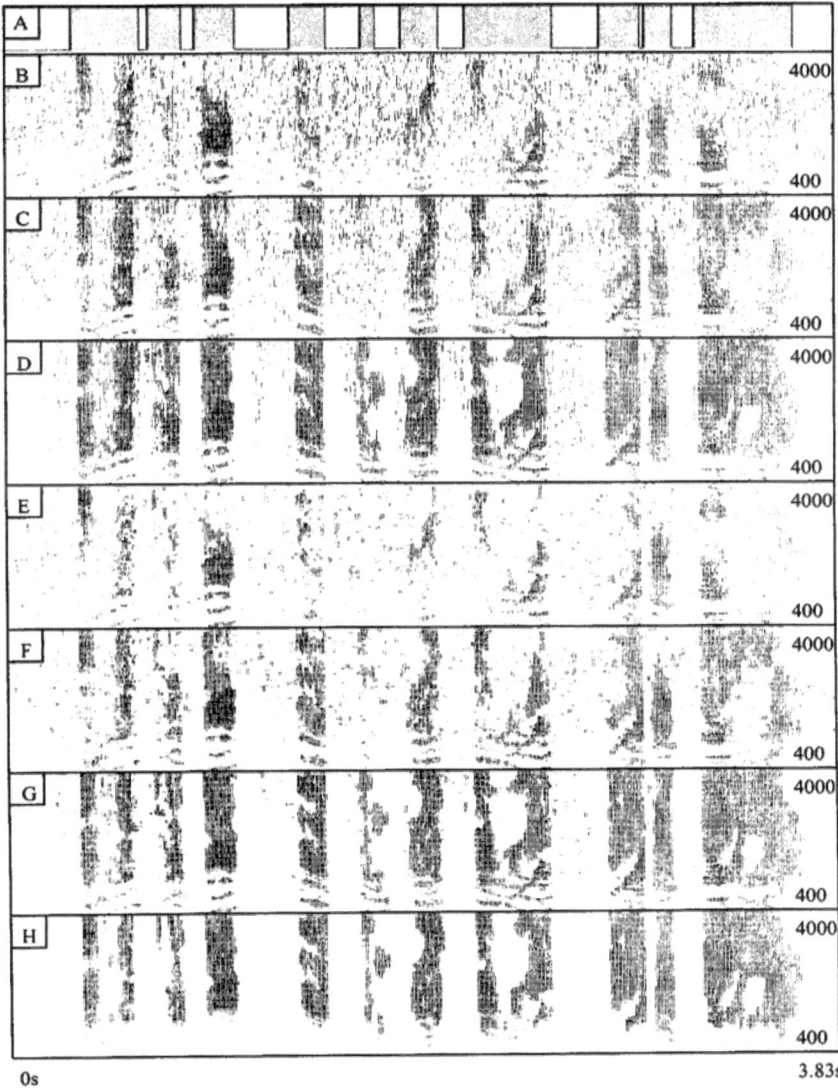

Figure 2: Effect of processing male TIMIT utterance "she had your dark suit in greasy wash water all year". dr3/mkls1/sa1. (A) dark sections mark voiced parts of the utterance. (B-D) Amplitude modulation pulses found. using 141 channels. 400-4000Hz. (B) with white noise added to give 5dB SNR. (C) with white noise added to give 10dB SNR (D) on original TIMIT signal (E-G) Amplitude modulation pulses retained when AM constrained to be in 80-140Hz region. (E) with white noise added to give 5dB SNR. (F) with white noise added to give 10dB SNR (G) on original TIMIT signal. Result of retaining only those pulses corresponding to AM between 80 and 140Hz. (H) Result of retaining only those pulses supported by 10 others within a radius of ±10 channels for original signal with no noise added.

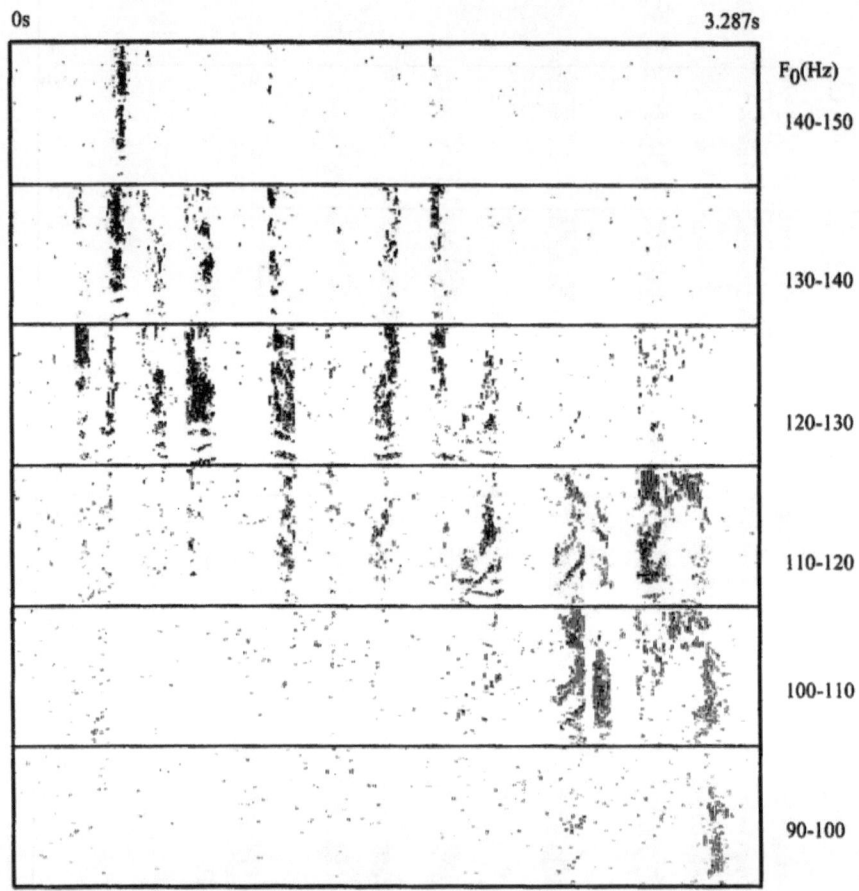

Figure 3: AM pulses retained for different bands of frequency of amplitude modulation. Processing is otherwise as in figure 2c (white noise. 10dB SNR).

those parts of the response in which the sound energy is concentrated. causing AM due to unresolved harmonics to occur at lower F_c. We have not been able to test this directly. although we have found that using a lower Q does permit AM to be found in female speakers speech at lower frequencies [27]. However. using a low Q throughout the spectrum hides the spectral structure of the amplitude modulation.

The most similar system is the stabilised auditory image [18]: however. our system works channel by channel. seeking amplitude modulation (partially a biologically motivated exercise). rather than buffering and triggering channel outputs to produce a visually inspectable image displaying the medium short-term structure of the sound.

Further work is required to find more effective ways of combining the information across multiple bands: we would particularly like to retain the formant structure while discarding isolated AM pulses caused by noise.

2.4   Fine short-term time structure

Fine time structure is used in binaural sound direction-finding [2]. This appears to be based on the phase locking of auditory nerve spiking for signals below about 2.5kHz in humans. Although exactly how one might extract useful information from the timing of AN spikes at this level is not clear. Rosen [22] identifies specific applications for this level of short-term time structure in speech interpretation.

The use of this level of time structure in the interpretation of sound or speech in unclear: nonetheless. applying auditory modelling does give some interesting pictures!

Figure 4 shows the result of applying cochlear filterbank followed by simple (i.e. half-wave) rectification to some sounds. The branching structure is characteristic of sounds with many pure sinusoidal frequency components: a simple tone results in a sequence of near-vertical stripes which are strongest (darkest) where the filter responds to that frequency. The precise structure is determined by the way in which the strongest frequency component in the bandpass filtered signal changes as the centre frequency of the bandpass filter changes. For wideband noise-based sounds with a flat spectrum. the strongest frequency component of the bandpass filtered signal will always be at the centre frequency of the bandpass filter. In this case. the pattern of branching will appear random. For voiced speech sounds. the branching reflects the strength of each harmonic: thus the branching has a regular structure and this structure is determined by the formants of the vocal tract. For bandpassed unvoiced sounds. like /s/. the branching has some degree of regularity. as can be seen from the bottom part of figure 4.

3   Discussion

Auditory modelling techniques retain more information about the short-term time structure of sound than techniques based on Fourier transforms. We have shown how certain features we believe to be useful in interpretation or streaming can be adduced from the coarse and medium scale short-term time structure. We have not identified how such features may be adduced directly from the

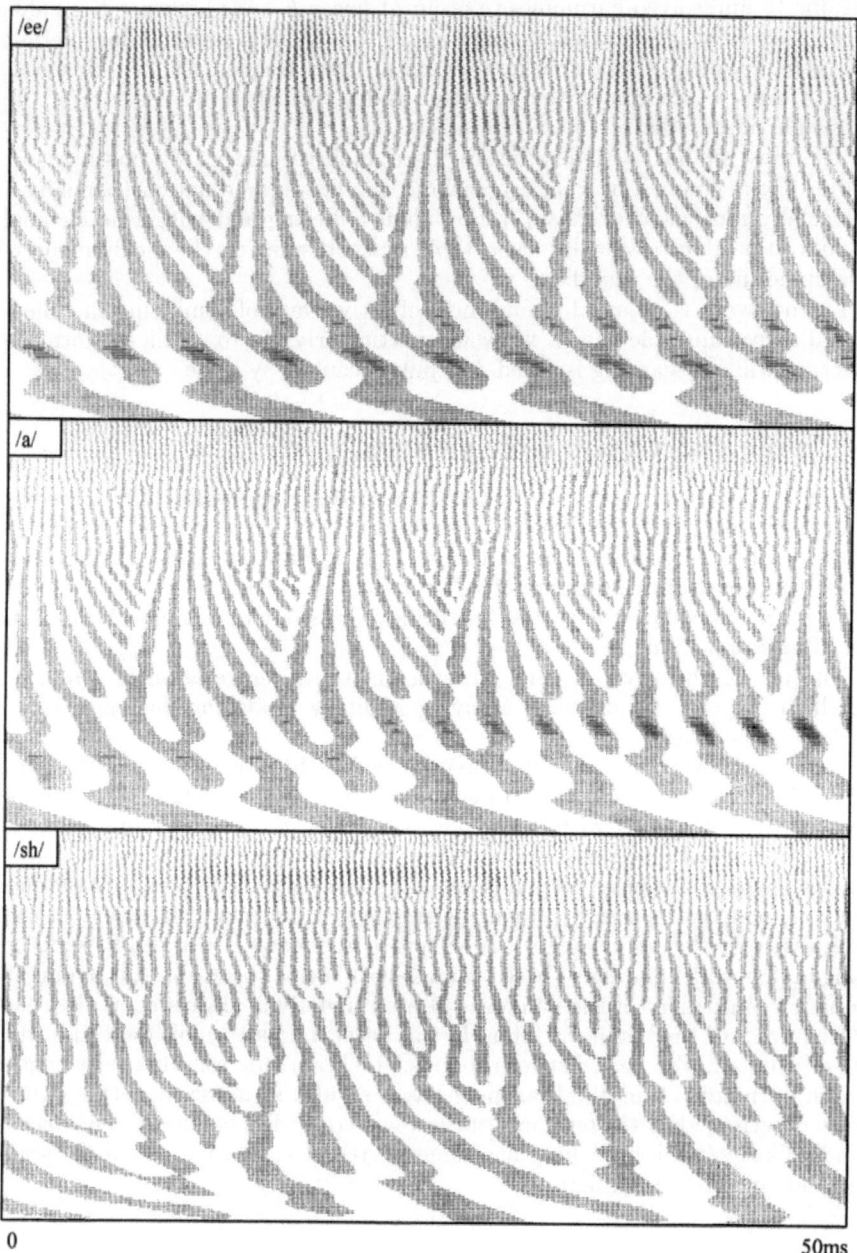

Figure 4: Fine time structure of two vowels and a sibilance. Channel centre frequencies range from 100Hz (bottom) to 6kHz (top).

fine scale short-term time structure. We note that Rosen [22] identifies more applications for each level of short-term time structure of speech.

For the coarse-scale time structure, we have shown that performing across-time processing before across-frequency processing can permit us to perform temporal and tonotopic clustering of onsets and offsets. Future work should consider exactly which channels are bracketed by the volleys of onset and offset firings, and concentrate attention on those channels during that segment. We note also that even when the spectral information is compressed down to 3 or 4 bands, envelope temporal cues suffice to permit high levels of word recognition [25], emphasising the importance of this level of structure.

For the medium-scale time structure, we have shown the usefulness of across-time processing on a channel by channel basis. However, we have yet to produce an effective method for across-frequency integration, and this is still under investigation: one possibility is to use lateral inhibition to sharpen the response profile. Using a cochlear filter/auditory nerve model whose response depends on the distribution of the energy of the sound in a more biologically realistic way would we believe, allow sounds with a higher frequency of fundamental to be processed in the same way as we have processed sounds with lower fundamental frequency. In particular, the widening of the peak level response of auditory nerve fibers with high spontaneous rates (reviewed in [23]) would allow unresolved harmonics to generate amplitude modulation pulses at lower F_c's. We are also interested in combining the features from different time-scales, with a view to performing feature-based sound streaming and interpretation.

Processing multiple channels produced by cochlear filtering is time consuming when performed with software. We are currently working with the department of Electrical Engineering at the University of Edinburgh to transfer some of the processing into analogue VLSI, in order to be able to perform these algorithms in real-time [10].

Acknowledgements

I am indebted to one of the referees, Professor Stuart Rosen, for his comments.

References

[1] J.B. Allen. How do humans process and recognize speech. *IEEE Transactions on Speech and Auditory Processing*, 2(4):567–577, 1994.

[2] J. Blauert. *Spatial Hearing*. MIT Press, 1983.

[3] A.S. Bregman. *Auditory scene analysis*. MIT Press, 1990.

[4] G. Brown. Computational auditory scene analysis:a representational approach. Technical report, Department of Computer Science, University of Sheffield, Sheffield, UK, 1992.

[5] G.J. Brown and D.L. Wang. Modelling the perceptual segregation of double vowels with a network of neural oscillators. Technical Report CS-96-07, Department of Computer Science, University of Sheffield, Sheffield, UK, 1992.

[6] C.E. Carr and M. Konishi. A circuit for the detection of interaural time differences in the brain stem of the barn owl. *Journal of Neuroscience.* 10:3227–3246. 1990.

[7] S.P. Dear and N. Suga. Delay-tuned neurons in the midbrain of the big brown bat. *Journal of neurophysiology.* 73(3):1084–1100. 1995.

[8] W. Gerstner. Time structure of the activity in neural networks. *Physical Review E.* 51(1):738–758. 1995.

[9] B.R. Glasberg and B.C.J. Moore. Derivation of filter shapes from notched-noise data. *Hearing Research.* 47:103–138. 1990.

[10] M.A. Glover. A. Hamilton. and L.S. Smith. Analogue VLSI integrate and fire neural network for clustering onset and offset signals in a sound segmentation system. Submitted to 1st European Workshop on Neuromorphic Systems. 1997.

[11] M.J. Hewitt and R. Meddis. A computer-model of amplitude-modulation sensitivity of single units in the inferior colliculus. *Journal of the Acoustical Society of America.* 95:2145–2159, 1994.

[12] G. Langner. Periodicity coding in the auditory system. *Hearing Research.* 60:115–142, 1992.

[13] J.C.R. Licklider. A duplex theory of pitch perception. *Experentia,* 7:128–133. 1951.

[14] R. Meddis and M.J. Hewitt. Virtual pitch and phase sensitivity of a computer model of the auditory periphery. I: Pitch identification. *Journal of the Acoustical Society of America,* 89(6):2866–2882. 1991.

[15] R. Meddis and M.J. Hewitt. Modelling the identification of concurrent vowels with different fundamental frequencies. *Journal of the Acoustical Society of America,* 91(1):233–245. 1992.

[16] A.R. Moller. *Auditory Physiology.* Academic Press. 1983.

[17] A.R. Palmer and I.M. Winter. Cochlear nerve and cochlear nucleus responses to the fundamental frequency of voiced speech sounds and harmonic complex tones. *Advances in the Biosciences,* 83:231–239, 1992.

[18] R. D. Patterson and J.W. Holdsworth. Generation of stabilised waveforms. UK patent GB 2212801 A. December 1990.

[19] R.D. Patterson. M.H. Allerhand, and C. Giguere. Time-domain modelling of peripheral auditory processing: A modular architecture and a software platform. *Journal of the Acoustical Society of America,* 98:1890–1894, 1995.

[20] J.O. Pickles. *An introduction to the physiology of hearing.* Academic Press. second edition. 1988.

[21] R. Plomp. The role of modulation in hearing. In R. Klinke and R. Hartmann, editors. *Hearing–physiological bases and psychophysics.* Springer-Verlag. 1983.

[22] S. Rosen. Temporal information in speech: acoustic, auditory and linguistic aspects. *Philosophical transactions of the Royal Society of London B.* 336:367–373. 1992.

[23] M.A. Ruggero. Physiology and coding of sound in the auditory nerve. In A.N. Popper and R.R Fay, editors. *The Mammalian Auditory Pathway: Neurophysiology.* Springer-Verlag. 1992.

[24] M.B. Sachs, H.F. Voigt, and E.D. Young. Auditory nerve representation of vowels in background noise. *Journal of Neurophysiology.* 50(1):27–45, 1983.

[25] R.V. Shannon, F.G. Zeng, V. Kamath, J. Wygonski, and M. Ekelid. Speech recognition with primarily temporal cues. *Science.* 270:303–304. 1995.

[26] M. Slaney and R.F. Lyon. On the importance of time–a temporal representation of sound. In M.Cooke, S.Beet, and M.Crawford, editors. *Visual representations of speech signals.* John Wiley and Sons. 1993.

[27] L.S. Smith. A neurally motivated technique for voicing detection and f_0 estimation in speech. Technical Report CCCN–22. Centre for Cognitive and Computational Neuroscience. University of Stirling. Stirling UK. 1996.

[28] L.S. Smith. Onset-based sound segmentation. In D.S. Touretzky, M.C. Mozer, and M.E. Hasselmo, editors. *Advances in Neural Information Processing Systems 8.* pages 729–735. MIT Press. 1996.

[29] L.S. Smith. A noise-robust auditory modelling front end for voiced speech. Accepted for ICANN97. Lausanne. October 8–10. 1997, 1997.

[30] N.P.McA. Todd. The auditory primal sketch: A multiscale model of rhythmic grouping. *Journal of New Music Research.* 23(1), 1994.

Representation in Working Memory and Attention

Representational Issues in Neural Systems: Example from a Neural Network Model of Set-Shifting Paradigm Experiments

Raju Surampudi Bapi
Michael J. Denham
University of Plymouth, UK

Abstract

Experiments in the Set-Shifting Paradigm (SSP) are used to test subjects' ability to acquire attentional sets and manipulate them. In normal primates, acquisition of discriminations requiring an intra-dimensional shift (IDS) is superior to that requiring an extra-dimensional shift (EDS). Further, damage to the prefrontal cortex is seen to impair EDS performance. We propose a bias theory to account for the IDS-EDS asymmetry. Uniform bias developed for exemplars from the relevant dimension makes it difficult to subsequently acquire exemplars from the previously irrelevant dimension. A neural network model embodying this theory replicates the experimental results. Prefrontal cortex is hypothesised to be involved in reward-based category learning which in turn facilitates EDS performance. Basic processes in neural systems that can support the formation of potentially higher-level representations are pointed out.

1 Introduction

In visual discrimination tasks animals or humans are required to discriminate between complex stimuli such as objects or complex two-dimensional visual stimuli. In these tasks, one possibility is that subjects may be associating positively reinforced compound stimuli with reward, using the configural properties of the stimuli (that is, subjects memorise stimuli as a whole without paying particular attention to the constituents). The other possibility is that discrimination is done by learning to attend to relevant dimension and then learning the rewarding exemplar within that dimension. In the latter case subjects are said to form an attentional set. As an example, consider the simple discrimination problem where green is associated with reinforcement and red with its absence, and that the shape of the stimuli (for example, squares and triangles) is unrelated to reinforcement. Subjects using configural properties would associate green square and green triangle individually with reward, whereas the other group would learn that colour is an important dimension and that green coloured stimuli are rewarding irrespective of shape. Tests using attentional set-shifting paradigm (SSP) are traditionally used to assess the ability of set learning, concept formation and categorisation in human and animal subjects. Another paradigm that has been used to assess set-shifting ability is the Wisconsin Card Sort Test (WCST). SSP is demonstrated to be more sensitive to damage to the prefrontal cortex than WCST [1] and hence is more useful in clinical assessment of prefrontal patients. Roberts [1] summarised that WCST requires several discrete cognitive processes in addition to attentional set-shifting, such as category/set identification and selective attention to one of the several categories. By controlling the number of categories and making them perceptually distinct (presented as foreground and background), SSP minimises requirements on other cognitive processes and selectively tests set-shifting ability. In the general area of set learning, there has been extensive research over the years on several fronts – behavioural experiments, theoretical accounts and mathematical and neural network modelling (see [2] for a general summary and for neural network modelling of reversal shifts). There have been modelling attempts of WCST, for example, see [3]; [4]; and [5]. However, there has been no systematic attempt so far at modelling the SSP deficits and linking model parameters to specific brain areas that are known to be involved in the task. In the study reported here, a first attempt is made in this direction.

2 Set-Shifting Task

2.1 Description of the Experiment

We use the experimental results reported by Trevor Robbins and colleagues of the Cambridge Experimental Psychology group. In this paradigm, subjects are required to perform a series of simultaneous compound visual discriminations using stimuli that are composed of white lines (foreground) superimposed on blue-filled shapes (background). The experiment uses total-change design where novel exemplars are used in the shift stage [6]. The test apparatus consists of a video screen display of patterns displayed to the right and left of a central area, a reinforcement delivery mechanism, and an automatic response monitoring mechanism. SSP experiments comprise the following three critical stages. For ease of discussion, examples based on figure 1 are used in the elaboration of various stages.

a) Simple discrimination: Simple stimuli of white lines or blue-filled shape exemplars are used. For example, in figure 1, triangle shape in any position is rewarding.

b) Compound discrimination: Compound stimuli with line and shape exemplars superimposed are used. For example, white lines are superimposed on the solid black shapes in figure 1. Subject needs to maintain responses to the triangle shape irrespective of the type of superimposed line and irrespective of the position of occurrence of the compound stimulus.

c) Dimensional shift: One of the two following shifts with a new set of exemplars is administered. The introduction of a totally new set of exemplars enables verifying if the subjects are attending to a relevant dimension (in this case, 'shapes') or simply discriminating based on configural cues.

(i) Intra-dimensional shift (IDS): A new exemplar from the *previously relevant* dimension is rewarded. As shown in figure 1, black diamond shape is

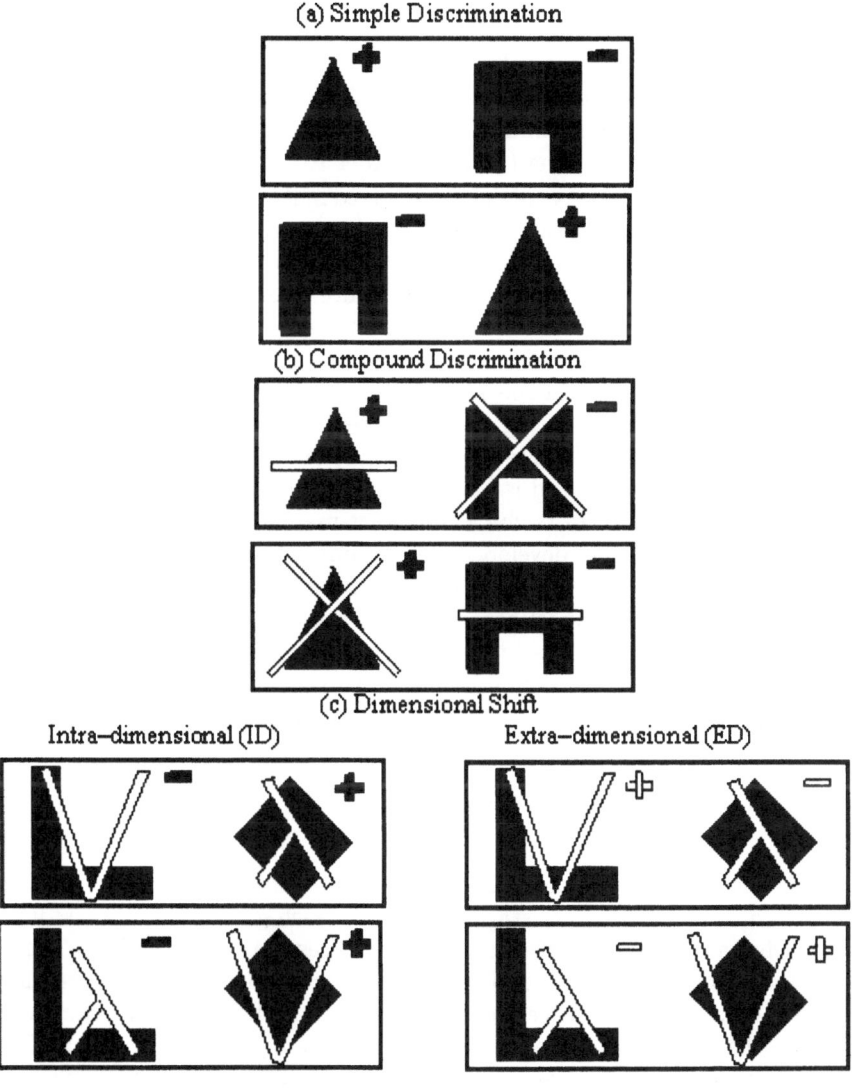

Figure 1: Experimental set-up illustrating the three stages – simple discrimination, compound discrimination, and dimensional shift – in the set-shifting experiment. Stimuli with 'plus' sign are rewarded and those with 'minus' sign are not rewarded. (Adapted from [6])

rewarding irrespective of the foreground white lines and position of occurrence of the compound stimulus. Subject needs to keep attending to the previously relevant dimension ('shapes') in order to be successful.

(ii) Extra-dimensional shift (EDS): A new exemplar from the *previously irrelevant* dimension is rewarded. As shown in figure 1, white coloured 'V' is rewarding irrespective of the background black shapes and position of occurrence of the compound stimulus. Subject needs to start attending to the previously irrelevant dimension ('lines') in order to be successful.

It is to be noted that the experiment reported in [6] consisted of other stages such as reversal and probe tests. Each of the above three stages is followed by a reversal stage, in which the reward contingency reversed between the exemplars in the relevant dimension. For example, in figure 1, during the reversal phase corresponding to the simple discrimination stage, square shape is rewarded instead of triangle. Additionally, a probe test using novel exemplars from the irrelevant dimension followed the second and third stages of the experiment. For example, in figure 1, during the probe test corresponding to compound discrimination stage, novel white line exemplars are superimposed on triangle and square shapes and reward is maintained for compound stimuli consisting of triangle shape. Probe tests check if subject maintained an attentional set. The neural network model developed here accounts for the shifts – IDS/EDS. Reversal shifts have not been modelled and probe tests are not conducted on the network model. NN model needs to be seen as a model of the brain areas subserving the attentional set-shifting function. Further, there is evidence for such a dissociation between the brain areas involved in attentional (IDS/EDS) and affective (reversal) shifts as observed by Dias, Robbins, and Roberts [7].

2.2   Results Of The Experiment

Subjects are divided into four groups depending on the type of stimuli used for initial simple discrimination and the type of subsequent shift: LineID, LineED, ShapeID, ShapeED. At every stage, subjects in each group were trained until they reached a criterion of 90% correct in any one session of 60 trials. The experimental results of Roberts et al [6] show that both monkeys and humans made more errors to reach the success criterion during the EDS stage as compared to either the pre-shift compound discrimination stage or the post-shift IDS stage. Results for monkeys are shown in figure 2. This IDS/EDS asymmetry is observed across three species [1]. Further, as shown in figure 3, performance on EDS is significantly impaired with damage to the prefrontal cortex but left performance on the IDS intact. In the following section a theoretical account for the IDS/EDS asymmetry is given.

3   Theory

As an exemplar of one category is being learnt, a category bias corresponding to that dimension will be strengthened. Hence all the exemplars from this *relevant*

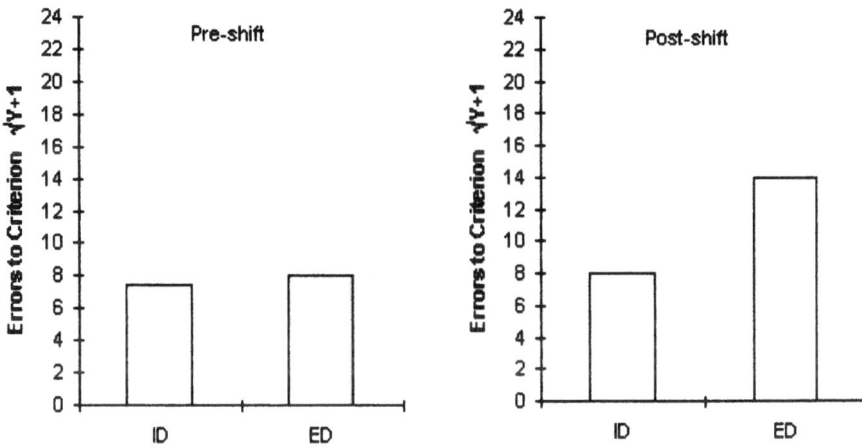

Figure 2: Experimental results on marmosets show a superior performance on the intra-dimensional shift than on the extra-dimensional shift. 'Y' represents the mean number of errors to criterion and the results shown are square-root transformed. Simulation results shown in later figures also follow the same notation. (Adapted from [6])

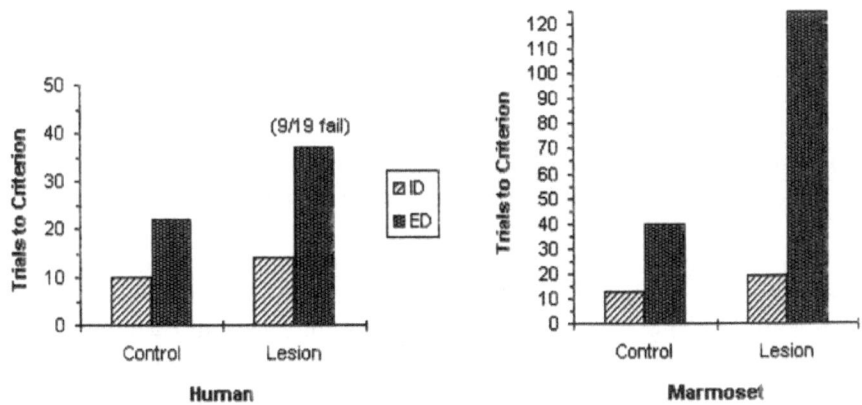

Figure 3: Prefrotnal damage enhances the normal IDS/EDS asymmetry both in humans and monkeys. (Adapted from [1])

dimension become equally associated with reward by way of uniform weighting bias (this feature will be subsequently referred to as *bias theory*). Thus the acquisition of discriminations requiring a subsequent EDS becomes difficult. A neural network (connectionist) model that embodies this theory is presented in the next section. Similar probabilistic accounts can be found in [8] and [9].

4 Neural Network Model

4.1 Network Architecture And Simulation Details

The neural network architecture consists of two categorisation modules - one for perceptual features and the other for exemplar response choices (see figure 4). Equations governing the activation of nodes in various layers are shown in the Appendix. Input stimuli representing the presence of lines and shapes are coded as binary vectors. Attentional competition at both the category and exemplar stages is assumed to be winner take-all (WTA). Binary inputs are presented at the input module and then the activation flows both to the category-bias and exemplar-bias modules. Because of the WTA dynamics at the category module, only one category is selected which in turn supplies a bias to the corresponding nodes in the exemplar module. Each node in exemplar module receives two inputs – one from the input module and the other from the category module. Competition at the exemplar level selects one of the exemplars to be active. The winner exemplar selectively gates (multiplicatively) the activity corresponding to that exemplar from the input module to the output module. The response module outputs a unit response from the side (left or right) corresponding to where the winning exemplar is located. If the response is correct, a reward signal of value 1 is given and for an incorrect response reward signal stays at a value of 0. There are two modifiable connections corresponding to attentional biases to categories and exemplars. Learning parameters control the rate of learning at both the modules. Learning is initiated upon the external reward signal and only weights corresponding to the winner categories and exemplars are reinforced. The absence of external reward initiates a decrement of these weights.

Lines and shapes are presented in different combinations and locations as in the original experiment. Simulation at each of the three stages (Simple, Compound, and Shift) continues for a maximum of 5 sessions each of 60 trials. Criterion is to reach 90% correct in any session in order to move to the next stage. Line and shape exemplar weights are initialised with small random numbers around $1/n$ (n: number of exemplars in each category, in this case four). Category weights are initialised to a random number near $1/2$. There are 15 NN subjects (initialised with different random initial weights) in each of four groups (LineID, LineED, ShapeID, ShapeED). All the results are calculated as a mean over all subjects in each of the IDS (total of 30 Ss) and EDS (total of 30 Ss) groups separately and square-root transformed as in the original experimental results [6].

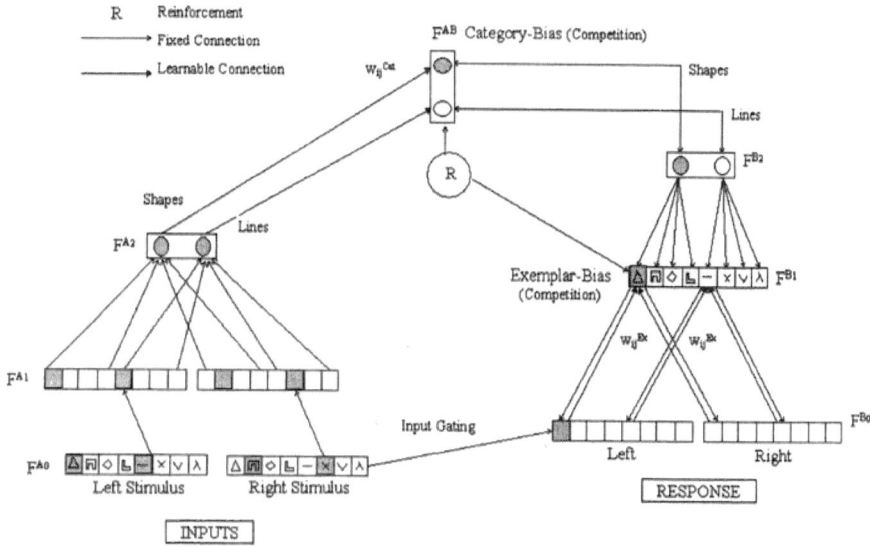

Figure 4: Neural Network Architecture. Category weights (w_{ij}^{Cat}) and exemplar weights (w_{ij}^{Ex}) for both shapes and lines are modified based on reinforcement signal. Category-bias and exemplar-bias are determined by competition. (See text for more details)

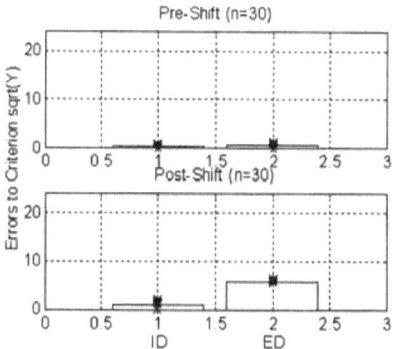

Figure 5: Simulation results with the category and exemplar learning rates set in the normal range (cLR=0.02; eLR=0.01) capture the IDS/EDS asymmetry observed during the post-shift phase in normal primates.

4.2   Simulation Results

When category learning rate (cLR) and exemplar learning rate (eLR) are set to zero, the network performance is at chance level (results not included here). Results in figure 5 establish the superiority of IDS performace over EDS when the learning parameters are in normal range (cLR=0.02, eLR=0.01) and compare with the experimental results in figure 2. With decreasing exemplar learning rate, overall errors to criterion are increased but the basic phenomenon of the superiority of the IDS performance over EDS is not affected (results shown in figure 6). In contrast, as the category learning rate is decreased (from 0.2 to 0.0002), response errors show a transition from approximately equal performance on the IDS and EDS to a situation where performance on the IDS is far superior to that of EDS (figure 7). In other words, the normal IDS/EDS asymmetry becomes enhanced as category learning rate is lowered and this result compares with the results of subjects with damage to the prefrontal cortex (compare figures 3 and 7). Extensive simulations over a wide range of values for both cLR and eLR were conducted and the basic qualitative pattern remained as indicated above.

4.3   Discussion

Damage to the Prefrontal Cortex (PFC) can be seen as lowering the category attentional learning rate thereby reducing learning of category bias on discrimination. Thus PFC is hypothesised to be involved in the reward association at the category level but not at the exemplar level. Further, in order to enhance a previously irrelevant dimension rapidly, it is hypothesised that a higher-level process is needed to destabilise the uniform bias developed at the category level during the initial simple and compound discrimination learning. We hypothesise that PFC is involved in this higher level function. Exemplar learning rate affected the overall number of errors and not the IDS/EDS asymmetry. In the network equations (see the Appendix), exemplar learning rate (γ) determines how fast a particular exemplar is learnt and thus functionally this parameter is related to aspects of reward learning related to individual exemplars. The learning of individual responses may not be solely dependent on the prefrontal cortex but is related more to the function of subcortical areas such as the basal ganglia, cerebellum, etc.

Based on the results, a prediction can be made that response errors made by subjects during any shift stage will be predominantly intra-dimensional in nature rather than extra-dimensional and that these errors occur because exemplars from the relevant dimension are uniformly biased and win the attentional competition.

4.4   Higher-Order Rule Formation

Higher-order rules such as "Line-Category is relevant" but "Shape-category is not relevant" are represented in the form of reward association combined with

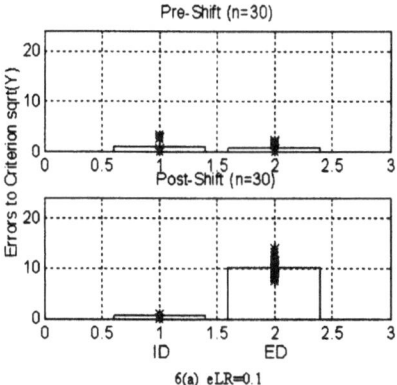

6(a) eLR=0.1

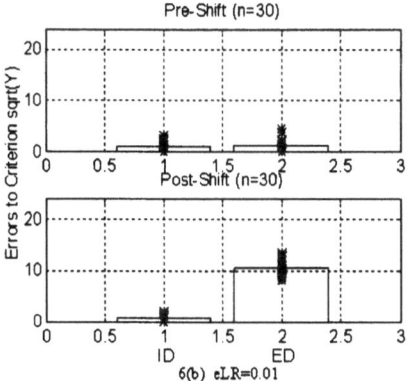

6(b) eLR=0.01

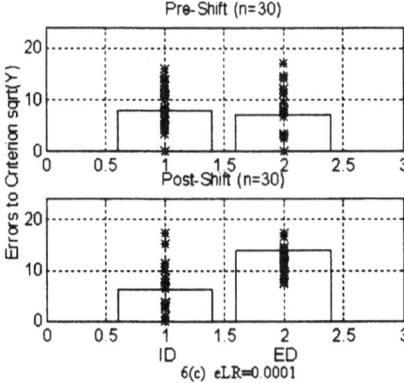

6(c) eLR=0.0001

Figure 6: Simulation results with a constant category learning rate (cLR=0.002) but with a decreasing exemplar learning rate (a) eLR=0.1 (b) eLR=0.01 and (c) eLR=0.0001. As eLR decreases, overall errors to attain the success criterion increase but the IDS/EDS asymmetry remains unaffected.

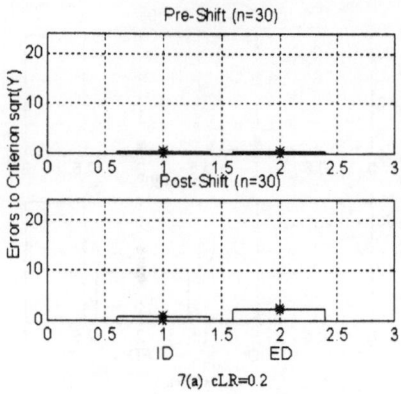

7(a) cLR=0.2

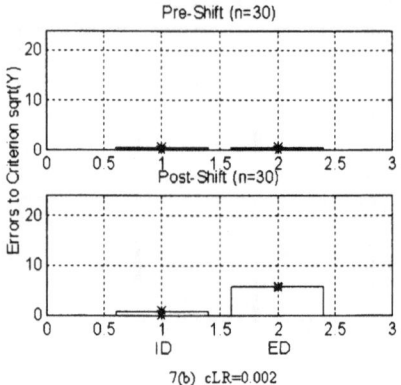

7(b) cLR=0.002

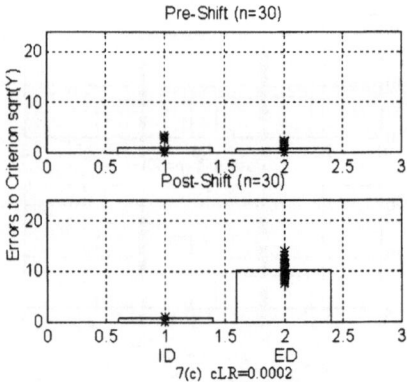

7(c) cLR=0.0002

Figure 7: Simulation results with a constant exemplar learning rate (eLR=0.1) but with a decreasing category learning rate (a) cLR=0.2 (b) cLR=0.002 and (c) cLR=0.0002. As cLR decreases, the IDS/EDS asymmetry grows bigger.

unequal biases triggering one category module and not the other. This simple representation leads to an apparent rule-like behaviour of the network. These rules do not yet offer the same manipulable access as higher-order rules. However this simple association learning is at the root of basic rule-like behaviour in animals and humans. As an example, consider learning to play a cards game where matching the colour of the card on the pile gets reward. Also, suppose that the rule of the game is not made explicit and needs to be discovered during the play. Subjects will only have information on what happened in each trial. Consider the following events — 2-of-spades matched with 9-of-hearts ended in no win, 3-of-diamonds matched with ace-of-hearts ended in a win, 5-of-diamonds matched with 6-of-hearts was successful, etc. Subject has to infer from these events that one of the common features of the two successful episodes is matching of colours. Further, this hypothesis needs to be tested in future trials to see if it is really a rewarding one. In time, if the colour matching is a successful strategy, it gets crystallised as a rule. It needs to be seen in this example that simple learning of association between various moves and reward is the first step in the complex process of inference and rule-formation. Damage to the PFC is known to cause breakdown in the use of strategy, so the study and modelling efforts of the PFC would throw light on generalised rule-representation in brain as well as connectionist systems.

5   Conclusions

In this study, we report a simple explanation of the asymmetry in intra-dimensional and extra-dimensional set-shifting performance in primates as due to uniform bias accumulation to the relevant category. A neural network model verifies this bias theory. Function role for the prefrontal cortex in attentional set-shifting experiments is hypothesised to be in the reward-association learning at the category-level. Higher-order rules are hypothesised to be represented in the form of associative memory combined with unequal biases triggering one memory module and not the other. It is suggested that these simple and basic processes in neural systems can support the formation of potentially higher-level representations.

Acknowledgements

RSB would like to acknowledge support from the UK Engineering and Physical Sciences Research Council (GR/J42151) for the work reported here.

References

[1] Roberts AC. Comparison of cognitive function in human and non-human primates. Cognitive Brain Research 1996; 3:319–327

[2] Kruschke JK. Dimensional relevance shifts in category learning. Connection Science 1996; 8(2):225–247

[3] Levine DS, Prueitt PS. Modeling some effects of frontal lobe damage: Novelty and perseveration. Neural Networks 1989; 2: 103–116

[4] Dehaene S, Changeux J-P. The Wisconsin card sorting test: Theoretical analysis and modeling in a neural network. Cerebral Cortex 1991; 1(1):62–79

[5] Monchi O, Taylor JG. A hard wired model of coupled frontal working memories for various tasks. King's College London preprint 1997; KCL-MTH-97-26

[6] Roberts AC, Robbins TW, Everitt BJ. The effects of intradimensional and extradimensional shifts on visual discrimination learning in humans and non-human primates. Quarterly Journal of Experimental Psychology 1988; 40B:321–341

[7] Dias R, Robbins TW, Roberts AC. Dissociation in prefrontal cortex of affective and attentional shifts. Nature 1996; 380:69–72

[8] Sutherland NS, Mackintosh NJ. Mechanisms of animal discrimination learning. Academic Press, New York, 1971

[9] Zeaman D, House BJ. A review of attention theory. In N. R. Ellis (Eds) Handbook of Mental Deficiency, Psychological Theory and Research 2nd Edition, pp. 63–120. McGraw Hill, New York, 1979

Appendix

Equations for the Neural Network Model

Input Layer:

$$x_i^{A_0} = \text{input stimuli} \in \{0, 1\}; \ i = 1, 2, \ldots, 16 \tag{1}$$

F^{A_1} Layer:

$$x_i^{A_1} = x_i^{A_0}; \ i = 1, 2, \ldots, 16 \tag{2}$$

F^{A_2} Layer:

$$x_i^{A_2} = \sum_{j \in F^{A_1}} x_j^{A_1}; \tag{3}$$

$$\text{where } i = 1(\text{Shape}), 2(\text{Line}); \ j = \left\{ \begin{array}{l} 1,\ldots,4 \ \& \ 9,\ldots,12 \ (\text{Shapes}) \\ 5,\ldots,8 \ \& \ 13,\ldots,16 \ (\text{Lines}) \end{array} \right.$$

F^{AB} Layer:

$$net_j^{AB} = \sum_{i \in F^{A_2}} w_{ij}^{Cat} \cdot x_i^{A_2}; \tag{4}$$

here $w_{11}^{Cat} = w_S, w_{22}^{Cat} = w_L,$ and other $w_{ij}^{Cat} = 0$

$$x_j^{AB} = \max_j(net_j^{AB}); \tag{5}$$

where max function sets node with max value to 1 and others to 0

$$w_{ij}^{Cat}(t+1) = w_{ij}^{Cat}(t) + \eta[x^r(t) - w_{ij}^{Cat}(t)] \cdot x_j^{AB}(t); \tag{6}$$

where $\eta = \text{CatLR} = \text{Category Learning Rate}$

$$x^r(t) = \text{External Reinforcement Signal} \in \{0,1\} \tag{7}$$

F^{B_2} Layer:

$$x_i^{B_2} = x_i^{AB} \tag{8}$$

F^{B_1} Layer:

$$\begin{aligned} net_i^B \ &= \text{category bias} + \text{exemplar bias} \\ &= x_i^{B_2} + \sum_{i \in F^{A_0}} w_{ij}^{Ex} \cdot x_i^{A_0} \end{aligned} \tag{9}$$

$$x_i^{B_1} = \max_i(net_i^B); \tag{10}$$

where max function sets node with max value to 1 and others to 0

$$w_{ij}^{Ex}(t+1) = w_{ij}^{Ex}(t) + \gamma[x^r(t) - w_{ij}^{Ex}(t)] \cdot x_i^B(t); \tag{11}$$

where $\gamma = \text{ExLR} = \text{Exemplar Learning Rate}$

F^{B_0} Layer (Input Gating):

$$x_i^{B_0} = x_i^{A_0} \cdot x_i^{B_1} \tag{12}$$

Models of Coupled Anterior Working Memories for Frontal Tasks

Oury Monchi & John G. Taylor*

Centre for Neural Networks, Department of Mathematics, King's College London
and * also at Institute for Medicine, Research Centre
Juelich, Germany

Abstract

We have previously developed a simple hard wired neural network which investigates the role of the dorsolateral prefrontal cortex, the ventrolateral prefrontal cortex and the Anterior Cingulate Gyrus, together with their associated basal ganglia-thalamocortical loops, in solving the classical delayed response task, Delayed visual matching and the Wisconsin Card Sorting Task. This was done by constraining the model to some of the known connectivity within these areas. Here an extension of this model is described which includes reinforcement of the Hebbian type as a mechanism to learn features as working memories. Lesions applied to the hard wired model are also discussed with respect to the deficits observed in various kind of patients while performing those tasks.

1 Introduction

1.1 Anatomical and Physiological Considerations

Cognitive and attentional frontal tasks such as the classical delayed response task (DRS), Delayed visual matching (DRO) and the Wisconsin Card Sorting Task (WCST) rely on anterior working memory (WM). WM has been associated with sustained activity from 2 to up to 60 seconds, as observed in single neurons in the Prefrontal Cortex [1]. It seems that the posterior visual system is involved in the building up of anterior WM via excitatory reciprocal connections to the prefrontal cortex (PFC) and it has even been proposed that these posterior regions are solely involved in the active maintenance of features. However, recent functional magnetic resonance imaging (fMRI) techniques [2] have shown the involvement of the PFC in the active maintenance of contextual features, at least for long enough delays. The cognitive processes required for the frontal tasks that are considered here include the access to contextual memory, selective attention, set shifting and decision making for action. Medial dorsal thalamic lesions in non human primates [3] have provided some evidence for the involvement of basal ganglia-thalamocortical loops in WM which is further suported by the cognitive deficits observed in patients with Parkinson's disease while solving frontal tasks [4]. Five such loops have been proposed in [5]. We suggest here that each of these loops selects and organises various features and strategies to be activated as WM when required. We investigate how the interaction of three of these loops, the dorsolateral prefrontal cortex (DLPFC) loop, the ventrolateral prefrontal cortex (VL) loop and Anterior Cingulate Gyrus (ACG) loop, could allow for solving the tasks mentioned above. We only consider the direct pathway of the basal ganglia. Thus each of these circuits involves a PFC area sending excitatory glutamatergic projections to its associated part of the caudate (CD). The latter sends inhibitory projections involving GABA and substance P to a corresponding area of the internal globus pallidus (Gpi) which sends GABA inhibitory projections to mediodorsal thalamus (MD) hence resulting in disinhibition. Reciprocal excitatory projections occur between MD and PFC involving glutamate. Of importance also are the strong long range inhibitory connections occurring within CD and GPi as a result of the principal spiny neurons, the inhibition occurring from interneurons within MD, the inhibition occurring from interneurons within PFC and the role of the nigrostriatal and mesolimbic dopamine. In the model the primary motor areas (PMA) are taken as the output. We therefore do not consider the whole motor loop. We examine here the role of the 3 loops mentioned above with respect to the DRS and DRO as they are a good way to probe the active maintenance of WM. We also examine those loops while performing the WCST as this is an attentional task which involves some higher level processes such as set shifting. PET studies [6] have shown the importance of the ACG, which projects to the Nucleus Accumbens (Nacc) with respect to selective attention. The basolateral amygdala-Nacc system has been associated with reward-related processes together with possibly the whole ACG loop. We suggest here that the ACG codes for possible strategies. Upon the detection of an error, the basolateral amygdala sends a penalty signal by firing so as to change the pattern of activity in Nacc which will result in a change of strategy choice occurring in ACG via the feedback projections occurring from posteromedial thalamus. It has been suggested (Gray, J., personal communication) that the error detection occurs in the hippocampal formation. This is not included in our model.

1.2 Learning Processes

Previous versions of the model [7] were hard wired. They proposed mechanisms for the active maintenance and the strategy selection involved in the frontal tasks without giving any insight into how they might be learned. Studies in non human primates [8] have given good evidence that long term synaptic changes involving dopamine occur in corticostriatal pathways during the learning of reward related and delayed response tasks. It is thought that some kind of reinforcement learning occurs in these pathways and we propose here that a similar type of learning also occurs in the cortico-thalamic pathways. This is supported by the fact that mediodorsal thalamic lesions impair the learning of reward related processes [3]. We suggest that reinforcement learning in corticostriatal and cortico-thalamic pathways in the DLPFC and VL loops allows for the organization of competing features to be activated as WM when required. This learning would be acquired while being trained to solve frontal tasks in monkeys and during infancy in humans as an infant explores its environment.

1.3 The Tasks

Delayed Response tasks have been extensively used to examine frontal lobe deficits in human and monkey. The basic procedure is the same for both the DRS and the DRO. A subject is cued with an object, followed by a variable delay period usually between 2 and 60 seconds. The subject is then presented with 2 objects situated at different locations and must choose one of them. In DRS the rule is to choose the object situated at the same location as the one cued before the delay. In the DRO task, 2 different objects are shown after the delay and the subject has to choose the object that was cued before the delay irrespective of its location.

In the WCST, a subject is shown 4 cards each inscribed with a set of objects. The cards vary in the number of objects they contain, their colours and their shapes. At each trial the subject is given a card to match with one of the four reference cards without being told what the rule of classification is. The experimenter chooses a feature (shape, colour or number) with respect to which the matching is to be done only telling the subject whether the classification is right or wrong after each trial. After a fixed number of correct classifications the experimenter changes the rule without telling the subject and the same procedure continues.

2 The Delayed Response Tasks Network

The architecture indicating the name of the layers and the connectivity of the delayed response tasks network model is as shown in Figure 1. The term grid here is defined to mean a group of units in the model with the same properties and a layer means a set of adjacent grids. Every grid in the network corresponds to a population of cells with the same properties. The grids in the input, DLPFC, VL, ACG, MC and PMA layers each contain 6 units while the grids in the other layers each contain 2 units. This is done to account for the smaller size of basal ganglia and thalamus than of PFC. The input layer contains 4 grids each containing 6 units which could represent 4 populations of cells lying in posterior visual cortex. Let A mean object A, B mean object B, L mean left location and R mean right location. The first grid in the input layer from the left codes for object A being at the left location (LA), and similarly the second grid codes for LB, the third for RA and the fourth RB. The DLPFC layer has 2 grids, one coding for L, the other for R. It is meant to represent 2 populations of cells within the DLPFC. Similarly the VL layer is meant to represent cells lying in the ventrolateral cortex with one grid coding for A and the other coding for B. LA in the input layer sends excitatory connections to L in DLPFC and A in VL and similarly for LB, RA and RB. The value of the lateral inhibitory weights in dlCD and ldmGPi are set twice as large as those in DLPFC and pcMD, since in the first 2 grids they represent the effect of the principal spiny neurons in the basal ganglia, whereas in the case of the other 2 grids they represent the effect of inhibitory interneurons. The connections within

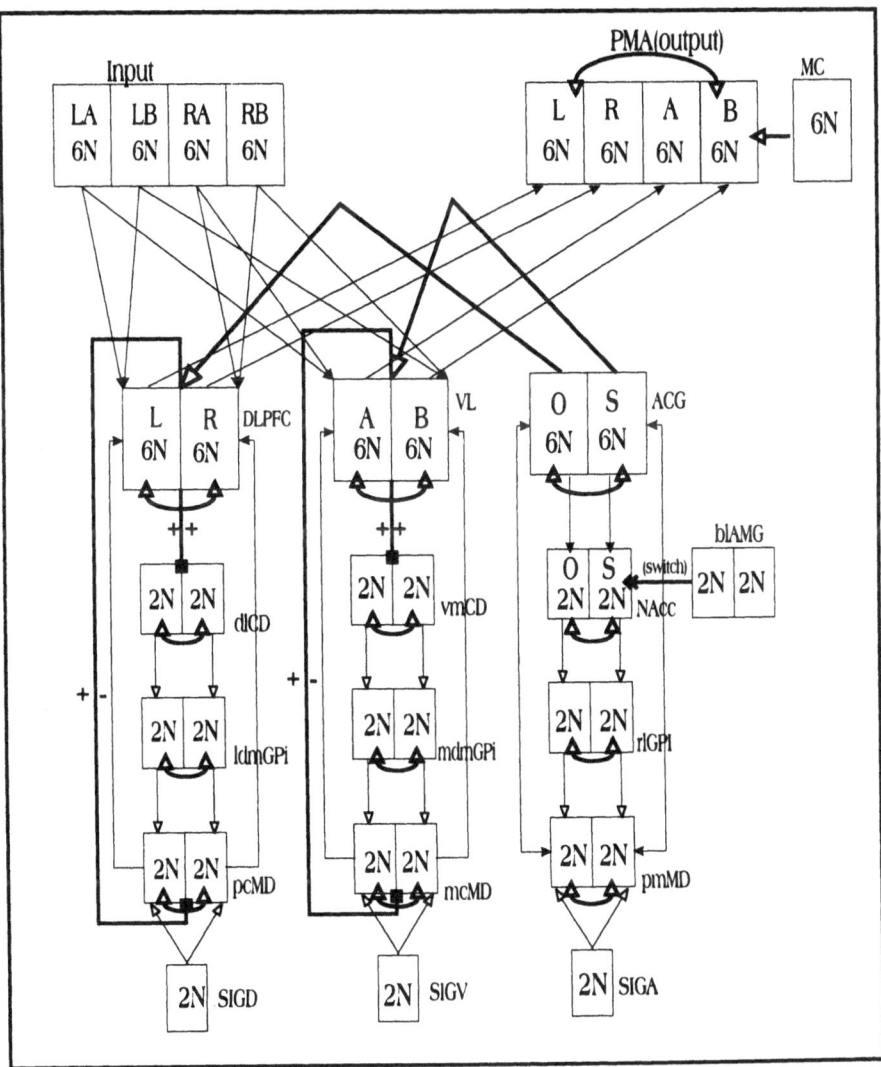

Legend: dlCD: dorsolateral CD, ldmGPi: lateral dorsomedial GPi, pcMD: medialis dorsalis pars parvocellularis, vmCD: ventromedial CD, mdmGPi: medial dorsomedial GPi, mcMD medialis dorsalis pars magnocellularis, rlGPi: rostrolateral GPi, pmMD: posteromedial dorsal thalamus. N: neurons.

Connections: ◭ ◭ : grid to grid all to all lateral inhibition, ──▷: grid to grid all to all inhibition, ──→ : grid to grid all to all excitation, ◄──► : grid to grid reciprocal all to all excitation
──▷ : grid to layer all to all inhibition, ──■ :all to all layer to layer learning, ──➤:switch.

Figure 1: The Delayed Response Tasks network

each of the DLPFC, VL and ACG loops in the model are the same except for the all to all learning weights from DLPFC to dlCD, from DLPFC to pcMD, from VL to vmCD and from VL to mcMD while the weights from ACG to Nacc and from ACG to pmMD are fixed. It has been postulated (Goldman-Rackic, PS, personal comunications) that the resetting of WM's could occur due to a cortical signal to the MD. We have explored this possibility further: the grids SIGD, SIGV, SIGA represent 3 populations of cortical cells which would excite the inhibitory interneurons of the appropriate partof MD, so as to inhibit MD during the reset of WM. In the model, these 3 grids send inhibitory connections to both grids in their corresponding MD. The "O" grid in ACG codes for "object strategy" and sends inhibitory projections to the whole DLPFC layer. Similarly the "S" grid in ACG stands for spatial strategy and inhibits the whole of VL. The grids of Nacc have been denoted "O" and "S" for ease of description. We do not suggest here that the Nacc codes for strategies, but that the competing populations in ACG coding for strategies send projections to competing populations of the Nacc. blAMG in the model plays the role of a switch, the left grid sending excitatory projections to the O grid of the Nacc and inhibitory connections to the S grid of the Nacc, while the right grid of the blAMG does the contrary. PmA in the model stands for premotor areas and represents populations responding to the fact that a movement has occurred and thus resetting activities in PMA.

All the neurons in the model except for the units in input, SIGD, SIGV, SIGA, MC and blAMG are Leaky Integrator Neurons (L.I.N). Their equations are the following:

$$\tau \, \dot{v}_i = -v_i + \sum_j w_{ji} u_j \text{ with } u_i = f(v_i - \vartheta) \text{ and } f(x) = 1/(1+e^{-\beta x}) \quad \text{eq.1}$$

where v_i is the potential of neuron i, u_i is its output, ϑ its threshold, β is the gain which is set to 1 for every L.I.N., u_j is the output of each unit j which feeds to unit i and w_{ji} are the weights connecting every neuron j to unit i. τ is the time constant which is set to 0.11 seconds for every L.I.N in the network . The remaining units in the grids mentioned above are input type neurons with their activity set to 1 when required, otherwise set to 0. All the L.I.N's are updated synchronously every 10 milliseconds.

2.1 Training the Network

The DLPFC loop and the VL loop are trained separately. In order to train the DLPFC loop the output of the neurons in the S grid in ACG are set to 1 for the VL loop to be inhibited. The network is then presented with trials of the DRS each consisting of a cue period which lasts for 1 second where one grid in the input layer is switched on, a delay period of 10 seconds where all units in the input layer have no output, and a response period of 2 seconds where the same object is switched on at 2 different locations in the input layer. There is an inter-trial period of 35 seconds where SIGD is switched on and the working memories are reset. Reinforcement learning occurs during the last 100 milliseconds of the response period between DLPFC and dlCD and between DLPFC and pcMD. The weights from DLPFC to pcMD are constrained to remain positive. Each grid in DLPFC sends projections to both grids in dlCD and both grids in pcMD. The learning equation is the following:

$$\left| w_{ij}(t+1) \right| = \left| w_{ij}(t) \right| + \rho \, R \, u_i(t) \, u_j(t) \qquad \text{eq.2.}$$

where R = 1 if the mean squared error at the DLPFC is less than 0.2, R = -1 otherwise. w_{ij} is the weight between units i and j, u_i and u_j their respective outputs. ρ is the learning rate. It is decreased slightly after each training cycle. The mean squared error being greater than 0.2 means that DLPFC is firing too strongly for the location oposite to the one cued during the response period. This causes the absolute value of the weights between currently active units to be reduced. After learning, the DLPFC distinguishes properly between the 2 features; that is it encodes the required location, keeps its activity sustained during the delay and outputs strongly for the cued location at the end of the response period.

Learning in the VL loop is done in the same way. It occurs from VL to vmCD which are kept positive and from VL to mcMD. The neurons in the O grid of ACG are now set to 1 in order to inhibit the DLPFC loop. The network is presented with trials of the DRO and is trained on delays of 10 seconds. Learning governed by eq.2 occurs during the last 100 milliseconds of the response period where 2 different objects are presented at the input. VL is trained to have a large output for the cued object and a small one for the other one, irrespective of their locations during the response period. After training the VL loop properly distinguishes the 2 objects as WM features.

2.2 Performing the Delayed Response Tasks

After training, the outputs of the S units in Nacc are set to 1, the others set to 0. After a few updates this causes the S units in ACG to have a strong output and therefore inhibits VL. The cue period lasts for 1 second with 1 grid in the input layer set to 1. This is followed by a delay period where all the input neurons are set to 0 which lasts 2 to 60 seconds. During the delay period sustained activity is observed in DLPFC for the cued location (L or R). The potential of one unit in the L grid of DLPFC is shown for a successful trial of DRS in Figure 2. The inter-trial period is not shown in full. A slight decrease of potential can be observed during the delay. It should be noted however that the resulting potential is much greater than the threshold which is set to 1. Also the L unit in DLPFC does not only represent context cells in DLPFC but all cells that are selective to the left direction in DLPFC. While the context cells reported in [1] fire strongly during the delay, the fixation cells and the visual tonic cells fire more strongly during the cue period and the response period. During the response period the network is presented with 2 units switched on in the input layer for a duration of 2.5 seconds. It is the output in PmA at the end of this period which is taken as the final output upon which performance is judged. There is an inter-trial period of 35 seconds during which SIGD, SIGV and MC are set to 1 and the WM's are reset. At this point the network classifies according to location correctly and solves the DRS. When the first trial of DRO occurs, the network still classifies according to location and an error occurs.

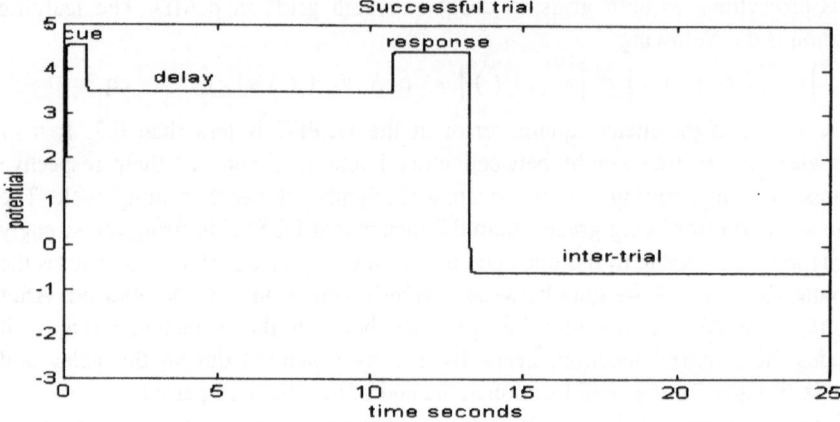

Figure 2: Potential of one unit in grid L during a succesful trial of DRS

This causes the grid in blAMG which inhibits S and excites O in Nacc and SIGA to activate during the inter-trial period. This results in O being activated in ACG. Thus, classification is sought by object from the second trial on. In this case, sustained activity is observed for the cued object (A or B) in VL. The DRO can also be solved when the objects are reversed during the delay. If this is followed by further trials of DRS then an error occurs as the network classifies according to object. This causes the S grid in blAMG to fire during the intertrial period switching the activity in Nacc to S again. It should be noted that after training no error within a loop can occur. An error only occurs when a shift of strategy is required.

3 The WCST Network

The architecture and the principles of the WCST network are very similar to the delayed response network. The architecture of the WCST network is shown in Figure 3. The network now contains one prefrontal loop for each attribute together with the ACG loop. The same areas as in the delayed response version are represented, with the subscript C indicating that an area is part of the colour loop, similarly for the subscript S for shape and N for number. The connectivity within each loop is the same as for the delayed response network. There are now 3 input layers, inputC codes for green, red and blue, inputS square, circle and triangle and inputN for 1, 2 and 3. PmA codes for colour (C), shape (S) and number (N) so that every units in FLC sends excitatory projections to the C node in PmA, similarly for every units in FLS to the S node in PmA and for every units in FLN to the N node in PmA. The C node in ACG sends inhibitory connections to FLS and FLN, the S node in ACG sends inhibitory connections to FLC and FLN and the N node in ACG sends inhibitory projections to FLC and FLS. Each node in blAMG sends

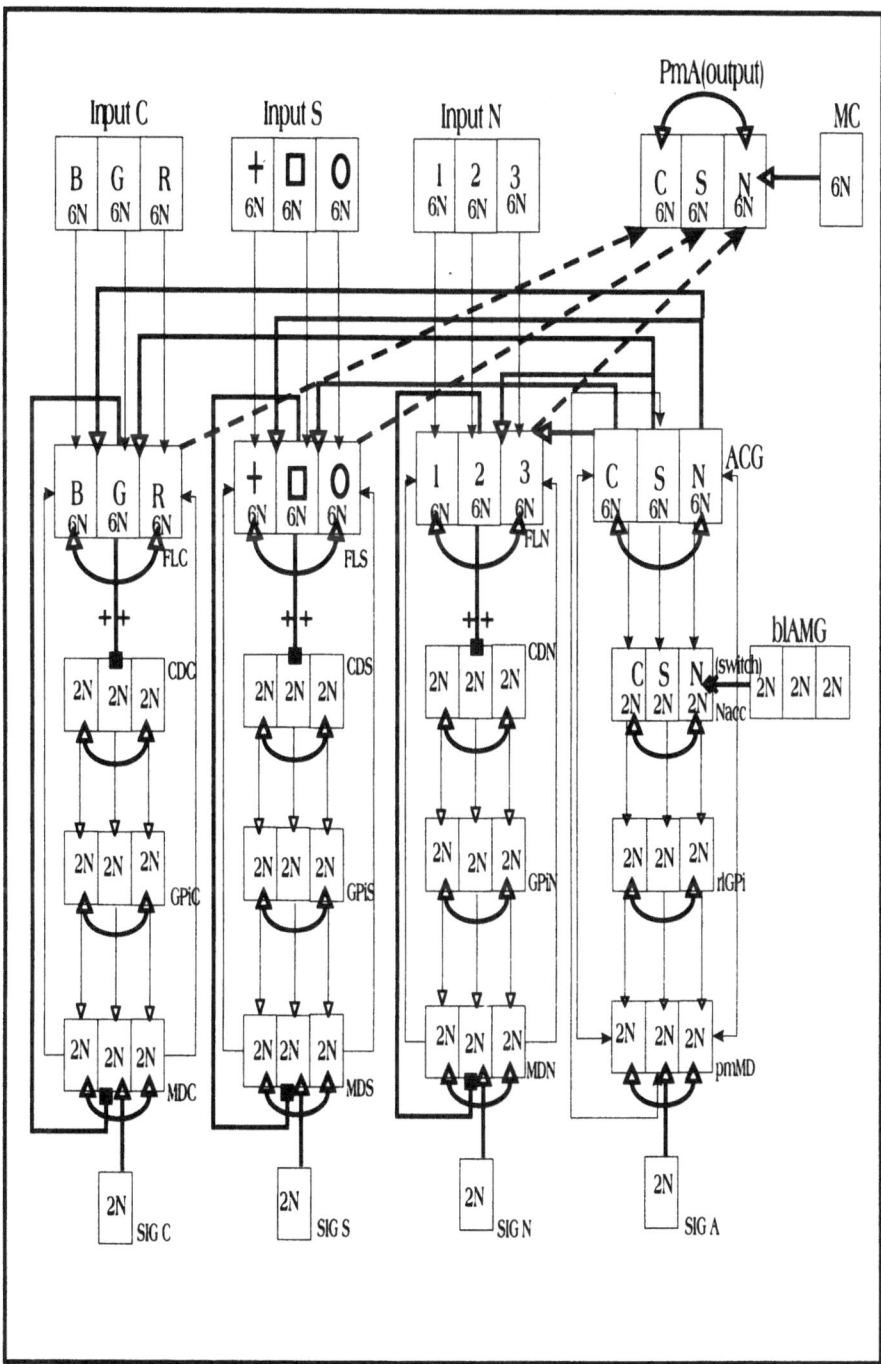

Legend: C: colour, S: shape, N: number, B: blue, G: green, R: red.

     ▬ ➤ : layer to grid all to all excitation. Rest of legend and connections same as figure1.

Figure 3: The WCST Network

excitatory projections to a single node in Nacc and inhibitory ones to the other two. The same neurons are used for both the WCST and the delayed response task versions of the model.

3.1 Learning Within the Loops

Each feature loop is trained on a delayed matching to sample task. For instance the colour loop is trained in the following manner. The C grid in ACG is activated in order to inhibit the other 2 loops. Then a single colour grid is activated in inputC during the cue period followed by a delay period of 10 seconds and then a response period where 2 colours are presented in inputC including the cued one. Reinforcement learning governed by eq.2 occurs between FLC and CDC, which are constrained to remain positive, and between FLC and MDC during the last 100 milliseconds of the response period. After training the colour loop is able to distinguish between the 3 colours and retrieve them when required. The FLS and FLN loops are trained in a similar fashion enabling each loop to distinguish and sustain each of its 3 features as WM.

3.2 Performing the WCST

A card is presented to the network by turning on one grid in each of the 3 input layers. Preceding the simulation, one grid in Nacc is turned on. The presentation period is 2.5 seconds. It is the output of PmA at the end of those 2.5 seconds which is taken as the response of the network. An inter-trial interval of 5 seconds occurs between each card presentation. Following a correct classification the neurons in SIGC, SIGS, SIGN and MC output 1 so as to reset the WM's of the features during the inter-trial period. Upon a wrong classification they also output 1 and so does SIGA and one grid in blAMG. This activity in blAMG causes a new grid in Nacc to be activated and thus a new strategy node C, S or N is activated in ACG via the effect of the whole ACG loop and a new strategy is chosen for classification. If following the next presentation another error occurs, the grid in blAMG that was last activated has its outputs set to 1. As such only a maximum of 2 errors in a row can occur. The strategy for classification is changed after 6 correct trials.

4 Lesion Studies

The lesion studies were performed on the hard wired versions of the network which have the same functionality as the 2 versions presented above except that every grid in the network contains only 1 unit.

Human infants of 7.5 months to 9 months and DLPFC lesioned monkeys have been reported to perform badly on the DRS. Furthermore they are known to make the classical $\overline{AB}$ error while performing the DRS for delays over 2 seconds. This error consists of the following: when a first location e.g. left is cued the subject correctly reaches the left location. If after the inter-trial period the subject is cued

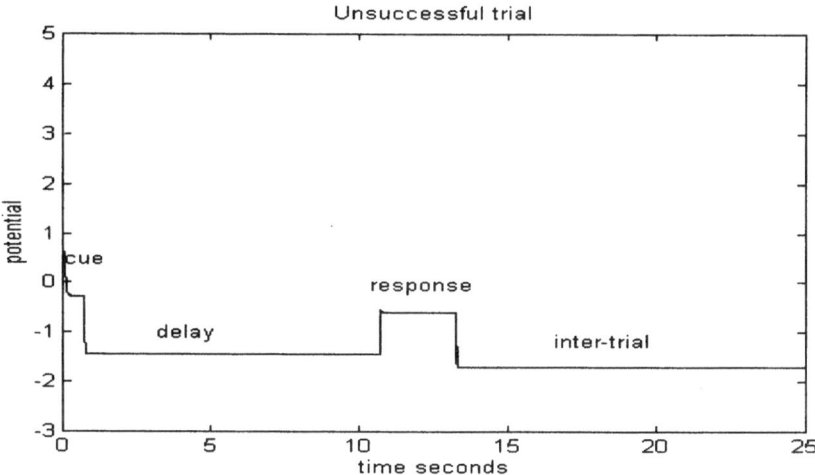

Figure 4: Potential of one unit in the R grid during an unsuccessful trial

for right the subject will wrongly reach for the previously cued left location. When the gains in the DLPFC of the delayed response model are reduced to a low value then an $\overline{AB}$ type of error occurs with respect to DRS. For instance, when the network is cued for LA, after the delay period, the L neuron correctly fires above 0.9 while the other neurons in PmA would fire below 0.1. Then following the inter-trial period, the network is now cued for RA and after the delay, the L neuron fires again above 0.9 and the other neurons fire below 0.1 in PmA instead of the R neuron firing above 0.9. During the delay preceding the error, sustained activity is not observed in the unit coding for the cued location. With the gains reduced in DLPFC, the inter-trial signal occuring from SIG D is not sufficient to reset the working memories properly in DLPFC: the previously cued unit L has a stonger activity and wins the competition over the unit R even after R is cued. The potential of the unit R in DLPFC with the gains set to 0.3 is shown during an error trial in Figure 4; it can be seen that the potential during the delay is very low. The inter-trial period is not shown in full in Figure 4. The same kind of error occurs with respect to DRO if the gains in VL are reduced. This result gives further support to our model.

Patients with Parkinson's disease are known to perform poorly on delayed response tasks (e.g. [4]). Parkinson's disease has been associated with a dopamine deregulation in the nigrostriatal pathway due to the degeneration of Basal Ganglia neurons. We have tried to model this deficit by reducing the weights exiting dlCD, ldmGPi, VmCD and mdmGPi in the hard wired Delayed Response network. The performance on DRS when these weights are significantly reduced in the model is as follows. During cue period, the right location is correctly encoded, but the activity in DLPFC during the delay is low and equal for both locations. At the end of the response period the PmA (which is effectively the output grid) fires equally for both locations. Similarly when performing DRO with the above mentioned weights significantly reduced, the right object is correctly encoded during the cue period, but both A and B in VL fire equally during the delay and the output in PmA at the end of the response period is equal for both A and B. Our model would suggest here that the degradation of the principal spiny neurons observed in Parkinson's disease causes a disruption in the active maintenance of a specific feature within a loop. This would assign an organising role to the basal ganglia with respect to WM.

Schizophrenic patients are known to perform poorly on the WCST. In normal subjects regional cerebral blood flow (rCBF) studies have shown increased activation in DLPFC while performing WCST. This result has been more recently confirmed by PET studies. rCBF studies reported in [9] have also shown a level of activity in DLPFC below baseline metabolic levels in schizophrenic patients. Schizophrenia has been associated with a dopamine deregulation of the mesocortical system which include the Nacc. Recently dopamine deregulation in Nacc has been proposed as one of the mechanism responsible for the lack of latent inhibition in Schizophrenics [10]. In order to investigate the mechanisms responsible for attentional and cognitive deficits in Schizophrenics we reduced the gains of all the units of Nacc in our WCST model. Reducing the gain is a method that was used [11] to model dopamine deregulation. We considered grids FLC, FLS and FLN to represent populations of cells in DLPFC and measured the sum of the outputs of all their neurons while performing a trial of WCST.

This total DLPFC activity was significantly reduced when the gains of FLC, FLN, FLS and Nacc were reduced. Figure 5 shows the high activity of the DLPFC neurons in the WCST model when all the gains are set to 1 while it shows the very low activity exhibited by these neurons when the gains of the grids mentioned were reduced to a value of 0.3. Our model further supports the claim that the PFC hypoactivity in schizophrenia may be linked to subcortical anatomic pathology [12]. When the gain of the neurons in Nacc are reduced to a value equal or below 0.4 in the network while performing WCST the network starts to respond equally to any strategy at a given trial, thereby not being able to decide upon a rule. Also all the nodes in all DLPFC respond equally and at a low level of activity. This causes more errors to occur and makes the blAMG fire more frequently than necessary causing even more disruption in Nacc making it impossible for the ACG to choose a strategy. Our model would predict that the lack of latent inhibition observed in patients with schizophrenia occurs from the fact that all stimuli are stored equally poorly in WM.

5. Conclusion and Discussion

The model presented here proposes mechanisms for basal ganglia-thalamocortical loops to learn features as WM's to be activated when required during attentional tasks. It is a first step in relating cognitive frontal tasks to the basal ganglia-thalamocortical loops and allows for more than one type of lesion to be performed in order to investigate the deficits occuring in more than one kind of patient. It is perhaps too strongly based on the parallel interpretation of the basal ganglia. This

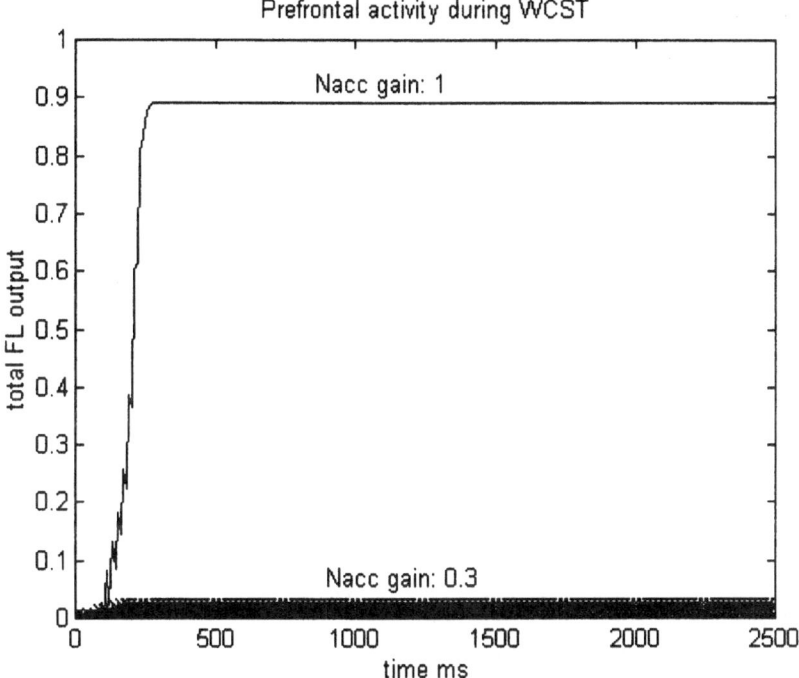

Figure 5: Total PFC output during WCST for Nacc gain 1 and 0.3

interpretation proposes that different PFC areas responding to different kinds of stimulus each project to a different area of the striatum. This is contrasted by the information funneling view of basal ganlia which proposes that the projections of various PFC areas coding for features of different dimensions could overlap on the striatum. The basal ganglia would then serve to reorganize this information by grouping different dimensions together. Both these interpretations are reviewed in [13] and it should be noted that they represent two opposite views that can be more contrasted.

Other models such as the ones presented and reviewed in [11] and [14] have well captured the various components of frontal lobe cognitive functions but have constrained themselves to explain cortical mechanisms only and have only application to one type of lesion study. Models such as the ones presented in [8] have dealt with similar cortical areas as the ones considered here. They have mainly dealt with active maintenance and serial order but have not tried to tackle the executive aspect of WM. Furthermore, no lesion studies were discussed there. Further expansion of the basal ganglia components and inclusion of dopamine modulation is a future step for the models presented here; this should include features noted in the recent reviews [15], [16] and [17].

References:

1. Barone, P; Joseph, J-P. Prefrontal cortex and spatial sequencing in macaque monkey. Experimental Brain Research. 1987; 78, pp.447-464.
2. Cohen, JD, Peristein, WP, Braver, TS, Nystrom, LE, Noll, DC, Jonides, J, Smith, EE. Temporal dynamics of brain activation during a working memory task. Nature 1997, 386, pp:604-608.
3. Goldman-Rackic, PS, Friedman, HR in Levin, HS, Eisenberg, HM, Benton, AL (eds), Frontal Lobe Function and Dysfunction O.U.P., 1991, pp.230-255.
4. Dubois, B, Pillon B. Do cognitive changes of Parkinson's disease result from dopamine depletion? Journal of Neural Transmitters 1995, 45, pp.27-34.
5. Alexander, GE, DeLong, MR, Strick, PL. Parallel organisation of functionally segregated circuits linking basal ganglia and cortex. Annual Review of Neuroscience 1986, 3, pp.357-381.
6. Posner, M I, Raichle, ME. Images of the mind. Scientific American Library. 1994.
7. Monchi, O, Taylor, JG. A model of coupled frontal working memories for delayed response tasks and the WCST in Wang, P (ed), Joint Conferences on Information Sciences 1997, 2, pp.34-37.
8. Dominey, P, Arbib, M, Joseph, JP. A model of corticostriatal plasticity for learning oculomotor associations and sequences. Journal of Cognitive Neuroscience 1995 7(3), pp.311-336.
9. Berman, FB, Barbara, PI, Weinberger, DR. Physiological dysfunction of dorsolateral prefrontal cortex in schizophrenia 1988, 45, pp.609-622.
10. Gray, JA, A model of the limbic system and basal ganglia: Applications to anxiety and schizophrenia in Ganzzagina, MS (ed), The Cognitive Neurosciences, MIT Press, 1995, pp.19-31.
11. Cohen, JD, Braver, TS, O'Reilly, RC. A computational approach to prefrontal cortex, cognitive control and schizophrenia: recent developments and current challenges. Philisophical Transaction of the Royal Society B 1996, 351, pp. 1515-1527.
12. Weinberger DR, Berman, KF, Daniel, DG in Levin, HS, Eisenberg, HM, Benton, AL (eds). Frontal Lobe Function and Dysfunction O.U.P., 1991, 275-287.
13 Parent, A, Hazrati, L-N. Functional anatomy of the basal ganglia (part 1 & 2). Brain Research Reviews 1995, 20, pp: 91-154.
14 Levine, DL, Prueitt, PS. Modelling some effects of frontal lobe damage. Novelty and Preservation. Neural Networks 1989, 2, pp:103-116.
15 Brown, LL, Schneider JS, Lidsky, TI. Sensory and cognitive functions of the basal ganglia. Current Opinion in Neurobiology, 1997, 7(2), pp:157-163.
16 White, NM. Mnemonic functions of the basal ganglia. Current Opinion in Neurobiology, 1997, 7(2), pp: 164-169.
17 Beiser, DG, Shua, SE, Houk, JC. Network models of the basal ganglia. Current Opinion in Neurobiology, 1997, 7(2), pp:185-190.

A Neurobiologically Inspired Model of Working Memory Based on Neuronal Synchrony and Rythmicity

Jacques Sougné & Robert M. French
Department of Psychology
University of Liège, 4000 Liège, Belgium
{J.Sougne, rfrench}@ulg.ac.be

Abstract

The connectionist model of reasoning presented here, INFERNET, implements a working memory that is the activated part of long-term memory. This is achieved by making use of temporal properties of the node spikes. A particular solution of the problem of multiple instantiation is proposed. This model makes predictions that have been tested experimentally and the results of these experiments are reported here. These results would seem to challenge modular models of memory.

1 Introduction

Connectionist models of working memory face two main problems. The first is the binding problem; the second is the problem of multiple instantiation. The model presented here draws its inspiration from neurobiology in an attempt to solve these problems. Different aspects of the same stimulus are not processed by the same neurons. The brain has to link together these various aspects (e.g., color, contours, movement) in order to differenciate them from other objects. This is referred to as variable binding and the present model achieves it through the use of temporal synchrony. In short, when one node (i.e., a group of neurons) fires in synchrony with another, they are temporarily bound together. This technique can be used to successfully represent n-ary predicates. This idea has been applied to "reflexive" reasoning [15], to natural language parsing [7], to analogical inferences [8], and to deductive reasoning [18]. Multiple instantiation involves simultaneous use of the same parts of the knowledge base in different ways. Connectionist models that define working memory as the activation of parts of representations in long-term memory must explain how multiply-instantiated entities are handled. In this paper we describe one such model, INFERNET, show how it simulates various aspects of human working memory, and demonstrate how it represents multiply instantiatiated concepts. Predictions will follow and experimental data will be presented which confirm predictions made by the model.

2 INFERNET description

2.1 Concepts and attributes

INFERNET is a connectionist model using integrate-and-fire nodes. Each concept is represented by a cluster of nodes firing in synchrony (figures 1, 2). Concepts are

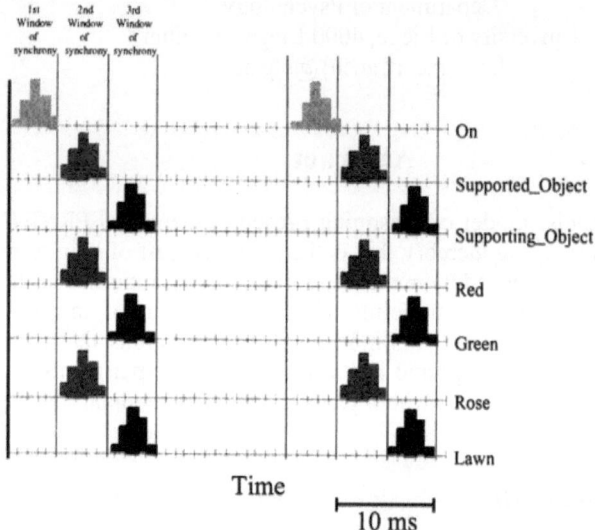

Figure 1: The "red rose on the green lawn" requires binding of concepts "red" and "rose" with the role "Supported_Object", followed by "green" and "lawn" with the role "Supporting_Object.

bound together by synchronous firing. For example, to represent the concept "red rose", nodes belonging to "red" must fire synchronously with nodes belonging to "rose" (figure 1). There is neurobiological evidence for considering synchrony as a possible binding mechanism in the brain. In particular, synchrony has been observed between distant cells in the same cortical area, between cells in different cortical areas and even between cells in different hemispheres. If a number of different objects make up a scene, distinct windows of synchrony are formed, each associated with a particular object. Individual cells can rapidly change partners of synchrony if the stimulus changes. Moreover the absence of synchronization has been observed to impair cognitive abilities. For a complete discussion on synchronization as a neural binding mechanism, see [16, 14].

2.2 Discrimination

Discrimination is achieved by successive synchronies, for example, to discriminate a red rose on a green lawn. The nodes belonging to "red" "rose" and "Supported_Object" must fire in synchrony and those corresponding to "green" "lawn" and "Supporting_Object" must also fire in synchrony. Further, these two sets of nodes must fire in close succession and after the nodes belonging to "On" for

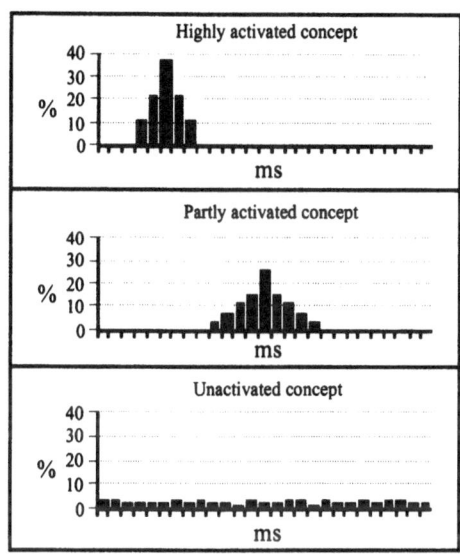

Figure 2: The temporal distribution of node-firing determines if a concept is activated.

"the red rose on the green lawn" to be perceived (figure 1). Engel and al. [6] provide evidence that shows that if several objects are present in a scene, several group of cells are grouped in distinct windows of synchrony.

2.3 Initial constraints

A number of neurobiological parameters are involved in this representation that rely on clusters of nodes firing simultaneously. The first is the frequency of oscillation. In INFERNET, as in SHRUTI [15], once a node is activated, it tends (but not necessarily) to fire rhythmically between 30 and 100 Hz. The temporal gap between 2 spikes of a node is therefore from 10 to 33 ms. This corresponds to the observed 30-100 Hz (γ wave) oscillations of certain types of neurons. These γ waves have been observed to be associated with attention [21] and with associative memory [22]. The second key parameter is the precision of the synchrony. According to [17] this precision is between 4 to 6 ms. For [1], the precision is about 5 ms and depends on the frequency of oscillation.

2.4 Windows of synchrony as working memory span

Since concepts are represented as a set of nodes, INFERNET focuses on the distribution of node-firing times. If the firing distribution is tightly concentrated about the mean, the concept is considered to be activated. In figure 2, three distibutions are depicted. The Y-axis represents the percentage of nodes belonging to a concept that are firing, the X-axis shows the time in ms. The top graph shows the distribution of a highly activated concept, all nodes pertaining to the concept fire within 5 ms. The middle graph shows a less activated concepts whose nodes all fire within 9 ms. The lower graph shows the distribution of an unactivated concept node. In this last case, too few of the concept nodes fire and what firing there is does not occur within a short interval.

In Figure 1, nodes corresponding to the concept "rose" are firing in synchrony and the firing-time distribution is concentrated around the mean. Nodes pertaining to "rose" fire in synchrony with nodes representing "red". This synchrony is distinguished from the synchrony between nodes pertaining to "green" and "lawn" within the same cycle. Their means are clearly different.

The temporal lag between 2 spikes of a node oscillating at γ frequency (30 - 100 Hz) is between 10 to 33 ms., and is typically about 25 ms. The precision or width of a window of synchrony is about 5 ms. and is proportional to the frequency [1]. This allows us to approximate the number of windows of synchrony that could be differentiated, i.e. $25/5 = 5$. If we assume that a window of synchrony corresponds to an item or a chunk in working memory, then this puts working memory span at approximately 5, with a small amount of variance since precision is proportional to oscillation frequency. This corresponds to current estimates of human working memory span. It has been suggested [4], that the traditionally accepted size of working memory (i.e., 7 ± 2 items [12]) may be too high. An item can be a word, an idea, an object in a scene or a chunk, i.e., a grouping of items. Similar explanations for the brain's ability to store approximately 7 short-term memory items can be found in [9, 10, 15].

2.5 Persistance in working memory

How can representations be maintained in working memory? The problem with γ waves is that they persist only a few hundred milliseconds. This is not long enough to reflect the time taken by people to draw inferences, nor does it correspond to standard estimates of working memory retention time (10 to 20 seconds). For this reason, following [10], γ waves in INFERNET occur in bursts which restart every 146 to 333 ms. This corresponds to θ waves [3 - 7 Hz] whose duration can exceed 10 seconds. The resulting temporal firing pattern for a single node is shown in Figure 3. The node shown fires at 50 Hz for the seven spikes that constitute a burst. This is followed by a resting period of 60 ms. Thereafter, the burst begins again. The burst interval is about 200 ms (5 Hz).

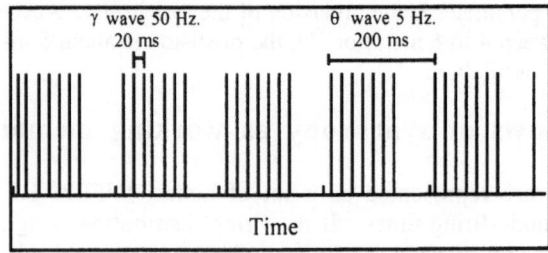

Figure 3: γ wave embedded in θ wave

There is neurobiological evidence for this rhythm in working memory. θ waves have been observed to be associated with visual short term memory task on a monkey [13]. This wave was maintained as long as attention was required.

2.6 Chunking

Working memory capacity is limited, and chunking increases the amount of information it can contain. In INFERNET, chunking is achieved by two processes:
1. Increasing the number of nodes — and, as a result, the number of concepts firing in synchrony. This is achieved by means of spreading activation.
2. Replacing the content of two or more windows of synchrony by a single one that sums them up. This is achieved by the use of excitatory and inhibitory connections.

2.7 Interference

Working memory is affected by interference. For example, when Working memory is successively tested by different words pertaining to the same category, the span decreases during the course of the trial. In INFERNET, concepts pertaining to the same category have nodes in common. Previously memorized items interfere with newly arriving ones if they share common nodes.

2.8 Memory scan

Sternberg [20] asked participants to rehearse lists of 1 to 6 items. At a non-predictable moment, participants received a probe item and were asked to decide as quickly as possible if the probe had been in the list of memorized items. Sternberg found that response time increased linearly according to the number of memorized items. For each additional item, reaction time increased by 38 ms. (see figure 4). Other replications showed a shorter increase of reaction time e.g. [11] found an increase of 22 ms.

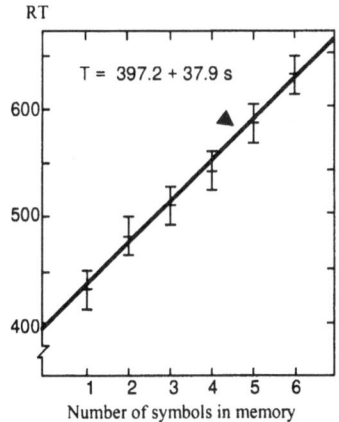

Figure 4 : Memory scan, Sternberg data

A closer look at the Sternberg data shows that, while overall reaction time increases with the number of items memorized, the variance remains constant. It is hard to see how this would be the case if the process was serial. If we consider each item as an independent random variable, then the total variance would be equal to the

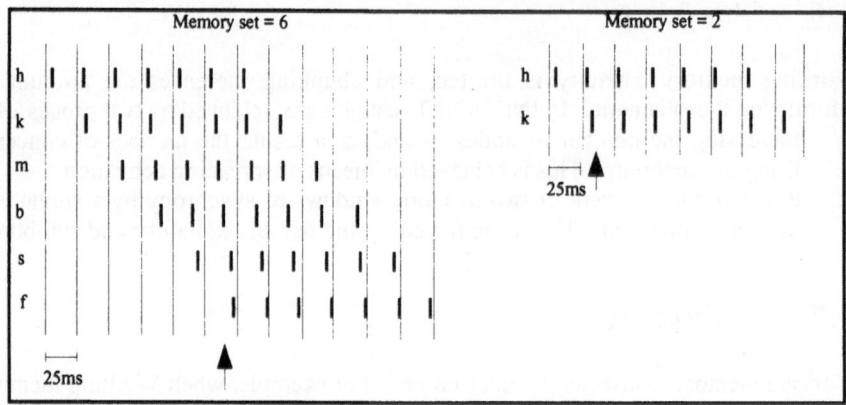

Figure 5 : Simultaneous activation of the memory set and starting point (arrow) of the parallel matching process in INFERNET.

sum of the variances associated with each of the variables. Just as measuring the length of a room by repeated ("serial") measurements with a six-inch ruler will produce a proportionately greater total error than measuring the room with a yardstick or a tape-measure, the same should hold for the Sternberg reaction-time data. If we have a serial process, then not only should the mean reaction time increase, *but the variance should as well*. But this is not the case.

In contrast to a serial recognition process, which would produce a linear increase in variance as the number of items increases, one solution compatible with INFERNET would produce the uniform variance that we observe in Sternberg's data. The actual implementation of this process is currently in progress. Recognition of previously seen items could involve a multi-phase process:

- Storage: the original items are inserted into memory and are refreshed once every every θ-wave cycle. At this point there is no need for the additional computational resources required by maintaining each item in a window of synchony.
- Simultaneous item activation (figure 5): The probe arrives: "Was the following item in the list?" followed by some item. At this point, the memorized items must be simultaneously activated in working memory. This involves the following serial process: one of the items in the list (for example, "h") will be associated with a particular window of synchrony (for example, the first window) and, thereafter, will appear in that position with every 25-ms cycle of the γ wave. Each of the other items in the originally learned list will be activated in the same manner, with its own window of synchrony and once every 25 ms. Once this process is completed — i.e., all of the letters in the list have been assigned to a window of synchrony — only then can the matching process begin. Thus, the length of time required to set up the matching process increases linearly with the number of items in the original list (approximately 25 ms. per item).
- Matching: This process occurs in parallel across all items and therefore takes a constant amount of time, independent of the number of items required in the matching.

As a result, reaction time would be a function only of the setup time required by the system once the probe has been presented. All of the elements must, in fact, be retrieved before the matching process can begin. A related explanation can be found in [10], although their work does not involve the problem of uniform variance with an increased number of items to be memorized.

2.9 Multiple instantiation

Multiple instantiation involves the simultaneous use of the same parts of the knowledge base in different ways. Knowing that "John is in love with Louise" and that "Louise is in love with John", one can easily infer that they should be happy. To arrive at this conclusion one must instantiate the predicate "is in love with" and the objects "John" and "Louise" twice. Precisely how this is done is the problem of multiple instantiation.

Traditional models (e.g. [2]) that load copies of pieces of knowledge into a working area before transforming them do not have any problem with multiple instantiation. They simply make several copies of the same content from the long-term knowledge base. However, for connectionists models that use the structure of the knowledge base itself as the place where concepts are associated, transformed and where inferences are drawn, multiple instantiation is a serious problem. How can the same part of the knowledge base be associated with different things at the same time without making several copies of the knowledge in question? This question is crucial for connectionist models of working memory. Multiple instantiation poses a significant problem for distributed representations. Two closely related concepts will, in principle, share nodes. If both concepts are needed simultaneously, their common parts must be instantiated twice.

However, some studies [3, 5, 19] show that humans handle at least double instantiation without difficulty. Experimental tasks using single and double instantiation are rare. One example is relational reasoning (three-term-series-problem). Singly-instantiated predicates in "A *is better than* B, C *is worse than* B" were compared to doubly-instantiated predicates in "A *is better than* B, B *is better than* C" and no difference in reaction times between these two situations was found [3, 19]. No difference of correctness can be found in [5]. These data seem to demonstrate that performance is not impaired by double instantiation. In other words, this would seem to imply that there is, in fact, no cost in terms of additional processing time for double instantiation. This property will emerge naturally from the underlying assumptions of INFERNET. However, this prediction should be assessed by further experiments.

The present model modifies the frequency of the γ wave to enable multiple instantiation. This means that neurons pertaining to a doubly-instantiated concept will oscillate twice as fast as singly-instantiated ones. If we assume a γ wave frequency between 30 and 100 Hz., the number of multiple instantiations should be limited to about 3 with little or no additional cost to the system. In this case, singly-instantiated nodes could fire at 30 Hz, doubly-instantiated ones at 60 Hz, and triply-instantiated ones at 90 Hz. Since the maximum oscillatory frequency of the γ wave is approximately 100 Hz, anything beyond triple instantiation will require chunking, and this would require extra time. INFERNET therefore suggests that the brain does multiple instantiation by replacing a number of windows of synchrony by a single "chunked" one. If the number of instantiations exceeds 3, an increase of processing time proportional to the difficulty of chunking should be observed.

3   Experiment 1

When the number of instances increases (beyond 2 or 3), a chunking process should reduce the number of instantiations in different windows of synchrony. Sometimes this process is easy, for example, when all instances can be grouped with one proposition. Sometimes it is more difficult, when no single proposition can be found that could chunk all instances. INFERNET predicts that in the latter case reaction time will increase. Experiment 1 will test this prediction.

3.1   Participants and design

The 30 participants were undergraduate psychology majors randomly assigned to each of two conditions that differed in their ease of chunking.

3.2   Material

Two sets of 4 premises (relational statements), using the same number of words, were constructed.

The easy chunking group set	The hard chunking group set
"Allan is in love with Mary",	"Peter is in love with Mary",
"Mary is in love with Allan",	"Barbara is in love with Allan",
"Peter is in love with Barbara",	"Allan is in love with Mary"
"Barbara is in love with Peter".	"Mary is in love with Peter".

The question asked of participants of both conditions was "Who is happy?" All material was presented by a computer program allowing reaction time to be recorded. Participants' conclusions were recorded manually.

3.3   Procedure

Each participant was seated approximately 50 cm from the monitor. The four premises appeared on the screen simultaneously in a random order. Participants were asked to read these 4 premises and to indicate when they had finished. Then a question appeared on the screen. Reaction time for answering the question was recorded. Before presenting the experimental material, participants received training exercises with the same procedure, but with an arithmetic content.

3.4   Results

Table 1 shows reaction times for all correct responses. Differences between groups are significant (Mann-Whitney $Z = -2.331$, $p= 0.019$).

	Mean	SD
Easy chunking group	3719	1025
Hard chunking group	7778	4312

Table 1: Reaction time in ms for hard and easy chunking of multiple instantiation

3.5   Discussion

For the easy chunking group where all relations are reciprocal, subjects can rapidly replace the relation "is in love with" by "love each other", and finally, by "are happy", therefore reducing the number of instantiations. By contrast, in the hard chunking group, subjects need to distinguish items for which the "love each other" relation is true from items for which this relation is false and maintain this distinction in working memory, before enabling the replacement process. This additional process takes time, explaining the significantly higher response times. Dealing with more than 2 or 3 instantiations (in this case, there were 4) seems to require additional processing resources, at least when no single property can be applied to all instances. One might reasonably object, for example, that Peter might not be happy because he was upset that Allan loves the person he loves and that Mary could be upset of the love of Peter. The point is well taken, but in this experiment we only considered response time for participants who replied that both Peter and Mary were happy. In addition, no participants replied that both Peter and Mary were unhappy.

4   Experiment 2

For a distributed connectionist model, multiple instantiation will also affect related concepts. Concepts that share properties most likely share something in the neurobiological substrate. The effect of multiple instantiation should be observable when related concepts are used together. The following experiment tests this hypothesis.

One of the key features of distributed connectionist models is that a single concept is represented by a large set of nodes, referred to here as a cell assembly. Moreover, a single node can participate in different cell assemblies. In INFERNET, a concept is represented by a set of nodes firing in synchrony. The distributed nature of each concept implies that closely related concepts have some nodes in common. If two related concepts are needed simultaneously, and if they cannot belong to the same window of synchrony, the nodes that they share must be instantiated twice. In the present experiment the number of closely related concepts was manipulated. The prediction was that if the number of instantiations of shared properties exceeded 2 or 3, a replacement process would be triggered. This replacement must take time and would be reflected in the subjects' response times.

4.1   Participants and design

The 40 participants were undergraduate psychology majors. They were randomly assigned to each of two conditions. These two conditions differed in the number of shared properties of concepts.

4.2   Material

Two rules of the type "if...then" (material implication), one for each condition, were constructed. These rules have the same length. The first rule assigned to the group of participants called "distant group" involved rather distant concepts: "If the lumberjack cuts down the oak tree, the farmer's tractor can use the pathway". The second rule assigned to the group of participant called "related group" used more closely related concepts: "If the lumberjack cuts down the oak tree, the carpenter can nail the oak boards". In the latter rule, there are 7 concepts related to wood. Four questions for each condition were designed. For the first condition, these were: "The lumberjack cut down the oak tree. What do you conclude?" "The lumberjack didn't cut down the oak tree. What do you conclude?" "The farmer's tractor can use the pathway. What do you conclude?" "The farmer's tractor can't use the pathway. What do you conclude?" For the second condition, they were: "The lumberjack cut down the oak tree. What do you conclude?" "The lumberjack didn't cut down the oak tree. What do you conclude?" "The carpenter can nail the oak boards. What do you conclude?" "The carpenter can't nail the oak boards. What do you conclude?"

The four questions and the rule correspond to the following logical forms: $A \supset B$, A; $A \supset B$, ~A; $A \supset B$, B; $A \supset B$, ~B. All material was presented by a computer program allowing response times to be recorded. Participants' conclusions were recorded manually.

4.3   Procedure

Each participant was seated approximately 50 cm in front of the monitor. One of the rules appeared on the screen. Participants were asked to read the rule and to indicate when they had understood it. The rule stayed on the screen during the entire experiment. Questions appeared on the screen, one at the time and in random order. Participants had to answer each question. The computer recorded the time required for them to respond. Before presenting the experimental material, participants received training exercises with the same procedure, but with an arithmetic content.

4.4   Results

There were no significant differences in betweeen-group reaction times (Table 2) for each type of inference, Modus Ponens (MP), Denying the antecedent (DA), Affirming the consequent (AC), and Modus Tollens (MT). Only reaction times for equivalent responses were considered.

	MP		DA		AC		MT	
	Mean	SD	Mean	SD	Mean	SD	Mean	SD
Group related	4031	1135	3898	982	4507	1518	5062	1844
Group distant	3526	1285	3685	1093	4177	1829	4298	1587

Table 2 : Mean reaction time for each inference type

Reaction times for each question presented in succession are considered. Table 3 shows the data (mean and SD) for the first, second, third and fourth question (questions were presented in random order). Only reaction times for equivalent responses were taken into account.

There was a significantly longer reaction time for answering the first question presented in the group "related" (Mann-Whitney Z = 2.994, p= 0.002). All other differences of reaction time were not significant. Reaction time for reading the rule does not differ significantly among groups for the related group: mean 8058 ms for the distant group 8243 ms. (Mann-Whitney Z = -0.132, p= 0.911).

	1st Question		2nd Question		3h Question		4th Question	
	Mean	SD	Mean	SD	Mean	SD	Mean	SD
Group related	4893	1426	3815	807	4204	1170	4322	1701
Group distant	3499	1024	3737	1197	4341	1960	3774	1456

Table 3: Mean reaction time by order of presentation.

There is no between-group difference regarding conclusion inferred, as Table 4 shows. Fisher exact probabilities are all not significant (.5, .7564, .3025, .6693, respectively).

	MP	DA	AC	MT
Group related	1.00	.95	.85	.85
Group distant	0.95	.95	.95	.85

Table 4: proportion of conclusions inferred

4.5   Discussion

There are no differences in the time required for participants to read one rule or another, but when they receive the first question, they must encode the rule in a particular way, thereby permitting an inference to be drawn. This encoding requires dealing with multiply-instantiated properties that share the concepts used in the rules. A replacement process is required, "the lumberjack cuts down the oak tree" must be assigned to a unique antecedent object, or window of synchrony. The two different consequents: "The farmer's tractor can use the pathway" and "The carpenter can nail the oak boards" must also be assigned to a single consequent object or window of synchrony. For these consequent parts, there is a crucial difference: the concepts in the sentence "The carpenter can't nail the oak boards" share properties with each other and with those used in the antecedent part of the rule. Multiple instantiations of these shared properties impair the replacement process, thereby increasing the time required to answer the first question. When the following three questions appear, this replacement has already been done, and reaction times no longer differ. The reaction time difference for the first question is not due to the type of question posed. The four different questions appear in random order for each participant and there is no significant difference in between-group reaction time for each of the question types A (MP), ~A (DA), B (AC) and ~B (MT). The only significant difference between the two groups occurs for the first question — when encoding occurs. In addition, the lack of any significant between-group difference related to the conclusions inferred, reinforces the idea that the only difference between groups involves multiple instantiation.

5   Conclusions

INFERNET attempts to simulate various aspects of a human working memory defined as the activated part of long-term memory. In particular, INFERNET predicts that multiple instantiation will not require additional processing time as long as the number of instantiations does not exceed 2 or 3. When the number of instantiations does exceed 2 or 3, INFERNET predicts a replacement process which requires additional processing time. The preliminary data reported here would seem to confirm this. INFERNET also predicts that dealing with closely related concepts will require multiple instantiation. The experimental results presented here would seem to confirm this hypothesis. These results seem to support distributed concept representations and challenge modular accounts of memory. For the latter models (e.g. [2]), working memory is distinct from long-term memory and the contents of LTM are loaded into WM when needed. According to modular memory models, multiple instantiation should not increase reaction time. The results reported here contradict this prediction.

Acknowledgments

This research was supported by the Belgian FNRS Grant D.4516.93 & PAI p4/19.

References

1. Abeles, M., Prut, Y., Bergman, H., Vaadia, E. & Aertsen, A. Integration, Synchronicity and Periodicity. In A. Aertsen (Ed.) Brain Theory: Spatio-Temporal Aspects of Brain Function. Amsterdam: Elsevier. 1993
2. Baddeley, A. D. Working Memory. Oxford: Oxford University Press, 1986
3. Clark, H.H. Linguistic process in deductive reasoning. Psychological Review, 1969, 76: 387-404.
4. Crowder, R. G. Principle of learning and memory. Hillsdale: LEA. 1976
5. De Soto, C. B., London, M. & Handel, S. Social reasoning and spatial paralogic. Journal of Personality an Social Psychology, 1965, 2, 513-521.
6. Engel, A. K., Kreiter, A. K., König, P., & Singer, W. Synchronisation of oscillatory neuronal responses between striate and extrastriate visual cortical areas of the cat. Proceedings of the National Academy of Science, 1991, 88: 6048-6052.
7. Henderson, J. Description Based Parsing in a Connectionist Network. PhD thesis, University of Pennsylvania, Technical Report MS-CIS-94-46. 1994.
8. Hummel, J. E. & Holyoak, K. J. LISA: A Computational Model of Analogical Inference and Schema Induction. Proceedings of the Eighteen conference of the Cognitive Science Society. Mahwah,NJ: LEA. 1996.
9. Jensen, O. & Lisman, J. E. Novel lists of 7±2 known items can be reliably stored in an oscillatory short-term memory network: Interaction with long term memory. Learning & Memory, 1996, 3, 257-263.
10. Lisman, J. E., & Idiart, M. A. P. Storage of 7 ± 2 Short-Term Memories in Oscillatory Subcycles. Science, 1995, 267: 1512-1515.
11. Marsh, G. R. Age differences in evoked potential correlates of a memory scanning process. Experimental Aging Research, 1975, 1, 3-16.
12. Miller, G. A. The Magical Number Seven, Plus or Minus Two. *Psychological Review*, 1956, *63*, 81-97.
13. Nakamura, K., Mikami, A. & Kubota, K. Oscillatory neuronal activity related to visual short-term memory in monkey temporal pole. Neuroreport, 1992, 3: 117-120.
14. Roelfsema, P. R., Engel, A. K., König, P. & Singer, W. The role of neuronal synchronization in response selection: A biologically plausible theory of

structured representations in the visual cortex. Journal of Cognitive Neuroscience, 1996, 8, 603-625.

15. Shastri, L. & Ajjanagadde, V. From Simple Associations to Systematic Reasoning: A connectionist representation of rules, variables and dynamic bindings using temporal synchrony. Behavioral and Brain Sciences, 1993, 16, 417-494.

16. Singer, W. Synchronization of neuronal responses as a putative binding mechanism. In M. A. Arbib (Ed.) The Handbook of Brain Theory and Neural Networks. Cambridge: MIT Press. 1995.

17. Singer, W. & Gray, C. M. Visual Feature Integration and the Temporal Correlation Hypothesis. Annual Review of Neuroscience, 1995, 18: 555-586.

18. Sougné, J. A Connectionist Model of Reflective Reasoning Using Temporal Properties of Node Firing. Proceedings of the Eighteen conference of the Cognitive Science Society. Mahwah,NJ: LEA. 1996.

19. Sternberg, R. J. Representation and process in linear syllogistic reasoning. Journal of Experimental Psychology: General, 1980, 109, 119-159.

20. Sternberg, S. High Speed Scanning in Human Memory. Science, 1966, 153, 652-654.

21. Wang, X. & Rinzel, J. Oscillatory and Bursting Properties of Neurons. In M. A. Arbib (Ed.) The Handbook of Brain Theory and Neural Networks. Cambridge: MIT Press. 1995.

22. Wilson, M. & Shepherd, G. M. Olfactory Cortex. In M. A. Arbib (Ed.) The Handbook of Brain Theory and Neural Networks. Cambridge: MIT Press. 1995.

Neural Networks and the Emergence of Consciousness

JG Taylor

King's College, London, UK

and Institut fur Medizin, Research Centre Juelich, Germany

Abstract

After a brief account of a two-stage model for awareness, the continuum neural field theory model is described as a possible neural network to help explain one of the most puzzling features of phenomenal experience, that of the relatively long temporal duration of the neural activity involved. The model allows for an explanation of this by means of long-lived 'bubbles' of activity caused by recurrence in the neural field; this is related to experimental data on traces observed in auditory and visual cortices, and also to some of the specific features of phenomenal experience.

1 Introduction

The race to understand consciousness is presently on. There is a large amount of interest in the neuroscience and neural network community on the topic. Various groups are seriously trying to understand its neural support better by the use of non-invasive instruments (PET, fMRI, EEG and MEG) [1]. The current body of knowledge on the subject is rapidly increasing. There is already a large reservoir of material on it discovered by psychologists over the last century and this is now being combined with the results coming from brain imaging to attempt to indicate where and how consciousness arises and is supported in the brain.

This paper will outline briefly a two stage neural model for the emergence of consciousness at its lowest level of phenomenal experience. In this model the lower first stage involves modules transforming inputs into various sensory codes. It is only at the second higher level that further modules are activated in a manner which brings about the emergence of phenomenal awareness.

The two-stage model will be developed by means of a detailed neural framework which will allow analysis of the extended duration of activity in posterior working memory sites (which are posited as being at the second stage in the model) using the notion of 'bubbles' of activity which are formed in neural modules with enough neurons and suitably strong recurrent excitatory and inhibitory connections. Such modules have recently been suggested as explaining the development of observed orientation sensitivity in primary visual cortex.

The purpose of the paper, after the presentation of the two-stage model, is to develop a brief analysis of the proposed neural underpinning noted above and

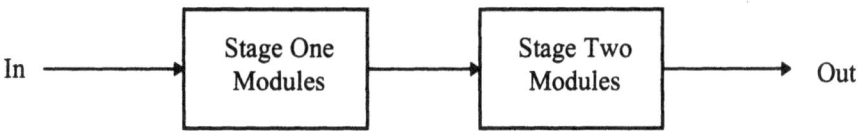

Figure 1. The basic two-stage model of awareness. Stage 1 performs preprocessing in various modalities; activity in stage 2 is that on which phenomenal awareness is based.

especially to consider the temporal duration of activities as described by the model. It will then present an even briefer discussion of the implications of the resulting dynamical activity of the two-stage model for the emergence of phenomenal consciousness.

2 The Two-Stage Model

The two-stage model of the emergence of awareness in the brain is shown in Figure 1. There is supposedly no direct awareness of the activity in stage 1 modules whilst it is the activity of modules at stage 2 that can enter awareness. Thus in vision the model is based on several recent demonstrations that there is not direct awareness of neural activity in striate visual cortex V1 [2], [3], [4]. There is similar experimental support in audition [5]. Thus phenomenal experience does not arise from activity in a monolithic neural network covering the whole brain, but there are special features of later processing in cortex which gives the added value termed consciousness.

What sort of neural networks would be suitable for such a separation between processing of which there is and there is not consciousness? There are spatial and temporal features of the networks which are of great importance. It is relevant to extend the 2-stage model to three stages so as to be able to specify more precisely the level of coding that outputs from the second (awareness) stage should have. There are spatial features which require localised representations in sets of well-connected modules which are also well coupled to modules involved in the higher cognitive processes, these being the modules C of the third stage of processing in Figure 2. This is an extension of the two stage model to higher cognition, where the third stage modules are those of 'active' working memory and motor set. The way that these higher order modules are fed smoothly from posterior cortices indicates that both the second and third stages are very well coupled together as well as the fact that the second stage modules are coded at the highest level so as to feed so smoothly to the frontal cortices; these latter are brought on-line for hard tasks, especially of long temporal duration, not able to be handled by the posterior sites.

Besides having the highest level of coding, the temporal features of the second stage modules are also very specific, requiring suitably long temporal duration of activity (of the order of 300 - 500 msecs) for phenomenal experience to arise but with little time between one experience and the next. Finally there are emergent

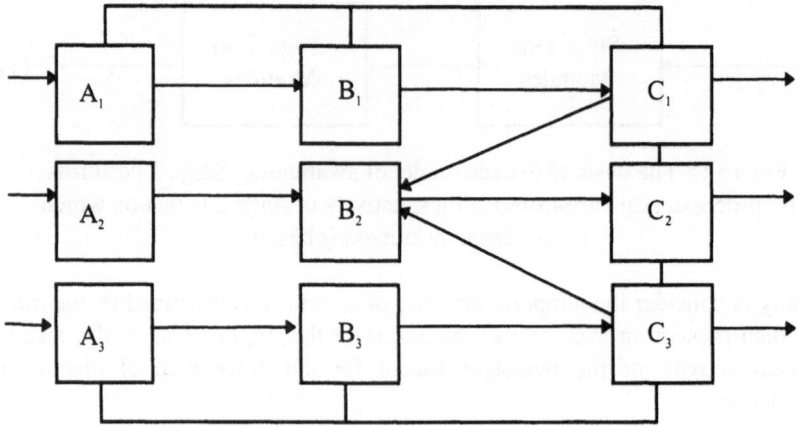

Figure 2. The three-stage model for the creation and control of awareness. The modules at the lowest or first stage are denoted A_1 , A_2 , ... and are involved only in low level feature analysis in the appropriate modality. A number of modules are involved in such processing. At the next stage are sites of 'buffer' memory in posterior cortex, denoted B_1, B_2, ... They are fed by preprocessed activity from first stage modules, and are coupled to each other so as to run a competition by lateral inhibition so as to select the most appropriate percept, given earlier context still present in activity traces on these modules, to enter phenomenal awareness. The final third stage is composed of modules which are frontal and possess attentional feedback control both to the second stage modules, so as to refresh activity there, and to the first stage modules to reduce or increase stimulus selectivity. Feedback is shown explicitly from the third to lower stages although it will also be present from the second to first stage .

features which are also non-trivial, involving one-way and rapid emergence of phenomenal experience at the highest level of a processing hierarchy with no ability to gain awareness of the activity of lower modules of stage 1.

Coding at the highest level of activity emerging into phenomenal experience is most simply obtained by assuming that it emerges at the second stage from those first stage modules which are also identically coded (or very closely so) as the second-stage level. Some form of selection amongst these well coded but non-conscious neural activations is initially at work in the second stage modules as part of the process of attaining consciousness. The other most important feature of the second stage modules, that of the temporal duration of activity, is a crucial part of the general features of the buffer stores in the psychologically-based working memory model [7], [8]. These buffers have input from semantic-level coding, where all possible interpretations (in the case of words) have already been accessed in the semantic memory, so at the end of the stage 1 processing, before the buffer store is attained [9], [10].

The two-stage model of Figure 1 has been developed in a neural network implementation elsewhere [11]. This model uses semantic-level coding of activity at stage 1 and then buffered activity at stage 2, with lateral inhibition at this second stage to achieve singling out the contextually appropriate representation at the higher stage. It is this activity which then enters awareness by gaining access to the anterior sites of working memory denoted in Figure 2. Once at that third level the material can be rehearsed or manipulated as desired.

Besides the construction of a model of the 2-stage process, and due to the plethora of buffer stores now observed in posterior cortex in various modalities and codes [12], [13], [14] there must be some way of combining their various activities so as to achieve a unified experience of consciousness. Control structures in the brain are thereby needed which produce global correlations between the various component working memories. As well as being involved in excitatory and amplification processes these control structures must also support competition between various inputs, when suitably encoded, and only allow certain, most relevant, memories to be activated and related to the corresponding winning input. This produces the 'filter' characteristic of attentional processing and awareness itself. The neural structures used in attentional processing may also be involved with assessing the level of discrepancy of new incoming input with that predicted from later parts of activated stored pattern sequences. These aspects were considered in [15], [16] (and earlier references quoted there) in terms of possible networks which could perform pattern matching and sustain competition. One of these involved the nucleus reticularis thalami (NRT), a sheet of mutually inhibitory neurons interposed between thalamus and cortex. Other systems include direct cortico-cortical interactions involving inhibitory interneurons.

In summary the proposed two-stage model has the following features:

- Coding occurs up to semantic level (denoted SM) in the first (preprocessing) stage.

- There is feedforward transfer of activity from the first to the second stage at approximately the same level of coding, with the feedforward map being SM → WM (in a given code).

- Duration of activity is longest of all posterior modules in the WM of the second stage.

- There is a process of global competition between activities on different WMs, supported by the TH/NRT/C system and cortico-cortical interactions.

- There is a strong reciprocal connectivity between the posterior WM sites and frontal areas at the highest level of coding (to allow rapid and effective access to the frontal 'active' working memory sites). Such connections are observed neuroanatomically.

We refer the reader to [6] for a description of some of the extensive experimental basis for the separation of the emergence of awareness in two parts, as the 2-stage model claims.

3 A Neural Network for the Two-Stage Model

3.1 The Basics of Bubbles

We now turn to the development of a neural model to help support the two-stage model of Figure 1 and use it to give tentative answers to the following questions :

1) What is the dynamical origin of the temporally extended memory traces residing in the buffer working memory sites?

2) What neural principles are behind creation of phenomenal awareness there?

To answer these questions we will employ continuum neural field theory (CNFT) which has been used over many years as a first approximation to cortical structure [17], [18], [19]. One of the important results of that period is the discovery of cortical "bubbles" of activity which are initially created by input but which persist after stimulus offset [17]. A brief introduction to bubbles and some of their properties in CNFT is given in this subsection, and their application to the analysis of the temporal duration of neural activity developed in the following one.

CNFT is based on a model of cortex as a continuous two-dimensional sheet of neurons with suitable lateral connections. This allows the creation of localised activity, the bubbles, which can persist, and remain localised in spite of the absence of input due to the recurrent activity causing repeated firing of the neurons initially activated. The basic CNFT equation is constructed in terms of the membrane potential of a neuron, denoted by $u(x,t)$, at the point x and time t. It will be assumed that there is lateral connectivity on the neural sheet defined by the lateral connection weight function $w(x-x')$ between the two neurons at the relevant points x. The connection weight will be taken to be of Mexican hat form as a function of the Euclidean distance $|x-x'|$. There is also an afferent connection weight function $s(x, y)$ from the thalamic position y to the cortical point x. The response function of a neuron will be taken to be determined by its mean firing rate, which is given as some function f of the membrane potential u of the relevant cell.

The membrane potential $u(x, t)$ will satisfy the CNFT equation [17]:

$$\tau \partial u(x, t)/\partial t = -u(x, t) + \int dx'\, w(x - x')\, f[\, u(x', t)\,] + \int dy\, s(x, y)\, I(y, t) + h \quad (1)$$

where $I(y, t)$ is the input to the thalamic position y at time t, h is the neuron threshold and integration with the lateral connection weight is over the cortical neurons.

There are well-known autonomous solutions to (1) in the case when M is one-dimensional [17], when equation (1), for a static solution and with no input, becomes:

$$u(x) = \int w(x-x')\, 1[u(x')]\, dx' + h \quad (2)$$

where the sharp threshold response function $f = \theta$ (the unit step function) has been assumed in (2). A 'bubble' is defined to have a positive membrane potential over an interval, independent of input. This is formalised as

Definition

A 'bubble' of neural activity is a localised persistent solution to the CNFT equations. Its size is in general dependent on input, but its continued existence is not (to within effects of adaptation, to be discussed in the following subsection).

Let us consider the bubble extending from x=0 to x=a:

$$u(x) > 0 , 0 < x < a; u(0) = u(a) = 0 \tag{3}$$

and otherwise u<0. From (2) and (3) u is obtained explicitly as

$$u(x) = \int_0^a w(x-x') \, dx' + h = W(x) - W(x-a) \tag{4}$$

where the function W is defined by

$$W(x) = \int_0^x w(x') \, dx' \tag{5}$$

Necessary conditions for the bubble to exist are that the membrane potential vanishes at the ends of the interval [0, a], so

$$u(0) = u(a) = 0 = W(a) + h \tag{6}$$

It is then possible to show that u(x) > 0 for 0<x<a if h<0; u(x)<0 otherwise. Stability of the resulting solution then requires

$$dW(a)/da < 0, \text{ or } w(a) < 0 \tag{7}$$

Thus the one-dimensional bubble exists under the conditions (6) and (7).

There are a number of further important results derived in [17] concerning the nature of bubble solutions and their extension to input dependence briefly summarised as:

a) The parameter ranges for h and for the parameters in W can be determined so as to allow for autonomous solutions of various types ($\varnothing$ or the trivial one, ∞ or the constant non-zero one, an a-solution as the bubble of finite length a described above, and a spatially periodic solution).

b) The complete determination of those patterns which are stable and those which are unstable, from amongst the stationary solutions described above.

c) Response to input stimulus patterns: a bubble of finite length moves to a position of maximum of the input.

d) Two bubbles interact, if close, with attraction (from the Mexican hat connection weight function), if more distant with repulsion, and if very distant with no effect on each other.

e) There can occur spatially homogeneous temporal oscillations (between a layer of excitatory and one of inhibitory cells).

f)   Travelling waves can persist.

Returning to the full two-dimensional bubble in the region D (a solution which will be called an R[2]-solution here), we define

$$W_\infty = \lim_{R \to \infty} W(R) \tag{8}$$

where

$$W(R) = \int_D w(\mathbf{x} - \mathbf{x'}) d\mathbf{x'} \tag{9}$$

where $\mathbf{x}$ is only allowed to be on the boundary of D, which has radius $|\mathbf{x}| = R$.

It is now possible to extend the methods of [17] to deduce the same results as in the one dimensional case for the questions (a) to (f) raised above to the two dimensional situation [20]. For case (a) above there is the two-dimensional extension:

a) Theorem 1. In the absence of input :

1. There exists a $\varnothing$ solution iff h < 0.
2. There exists an ∞-solution iff W_∞ > - h.
3. There exists an R[2]-solution iff h < 0 and R > 0 satisfies

$$W(R) + h = 0 \tag{10}$$

Extension of the other features (b) to (f) above is treated in [20].

3.2 Bubble Lifetimes

We will apply the bubble solutions only to the case of the lifetime of bubbles in cortex. Bubbles have also been applied to a variety of cortical processes: the development of topographic maps in the one dimensional case [21], control of saccades by the superior colliculus, on which the bubbles are supposed to form [22], the modifications of the somatosensory constant topographic map by relearning [23], the guidance of head-directed cells [24] and in explaining pre-attentive auditory memory [25]. The case considered here is that of the temporal duration of neural activity, and is closely associated with the possible manner in which bubbles could enter directly into perception, as mentioned earlier.

Here we consider how bubbles might disappear It is very unlikely that they persist for ever, and if they did so then they would present an ever increasing background of 'noise' interfering with current ongoing processing.

There is evidence for bubbles possessing a finite lifetime from work of Williamson & colleagues [26]. They exposed subjects to a sequence of sounds with the interstimulus interval (ISI) being gradually increased. They discovered that the amplitude of the N100 response (100 msecs after stimulus onset) reached saturation at suitably long ISI in both primary and secondary auditory cortex, with the rise to saturation corresponding to a decaying trace with lifetime of about 3 seconds in primary and 5 in secondary auditory cortex; visual stimuli led to even longer lifetimes. The results of [26] (& earlier references of the group) will be interpreted here in terms of the decay of a lasting trace of activity in the region from which the magnetic field was measured.

What mechanism could cause the decay of the bubbles which the traces represent? The most likely answer is that of adaptation of the responses of the neurons in the CNFT. Spike adaptation is a well-studied phenomenon arising from slow after-hyperpolarizing currents I_{AHP} and I_M , which can last for several seconds. These after-currents raise the threshold for neuronal response. There may also be an effect from previous traces of neural activity which shunt out later activation [27].

We will consider this here by using a very simple model of the response of a neuron, that of the leaky integrator (Hodgkin-Huxley) neuron, with an additional after-hyperpolarizing current. The equation for the membrane potential u of this neuron is

$$\tau \, du/dt = -u + I(t) - \lambda \int_0^t \exp[-(t-t')/\tau'] \, f[u(t')]dt' \qquad (11)$$

where $I(t)$ is the input current at time t, λ is the strength of an after-hyperpolarising current dependent on the response $f[u(t)]$ integrated over the time the neuron is active with an exponential decay of lifetime τ', and τ is the intrinsic lifetime of activity on the surface of the neuron (assumed to have no internal structure).

Under the experimental paradigm of [26] the input is on for the time T and off for the time which we denote by the value ISI.

During the period that the input is on, u builds up its value driven by the input I. Let us suppose that the hyperpolarising lifetime τ' is much longer than the time T of duration of the input. This is valid for the long-lasting potassium-dependent hyperpolarisations, which we assume to be the one of equation (11). At the end of the input period the membrane potential begins to decay exponentially, so behaves as $\exp[-t/\tau]$ (multiplied by a suitable constant, and to within an additive constant).

We now assume that the term on the left-hand side of (11) can be neglected (in other words the time constant τ is relatively short) with the result that the time dependence of u at (or close to) the beginning of the next input, say at the N100 response, has the value (to within a constant initial value from t=T)

$$- \lambda \tau' \int \exp[-(t-t')/\tau'] \, f[u(t')]dt' \qquad (12)$$

where t=T+ISI and the integration is from t=T to t=T+ISI. For f chosen to be the step-function $f(x) = \theta(x)$ and assuming that the membrane potential is positive through the ISI (so that f is unity) then the membrane potential at t= (T+ISI) is, from (12), equal to

$$\text{constant} - \lambda \tau' \exp[-(T+ISI)/\tau'] \qquad (13)$$

For an ISI=0 there will be no N100 so (13) must be equal to zero, giving (for fixed T)

$$u(T+ISI) = A(1 - \exp[-ISI/\tau]) \qquad (14)$$

Formula (14) fits the results of [26]. This justifies interpreting the value of the time constant τ' as the duration of the neural trace of activity in the measured cortical site. A more complete analysis can be given, under other assumptions on the relation between τ and τ', with a similar result to that presented above.

There is the further question as to how neurons can possess the large and variable time constants, both across areas and across subjects, as have been measured [26]. We will now show that these variations are to be seen as arising from variable levels of recurrence, giving an increase to the intrinsically identical time constants of each neuron by an amount dependent on the amount of recurrence; this level of recurrence can vary from one cortical region (and from one subject) to another, and is crucially dependent on the cell density in the short-term memory stores.

In order to consider bubble decay we will consider the effect of the long-lasting after-hyperpolarisation current used in equation (11) on bubble lifetime. The two-dimensional expression replacing equation (11) is

$$\tau \partial u(x, t)/\partial t = - u(x, t) + \int dx' \, w(x - x') \, f[\, u(x', t) \,] + \int dy \, s(x, y) \, I(y, t) + h$$

$$- \lambda \int_0^a \exp[-(t-t')/\tau'] \, f[u(x, t')] \, dt' \qquad (15)$$

We now calculate the lifetime of a bubble created using equation (15 firstly for the one-dimensional case; that for two dimensions will follow straightforwardly.

A particular case of interest is when a bubble has initially been created by an input, which is then removed. That could be due, for example, to that neural module acting as the source of the input having a shorter lifetime for the persistence of bubbles than the module under consideration. It would also occur if the bubble is created in a primary sensory module and the input itself has been modified.

To discuss this case it is appropriate to first reduce even further to a single recurrent neuron. For that case the membrane potential equation, from (15), is:

$$\tau \partial u(t)/\partial t = - u(t) + w \, \theta[\, u \, t) \,] + h - \lambda \int_0^a \exp[-(t-t')/\tau'] \theta[u(t')] dt' \qquad (16)$$

where a step function response has been taken for the neuron. From equation (16)

$$u(t) = u(0) + [1-\exp(-t/\tau)][h+w] - \lambda \int_0^t \exp[-(t-t')/\tau] dt' \int_0^t \exp[-(t'-t'')/\tau'] dt'' \qquad (17)$$

From (17), with $u(0) > 0$, $u(t)$ will remain positive in time & reduces to the expression

$$u(t) = u(0) + [1-\exp(-t/\tau)][h + w -\lambda\tau\tau'] + \lambda\tau(\tau')^2[\exp(-t/\tau') - \exp(-t/\tau)]/(\tau' - \tau) \qquad (18)$$

where the last term on the right hand side of (18) is replaced, for $\tau = \tau'$, by the expression $\lambda\tau\tau'\exp(-t/\tau)$. The last term in (18) may be neglected if $\tau'<<\tau$, so that if

$$\lambda\tau\tau' > h + w + u(0) \qquad (19)$$

then for suitably large t, $u(t)$ will become negative and the firing of the neuron will then cease. If no new input arrives then no further activity will ensue from the neuron.

The initial lifetime of the bubble is given by equating the right hand side of (18) to zero. For $\tau' >> \tau$ in (18) the approximate value for the life-time T is

$$T = -\tau'\ln\{1 - u(0)/\tau[\lambda\tau\tau' - h - w]\} \tag{20}$$

where the factor $[\lambda\tau\tau' - h - w]$ is positive, by (19). Equation (20) is the formula we wish to extend to the case of a one- and then a two-dimensional CNFT.

Firstly the case of a bubble solution infinitely extended in either dimension reduces to the above analysis with the constant w in the single neuron case being replaced by $w=\int w(x)dx$, $w=\int w(x)dx$ in the one and two dimensional cases respectively.

The equation in one dimensions, for a finite-sized bubble, has the adaptation term

$$-\lambda\tau\tau' \tag{21}$$

(dropping the term of $O(\tau')$ in (18)) and the added initial value $u(l(0), 0)$, where $l(t)$ is the size of the bubble at time t; the input term involving S has also to be dropped. The bubble will have a finite lifetime if the adaptation term is so negative that there exists a solution to the resulting equation for the asymptotic size of the bubble [20]:

$$h - \lambda\tau\tau' + W(2l(\infty)) = 0 \tag{22}$$

where $W(x)$ is the first integral of the connection weight w over the bubble domain. Such a solution could arise if

$$\lambda\tau\tau' - h > W_m \tag{23}$$

where W_m is the maximum value of W Thus if (23) is true then the bubble will have a finite lifetime given, under the same approximation as for the single neuron, by

$$T = \tau'\ln[-h/(\lambda\tau\tau' - h - W_m)] \tag{24}$$

This approximation should hold for both the one and two dimensional cases. In both cases we note that as W_m is increased, say by increase of cell density, the corresponding lifetime increases.

For the other extreme $\tau >> \tau'$ then τ and τ' must be interchanged in the lifetime formulae (22) and (24).

In conclusion, for the case $\tau >> \tau'$ the bubble lifetime is effectively proportional to τ, so dependent on whatever mechanism produces the bubble itself. In the opposite case the bubble lifetime is proportional to τ'. The latter quantity is expected to be an intrinsic characteristic of the single (pyramidal) neuron, so very likely constant throughout cortex.

Finally the lifetime is seen to increase (logarithmically) as the lateral connection strength (so W_m in (24)) increases. Such an increase is slow, according to the formula (24), but this may be only a result of the assumption of a hard limiting threshold output function for the neurons. A smooth sigmoid response (which can still support bubble creation) can lead to a linear increase in lifetime. This may therefore explain the observed increase of lifetime as observed in [26] as well as be the source of the buffer capability of working memory modules.

4 The Buffer Stores

A simple explanation of the recency effect, that more recent items in a short list are remembered better and faster, has been given by many groups; one of these, with a useful 'universal forgetting formula' was in [28]. This models the short-term buffer store as a set of dedicated nodes which have decaying activity on them. A short list of items coded by these nodes has decaying activity on the store in which the strongest activity is that for the latest input. Recognition of the items presented then occurs from probe inputs which cause a temporal increase in activity until it reaches some criterial threshold for response. The most recent input reaches the criterial threshold soonest, the earliest one taking the longest time. The resulting set of reaction times RT(n, N) for the n'th item in a list of length N may be shown to be given by the 'universal forgetting' formula

$$RT(n, N) = a.\ln\{b + c.\exp[d(n-N)]\} \tag{25}$$

where a, b, c, d are constants and in particular d is determined by the decay constant of the nodes. A very good fit to the experimental observations leads to a value of the lifetime of the activations on the nodes of about 1.5 seconds, which is the same order of magnitude as the lifetimes observed in [26] noted above.

We conclude that there is support for the existence of bubbles in cortex at the basis of phenomenal experience and that these can help to explain the somewhat activity-independent lifetimes observed in short-term memory tests and modelled by very simple dedicated nodes with lifetimes of about 100 times the decay constant of the single neurons themselves. This latter feature is explicable in terms of adaptation-driven bubble decay. The resulting lifetime of a bubble depends on the density of the cells in the area supporting it, with the longest lifetime occurring for highest density. Finally we note that these bubble may be used to help explain the nature of the 'qualia'-like aspects of phenomenal experience, in particular its apparently intrinsic and non-relational characteristics mentioned in [6].

5 Discussion

5.1 The Emergence of Phenomenal Awareness by Means of Bubbles

Let us restate the model presented so far for the emergence of phenomenal consciousness. The nature of primary awareness of the various modalities is suggested to occur after coding at a lower order feature analysis level. There may be a number of such stages, both in serial and in parallel. Consciousness only then arises in those modules which possess sufficiently long time constants (from the recurrent excitation, using the bubbles of section 3) and suitably strong inhibitory/excitatory connections for intra-module competition so as to allow a unique winner to emerge, by its activity being above some criterial level. The model has been suggested by the empirical fit of [11] to Marcel's (1980) data [9] for words, and can also be used to give a more qualitative explanation of the emergence of visual awareness being explored in a number of paradigms. There is no space to discuss that here so we turn to the most important question not so far addressed: how may the properties of qualia be seen to arise from the specific process of neuronal computation in the model? Especially why should consciousness arise from a simple thresholding of activity on a working memory module? There must be more to consciousness than that! In particular how may the properties of qualia, such as those of transparency, ineffability and presence be expected to occur [29]?

The first of these is 'presence', and includes the sense of the subjective present. The involvement of self is not part of our discussion in this section, but the temporal component of phenomenal awareness is. The latter has three characteristics: persistency, latency and seamlessness. The first of these, that of the temporal extension of phenomenal experience, is a very important component of the sense of the 'subjective now'. Such persistence is expected to be an intrinsic part of the process of winning a competition. This is the opposite side of the coin to latency (the delay of the onset of consciousness after input occurs); until another winner arises the earlier one is still 'king'. In the competitive model latency will arise as the time needed for a competition to be won on a working memory site. There is also the further property that we will call 'seamlessness': that the transition from one content of awareness to another happens rapidly enough to provide a sense of continuity in awareness.

Both latency and seamlessness were probed by in Libet's experiments [30] (and earlier references). In the former it was shown that about 500 msec is needed to cause the 'artificial' arousal of consciousness by direct electrical stimulation of somatosensory cortex as already discussed in section 3. It was also noted by Libet that the change-over process of consciousness was brief, occurring in less than a tenth of the time it took for the total process of changeover. That this could occur, along with the detailed features of the dependency of the length of the latency on the stimulation parameters, was shown in a neural system by the simulation of a simplified version of the Thalamus/NRT/Cortex system (noted in [6]). Thus seamlessness arises in the competitive model provided the competition, once started, is concluded suitably rapidly.

The next notion of transparency may be seen as arising from the well-connected system of working memories, for which there must be easy transfer of correlated information once a winner has occurred. Such transfer would also carry along with it correlated preconscious material across different codes, since there are good connections between modules at the same level of complexity, defined earlier in terms of either transience of activity or cell density in layers 2/3.

Such parallel processing would be expected especially to arise if anterior attention were focused, so that there is a suitable persistence of the lower area activity alongside that on the working memory.

In conclusion transparency is achievable by the crucial well-connectedness of the heteromodal regions, thus giving a transparent 'feel' to the activity.

It is important to follow up the feature that is posited as being played by anterior attention in the above emergence into awareness of activity on sites of working memory. If such attention is not being used then the working memory activity will not have the back-up of its related underlying preconscious activity which produced it in the first place. Both the working memory and the preconscious activity are posited as being needed for laying down a permanent memory of the event, so that it can be recalled in suitable detail and at various scales. Such encoding may be unavailable if only working memory itself is available, without its back-up; this may explain the lack of memory of any awareness experienced whilst performing so-called automatic acts, such as driving a car, in spite of there being phenomenal experience itself during the activity.

There is also the 'fully interpreted' character of qualia claimed to be part of transparency [29]. Such a property could arise from the fact that the working memory sites are at the highest level of the posterior processing hierarchy. Thus all the coding and 'interpretation', in informational terms, has been achieved when the competition has been won and incompatibilities ironed out. Indeed it would seem that such competition is indeed the final step in the interpretation process, achieved, it is claimed in the model presented here, as part of awareness being reached.

The third property of qualia is ineffability, that qualia are impossible to probe and 'get behind'. They are 'atomic' or intrinsic. This property is well mirrored in the one-way character of activation on working memory sites posited in the mode.

Thus in conclusion all of the characteristics of qualia suggested in [29] (except perspectivalness) have been seen to be mirrored in the properties of activity emerging onto the well-coupled working memory system of heteromodal cortical sites in posterior cortex. This gives support to the suggestion that the model is indeed one for the emergence of phenomenal awareness. In particular it may help towards answering the 'what is it like to be?' question for animals with no sense of self.

5.2 Are There Really 'Bubbles' in Cortex?

The hypothesis of the existence of bubbles in cortex as the source of phenomenal awareness can be criticised on a number of points:

1) The only evidence for them is from [26], which is indirect.

2) Counter-evidence has been brought forward in [31], in which only short-lived aperiodic wave-forms were observe in rabbit visual and auditory cortex.

3) The main temporal features of processing have been claimed to be carried 40-Hz wave-forms, which are not yet incorporated in the CNFT framework.

4) No analysis has been given of the N1 response or later peaks, used in the measurements of [26].

To answer these points, data analysis at the single trial level is needed; in both [26] and [31] ensemble averages were used. If there is jitter in 'bubble' production, signal averaging could cause loss of any trace activity present in single trials.

Finally the 40-Hz story does need to be incorporated into the CNFT framework, but until that us done such a criticism cannot be met. Nor can the criticism (4), although this is being considered [25].

Acknowledgements

I would like to thank A Ioannides and M Himmelbach of IME, P May of KCL and S-I Amari of BSI, Tokyo for useful discussions.

References

[1] Posner M & Raichle P. Images of Mind, San Francisco: Freeman. 1994.
[2] He S, Cavenagh P and Intrilligator J. Attentional resolution and the locus of visual awareness. Nature 1997. 383:334-7.
[3] Weiskrantz L, Barbur JL and Sahrie A. Parameters affecting conscious versus unconscious visual discrimination with damage to the visual cortex (V1). Proceedings of the National Acadademy of Science (USA) 1995;92: 6122-6.
[4] Kolb FC and Braun J. Blindsight in normal observers. Nature 1995; 377: 336-8.
[5] Taylor JG, Jaencke L, Shah NJ, Noesselt T, Schmitz N, Himmelbach T & Mueller-Gaertner H-W. A Three-Stage Model of Awareness: Formulation & Initial Experimental Support. Society for Neuroscience. Abstracts.1997.
[6] Taylor JG. Neural Networks for Consciousness. Neural Networks (to appear),1997.
[7] Baddeley A D and Hitch G. Working memory. in Bower G A (ed) The Psychology of learning and motivation, 1974; 8:47-89, Academic Press, New York.
[8] Baddeley AD. Working Memory, Oxford: Oxford University Press. 1986.
[9] Marcel A. Conscious and preconscious recognition on polysemous words: Locating selective effects of prior verbal contexts. in Nickerson RS (ed) Attention and performance VIII; Hillsdale NJ: Erlbaum Assoc. 1980
[10] Levelt WJM, Schriefers H, Vorberg D, Meyer AS, Pechmann T and Havinga J. The Time Course of Lexical Access in Speech Production: A Study of Picture Naming. Psychological Review 1991; 98: 122-142.
[11] Taylor J G. Breakthrough to Awareness. Biological Cybernetics 1996; 75: 59-72.
[12] Salmon E, Van der Linden M, Collette F, Delfiore G, Maquet P, Degueldre C, Luxen A and Franck G. Regional brain activity during working memory tasks. Brain 1996; 119: 1617-1625.
[13] Paulesu E, Frith C and Frakowiak RSJ. The neural correlates of the verbal components of working memory. Nature 1993;362: 342-5.
[14] Smith EE and Jonides J. Working memory in Humans: Neurophysiological Evidence. The Cognitive Neurosciences. 1995; Boston: MIT Press. pp 1090-1020

[15]Taylor J G. Goals, Drives and Consciousness. Neural Networks 1994; 7:1181-1190.

[16]Taylor JG and Villa AEP (1997) The Conscious I-A Neuro-Heuristic Approach to the Mind. To appear in The Brain of Homo Sapiens, Rome: Istituto della Enciclopedia Italiana.

[17]Amari S-I. Dynamical study of formation of cortical maps. Biological Cybernetics 1977; 27: 77-87

[18]Beurle RL. Properties of a mass of cells capable of regenerating pulses. Transactions of the Royal Society London 1956; B 240: 55-94.

[19]Ermentrout GB and Cowan JD. Studies in mathematics, The Mathematical Association of America 1978; 15: 67-117.

[20]Taylor JG. Neural 'Bubble' Dynamics in Two Dimensions I: Foundations. Biological Cybernetics (to appear) 1997.

[21]Takeuchi A and Amari S-I (1979) Formation of Topographic Maps and Columnar Microstructures in Nerve Fields. Biological Cybernetics 1979; 35: 63-72.

[22]Kopecz K and Schoner G. Saccadic motor planning by integrating visual information and pre-information on neural dynamic fields. Biological Cybernetics 1995; 73: 49-60.

[23]Petersen R and Taylor JG Reorganisation of somatosensory cortex after tactile training. In D Touretzky, M Moser & M Hasselmo (eds) Neural Information Processing Systems 8, 1996. Boston: MIT Press.

[24]Zhang K. Representation of Spatial Orientation by the Intrinsic Dynamics of the Head-Direction Cell Ensemble: A Theory. Journal of. Neuroscience 1996; 16: 2112-2126.

[25]May P, Himmelbach M & Taylor JG (in preparation).

[26]Uusitalo MA, Williamson S.J & Seppa MT. Dynamical organisation of the human visual system revealed by lifetimes of activation traces. Neuroscience Letters 1996; 213: 1149-152.

[27]Taylor JG. The Race for Consciousness, Boston: MIT Press. 1998.

[28]Hastings S and Taylor JG. Modeling the Articulatory Loop. In Morasso P and Marinaro M (eds), Proceedings of the International Conference on Artificial Neural Networks (ICANN'94), 1994; pp 1452-1455.

[29]Metzinger T. The Problem of Consciousness. In Metzinger T, Thorverton (eds) Conscious Experience. UK: Imprint Academic. 1995. pp3-40

[30]Libet B, Wright Jr E W, Feinstein B and Pearl D K. Subjective Referral of the Timing for a Conscious Sensory Experience. Brain 1979; 102: 193-224.

[31]Barrie JM, Freeman WJ & Lenhart MD. Spatiotemporal Analysis of Prepyriform, Visual and Somesthetic Surface EEGs in Trained Rabbits. Journal of Neurophysiology 1996; 76: 520-539.

Selective memory loss in aphasics: An insight from pseudo-recurrent connectionist networks

Robert M. French

Psychology Department, B32
University of Liège, Liège, Belgium
rfrench@ulg.ac.be

Abstract

McClelland, McNaughton, O'Reilly [15] suggest that the brain's way of overcoming catastrophic interference is by means of the hippocampus-neocortex separation. French [8] has developed a memory model incorporating this separation into distinct areas, using pseudopatterns [23] to transfer information from one area to the other of the memory. This network gradually produces highly compact representations which, while they ensure efficient processing, are also highly susceptible to damage. Internal representations of categories must reflect the variance within the categories. Because the variance within biological categories is, in general, smaller than that in artificial categories and because memory compaction gradually makes all representations proportionately less distributed, representations of low-variance biological categories are likely to be the most adversely affected by random damage to the network. This may help explain the selective memory loss in aphasics of natural categories compared to artificial categories.

1 Introduction

This paper is an attempt to bring together three ideas. The first is that the human brain evolved a particular means of overcoming the problem of catastrophic interference [16, 22] — namely, two separate systems of processing information: the hippocampus in which fast learning takes place and the neocortex where the information learned by the hippocampus is gradually consolidated [15]. A "pseudo-recurrent" connectionist model [8], based on this kind of separation, is described. The second key idea is that connectionist networks reflect the variability of categories in the environment in their internal representational organization. The greater the variability of a category, the greater the variance of the corresponding internal representations. And third, we will extend these ideas to the case of selective memory loss in aphasics. Our ultimate conclusion will be that differences in the variability of various categories may be implicated in preferential memory losses in aphasics of certain categories over others, in particular, the greater loss of natural kinds categories compared to artificial kinds.

In the first part of the paper, we explain the pseudo-recurrent connectionist model [8] that incorporates the idea of two separate storage and processing areas in the human brain in order to prevent catastrophic forgetting. Catastrophic forgetting (also referred to as catastrophic interference) is the tendency of neural networks — whether artificial or natural — to abruptly and completely forget previously learned information upon the learning new input [16, 22]. The vast majority of connectionist networks suffer from this problem because of the highly distributed nature of their internal representations. As French has shown [6], the degree to which networks suffer from catastrophic interference is in part a function of the amount of overlap of internal representations. In other words, the very feature that makes artificial neural networks so powerful and gives them the all-important ability to generalize is the same feature that causes catastrophic interference.

The most generally applied method of avoiding this problem requires a cognitively implausible means of learning new patterns. Whenever the network must learn a set of new patterns, *all* of the patterns it has ever learned in the past must be relearned by the network along with the new ones to be learned. This a far cry from how humans learn new patterns, however. Much of human learning tends to be *sequential*. A particular pattern is learned, then another, and another, and so on. While some of the earlier patterns may be seen again, this is not necessary for them to be retained in memory. As new patterns are learned, forgetting of old, unrepeated patterns occurs gradually as a function of time.

The connectionist architecture presented here is designed, like the brain, to not have to resort to this re-presentation of all of the past patterns it has learned. This means that the network, because it will not catastrophically forget previously learned information like a standard backpropagation network, will be capable of effective sequential learning. This architecture is based on two crucial techniques:

- separating the previously learned internal representations from those that are currently being learned;
- a method of *approximating* the previously learned data (not the original patterns themselves, which the network will not see again) and interleaving these approximations with the new patterns to be learned.

2 The need to separate old and new representations

The most common techniques for reducing catastrophic interference in traditional connectionist architectures have relied on reducing the overlap of representations either by orthogonal recoding of the input patterns [11, 13] or, alternately, by orthogonalizing the network's hidden layer representations [6, 7, 12, 17, 19]. A thorough discussion of these techniques and an analysis of the underlying causes of catastrophic interference can be found in [9, 26]. Pushing the logic of reducing representational overlap to its ultimate conclusion, McClelland, McNaughton, and O'Reilly [15] have argued that the evolution of two separate memory structures, the hippocampus and the neocortex, might have been brain's solution to the problem of new information completely destroying previously learned information. But this stills leaves unanswered a crucial question— namely: *How* does the neocortex store new information, whether it comes from the hippocampus or elsewhere, without disrupting information already stored there? Their solution involves the very gradual incorporation of the new information into the neocortical structure (i.e., long-term memory). Hippocampal representations very gradually train the neocortex. The problem is that no matter how slowly the hippocampal information is passed to the neocortex, radical forgetting of the old information may still result, *unless a way is found to interleave the already stored neocortical patterns* with the new patterns being learned. This interleaving cannot always use "the rest of the [original] database" [15] of previously learned patterns because many of these patterns will no longer be explicitly available for re-presentation to the network. For example, I have not seen a porcupine in at least ten years, so there has been no re-presentation of this item to my sensory interface during that time and thus no possibility for the corresponding long-term memory concept to be "refreshed" by seeing a real porcupine. Nonetheless, I would have no problem whatsoever recognizing one. There are a great many concepts like this, ones which are not continually refreshed via the environment, but that we still remember without difficulty.

This problem was the reason for the development of the pseudo-recurrent model developed in detail in [8] and exposed briefly here. This architecture has a way to automatically refresh the network without recourse to the original patterns. Instead of the original patterns, internally-produced *approximation*s of these patterns, called pseudopatterns [23], will be used and interleaved with the new patterns to be learned. The architecture proposed will argue for two functionally distinct areas of long-term memory: one, an "early-processing area" in which new information will be initially processed and a second, a "final-storage area," in which information will be consolidated. This model of long-term memory will suggest a natural means of consolidation of information in long-term memory that supports the neurobiologically motivated conclusions of [24].

The ideal way, of course, to solve the problem of catastrophic interference would be to store all previously learned patterns out of harm's way until new input was presented to the system. At that point, all of the previously learned patterns would be taken out of storage, so to speak, and would be mixed with the new patterns. The system would then learn the mixed set of old and new patterns. After the augmented set of patterns had been learned by the network, they would all be put in storage, awaiting the next time new information was presented to the network. There would be no forgetting, catastrophic or otherwise, in this ideal world and new input would have no deleterious effect on the network's ability to generalize, categorize or discriminate.

Unfortunately, this way of learning new data is rarely possible in the real world except in the most artificial situations. It is in essence impossible to explicitly store all, or even a reasonable fraction of previous training exemplars for future learning. I will suggest that *internal approximations* of the original patterns are generated in long-term memory and it is these approximations that, in the absence of the real patterns in the environment, serve to continually reinforce the long-term memory traces of the original patterns. The use of pseudopatterns to improve performance of connectionist networks on catastrophic interference was first proposed by Robins [20] and their plausibility has been further explored in [5, 24].

3 The "pseudo-recurrent" architecture

The architecture discussed in this paper consists of a feedforward backpropagation network that is divided into two parts, one used to help train the other (Figure 1). We will call the left-hand side of the network the "early-processing memory" and the right-hand side the "final-storage memory." It is perhaps easiest to explain how the network works in terms of a specific example.

Suppose that the "final-storage" area contains what the network has learned up to the present time. The network is then asked to sequentially learn 20 new patterns, P_1, P_2, ... P_{20}. Each of these patterns, P_i, consists of an input and an output ("teacher") association: (I_i, T_i). By sequentially learning these patterns we mean that each individual pattern must be learned to criterion before the system can begin to learn the subsequent pattern. To learn pattern P_1, its input I_1 is presented to the network. Activation flows through both parts of the network, but the output from the final-storage part is prevented from reaching the teacher nodes by the "real" teacher T_1. In other words, the teacher pattern T_1 fills the teacher nodes. The early-processing network then adjusts its weights with the standard backpropagation algorithm using as the error signal the difference between T_1 and the output O_1 of the early-processing network. Crucially, however, the early-processing network does not only learn the pattern P_1. Internally created *pseudopatterns*, reflecting the contents of final-storage, are also generated by the final-storage memory and will be learned by the early-processing memory along with P_1.

Pseudopatterns are generated by final-storage and learned by the early-processing memory as follows. A random input pattern, i_1, is presented to the input nodes of the system. This input produces an output, o_1, at the output layer of the early-processing memory and also produces an output, t_1, on the teacher nodes of the final-storage memory. This input-output pair (i_1, t_1) defines a pseudopattern, ψ_1, that reflects the contents of the final-storage memory. The difference between t_1 and o_1 determines the error signal for changing the weights in the early-processing memory. Similarly, the other random inputs, i_2, i_3, . . . i_n, produce pseudopatterns, ψ_2, ψ_3, . . . ψ_n that are also be learned by the early-processing memory. Once the weight changes have been made for the first epoch for the set of patterns $\{P_1, \psi_1, \psi_2, . . . \psi_n\}$, the early-processing memory cycles through this set of patterns again and again until it has learned them all to criterion. By learning the pattern P_1 the early-processing memory is learning the new information presented to it; by learning the pseudopatterns $\psi_1, . . ., \psi_n$, the early-processing memory is, in addition, learning an approximation of the information previously stored in final storage. Obviously, the more pseudopatterns that are generated, the more accurately they will reflect the contents of final storage. Once learning in the early-processing network has converged for P_1, ψ_1, $\psi_2, . . . \psi_n$, the early-processing weights then replace the final-storage weights. In other words, the early-processing memory *becomes* the final storage memory and the network is ready to learn the next pattern, P_2. (Note that this weight-copying strategy is certainly not biologically plausible. However, it has been shown [8] that

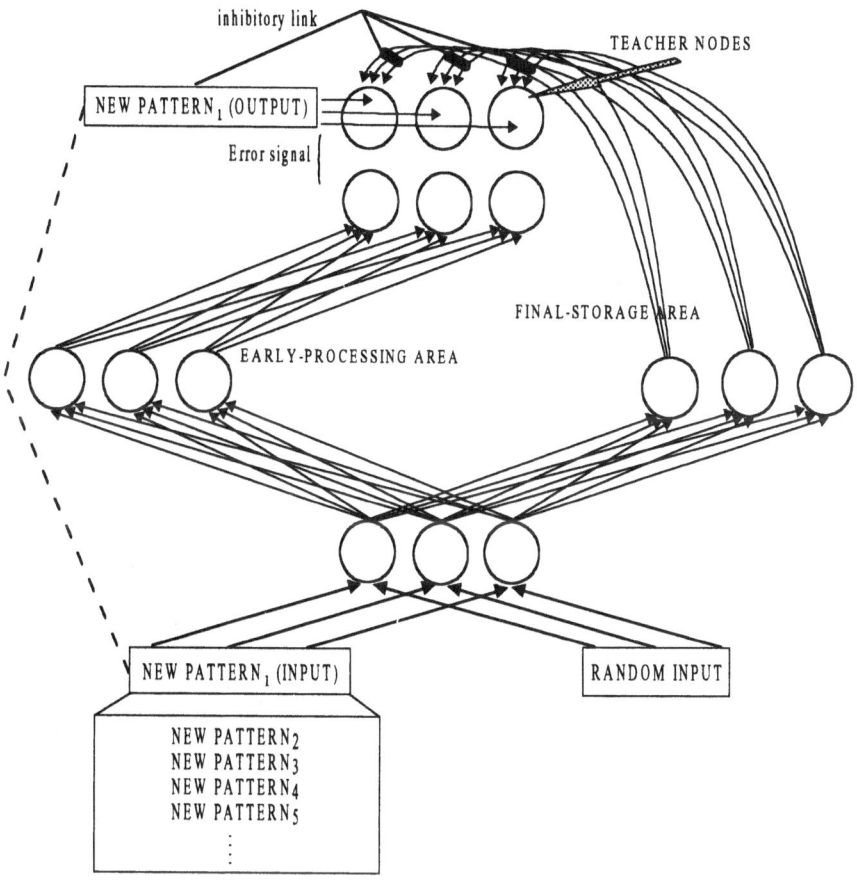

Figure 1. The pseudo-recurrent network architecture

information transfer can also be effectively done from early-processing to final-storage by means of the above type of pseudo-pattern transfer.)

The essence of this technique is to interleave new information to be learned with pseudopatterns that reflect the contents of final-storage. Thus, rather than interleaving the real, originally learned patterns with the new input coming to the early-processing memory, we do the next best thing — namely, we interleave pseudopatterns that are *approximations* of the previously stored patterns. Once the new pattern and the pseudopatterns are learned in the early-processing area, the weights from the early-processing network are copied to the corresponding weights in the final-storage network (or, more plausibly, the early-processing area trains the final-storage area using its own set of pseudopatterns).

The model is called "pseudo-recurrent" not only because of the recurrent nature of the training of the early-processing memory by the final-storage memory — approximations of previously learned information is continually fed back into the early-processing area from final-storage —, but also as a means of acknowledging the all-important mechanism of information transfer from final-storage to early-processing storage — namely, pseudopatterns.

3.1 Testing the pseudo-recurrent network

This type of network has been extensively tested and it has been shown not to suffer from catastrophic interference [8]. As a result, it is able to do sequential learning in a cognitively plausible manner. In Figure 3 the performance difference of the pseudo-recurrent network on a sequential learning task is compared with standard backpropagation. We will briefly describe this experiment designed to illustrate the pseudo-recurrent network's crucial ability to do sequential learning.

In these tests on the pseudo-recurrent network, we will show that it does two things that will allow us to use this model to provide a possible insight into selective memory losses in aphasics — namely:

- Sequential learning: The network does not forget catastrophically and, as a result, can learn sequentially. It is, therefore, a more cognitively plausible memory model than standard backpropagation networks, both in terms of its architecture and its performance.
- Emergence of compact representations: Over time, the network automatically develops "compact" internal representations in the final-storage area. This gradual representational compaction has numerous desirable effects, especially in terms of resource utilization, but has a major negative consequence: compact representations are more easily damaged by any damage to the network.

3.1.1 Sequential Learning

To test the network on sequential learning, we used the 1984 U.S. Congressional Voting Records database from the University of California at Irvine repository of machine learning databases [18]. Twenty members of Congress (10 Republicans, 10 Democrats, defined by their voting record on 16 issues) were chosen randomly from the database. Each of the 20 patterns presented to the network therefore consisted of 16 binary inputs and a single binary output. The 20 patterns were presented *sequentially* to the network. In other words, a new pattern was presented only after the previous one had been learned to criterion (i.e., the output on the single output node was within 0.2 of the desired output). After all twenty patterns had been sequentially learned by the network, a test was made of the percentage of these patterns that the network still correctly remembered. A pattern was considered to have been exactly remembered by the network if, when it was presented to the network, the output that was produced on the single output node remained within 0.2 of the desired output for that pattern. After sequentially learning the 20 patterns, Figure 2 shows that a standard backpropagation network can exactly remember about 40% of the them. This figure climbs rapidly to 65% when 5 pseudopatterns from final-storage are added along with each new pattern to be learned. With 50 pseudopatterns added to each new item to be learned, exact recognition of all of patterns climbs to 85%.

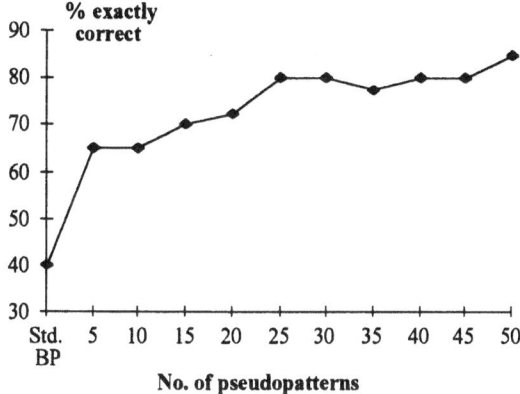

Figure 2. Percentage of all data exactly recalled by the network after serial presentation of all 20 patterns (median data).

After the network learned the twenty items sequentially, each item was tested to see how well the network remembered that individual item. The hypothesis was that forgetting would be more gradual when pseudopatterns were used compared to standard backpropagation. Figure 3 shows that this is indeed the case. Of particular importance is the difference in amount of forgetting between the final item learned and the penultimate one for both standard backpropagation and the 25-pseudopattern network. Further, as can be seen in the figure, the standard backpropagation network is, on average, significantly above the 0.2 convergence criterion for *all* of the previously learned items, whereas the pseudo-recurrent network is at or below criterion for the last eight items learned (items 13-20) and within 0.05 of the criterion for items 7-12.

Clearly, forgetting is taking place more gradually in the pseudo-recurrent network than in the backpropagation network, where *none* of the 19 previously learned items are below criterion after the 20th item has been learned (Figure. 3).

This experiment shows that the forgetting curves for this type of network are considerably more gradual than with standard backpropagation. This experiment also points out the importance of interleaving approximations of the already-learned patterns with the new patterns to be learned.

3.1.2 The emergence of compact representations

During sequential learning, information is continually passed back and forth between the two memory areas by means of pseudopatterns. (In the version of the model described above pseudopatterns are used only to transfer information from final-storage to the early-processing area. Weight copying is used in the other direction. This constraint has been successfully relaxed and pseudopatterns have been used to pass information in both directions. A detailed discussion of these results can be found in [8].) It turns out that one unanticipated result of this use of pseudopatterns is the "compaction" of the representations that develop in final storage. This has numerous advantages, among them, a decrease in the number of

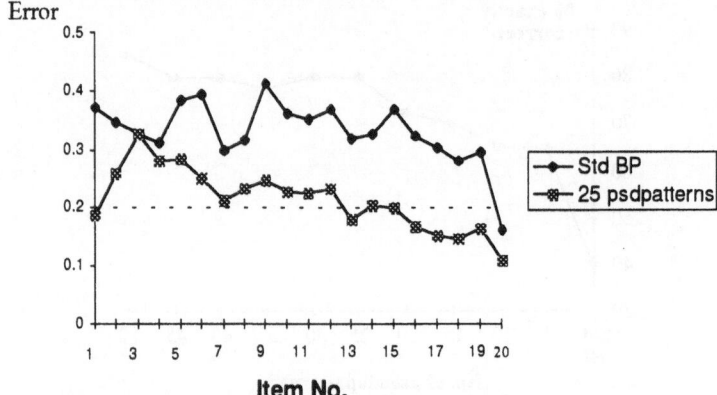

Figure 3. Amount of error for each of the 20 items learned sequentially after the final item has been learned to criterion (in this case, 0.2).

resources required to activate any given concept, a decrease in the amount of overlap in final storage, etc. On the other hand, compact representations are more likely to be destroyed if the network is lesioned.

This suggests an interesting possibility for the human brain. It has been shown that there is continual interaction between the hippocampus and the neocortex and that this interaction is almost certainly involved in long-term memory consolidation. If this interaction is indeed mediated by pseudopatterns, as suggested by Robins [24], then it would not be unreasonable to think that the representational compaction observed in the pseudo-recurrent model might also occur in the brain. Compact representations would, presumably, allow for more efficient processing of incoming stimuli because of their reduced demand on system resources (i.e., less activation is required to fully activate a compact representation, fewer connections are involved, etc.). On the other hand, the more compact these representations, the more difficult it would be to make category distinctions (see [7] for a discussion of this problem). This would also lead to the category brittleness that occurs as people grow older, a phenomenon whose description dates at least to James [10], and results in a loss of the capability of "assimilating impressions in any but old ways." [10] Finally, highly compact representations would presumably be more vulnerable to severe disruption than highly distributed representations. This, too, would seem to be consistent with selective memory loss with aging.

The data used to test the network were obtained from measurements of the original Cat and Dog pictures used by Eimas, Quinn, and Cowan [4, 21] and by Mareschal and French [14] to study infant categorization. They included 18 dogs and 18 cats classified according to head length, head width, eye separation, ear separation, ear length, nose length, nose width, leg length vertical extent, and horizontal extent.

A 10-30-10 autoassociator was used in learning these two categories of animals. We compared the hidden unit representations in networks that had sequentially learned 6 pairs of cats (i.e., a total of 12 cats) using differing numbers of pseudopatterns. The network was then tested on its ability to correctly autoassociate

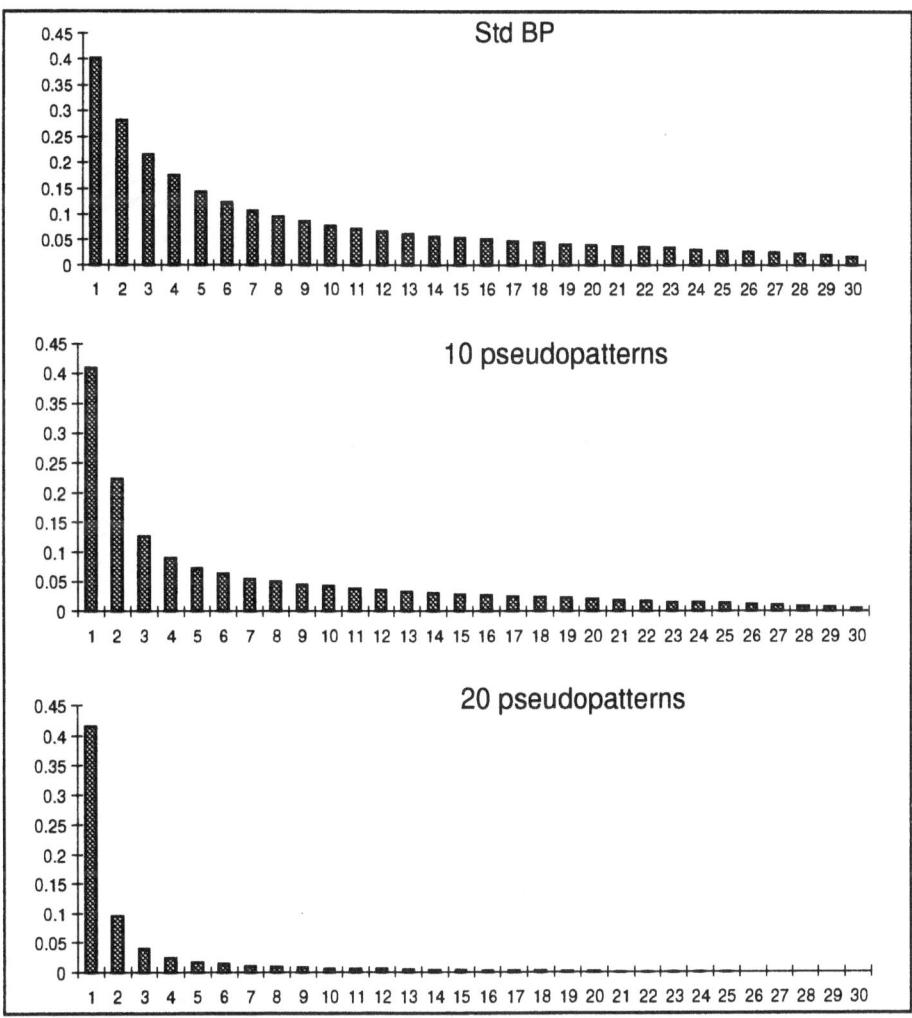

Figure 4. Pseudopatterns gradually produce highly "compact" representations for the categories in final storage (in this case, for the category "cat"). The greater the number of pseudopatterns, the more compact the representations becomes.

the previously learned cats. As the number of pseudopatterns increases, the network's internal representation of the concept "cat" undergoes compaction (Figure 4).

It is the continual interaction between the two processing areas of the pseudo-recurrent memory that gives rise to these more compact (i.e., less distributed) internal representations. These are the same types of representations that have been shown in other work to reduce catastrophic interference [6, 7]. Unlike this earlier work in which explicit algorithms produced this type of representation to reduce catastrophic interference, in this memory model — and conceivably in the brain as well — they emerge naturally from the mechanisms underlying the model.

4 Selective memory loss in aphasics

Natural kinds are categories like "cat", "bird", "horse", etc., while artificial kinds are categories like "chair", "house", "clothes", etc. It has been repeatedly shown [1, 25, 28] that there can be selective memory loss in certain aphasics for natural-kinds compared to artificial-kinds categories. In contrast to explanations that rely on the form/function distinctions in their attempts to explain the observed selective anomia (for example, [3]), I will suggest that this selective memory loss is due, at least in part, to the considerable difference in the average variability within most biological and artificial kinds. This difference, combined with the phenomenon of gradual compaction of representations as they are consolidated in final-storage — making them increasingly susceptible to damage — will provide a simple, if undoubtedly partial and speculative, account for this type of aphasia.

If two real-world categories that have very different variance are stored in a network — connectionist or human — this difference in variance must be reflected in a difference in the variance of the internal representations of the two categories. The greater the variance in the real-world category, the greater the variance in the internal representation of that category, where the variance of an internal representation is determined by the "spread" of the distribution of hidden-unit activation pattern corresponding to a representation when it is activated. The more spread out the distribution, the greater the variance. Consider, for example, the artificial-kind category "house" and the natural-kind category "cat." The former has greater variance than the latter. The folk observation that "If you've seen one cat, you've seen 'em all" translates more rigorously into a statement about the lack of variability within the category of cats. On the other hand, the same could never be said about all houses, which certainly *do not* all look the same. Some are brick, some wood, some tall, some wide, some are made of logs, some of stone, some even of cloth (a "teepee," for instance) or animal hides, etc. This greater category variance will be reflected in a greater amount of variance in the internal representations for each category [14]. So, for example, we might have internal representations for "house" and "cat" similar to those in Figure 5.

But if, as it has been suggested [24], neural pseudopatterns are used to consolidate the long-term memory trace, the representations shown in Figure 5 will gradually become more and more compact, giving rise to representations like those in Figure 6. And, since compaction occurs in a uniform manner, the representations that were more highly distributed initially will remain so as compaction progresses.

The problem, though, is that, while these more compact representations will certainly be more efficient in terms of overall processing demands, they are also more easily disrupted. If we randomly remove, say, four nodes from the hidden-layer of the above network, the chances of destroying the internal representation for "cat" will be far greater than for destroying "house." Of course, one prediction of the pseudo-recurrent model is that, on rare occasions, we should also see an anomia for an artificial-kind category, but that this should be far less frequent than for natural-kind categories. Anomia of this kind has been observed, but is, indeed,

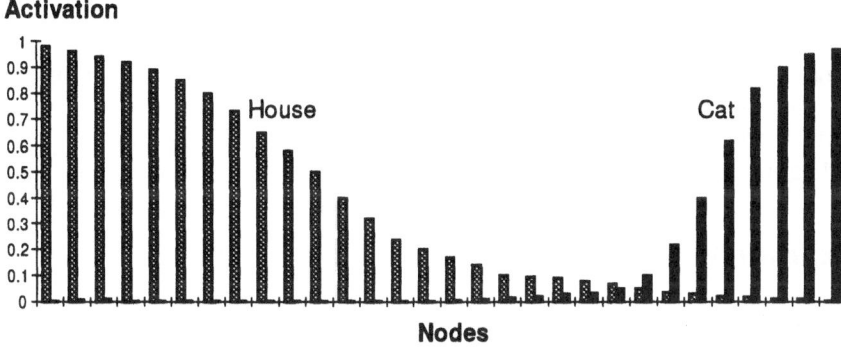

Figure 5. The internal representations of the categories "house" and "cat" before the gradual effect of pseudopattern transfer transforms them into the more compact representations shown in Figure 6.

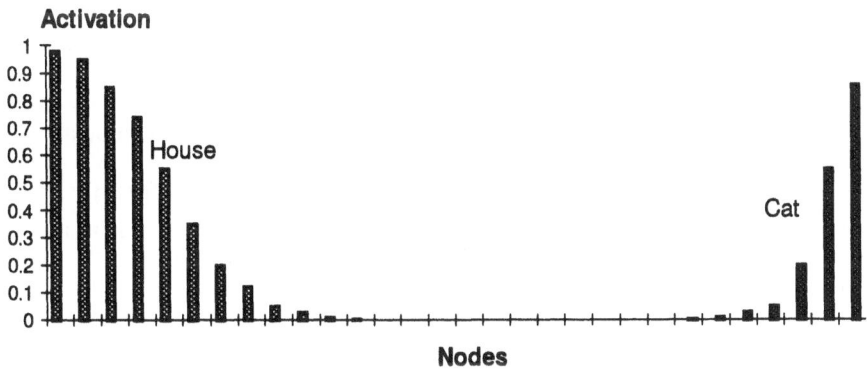

Figure 6. The representations for "house" and "cat" after undergoing gradual compaction due to the effect of pseudopattern transfer.

exceedingly rare. While there is a growing body of research using connectionist models to understand category-specific deficits [2, 3, 20, 27, etc.], the above model is unique in suggesting that this phenomenon might, at least in part, be related to gradual representational compaction in long-term memory and subsequent damage to these compact representations.

5 Conclusion

This paper proposes a "pseudo-recurrent" connectionist model of long-term memory in which an "early-processing" memory and a permanent, "final-storage" memory continually exchange information by means of pseudopatterns [8]. Some form of neural pseudopatterns arguably play a role in long-term memory consolidation [24]. However, one of the consequences of pseudopattern transfer is a gradual compaction of the representations stored in long-term memory. I argue that this compaction, along with the fact that the internal representation of a category must reflect the amount of variance of that category in the environment, may contribute to the observed selective memory losses in aphasics. In particular, the greater variance, on average, of artificial kinds compared to natural kinds would predict greater losses of the latter kind of category, which corresponds to aphasia data. This is certainly not the whole story on selective memory loss in aphasics, but this paper suggests that it could be an important part of it.

Acknowledgments

This work was supported in part by Belgian National Science Grant PAI P4/19. The author also wishes to thank Jean-Pierre Thibaut for his significant contribution to the ideas of this paper.

References

1. Brandt, R. (1988). Category-specific deficits in aphasia. *Aphasiology, 2*(3-4) 237-240.
2. Devlin, J., Gommerman, L., Anderson, E., Seidenberg, M. (1997). Category specific deficits in focal and widespread brain damage: A computational account. (Submitted to *Journal of Cognitive Neuroscience*).
3. Durrant-Peatfield, M., Tyler, L., Moss, H. & Levy, J. (1997). The distinctiveness of form and function in category structure: A connectionist model. *Proceedings of the Nineteenth Annual Conference of the Cognitive Science Society*, Mahwah, NJ:LEA.
4. Eimas, P. D., Quinn, P. C., & Cowan, P. (1994). Development of exclusivity in perceptually based categories of young infants, *Journal of Experimental Child Psychology, 58*, 418-431.
5. Frean, M. and Robins, A. (1996). Catastrophic forgetting: A review and an analysis of the pseudorehearsal solution. (under review).
6. French, R. M. (1992). Semi-distributed representations and catastrophic forgetting in connectionist networks. *Connection Science, 4*, 365-377.
7. French, R. M. (1994). Dynamically constraining connectionist networks to produce orthogonal, distributed representations to reduce catastrophic interference. In *Proceedings of the 16th Annual Cognitive Science Society Conference*. Hillsdale, NJ:LEA, 335-340.
8. French, R. M. (1997). Pseudo-recurrent connectionist networks: An approach to the "sensitivity–stability" dilemma. *Connection Science, 9*(4) (in press).
9. Hetherington, P. A. (1991). The sequential learning problem in connectionist networks. Unpublished Master's Thesis, Psychology Department, McGill University, Montreal.
10. James, W. (1890). *Psychology, The Briefer course*. New York: Holt.
11. Kortge, C. (1990). Episodic Memory in Connectionist Networks, In *Proceedings of the 12th Annual Conference of the Cognitive Science Society*, Hillsdale, NJ: LEA, 764-771.

12. Kruschke, J. K. (1993). Human Category Learning: Implications for Backpropagation Models. *Connection Science, 5*(1), 1993.

13. Lewandowsky, S. & Shu-Chen Li (1993). Catastrophic Interference in Neural Networks: Causes, Solutions, and Data. In *New Perspectives on interference and inhibition in cognition* F.N. Dempster & C. Brainerd (eds.). New York, NY: Academic Press.

14. Mareschal, D. & French, R. (1997). A connectionist account of interference effects in early infant memory and categorization. In *Proceedings of the 19th Annual Cognitive Science Society Conference*, New Jersey: LEA (in press).

15. McClelland, J., McNaughton, B., & O'Reilly, R. (1995). Why there are complementary learning systems in the hippocampus and neocortex: Insights from the successes and failures of connectionist models of learning and memory. *Psychological Review. 102*, 419–457.

16. McCloskey, M. & Cohen, N. (1989). Catastrophic interference in connectionist networks: The sequential learning problem. *The Psychology of Learning and Motivation, 24*, 109-165.

17. McRae, K. & Hetherington, P. (1993) Catastrophic interference is eliminated in pretrained networks. In *Proceedings of the 15h Annual Conference of the Cognitive Science Society.* Hillsdale, NJ: LEA. 723-728.

18. Murphy, P. & Aha, D. (1992). UCI repository of machine learning databases. Maintained at the Dept. of Information and Computer Science, UC Irvine, CA.

19. Murre, J. (1992). The effects of pattern presentation on interference in backpropagation networks. In *Proceedings of the 14th Annual Conference of the Cognitive Science Society.* Hillsdale, NJ: Erlbaum. 54-59.

20. Plaut, D.C. (1995). Double dissociation without modularity: Evidence from connectionist neuropsychology. *Journal of Clinical and Experimental Neuropschology, 17*, 291–326.

21. Quinn, P. C., Eimas, P. D., & Rosenkrantz, S. L. (1993). Evidence for representations of perceptually similar natural categories by 3-month-old and 4-month-old infants, *Perception, 22*, 463-475.

22. Ratcliff, R. (1990). Connectionist models of recognition memory: Constraints imposed by learning and forgetting functions, *Psychological Review, 97*, 285-308.

23. Robins, A. (1995). Catastrophic forgetting, rehearsal and pseudorehearsal. *Connection Science, 7*(2), 123–146.

24. Robins. A. (1996). Consolidation in Neural Networks and in the Sleeping Brain. (under review).

25. Sartori, G., Miozzo, M., & Job, R. (1993). Category-specific form-knowledge deficit in a patient with Herpes Simplex Virus Encephalitis. *The Quarterly Journal of Experimental Psychology, 46A*(3) 489-504.

26. Sharkey, N. & Sharkey, A., (1995). An analysis of catastrophic interference. *Connection Science, 7*(3-4), 301–329.

27. Small, S. (1994) Connectionist networks and language disorders. *Journal of Communication Disorders, 27*, 305-323.

28. Temple, C. (1986). Anomia for animals in a child. *Brain, 106*, 1225-1242.

Lexical/Semantic Representations

Extracting Semantic Representations from Large Text Corpora

Malti Patel
Department of Computing, Macquarie University
Sydney, Australia

John A. Bullinaria & Joseph P. Levy
Department of Psychology, Birkbeck College
London, UK

Abstract

Many connectionist language processing models have now reached a level of detail at which more realistic representations of semantics are required. In this paper we discuss the extraction of semantic representations from the word co-occurrence statistics of large text corpora and present a preliminary investigation into the validation and optimisation of such representations. We find that there is significantly more variation across the extraction procedures and evaluation criteria than is commonly assumed.

1   Introduction

How to represent semantics has been a difficult problem for many years, and as yet there is no consensus as to exactly what is stored and how. With the rise of cognitive modelling, the problem of representing semantic information must now be addressed if any headway is to be made. Although semantics obviously plays a very important role in language, cognitive models concerned with language have either not attempted to implement this component [2, 20], or implemented it only on a small-scale [3, 4, 6, 7, 16, 17, 18]. If the experimental results from tasks such as reading and lexical decision are to be simulated, there must be serious investigations into how semantics can be represented on a large scale, e.g. for thousands of words.

Recently, work has begun on using large corpora to extract semantic information in the form of vectors of word co-occurrence statistics. In this paper, we shall discuss the results obtained from a preliminary study of extracting co-occurrence vectors from the British National Corpus (BNC) – a large corpus consisting of 100 million words, both written and spoken [9]. These vectors are obtained by counting how often words occur near each other in a corpus to give a vector of probabilities for each word with components corresponding to the different words in the corpus. There are a number of parameters which specify the vector creation process and their values will affect the resultant vectors. We describe some simple evaluation procedures with the aim of optimising these parameters to give the best semantic representations.

This kind of analysis seeks to investigate the degree to which aspects of the meaning of a word are reflected in its tendency to occur around certain other words.

This may give insights into how semantics may be learnt by humans through exposure to language and stored in the brain [8]. These vectors will also be of great use for representing semantics in models of various psychological processes, such as reading and lexical decision. The current methods are somewhat inadequate since the semantic representations are randomly generated or hand-crafted. Randomly generated vectors clearly have no relation to real semantics. Hand-crafted representations are subjective in that the modellers concerned decide how the meaning of a word, and also what features of the meaning, should be stored. For example, different people will have different ideas on how to best represent the meaning of *dog*. Also, creating semantic representations for thousands of words would be a time-consuming task. Hence, we need a technique which captures meanings in an objective fashion and one which would allow us to easily create semantic representations for many words.

We shall first briefly describe work already performed in this area of corpus analysis and then describe how semantics has been represented previously in various psychological models and why the corpus based approach for obtaining semantic representations has advantages over these. Our main focus will be on how the various parameters involved in the corpus analysis can be optimised to produce the best co-occurrence vectors. This will hopefully lead to a greater awareness of which parameter values give what types of results. In the process, we will define evaluation procedures which can be used by other researchers working on corpus analysis.

2 Previous Corpora Work

Various relevant results have already been obtained from corpus analysis [8, 11, 12, 19]. Lund and Burgess [11, 12], for example, derived co-occurrence vectors with 200 components from a 160 million word corpus, based on words occurring within a weighted window of ten words around the target word. Amongst other things, their analyses showed that vectors derived for semantically related words tended to be closer in Euclidean space than was the case for semantically unrelated words, e.g. the semantic vector for *cat* was closer to other co-occurrence vectors representing animals, such as *lion*, than to vectors representing body parts, such as *ankle*. Schütze has carried out numerous experiments on extracting semantics from corpora. His initial work [19] involved creating co-occurrence vectors from letter four-grams as opposed to words. He showed that semantically related vectors tended to be close in distance and demonstrated successful semantic disambiguation. Together, these investigations have indicated that useful semantic representations can be produced from corpora. Moreover, Bullinaria and Huckle [5] have already used semantic vectors of this form with some success in connectionist models of lexical decision.

Although these studies have shown this approach to be useful, no systematic and rigorous evaluations have yet been performed. There are a variety of parameters which specify how the co-occurrence vectors are created, for example, different window shapes and sizes, different numbers of vector components, different corpora sizes, and so on. Here we shall create co-occurrence vectors for the same groups of words for different parameter values. These vectors will be then be evaluated using two different criteria to optimise the parameter values and assess how good the best resultant semantic representations really are.

3 Implementation of the Semantic Component of Reading and Lexical Decision Models

Psychological models of reading and lexical decision have been implemented using neural networks with varying degrees of success [2, 3, 4, 7, 16, 17, 18, 20]. A major problem has been in implementing the semantic component of such models since there is no established theory of what should be represented or how. Modellers have tended towards using simple notions of semantic micro-feature representations as a practical way of implementing the lexical semantics of small sets of words. For example, Hinton & Shallice [7] generated their own semantic micro-features by hand such that each stood for a specific concept such as *has-legs* or *indoors*. A semantic vector consisted of 30 components with each representing one semantic micro-feature. Similarly, Plaut & Shallice [17], used 86 semantic micro-features split into categories such as *visual characteristics, where found*, etc. Others have shown that realistic patterns of performance can be obtained simply by using randomly generated semantic representations, for example, both Plaut [16] and Bullinaria [3] in their lexical decision models and Bullinaria [4] in his reading model.

A somewhat different approach investigated by Patel [15] involved using WordNet definitions to represent semantics. WordNet is a dictionary based on psycholinguistic principles, developed at Princeton University by Miller et al. [13], that contains approximately 57,000 nouns, 21,000 verbs and 19,500 adjectives. For each word, WordNet gives all possible meanings in terms of a number of definitions. For example, the WordNet representation for Sense 2 of *hand* is:

HAND : Sense 2 : hired hand, hand, hired man -- (a hired laborer on a farm or ranch)

=> laborer, manual laborer, labourer -- (works with hands)
  => workman, working man, working person
   => employee -- (a worker who is hired to perform a job)
    => worker -- (a person who has employment)
      => person, individual, someone, man, mortal, human, soul -- (a human being)
        => life form, organism, being, living thing -- (any living entity)
          => entity -- (something having concrete existence; living or nonliving)

In the semantic vectors developed by Patel, each component corresponded to one WordNet definition. The component was *on* if the meaning contained that definition otherwise it remained *off*. Although, some promising results were obtained with this approach, problems did occur occasionally with the total number of definitions used to define a meaning. In some cases for polysemous words, the wrong meaning had a higher activation that the correct meaning simply because it consisted of more WordNet definitions than the correct meaning. Hence, for these cases, the more components a vector had *on*, the greater advantage the corresponding meaning had of gaining more activation.

The appealing factor of the above vector based approaches is that they are simple and intuitive. However, in the long-term, they have no external validity, except perhaps the WordNet approach which is at least based on psycholinguistic data. The corpus based approaches for representing semantics may prove to be better if, after rigorous evaluation, it can be shown that co-occurrence vectors do have some interesting and psychologically realistic properties. A technique will then have been found which has many advantages over the usual hand-crafted approach towards semantic representation. For example, it does not rely on subjective judgements, it is automatic and it produces data that are derived from genuine linguistic performance. These co-occurrence vectors could then be used reliably in the semantic components of connectionist language processing models.

4 Optimising the Vector Creation Parameters

The semantic vectors derived from corpus analysis are produced by simply counting the occurrences of neighbouring words, e.g. by counting the number of occurrences of the context words which neighbour *flower* to create the semantic vector for *flower*. There are clearly a number of parameters that need to be specified to uniquely determine this counting and vector creation process. In this section we briefly discuss five of the main parameters that we wish to vary in this preliminary study.

4.1 The Vector Creation Process

We begin with a simple illustration to show the roles the various parameters play in creating the vectors. Suppose we are producing the semantic vector for the word *girl* using a *window size* of two words on either side of the *target* word *girl*. Then suppose that the phrase "the little girl said that ..." is the next one to appear in the corpus. The values below show the increments that will be given to the already accumulated frequency counts of these words. For a *rectangular* window, the current total for each word around *girl* will be incremented by one, whereas for a *triangular* window, the increment is larger the closer the word is to *girl*.

- *Rectangular Window* (each word carries the same weight)

the	little	girl	said	that
1	1	0	1	1

- *Triangular Window* (closer words carry more weight)

the	little	girl	said	that
1	2	0	2	1

Then, how we use these increments depends on the *window types*:

- *Left only* - count words to left of target, e.g. "the little".

- *Right only* - count words to right of target, e.g. "said that".

- *Left plus Right* - count words on both sides of target, e.g. "the little said that".

- *Left and Right* - concatenate left only and right only vectors from above.

The final value of these frequency counts will then be used to calculate the co-occurrence vector for *girl*, first by normalising to take account of the total window size, and then dividing by the target word frequencies to give the probabilities of co-occurrence. We can now look at the main parameters in more detail.

4.2 The Main Parameters

Window Size

This defines the number of neighbouring words that we count as occurring "near" to the target word, e.g. do we count the two words immediately next to it, or the five words next to it, or the fifty words next to it, etc. One might conjecture that a large window size gives more semantic information whereas a small window size gives more syntactic information.

Window Type

This refers to which side of the target word we count the neighbouring words:

• *Left only* - count only words occurring to the left of the target word, producing vectors with one component for each of the D different words in the corpus.
• *Right only* - count only words occurring to the right of the target word, again producing vectors with D components.
• *Left plus Right* - count words occurring to the left and right of the target word, still producing vectors with D components.
• *Left and right* - concatenate the vectors formed by looking at just the left and right sides, i.e. the vectors from left only and right only, producing vectors with $2 \times D$ components.

We shall not investigate the possibility here, but one might also wish to consider treating the left and right contexts asymmetrically.

Window Shape

It might be appropriate to treat the context words differently depending on how far away they are from the target words, so we have windows of different shape:

• *Rectangular/Flat* - each neighbouring word around the target word is given the same weight.
• *Triangular/Weighted* - as a neighbouring word gets further from the target word, it is given linearly less weight - a technique used by Lund and Burgess [8].

and one can imagine other possibilities that we shall not consider in this paper.

Number of Vector Components

Clearly we generally do not want to use all D components of our vectors, because D will be a very large number and the resultant vectors would be too large and very difficult to process. Hence some analysis must be carried out to determine how many vector components are appropriate to obtain the best results, e.g. does restricting ourselves to 100 components give better results than, say, using 1000 components? In this paper we shall use the components corresponding to the context words of the highest frequency. In future work we shall need to consider if it is more appropriate to use the components with the highest variance, or if we should use something like principal component analysis to reduce the dimension of the space.

Corpus Size

We would expect the vectors produced from a large corpus to be better than those produced from a smaller one, simply because the relative noise in the frequency counts will fall with the counts themselves and these will clearly increase with the corpus size. We need to determine how crucial this factor is and how it depends on the frequencies of the target and context words and on the evaluation criteria.

5   Evaluation Criteria

We thus have five main parameters whose values can be varied. Obviously, changing these values will produce differing co-occurrence vectors for the same set of words. Hence, evaluation techniques need to be formulated to decide which parameter values give the best set of co-occurrence vectors and how good these best vectors really are. In this section we begin a systematic investigation by describing two simple criteria for evaluating the different sets of co-occurrence vectors and in the next section we present some preliminary results.

The most natural conjecture is that if we define some distance metric on our semantic vector space, then the vectors corresponding to semantically unrelated words should be further apart than those for related words. Since there are numerous normalisation artefacts that may arise when we compare vectors derived using different values of the above parameters (e.g. different amounts of baseline noise), the natural dimension free quantity to compare is the relatedness ratio:

$$R = \frac{\text{Mean distance between control words}}{\text{Mean distance between related words}}$$

The larger this ratio, the relatively closer are the related words, and the better our semantic representations. We chose a representative set of 100 pairs of words that had been judged by human subjects to be near synonyms [14] and for each pair we took eight frequency matched random pairs of words to act as our controls. We then created the co-occurrence vectors and calculated the ratio R using simple Euclidean distances for these pairs for a range of parameter sets.

To check the extent to which our results depended on the details of the chosen evaluation criterion, our second criterion was based on a somewhat different idea. Given a set of words which human subjects have assigned to different categories, we can define category centres in the semantic vector space and ask how many of the vectors do actually fall closer to the correct category centre than to any of the other centres. If our vectors really are a good representation of semantics, we would expect all the vectors to fall closer to an appropriate category centre than to an inappropriate

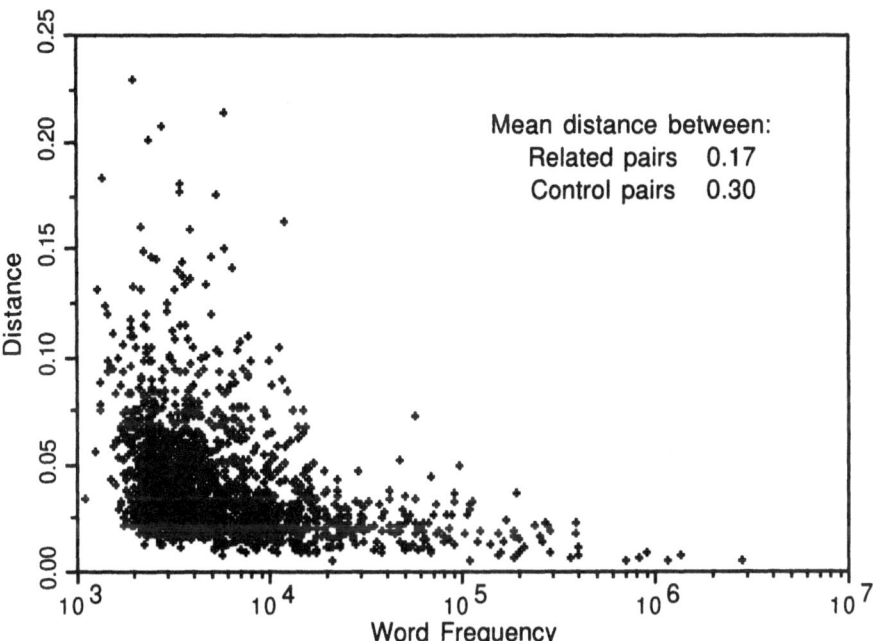

Figure 1: The distances between vectors created from different halves of the corpus showing that the higher frequency word vectors tend to be more reliable.

centre. We took ten words for each of ten Battig and Montague [1] categories which had minimal category overlap and counted the number of correct classifications for each parameter set.

6   Results

The first thing we need to consider is the reliability of the vectors we create. We are estimating probabilities by counting the word occurrences in a finite corpus, and we therefore expect the random variations in the vectors to be smallest for the high frequency words and for very large corpora. The important questions are how small can the corpus be and how low can the frequencies be before we start running into problems. We begin by checking that our full corpus of 89 million written words is large enough and that the frequencies of our chosen words are high enough, and consider what happens for smaller corpora at the end of this section. We generated vectors of the *left & right* type using a weighted window of size two with components corresponding to the 128 highest frequency words. Figure 1 shows that the distances between vectors for the same word created from different halves of the full corpus are small compared with the mean distances between different related and control words within the corpus. Figure 2 confirms this for the actual word pairs we used and shows the distribution of related and unrelated distances which is our first indication that we really are extracting semantic effects. Together these Figures give us confidence that our results are not going to be swamped by statistical noise.

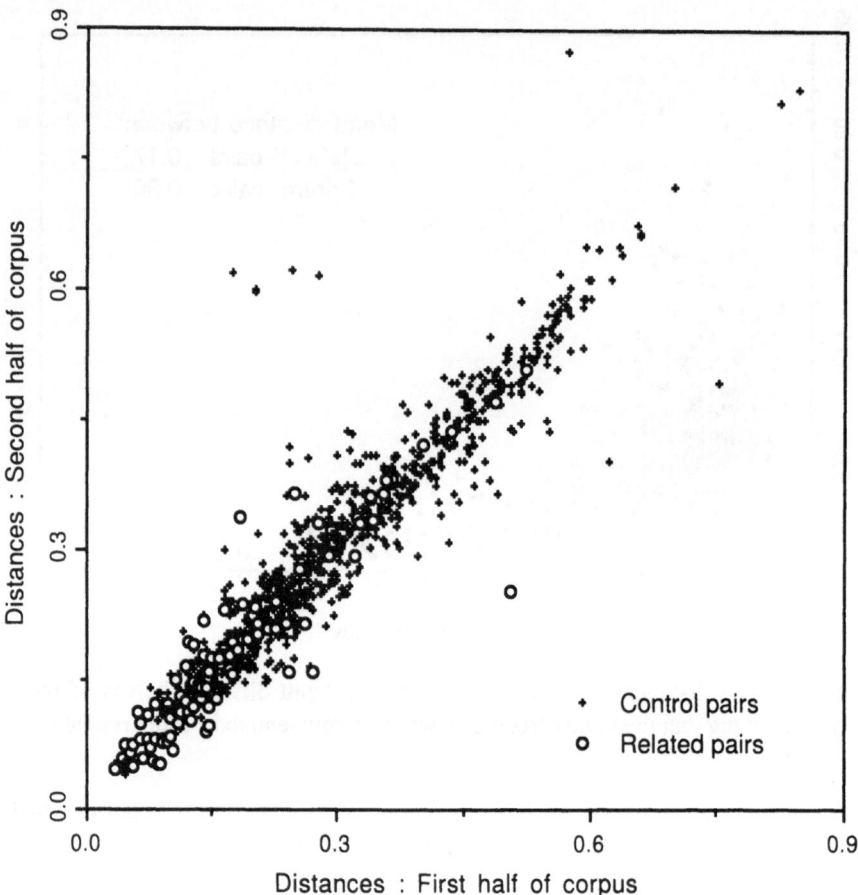

Figure 2: A comparison of the inter-word distances for vectors derived from different halves of the corpus. As one would hope, semantically related word pairs tend to be closer together than random control word pairs.

The following graphs showing how our two performance measures vary with our main parameters are fairly self explanatory. Figures 3 and 4 show how our criteria vary with the number of frequency ordered vector components. We used *left & right* type vectors for flat and weighted windows of size two. We see that the ratio measure has a peak at around a hundred components and then falls slowly, whereas the classification measure increases rapidly up to about 64 components and then remains fairly level. Figures 5 and 6 show the variation with the window size and between flat and weighted windows for *left & right* type vectors of 128 components. The ratio measure has a peak at window size two whereas the classification measure peaks nearer sixteen. In each of these graphs we have a trade-off between acquiring more information against more noise from the extra vector components or window positions. For both measures, we can see that large weighted windows behave equivalently to a flat window of about half the size.

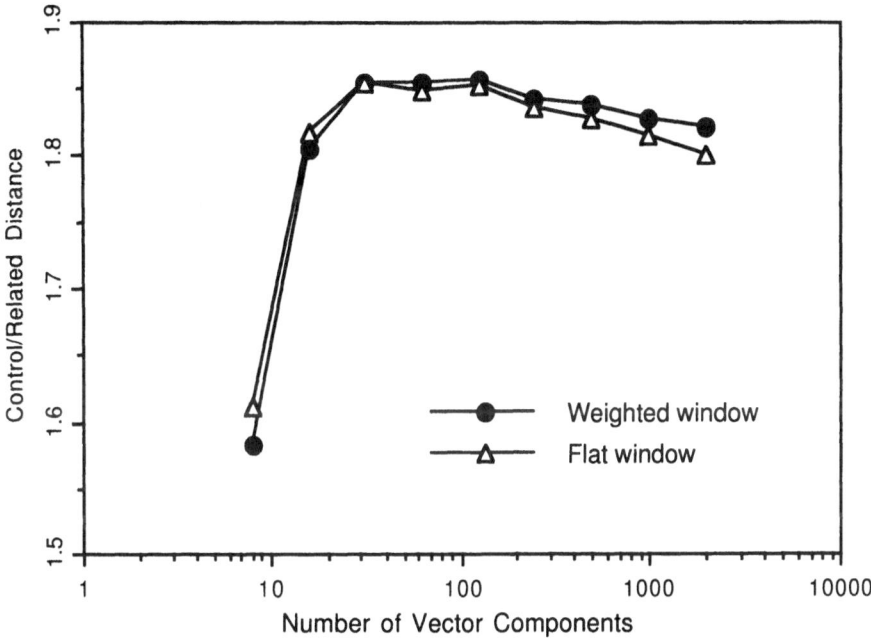

Figure 3: The plot of our Control/Related distance ratio as a function of the number of frequency ordered vector components has a maximum and then falls.

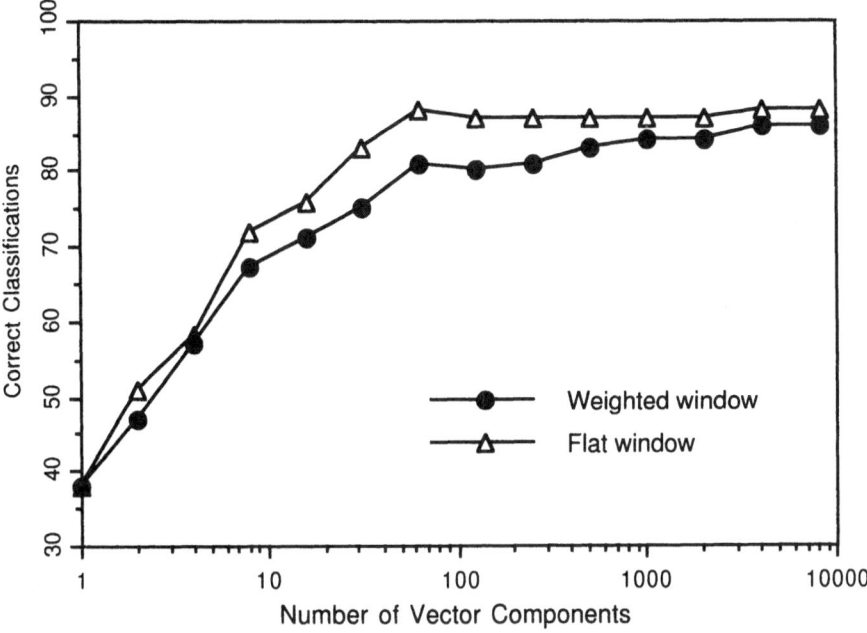

Figure 4: The plot of the number of correct classifications as a function of the number of frequency ordered vector components rises and eventually levels off.

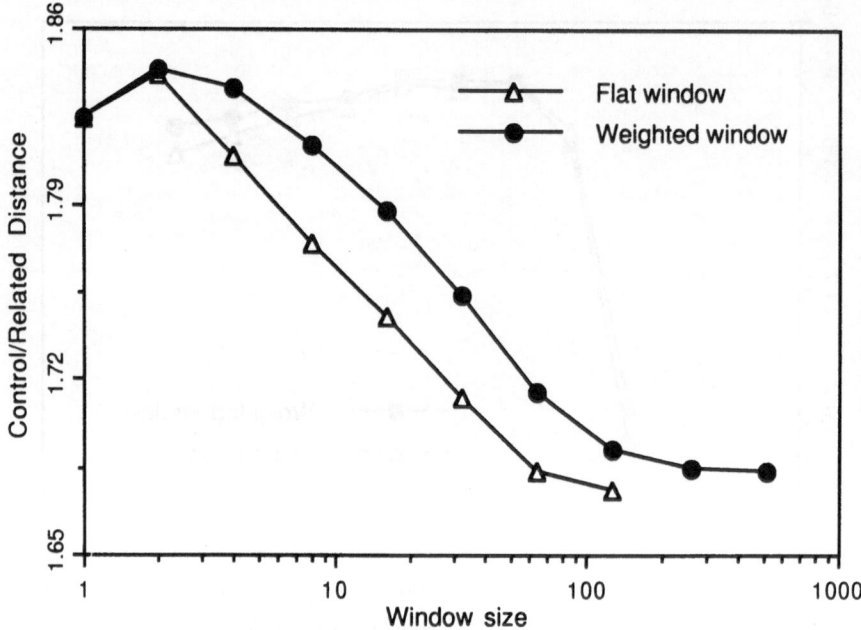

Figure 5: The plot of our Control/Related distance ratio as a function of window size has a maximum at 2 and then falls till it levels off at around 100.

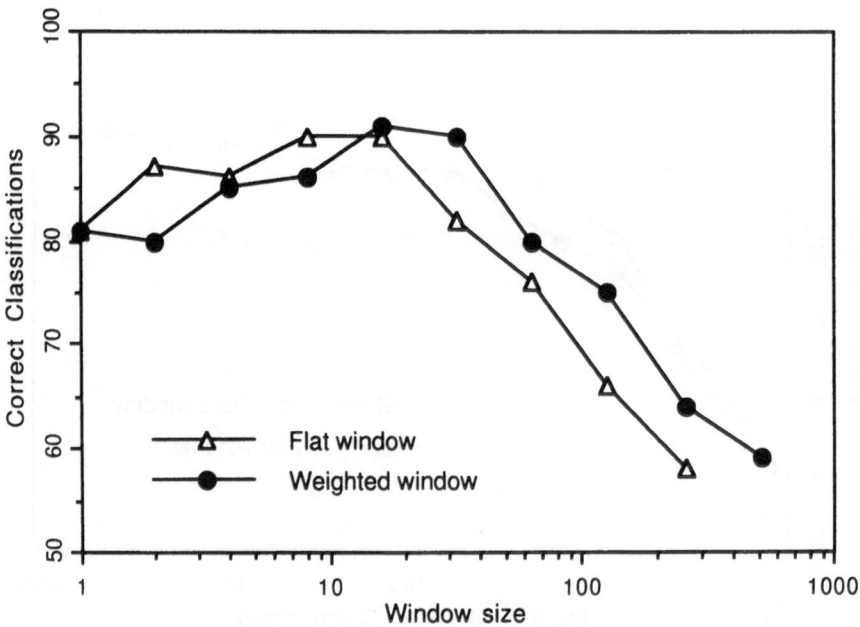

Figure 6: The plot of the number of correct classifications as a function of window size has a maximum around 16 and falls for larger windows.

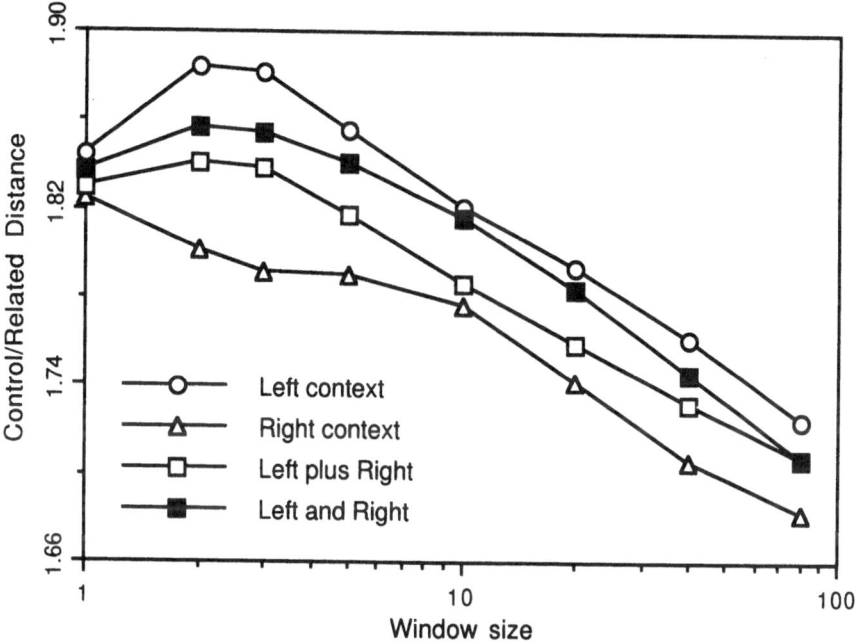

Figure 7: The plot of our Control/Related distance ratio for the four main window types as a function of window size.

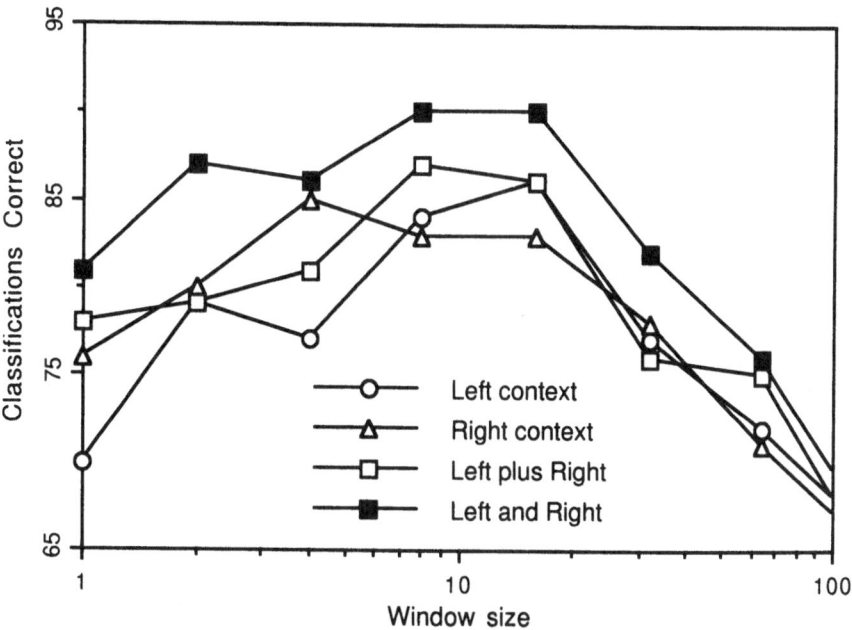

Figure 8: The plot of the number of correct classifications for the four main window types as a function of window size.

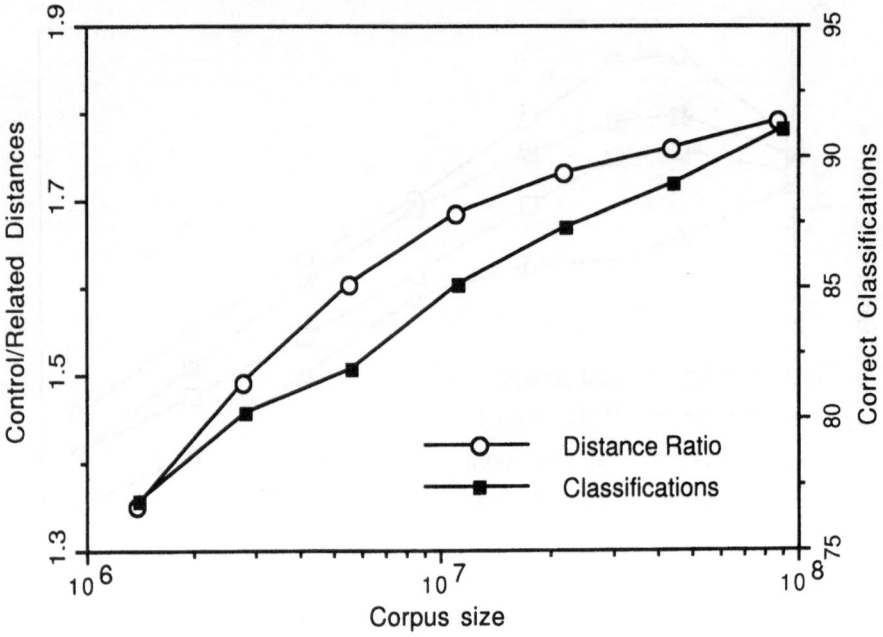

Figure 9: Both criteria for validating our semantic vectors show the expected improvement in vector quality as we increase the size of the corpus.

Figures 7 and 8 show the differences between the window types for weighted windows of different sizes for vectors of 128 components. For the ratio measure, the performance ordering is independent of the window size with the *left* contexts always giving the best vectors and the *right* contexts the worst. For the classification measure, the combined *left & right* context vectors are always the best, but the window size has a more variable effect on the others. Again, we see that the optimal choice of parameters depends on what you want to do.

Finally, Figure 9 shows how the quality of the *left & right* type vectors vary with corpus size for 128 vector components. We used near optimal weighted window sizes of 2 for the distance ratio and 16 for the classification measure. This confirms our natural expectation that, for both performance measures, the vectors do improve as we increase the corpus size, but it is slightly worrying to see that they are still improving even at the 89 million words which is the whole of the written BNC.

7 Conclusions

We have discussed how we can derive semantic representations for use in connectionist models from the word co-occurrence statistics of large text corpora. Arguments concerning their psychological realism have been suggested elsewhere [8]. Here, we have been concerned with optimising a number of parameters that affect the quality of the representations obtained from this approach, and have suggested and investigated two simple criteria for evaluating this quality.

Already we have seen that the optimal values of the various parameters will be dependent on the criteria we use. For example, our simple ratio of mean Euclidean distances between semantically related and unrelated words tells us that a co-occurrence window of two words produces the best results, whereas our measure of correct category classification suggests that a window some eight times larger is best. Preliminary analysis of other distance measures and criteria [10] suggest there is even more variability to be found. We have also seen that even with corpora of tens of millions of words, there is still room to improve our results by using still larger corpora. Clearly there is significantly more variation across the vector creation procedures and evaluation criteria than is commonly assumed.

This work, together with the preliminary application of similar corpus derived semantic representations in a connectionist lexical decision model [5], gives us confidence in the usefulness of this approach, but clearly we need more extensive analysis to determine exactly how these representations relate to those employed in real brains. For example, it does not seem appropriate to use different semantic representations for different tasks, and it is difficult to argue that our corpus derived representations are realistic if they require a corpus much larger than the total amount of written and spoken input experienced in a whole lifetime. However, variations on this theme are already looking promising [8, 10].

References

1. Battig WF & Montague WE. Category norms for verbal items in 56 categories: A replication and extension of the Connecticut category norms. Journal of Experimental Psychology Monograph 1969; 80

2. Bullinaria JA. Modelling Reading, Spelling and Past Tense Learning with Artificial Neural Networks. Brain and Language 1997; in press

3. Bullinaria JA. Modelling Lexical Decision: Who needs a lexicon? In Keating JG. (Ed) Neural Computing Research and Applications III, 62-69. Maynooth, Ireland: St. Patrick's College, 1995

4. Bullinaria JA. Connectionist Models of Reading: Incorporating Semantics. In Proceedings of the First European Workshop on Cognitive Modelling, 224-229, Berlin: Technische Universitat Berlin, 1996

5. Bullinaria JA & Huckle CC. Modelling Lexical Decision Using Corpus Derived Semantic Representations in a Connectionist Network. In Proceedings of the Fourth Neural Computational and Psychology Workshop 1997

6. Coltheart M, Curtis B, Atkins P & Haller M. Models of Reading Aloud: Dual-Route and Parallel-Distributed-Processing Approaches, Psychological Review 1993; 100: 589-608

7. Hinton GE & Shallice T. Lesioning an Attractor Network: Investigations of Acquired Dyslexia. Psychological Review 1991; 98:74-95

8. Landauer TK & Dumais ST. A Solution to Plato's Problem: The Latent Semantic Analysis Theory of Acquisition, Induction and Representation of Knowledge. Psychological Review 1997; 104: 211-240

9. Leech G. 100 million words of English: the British National Corpus. Language Research 1992, 28:1-13

10. Levy JP, Bullinaria JA & Patel M. Evaluating the Use of Word Co-Occurrence Statistics as Semantic Representations, in preparation
11. Lund K, Burgess C & Atchley RA. Semantic and Associative Priming in High-dimensional Semantic Space. In Moore JD & Lehman JF (Eds), Proceedings of the Seventeenth Annual Meeting of the Cognitive Science Society, 660-665. Lawrence Erlbaum Associates, Pittsburgh PA 1995
12. Lund K & Burgess C. Producing High-dimensional Semantic Spaces from Lexical Co-occurrence. Behaviour Research Methods, Instruments and Computers 1996; 2:203-208
13. Miller GA & Fellbaume C. Semantic networks of English. Cognition 1991; 41:197-229
14. Moss HE, Ostrin RK, Tyler LK & Marslen-Wilson WD. Accessing Different Types of Lexical Semantic Information: Evidence From Priming. Journal of Experimental Psychology: Learning, Memory and Cognition 1995; 21:863-883
15. Patel M. Using Neural Nets to Investigate Lexical Analysis. PRICAI'96: Topics in Artificial Intelligence 1996; 241-252
16. Plaut DC. Semantic and Associative Priming in a Distributed Attractor Network. Proceedings of the Seventeenth Annual Conference of the Cognitive Science Society 1995; 37-42
17. Plaut DC & Shallice T. Deep Dyslexia: A case study of connectionist neuropsychology. Cognitive Neuropsychology 1993; 10:377-500
18. Plaut DC, McClelland JL, Seidenberg MS & Patterson KE. Understanding Normal and Impaired Word Reading: Computational Principles in Quasi-Regular Domains. Psychological Review 1996; 103:56-115
19. Schutze H. Word Space. In Hanson SJ, Cowan JD & Giles CL (Eds), Advances in Neural Information Processing Systems 5, 895-902. Morgan Kaufmann, San Mateo CA, 1993.
20. Seidenberg MS & McClelland JL. A Distributed, Developmental Model of Word Recognition and Naming. Psychological Review 1989; 96:523-568

Modelling Lexical Decision Using Corpus Derived Semantic Representations in a Connectionist Network

John A. Bullinaria & Christopher C. Huckle
Department of Psychology, Birkbeck College
London, UK

Abstract

Connectionist models of the mapping from orthography or phonology to random binary semantic vectors allow the simulation of lexical decision with reaction times that show patterns of semantic and associative priming similar to those found experimentally with human subjects. The co-occurrence statistics of words in large corpora allow the generation of vectors whose distribution correlates with the perceived semantic relatedness of the words. Here we discuss the use of these more realistic corpus derived semantic representations in connectionist models of lexical decision. We find lexical decision priming that correlates with distances in the semantic vector space, but the reaction times are very noisy. Averages over many words and/or many networks are required for the relationships to become clear. The question of associative priming remains open.

1 Introduction

Connectionist models of many language processing tasks have now reached a level of sophistication whereby reasonably realistic distributed representations of semantics are required. Lexical decision (i.e. the task of deciding whether a given string of letters or phonemes is a real word) is widely used in psychological experiments to investigate the processes and representations employed in basic human language processing [1, 2, 3]. Of particular interest is the study of priming (i.e. the effect by which response is speeded through prior presentation of certain related words). The fact that we observe facilitation by semantically related words (e.g. 'jump' primes 'leap') suggests that the lexical decision process taps into some underlying semantic representation and that lexical decision experiments can be designed to explore these representations. However, priming is also found to be produced by words that are associated but not semantically related (e.g. 'pillar' primes 'society'). It is not yet clear if such associative priming needs to be explained by a different mechanism to semantic priming or if it is inherent in the properties of the same semantic representations.

Recently, connectionist models of the lexical decision process have been constructed that account for many aspects of semantic and associative priming [4, 5].

The semantic priming arises due to the overlap of distributed semantic vectors and the associative priming arises due to word co-occurrence during learning. However, these models have been based on hand-crafted and/or random binary semantic vectors. Other researchers [6] have derived semantic vectors from large text corpora and have suggested that the distances between words in this semantic vector space can account for the experimental priming results. In this paper we put these two approaches together and investigate the properties of connectionist lexical decision models based on corpus derived semantic representations. In particular, we question whether it is really possible to obtain useful results *without* considering the two approaches together.

2 Modelling Lexical Decision

Given the experimental evidence that semantics has an effect on lexical decision reaction times, it is natural to assume that the time taken to activate the appropriate semantic representation provides at least one factor in the lexical decision process. Within the conventional connectionist framework we model this by choosing (simplified) representations for the orthography/phonology and semantics of words and setting up a network to map between them. Plaut [4] chose to do this with a recurrent network trained with continuous back-propagation through time. Bullinaria [5] used a cascaded feed-forward network trained in a similar manner. Both approaches led to similar (though experimentally distinguishable) patterns of reaction times and priming. Here we shall adopt the Bullinaria [5] approach. The idea is that we explore these simple models first and only add in complicating factors as they are required by the experimental data.

For simplicity, we restrict ourselves to mono-syllabic words and represent phonology by having one unit for each possible onset, vowel and offset phoneme cluster. Each word then has three phonological input units activated. Since the phonology to semantics mapping in English is essentially random (ignoring morphological effects) it is not unreasonable to represent the semantics by random binary vectors with the interpretation that activated units correspond to the small number of relevant semantic micro-features [7]. The network will then require a sufficiently large layer of 'hidden units' in order to handle the random and non-linearly separable associations between this phonology and semantics.

Since we are aiming to model reaction times (RTs), it makes sense to think in terms of activation cascading through the network [8] as in recurrent networks rather than the typical one pass approach of standard feed-forward networks. To simulate this we discretize the time and at each time slice t take:

$$Out_i(t) = Sigmoid(Sum_i(t))$$

$$Sum_i(t) = Sum_i(t-1) + \lambda \sum_j w_{ij} Prev_j(t) - \lambda Sum_i(t-1)$$

with the output $Out_i(t)$ of each unit i the usual sigmoid of the sum of the inputs into that unit at that time. The sum of inputs $Sum_i(t)$ is given by the existing sum at time *t*−1 plus the additional weight w_{ij} dependent contribution fed through from the activation $Prev_j(t)$ of the previous layer and a natural exponential decay of activation depending on some time scale λ.

There are now two broad approaches to training the network. The quick and easy way is to note that, as long as we have static inputs, the asymptotic state of the above equations reduce to:

$$Out_i(t_\infty) = Sigmoid(Sum_i(t_\infty)) \quad , \quad Sum_i(t_\infty) = \sum_j w_{ij} Prev_j(t_\infty)$$

which are the equations for a standard non-cascaded feed-forward network. It follows that, if we only require the network to produce correct outputs for individual words, we can simply train on this asymptotic state using a standard gradient descent algorithm (such as back-propagation). The resultant trained network can then be used in a cascaded fashion to extract the RTs. If, however, we want the network to respond efficiently to sequences of words, we need to train *during* the cascading process so that the network can *learn* to make quick transitions from one set of activations to another. The network can still be trained using a standard gradient descent procedure to modify the weights w_{ij} iteratively so that the output activation errors are reduced. However, for each input word, we now need to repeat this process over many time slices as the network settles into a stable state. If we present the training words in random order, and keep the time parameter λ and learning rate η sufficiently small that large fluctuations in the weights and activations do not occur, then the network eventually learns to produce the correct outputs for any input word without any resetting of the network after the previous word.

Reaction times can then be defined in terms of time slices in a number of ways. We could simply take the time required for the network to settle into a stable output semantic state (as used by Plaut, [4]). Alternatively, we could attempt to be more explicit about modelling the lexical decision process by timing the consistency checking between the input phonology and the phonology produced by allowing activation to flow from phonology to semantics and back to phonology. This simple 'activate and check' mechanism was shown by Bullinaria [5] to be able to provide a reliable method for performing lexical decision in this kind of model, whereas details of the pattern of semantic activation alone were not sufficient. Finally, we could argue that the semantic output activations need to drive some later decision process, and that we can ignore the details of this process and take the time required for the integrated output activations to reach some threshold. This may be feasible if all the semantic vectors had equal numbers of fully activated units, but if different words have unequal numbers of activated units (e.g. to represent word concreteness [7]) or if they have non-binary activations (as we shall consider later), then this approach makes less sense. In the following we shall consider both the settling and consistency checking times, and compare their results. In each case we first activate the network for the prime input word and then, without resetting the other network activations, present the target input word and measure the RT.

In this framework, semantic priming arises naturally due to overlap of the semantic vectors. If the network activations due to the prime word are already close to that which will be activated for the target word, then it will take fewer time slices

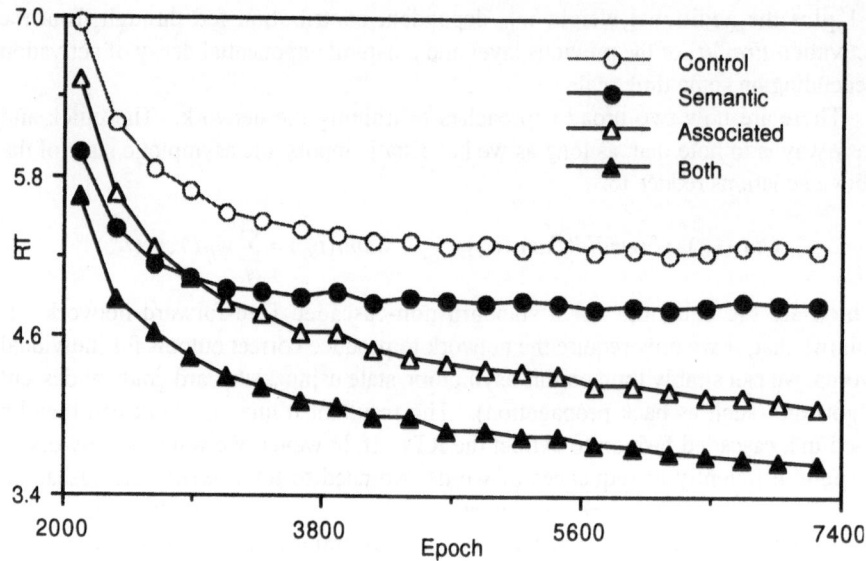

Figure 1: Semantic and associative RT priming effects during the training process.

for the target word to be activated from this state than if it were starting from the activation pattern of some unrelated control word. Associative priming may be caused by properties of the semantic vectors in a similar way, but it has been shown explicitly in connectionist models [9, 4, 5] how the facilitation can also arise purely due to co-occurrence of words in the training data. If, for example, 'society' follows 'pillar' much more often during training than would be expected by chance, then it is not surprising that an efficient learning system will be able to make use of this fact to speed its response times.

To confirm these ideas explicitly, such a phonology to semantics to phonology network with 50 phonological units, 400 hidden units and 27 semantic units was trained by back-propagation throughout the cascading process on 200 mono-syllabic words split into 40 sets of five [5]. Each set consisted of one target word, one unrelated control prime word, one semantically related prime word (with two out of three activated semantic units in common), one associated prime word (that preceded the target word 25% of the time during training) and one prime word that was both semantically and associatively related. Figure 1 shows how the mean primed target word consistency RTs varied for the four prime types during training from the point at which the network had learnt to perform the lexical decision task reliably. We find clear and highly significant ($p < 0.0001$) semantic and associative priming, but there is still a large overlap between individual RTs for the different prime types, for example at epoch 5000 we have mean RTs and standard deviations of 5.28 ± 0.30 for the control primes, 4.84 ± 0.40 for semantically related primes, 4.33 ± 0.47 for associated primes and 3.90 ± 0.32 for semantically related and associated primes. Models of this type also allow us to easily investigate various more detailed RT effects such as prime duration, target degradation, priming spanning unrelated items and mediated priming [5].

3 Corpus Based Semantic Vectors

As noted above, there has been considerable interest recently in using the vectors of statistics that describe the contexts in which words occur in large text corpora to provide a representation of their semantics. The idea is that words which occur in similar contexts will naturally tend to have similar meanings. The obvious advantages of this approach include the elimination of the need for semantic features to be generated randomly (e.g. as done by Plaut [4] and Bullinaria [5]) or by hand (e.g. as done by Plaut & Shallice [7]) and the parsimony of being able to use that statistical structure latent within the language itself. Work of this type has often been pursued from the perspective of computational linguistics [10], but Huckle [11] and Landauer & Dumais [12] have recently noted that it is also of importance for exploring psychological questions concerning human acquisition and representation of word meanings, and have discussed such methods in conjunction with the use of neural network models.

The general approach is to represent each word's distributional context using a vector of probabilities obtained by 'reading' large samples of natural language text. For every 'target word' $word_p$ being represented, each component of its semantic vector contains the probability that some other 'context word' $word_q$ will occupy a particular relationship to $word_p$ in the text. This relationship is typically one which concerns the physical distance between the two words, such as one word occurring within a window of a particular size around the other. Once vectors of this general type have been obtained, the distances between them can be calculated using various metrics to reveal similarities between word meanings and suitable transformations may be applied to provide useful semantic representations for neural network models (e.g. as discussed by Schütze [13]). Alternatively, the inter-word distances in the semantic space can be used directly as a basis for investigating psychological phenomena such as semantic priming (e.g. as suggested by Lund et al. [6]).

For reliable statistics to be obtained, an appropriately large corpus must be used, (e.g. [14]). It was convenient here to use a 10 million word corpus taken from issues of the Wall Street Journal published in 1988 and 1989. Since Zipf's law [15] informs us that the probabilities for less frequent words in a corpus of this size will rapidly become less reliable, we restricted ourselves to using only the highest frequency items. We actually used the most frequent 1000 words in the corpus as our target words and the most frequent 200 words as our context words.

This still left us with many possibilities for deriving useful semantic vectors and choosing different values for the various parameters that specify the vector extraction process will affect the quality of the vectors obtained [14]. For the purposes of this paper, however, it was not crucial that we used the best vectors possible, as long as their distributional properties were sufficiently typical. For each of the 1000 target words, we calculated the 200 dimensional vector in which each component contained the probability that a particular context word would occur within a window of two words to the left of the target word in the corpus, and a similar vector for a window of two words to the right. The window length of two words was chosen following exploratory work which suggested this captured the words' semantics reasonably well. Finally, we concatenated our left and right context vectors to give a 400 dimensional vector of probabilities for each of the target words. This approach to representing the target words' semantics is thus similar to that adopted by Lund et al. [6].

4 The Combined Model

Unfortunately, using our corpus derived vectors in the existing lexical decision model described above was not a totally straightforward matter. Our first problem was that, if we are to train our networks in a reasonable amount of time, we need to keep the networks as small as possible, which in turn means minimising the dimensionality of our semantic vector space. For our purposes, principal component analysis proved to be a convenient procedure. The 400 dimensional semantic vectors were projected onto the 30 dimensional sub-space containing the maximum variance. This provided much lower dimensional vectors with relatively little loss of information and had the added advantage that we lost a lot of the noise in the process. The inter-word distances in the original space and the sub-space correlated well (Pearson $r = 0.94$). The psychological relevance of this dimensional reduction procedure for corpus derived semantic representations has been discussed recently by Landauer & Dumais [12].

The second problem arose with the standard use of sigmoidal activation functions in our network. For our non-binary outputs it was appropriate to use a linear activation function for the network outputs rather than sigmoids. Since the distribution of vector components was rather skewed towards small values anyway, which corresponds to the central linear region of the sigmoid rather that the saturated extremes, this difference is probably not crucial.

What might be more crucial however, is the decision to use the non-binary components that come naturally out of the corpus analysis rather than attempting to convert them into the binary form commonly used in connectionist systems. Since we already know that we can get semantic and associative priming using random binary semantic vectors [4, 5], it seemed appropriate go on to investigate the more ambitious case of non-binary vectors. Moreover, in the human case, it would be natural to consider our semantic representations to be 'hidden representations' that are learnt by the brain, and it is rare to find hidden representations developing purely binary values in connectionist models. We shall see later how our networks behave rather differently when based on real, rather than binary, outputs.

The next thing we have to consider is that the Wall Street Journal is a rather atypical source of the English language. Certain word pairs (such as 'wall street' and 'dow jones') occur together much more frequently than in normal English, and other words (such as 'bush' and 'ford') are often used in atypical ways. In general, it is interesting and important to study such words, since they are simply extreme examples of what does happen in real language, but to avoid possible artefacts that these words may cause in the current study, we simply removed them from our network training set. We also removed 16 homographs (e.g. 'lead' and 'row') which would clearly have problematic semantic vectors.

In the original model reviewed in Section 2, Bullinaria [5] simulated mappings between phonology and semantics. Here (as Plaut did in his model [4]) we consider the mappings between orthography and semantics. Given our simplified abstract input representations and the regularity of the orthography to phonology relationship, the distinction is unlikely to be crucial, but it should be kept in mind. As with other models that map to semantics, the randomness of the mapping means that in order to train the network in a reasonable amount of time, we need to restrict the number of training words, which also allows us to use less hidden units. It then follows that we have to reduce the size of the input space so that the word distribution does not become unnaturally sparse. To this end we restricted ourselves to monosyllables with orthography made up of the most common onset consonant clusters (30), vowel clusters (18) and offset consonant clusters (38) plus two units to code for the presence or absence of a final 'e'. Our highest frequency set of 1000 target words contained 270 words consistent with all the above restrictions. These all occurred at least 1297 times in the corpus and were within the most frequent 993 words. Finally, in an attempt to keep the weights and weight changes at values comparable to the binary output networks, we set the arbitrary scale and origin of the semantic vector space so that the mean activation of each semantic unit was zero and the overall standard deviation was 0.14, with maximum component 1.95 and minimum component −1.27.

Since all our 270 words are classed as high frequency in the experimental studies, we did not attempt to impose a word frequency structure on our network training regime. We trained our main network for 75000 epochs on these words using back-propagation on the asymptotic output patterns (with 270 hidden units, sum squared error measure, learning rate $\eta = 0.01$, no momentum). By this point the network was able to perform reliable lexical decision by input-output orthography consistency checking. The RTs were then extracted as above, except that we used a reduced $\lambda = 0.01$ to give a more accurate approximation to the continuous process. The settling RTs were defined as the number of time slices required for all output activation changes per time slice to fall below 0.0001. The consistency RTs were defined as the number of time slices required for the total difference between the input and output orthography activations to fall below 0.1. Note that the precise RT criteria are somewhat arbitrary. The way to proceed is (as in [16]) to vary the various parameters and criteria and show that the resultant RTs are highly correlated over a wide range of reasonable values, and then pick central values within that range. The values used here were also chosen to result in similar RT means and standard deviations for the two RT approaches.

Finally, we also attempted to train an identical network on the same words throughout the cascading process with no resetting of activation between words (150 time slices per word, $\lambda = 0.1$, sum squared error measure, learning rate $\eta = 0.0001$, no momentum), though, as we shall discuss in Section 6, the network never managed to learn to perform reliable lexical decision.

5 Semantic Priming

Needless to say, we checked that our closest semantic vectors (defined in terms of Euclidean distances) did actually correspond to words that were semantically related (the shortest distances were 21 between 'will' and 'would', and 21 between 'three'

Prime Set	Distances	Settling Times	Consistency Times
C1	561 (42)	669 (44)	709 (77)
C2	459 (43)	655 (58)	699 (75)
C3	399 (53)	638 (47)	676 (83)
P3	96 (54)	591 (72)	586 (91)
P2	86 (52)	586 (71)	569 (93)
P1	71 (44)	581 (78)	570 (101)

Table 1. The simulated primed RTs compared with distances in semantic space.

and 'four') and the most distant words really were unrelated (the longest distances were 737 between 'lot' and 'past', and 646 between 'same' and 'try') though in this paper we shall not attempt to match our network results to real lexical decision experiments. To do that reliably we would need to train a much larger number of considerably more realistic networks on many more words and use semantic vectors derived from significantly more representative corpora.

As we discussed in Section 2, semantic priming has been found before in network models such as ours [5]. In these random binary target networks, the semantic Euclidean distances were all $\sqrt{2} \sim 1.41$ between semantically related words and $\sqrt{6} \sim 2.45$ between un-related words, yet there was still a large distribution of RTs and varying degrees of priming. Clearly factors other than simple semantic distances are determining these results. Inevitably, each RT will be determined by the unit i that is the slowest to update its activation. Looking at the above cascade equations we see that, to first approximation, the number of time slices required to move from the prime output to the settled target output will be given by the difference of the final $Sum_i(t_\infty)$ between the prime and target divided by the average step size which will be related to the $Sum_i(t_\infty)$ for the target. Unfortunately, we cannot use this as an easy way to predict the RTs, because determining the average step size is harder than actually running the network, but it does tell us something useful about the RTs. The problem with sigmoids and binary output targets is that the sigmoids saturate, which means that very large random variations may arise in the Sum_i's during learning without affecting the actual network outputs very much and hence without being constrained by the training algorithm. Given that the values of the Sum_i's have such a big influence on the RTs, it is no wonder that the RTs are so noisy. With our non-binary semantic vectors we have no output sigmoids and the output activations are the Sum_i's themselves which are learnt to be particular values. We may thus expect to suffer less seriously from random effects than the binary case. But is this true (given that we still have sigmoids at the hidden layer) and does it really allow the simulated priming results to correlate better with the distances between our semantic vectors?

There are many ways in which we can illustrate our network priming results. One useful approach is to look at the RTs for each of our 270 words when primed by the three closest words in semantic space (sets P1, P2, P3) compared to the RTs when primed by the three furthest words (sets C1, C2, C3). The mean distances and RTs are shown in Table 1 (with standard deviations in brackets). The first thing to notice is that both forms of simulated RT show faster times for the prime sets (P's)

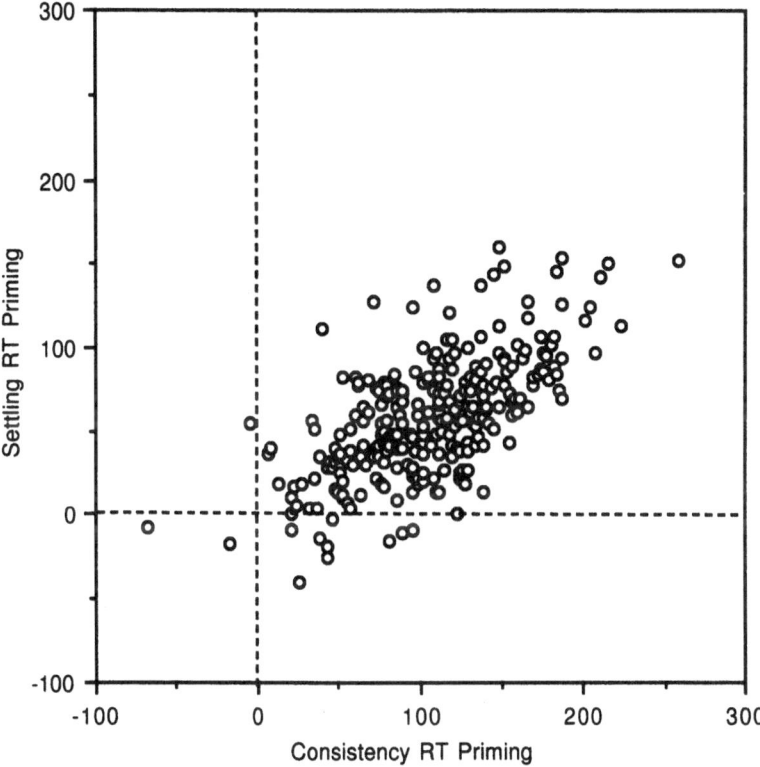

Figure 2: Comparison of priming results for settling and consistency RTs.

than the control sets (C's), so we do find semantic priming (and this is highly significant, $p < 0.0001$). However, it is clear from the standard deviations that the RTs are very noisy and that, as we also found in the binary target networks, there is no simple relationship between the Euclidean distances and the RTs. Indeed, if we take what we would expect to be the maximum priming result, i.e. the differences in RTs between control prime set C1 and semantically close prime set P1, we find the effect is not always even in the right direction. Not only do both RT approaches show some negative priming, but they also fail to agree on which words this happens for. For the settling RTs we have a mean priming of 88 (standard deviation 76), minimum −72, maximum +293. For the consistency RTs we have 140 (101), −135, +429. If we average over all three sets of primes and control primes, the priming is only slightly more reliably positive: 68 (48), −69, +205 for settling and 119 (61), −38, +322 for consistency. At least every time we test a given trained network on a particular prime-target pair, we get the same RT. In experiments on human subjects, noise arises even here (e.g. due to effects such as concentration, tiredness, episodic memory recall, and so on) to give a distribution of RTs. Since distributions of priming results are also found in humans, there is no real problem for our models in that respect, but it does make it rather difficult to uncover the precise relationship between the semantic space distances and the network priming results.

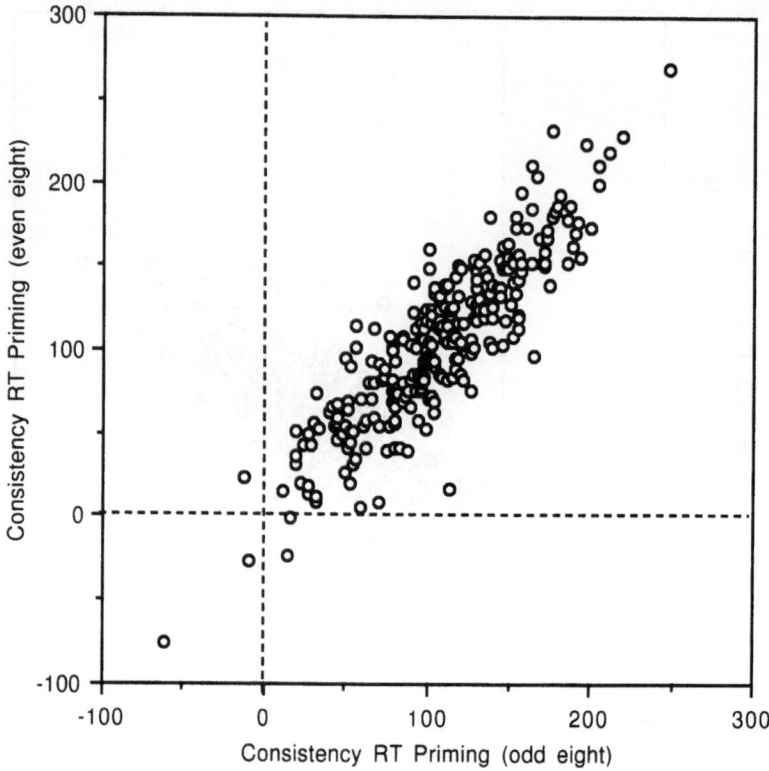

Figure 3: Reliability of consistency RTs for individual words.

To see past the random noise and to reveal the reliable underlying effects we really need to look at many networks in the same way that experimental results are averaged over many human subjects. We therefore trained another fifteen networks with exactly the same architecture and words, but with different random initial connection weights and learning rates, and obtained results similar to those of our original network. The individual word primings did not correlate particularly well between the networks – we typically found Pearson r ~ 0.4 to 0.5 for consistency priming and Pearson r ~ 0.5 to 0.6 for settling priming across networks. This was comparable to the correlation between the consistency and settling priming within an individual network – typically Pearson r ~ 0.45 to 0.55. However, each network did show a similar, and highly consistent, average semantic priming effect for both settling and consistency RTs. Averaging over all sixteen networks and the three primes and controls per word gave a settling priming of 58 (36), –40, +160 and a consistency priming of 106 (47), –69, +257. Figure 2 shows the actual distributions of average priming and compares the settling and consistency results. The correlation between the two approaches has now risen to Pearson r = 0.65.

We can get a fair indication of the reliability of these average priming results by comparing the results obtained from two disjoint random subsets of eight of our sixteen networks. Figure 3 shows how well the consistency primes correlate

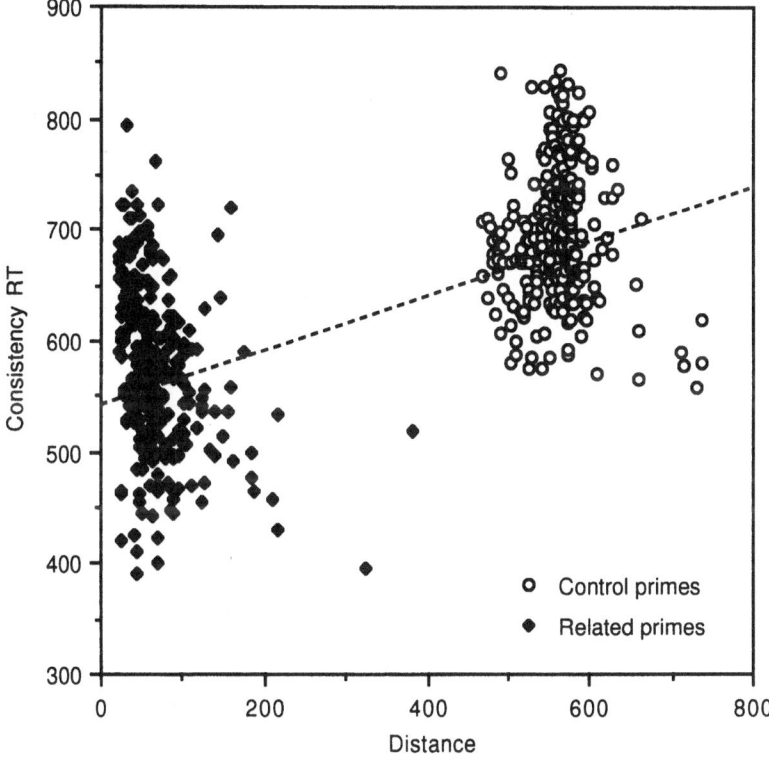

Figure 4: Comparison of the semantic vector space distances with consistency RTs showing a significant, but very noisy, semantic priming effect.

(Pearson $r = 0.88$) and we get a very similar pattern for the settling primes (Pearson $r = 0.91$). These results suggest that averages over sufficiently many networks and/or primes can cancel out the noise to leave reliable semantic relatedness effects together with any other (e.g. orthographic, consistency, neighbourhood, RT approach) effects not inherent in individual semantic vectors themselves. It is unfortunate, given the computational resources necessary to train the networks to map between the orthographic and semantic representations, that so many networks are required in order to obtain a clear picture of what is going on.

The final question we need to ask is what exactly is causing the spread of priming that is becoming clear in plots such as Figure 3. The natural first guess is that it is simply the Euclidean distances between the words in our semantic vector space [6]. Figure 4 shows how these distances for individual word pairs (the P1's and C1's) compare with the consistency RTs averaged over all sixteen networks. We get a similar pattern for the settling RTs. Once again we can see that there is more involved than simple Euclidean distances. It may well turn out that city block distances or particular information theoretic measures can provide a better indicator of priming, but, since these are not preserved by the principal component dimensional reduction, it is rather difficult to investigate this reliably.

In the long term, we really need to investigate the networks' performance much more closely. One approach is to look at the words which stand out as being reliably good or bad primers and see what is special about them. Unfortunately, the variability between networks makes this rather difficult and we often find that a given RT is determined by one particular output unit that has no obvious significance. Another problem is that the current networks are still far too small scale. Despite our restrictions on the orthographic space, there are still some graphemes that only occur in two of the training words, whilst others occur up to 57 times. Similarly some words occur in sparsely populated areas of semantic space whereas others have several close neighbours. These factors, which presumably contribute to the spread of priming results, may well disappear in more realistic networks. It is clear that there is much more work to be done in this area.

6 Associative Priming

As we discussed in Section 2, for random binary semantic vectors, we find that training our networks throughout the cascading process allows them to use any frequent word co-occurrences that arise during training to speed their RTs, and hence they automatically exhibit associative priming [5]. This is largely because such sigmoidal networks with binary output targets have an inbuilt flexibility that enables them to make the weight adjustments appropriate for an advantage in RT with little increase the output error. For example, weight changes could be made that result in a large shift (from -15.0 to -5.0 say) in a $Sum_i(t_\infty)$, with only a small increase (~ 0.007) in the activation error $Out_i(t_\infty)$.

In our linear non-binary output networks it is much harder to gain an RT advantage in this way, since any significant change to an output $Sum_i(t_\infty)$ will directly introduce a significant error into the $Out_i(t_\infty)$. When using the standard cascaded learning approach described in Section 2 in this case, the output errors that inevitably occur during the word transitions cause weight changes that disrupt the networks' output performance to such an extent that it is very difficult for the networks to learn accurate semantic representations (as checked by testing them on the orthography to semantics mapping) and they are hence unable to perform reliable lexical decision by input-output orthography consistency checking. However, if we artificially reduce the disruption by increasing λ (to 0.5), the network *is* able to learn sufficiently well to end up performing lexical decision reasonably reliably, and the RTs do exhibit semantic and associative priming. Both types of priming are significant but, compared with human experimental results, the associative priming is too small in comparison to the semantic priming.

It thus remains a rather open question as to whether human brains are able to exploit this word co-occurrence mechanism with fixed semantic representations (such as derived from corpus statistics) and hence exhibit associative priming. It is possible that the semantic representations must themselves be subject to adjustment during training in order to show this effect. It is also possible that the experimental associative priming is already inherent in the 'semantic' vectors without the need for any additional training effects. It may even be possible that additional connections between associated words (i.e. their semantic micro-feature units) are employed.

Clearly, many more network simulations are required to resolve this matter. Of course, it should be noted that the corresponding experimental results are far from clear cut either. Separate claims have been made that all associative priming is really a form of semantic priming (e.g. by Lund et al. [6]), that all semantic priming is actually associative priming (e.g. by Shelton & Martin [2]), and that both forms of priming exist in their own right (e.g. by Moss et al. [3, 9]).

7 Conclusions

The use of a cascaded activation approach in neural network models of simple mappings provides a natural procedure for simulating realistic distributions of RTs including priming and speed-accuracy trade-off effects [16]. Previously this approach has been used to show how connectionist models of the mappings between simplified representations of orthography/phonology and random binary vector representations of semantics can account for many experimental results concerning semantic and associative priming of lexical decision RTs [5]. In this paper we have investigated the use in these lexical decision models of non-binary semantic vectors derived from the word co-occurrence statistics of large text corpora. Our main conclusion is that there *is* a significant relationship between the prime-target distances in the underlying corpus derived semantic vector spaces and the priming in the connectionist networks that use these vectors, *but* the relationship is very noisy. In the same way that experiments need to control for many other factors and average over many test words and many subjects to show clear priming results, so do the connectionist simulations.

We believe that the simplified and small scale connectionist lexical decision models presented here show much promise and already exhibit many of the essential features required of a complete model of this task. We have also identified and solved a number of problems inherent in this class of model. However, it is clear from the preliminary results presented here that further investigations employing larger and more representative corpora and many larger and more realistic networks will be required before we can be confident of the precise relationships between the various corpus, neural network and experimental results.

References

1. Neely JH. Semantic Priming Effects in Visual Word Recognition: A Selective Review of Current Findings and Theories. In Besner D& Humphreys GW (Eds) Basic Processes in Reading: Visual Word Recognition. Erlbaum, Hillsdale NJ, 1991, pp 264-336
2. Shelton JR & Martin RC. How Semantic is Automatic Semantic Priming? Journal of Experimental Psychology: Learning, Memory and Cognition 1992; 18:191-210
3. Moss HE, Ostrin RK, Tyler LK & Marslen-Wilson WD. Accessing Different Types of Lexical Semantic Information: Evidence From Priming. Journal of Experimental Psychology: Learning, Memory and Cognition 1995; 21:1-21

4. Plaut DC. Semantic and Associative Priming in a Distributed Attractor Network. Proceedings of the Seventeenth Annual Conference of the Cognitive Science Society. Erlbaum, Mahwah NJ, 1995, pp 37-42

5. Bullinaria JA. Modelling Lexical Decision: Who Needs a Lexicon? In Keating JG (Ed) Neural Computing Research and Applications III. St. Patrick's College, Maynooth Ireland, 1995, pp 62-69

6. Lund K, Burgess C & Atchley RA. Semantic and Associative Priming in High-Dimensional Semantic Space. Proceedings of the Seventeenth Annual Conference of the Cognitive Science Society. Erlbaum, Mahwah NJ, 1995, pp 660-665

7. Plaut DC & Shallice T. Deep Dyslexia: A Case Study of Connectionist Neuro-psychology. Cognitive Neuropsychology 1993; 10:377-500

8. McClelland JL. On the Time Relations of Mental Processes: An Examination of Systems of Processes in Cascade. Psychological Review 1979; 86:287-330

9. Moss HE, Hare ML, Day P & Tyler LK. A Distributed Memory Model of the Associative Boost in Semantic Priming. Connection Science 1994; 6:413-427

10. Brown PF, Della Pietra VJ, deSouza PV, Lai JC & Mercer RL. Class-based n-gram models of natural language. Computational Linguistics 1992; 18:467-479

11. Huckle C. Grouping Words Using Statistical Context. Proceedings of the Seventh Conference of the European Chapter of the Association for Computational Linguistics. Morgan Kaufmann, San Francisco CA, 1995, pp 278-280

12. Landauer TK & Dumais ST. A Solution to Plato's Problem: The Latent Semantic Analysis Theory of Acquisition, Induction and Representation of Knowledge. Psychological Review 1997; 104: 211-240

13. Schütze H. Word Space. In Hanson SJ, Cowan JD & Giles CL (Eds) Advances in Neural Information Processing Systems 5. Morgan Kauffmann, San Mateo CA, 1993, pp 895-902

14. Patel M, Bullinaria JA & Levy JP. Extracting Semantic Representations from Large Text Corpora. Proceedings of the Fourth Neural Computation and Psychology Workshop. Springer Verlag, London, 1997

15. Zipf GK. The Psycho-biology of Language. Houghton Mifflin, Boston, 1935

16. Bullinaria JA. Modelling Reaction Times. In Smith LS & Hancock PJB (Eds), Neural Computation and Psychology. Springer, London, 1997, pp 34-48

Semantic Representation and Priming in a Self-organizing Lexicon

Will Lowe

Centre for Cognitive Science, Edinburgh University
Edinburgh, Scotland

Abstract

This paper presents a model of the mental lexicon and its formation, based on the self-organizing neural network. When exposed to raw text, the model clusters words according to their semantic relatedness to form a semantic network [7]. Simulations using artificial data are described that show how co-occurrence information can be used to create a low-dimensional representation of lexical semantics. The model also suggests a novel explanation of semantic priming based on topographic organization and co-occurrence statistics. A simulation that implements this explanation is presented, and the model is tested against priming effects found in Moss *et al.*'s [25] semantic priming experiment.

1 Introduction

Priming studies are an important source of evidence for the structure of the mental lexicon. When subjects are presented briefly with a letter string, followed by another, and asked to decide whether the latter is a real word, the response time is reliably faster when both strings are related than when they are unrelated. Priming effects can be found using stimuli that are graphemically, syntactically or semantically related [26, 35].

There has been substantial progress in modelling lexical representations using neural networks [31, 28]. However, the question of lexical-*semantic* representation has been mostly overlooked. In particular there are few computational models of where semantic representations come from, and how they can be acquired ([23] but see [17, 3]).

The model presented here is an attempt to address these issues. It is inspired by two rather different approaches to semantic representation from cognitive psychology and computational linguistics. In the next section I consider two approaches to lexical-semantic representation from cognitive psychology. In section 3, I discuss techniques and results from statistical natural language processing that are drawn upon in subsequent sections. Section 4 contains a short description of the model and presents simulations using artificial and then real stimuli. There is a short conclusion.

2 Network Models of Lexical-semantics

2.1 Localist Models

One influential theory of lexical-semantic representation from cognitive psychology is based on the semantic network. A semantic network consists of a set of nodes and connections of varying strengths, or lengths, between them [7, 1]. Each concept is assigned a node, and connection strengths reflect the amount of conceptual relevance each node has to its partner. The stronger, or shorter, connections represent a high degree of semantic relatedness. Weaker, or longer, connections hold between less related nodes. In a lexical-semantic network (LSN), each node represents a word and the distance between nodes reflects the amount of semantic similarity between each word [24].

LSN theories explain semantic priming effects in the following way: Each node has an activation level. When a stimulus is presented it activates all nodes in the network to some degree. If one node is activated strongly enough its activation will pass a threshold and fire. The stimulus will be recognized as that word. Each time a word is presented, activation spreads from the most activated node to nearby nodes, decaying over time. For example, if 'doctor' is presented shortly before 'nurse', the node associated with 'nurse' will reach threshold faster and fire sooner. Its resting activation level is raised by activation spreading from 'doctor' during the inter-stimulus interval [35].

LSN theories provide a straightforward and intuitive account of how semantic relatedness is represented, and how priming occurs. However, there are a number of unresolved problems with the approach. First, what information determines whether words are semantically related or unrelated, and therefore determines the connections between nodes ? In the light of this problem it is difficult to explain how an LSN could be formed during development [23]. Second, it is not clear how an LSN should be implemented in the brain — are nodes best understood as individual neurons, as cell-assemblies [29] or as functional objects, implemented in a distributed manner at the level of cortical structure ?

A full LSN theory should give an account of the evidence that determines the organization of the network. It should also show how this information can be used to create the network during development.

2.2 Distributed Models

An alternative model of lexical semantic representation describes a word not as a single node, but as a pattern of activity across many nodes [21]. Representing meaning as a set of values over a large number of dimensions is also appealing, since it allows a computational interpretation of feature-based semantic theories. In a feature-based theory, each concept is represented by a distribution of numerical values over a set of semantic features (usually perceptual properties possessed by instances of the concept). The values ascribed to each feature can be treated as a vector that determines the location of the concept in feature space.

Distributed semantic representations can be used as target values in a multi-layer perceptron trained with a gradient-descent algorithm [28, 3]. Alternatively they can be associated with feature vectors for each word using a Hopfield net [20]).

In these models of semantic priming, a stimulus vector representing the prime is presented, and the network begins to settle onto the semantic vector that has been associated with it during training. If the stimulus vector representing the target is then presented, before the network has settled fully, then the time taken for the network to settle on the new target semantic vector is less if the two semantic vectors are similar. Similarity can be understood as the number of shared values (for binary vectors) or as the Euclidean distance between vectors (for continuous values). In Hopfield net models which use binary values [20] the settling time of the network after the target presentation will tend to be proportional to the Hamming distance between the prime and target semantic vectors. In continuous models [28, 3], the settling time will tend to be a function of the Euclidean distance between the prime and target semantic vectors. However, many network models either use hand-coded or arbitrary feature sets to represent word meaning (eg. [20, 28]). This makes it difficult to test the model against particular experimental results.

It would be desirable to have a model that maintains the intuitive aspects of LSN theories, and provides a biologically reasonable explanation of how the network is formed. Such a model would necessarily include a theory of what information determines the final shape of the network. It should then be possible to relate the model to experimental data.

3 Statistical Natural Language Processing

Recent work in computational linguistics suggests that large amounts of semantic information can be extracted automatically from large text corpora on the basis of lexical co-occurrence information [6, 30]. Since co-occurrence information is typically continuous valued and of high dimensionality, this approach is well suited to neural network implementation [10, 11].

The motivation for this approach comes from the following inference: The structure of a speaker's semantic representations determine, in part, the distributional patterns that are present in her speech. These distributional patterns show up as statistical regularities in the co-occurrence patterns of single words. We ought, therefore, to be able to infer the distributional regularities of speech from the patterns of individual word co-occurrences. From this distributional information it should be possible to create a language model that is functionally similar to the semantic system of the speaker, in the limit of many samples. This approach is attractive since it may be pursued automatically, using only text or speech corpora as data.

The approach has enjoyed considerable success in the fields of speech recognition and machine translation ([6] for a review) With a large enough sample, there is sufficient information in a strictly linguistic environment to recover much useful semantic structure. It seems reasonable to investigate how the the brain could make use of such information.

This research has become relevant to psycholinguistics since the discovery that semantic and associative priming effects in lexical decision are significantly correlated with co-occurrence statistics [19, 34]. Lund, Burgess and Atchley [19] constructed a high-dimensional space on the basis of lexical co-occurrence statistics extracted from the Usenet. In a comparison with stimuli from Shelton and Martin's [32] semantic priming experiment, Lund *et al.* found that words that were close together in their co-occurrence space gave larger priming effects than those further away. Similar results have also been observed for off-line measures of semantic similarity [17, 22].

It seems reasonable to take these observations as converging evidence that language users make use of co-occurrence information latent in the linguistic environment. The model presented here is an attempt to explore how much semantic representation can be extracted from *only* this type of information.

One practical problem with the statistical NLP approach, and with its psychological counterparts, is that very high-dimensional spaces are difficult to work with; computations suffer from the 'curse of dimensionality' [2], which necessitates complex smoothing techniques to deal with unseen co-occurrences.

In this paper, we explore the possibility that *two* dimensional spaces are adequate to represent semantic relatedness between words, at least for the purposes of modelling lexical decision. The two dimensions are intended to represent the dimensions of the cortex.

4 Model

The following section describes a model of lexical-semantic representation based on the self-organizing map. The aim of the model is to explain how a semantic network can be formed in a biologically reasonable way, on the basis of readily available linguistic information.

4.1 The Self-organizing Map

The Self-organizing Map (SOM) is a neural network intended to explain how the cerebral cortex can become organized topographically [13, 14, 16]. Topographic organization is present when the implicit spatial structure of an input signal is retained in a low-dimensional neural representation, such that nearby points in the neural representation refer to nearby points in the input space [13]. Topographically organized cortex is ubiquitous in mammalian nervous systems; it reflects simple input signals in early sensory processing [12] and complex signals such as geometrical shapes, individual faces and gestures in the temporal cortex [36, 27].

The SOM consists of a two-dimensional grid of output units, fully connected to an input signal. By the end of training the SOM defines a smooth non-linear mapping from the input space onto the grid of output units (see [14] for details of the algorithm). The SOM has a straightforward physiological interpretation: it models the development of feature selectivity and topographic organization due to lateral connectivity among cortical nerve cells [33, 15].

In the simulations described below, two versions of the model are used. The first simulation is intended to show how semantic representations for words from artificial grammar can be developed from scratch by training an SOM on successively re-estimated co-occurrence vectors (see [18] for details). The second simulation trains a SOM on pre-computed co-occurrence vectors derived from a real corpus and is used to replicate part of a priming experiment.

4.2 Artificial Corpus Simulation

4.2.1 Input data

In this simulation, input data for the network are taken from a corpus generated by a small stochastic context-free grammar [9]. The grammar was used to create a 10,000 word corpus with simple distributional properties [1]. The corpus contains no punctuation or other clues to sentence structure. An example of the text is shown below:

dragon eat man girl like boy

Using an artificial grammar makes it possible to systematically alter the distributional properties of the input data, and to verify that the network is in fact extracting relevant information.

4.2.2 Training

Each word in the 29 word vocabulary is associated with a 58 element co-occurrence vector. The value of element n ($1 \leq n \leq 29$) reflects the number of times the nth word in the vocabulary has occurred directly *before* the word in question. The value of element n ($30 \leq n \leq 58$) reflects the number of times word $n - 29$ has occurred directly *after* the word in question. Since the model starts with no prior semantic information, all co-occurrence vectors contain zeros before training.

Training vectors are generated by passing a three word window over the corpus, advancing one word at a time. Each time the window moves forward, a new word appears at its centre and the vector for that word is updated. The vector elements representing the previous and following words are incremented by one, the vector is normalized to unit length, and it is presented as a training pattern to the SOM. The process continues until the end of the corpus is reached.

The co-occurrence vectors associated with each word are increasingly accurate unnormalized estimates of the probability of word n occurring before the

---

[1] Thanks to Martin Redington and Chris Huckle for providing a PROLOG implementation of the grammar.

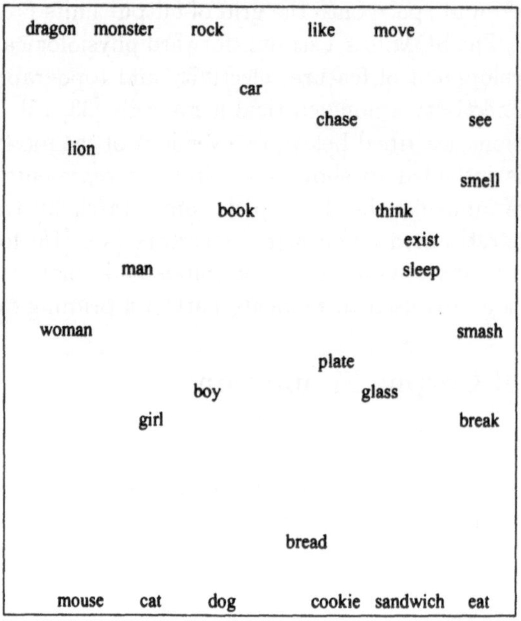

Figure 1: Most activated units for each word in the vocabulary after training

current word, and the probability of word n occurring after the current word, for all words n. Note that the network sees statistically accurate co-occurrence information only towards the end of training. For the majority of the training time, the information is inaccurate and noisy, though this does not appear to compromise the final performance.

4.2.3 Results

Figure 1 shows which units is most active when the co-occurrence vector for each word is presented at the end of training. The coordinates of the output unit grid have been removed. Consistent with the LSN approach, the network clusters each word with other words that are used in similar contexts. Similar words tend to be nearer to one another than to dissimilar words. Verbs have been represented together on the right side: Psychological verbs 'see' and 'smell' are represented together, as are destructive verbs 'smash' and 'break' within the main verb group. On the left side, categorical similarity among the nouns is equally well preserved — human and animal nouns group separately, adjacent to one another.   However, Figure 1 does not reflect the full extent of the net's categorization. 'Man' is equidistant from 'boy' and from 'book', but is related much more closely to one than the other. This fact is represented by the network, not in the pattern of most active units, but by the pattern of activation across *all* output units. Each unit is partially activated by all words, though it responds most strongly to one. In this sense, the output representation contains

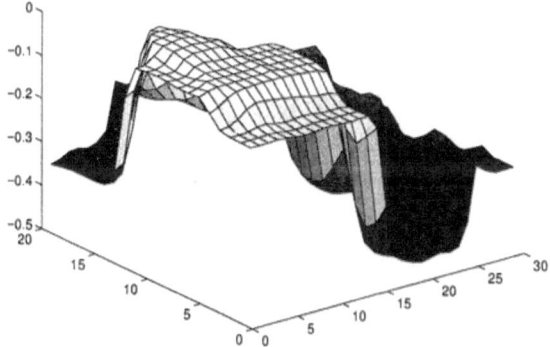

Figure 2: Activation plot for the word 'man'.

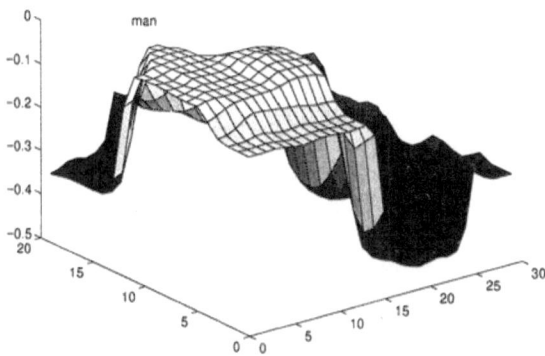

Figure 3: Activation plot for the word 'boy' with 'man' marked.

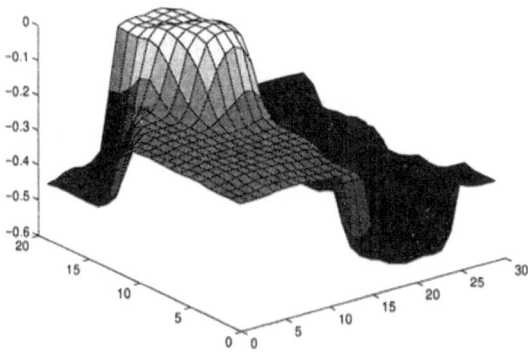

Figure 4: Activation plot for the word 'book' with 'man' marked.

elements of both localist and distributed coding. The network is localist to the extent that each word has a unit that is most active when that word appears, but distributed to the extent that the number and activation of units *between* each most active unit reflects semantic relatedness; the identity of the most active unit for a word only reflects that word's semantics if the state of other units is known.

Figures 2, 3 and 4 show activation plots for 'man', and for 'boy' and 'book' with the unit most active for 'man' marked. The x and y axes show the indices of each SOM unit. The z axis represents the amount of activation in each unit for a given stimuli (the activation values for each unit are given by the z values at the intersections of the surface grid-lines). The z axis has a maximum value of 0 because the map units are active in proportion to the Euclidean distance between their weight vectors and the input vector. Since units that are specialized to a particular word vector have weight values that are nearly identical to that vector, the Euclidean distance between the weight vector and the word vector is small. In Figures 2, 3 and 4 the indices of each SOM unit are plotted against the inverse of its activation so that it is easy to locate the most active unit and its neighbours. Note the smooth transitions between activation values across units.

4.2.4 Semantic Priming

The activation patterns shown in Figures 2, 3 and 4 allow an explanation of priming that is influenced by both localist and distributed theories.

We assume that word recognition advances all unit activations to the levels particular to the recognized word in small amounts over a brief time period, and that unit activations then decay over time until the activation surface is flat. The explanation of semantic priming is then straightforward: If a prime word is presented before activation levels have fully decayed, then residual activation will still be present in some units. For example, let 'man' be the target word, and let the related word 'boy' and the unrelated 'book' be primes. 'Man' will take longer to be recognized as a word when preceded by 'book' than when it is preceded by 'boy' because the activation surface for 'man' is almost identical to that of 'boy', but quite different from the activation surface for 'book'; fewer increments are necessary to convert the activation surface for 'boy' into the surface for 'man' than to convert the surface for 'book' into the surface for 'man' (a network implementation with explicit lateral inhibition and excitation is in progress).

This account of priming is similar to LSN models, but settles in a similar manner to distributed models. Priming effects depend essentially on the distance between the prime and target words because the the map is organized such that activation tends to drop off with distance from the winning node. Thus topographic organization is essential to the explanation.

Since the stimuli used in this simulation are artificial and extremely simple, it is not very illuminating to pursue a detailed priming explanation. Real stimuli provide a better test of priming behaviour, since they can be compared with human data.

4.3 Real Corpus Simulation

4.3.1 Input data

The second simulation used the first 10 million words of the British National Corpus [4] to create co-occurrence vectors for the first 14 prime-target pairs from a semantic priming experiment by Moss, Ostrin, Tyler and Marslen-Wilson [25]. The stimuli are associatively and semantically related category coordinate pairs. Subjects were required to make lexical decisions on the second word. Examples of prime-target pairs are shown below:

square circle
black white

In this simulation, input vectors were provided by Scott McDonald. Each vector consisted of 446 elements, corresponding to the 446 most frequent open class words in the British National Corpus. Each vector was created by counting how many times the target word co-occurred with each of the 446 open class words in a three word window. Dunning's g-statistic [8] was then applied to each co-occurrence count. The g-statistic is similar to a measure of mutual information [5]: for any amount of co-occurrence between two words in a corpus, it states how likely that amount of co-occurrence is, given the frequencies of each word. Unlike mutual information, however, it is accurate for very low frequency items that constitute the majority of data encountered in corpora.

4.3.2 Training

To decrease the amount of time spent training the network, precomputed and reduced vectors were used to train the SOM. Each vector was reduced to 10 dimensions using principal component analysis. The results presented below were acquired using reduced vectors (full-size vectors were also used as a comparison, but the results were almost identical).

4.3.3 Results

Figure 5 shows the most active unit for each prime and target word, where output unit indices have been removed. Note that intuitively related pairs are mostly adjacent to one another.

4.3.4 Semantic Priming

The simulation of semantic priming effects proceeds as follows: The SOM is first presented with the prime word's vector. Each unit on the map is partially activated, including the unit that is most activated by the target word. When the prime vector is presented, the activation values for each unit associated most strongly with a word (labeled in Figure 5) express how much activation

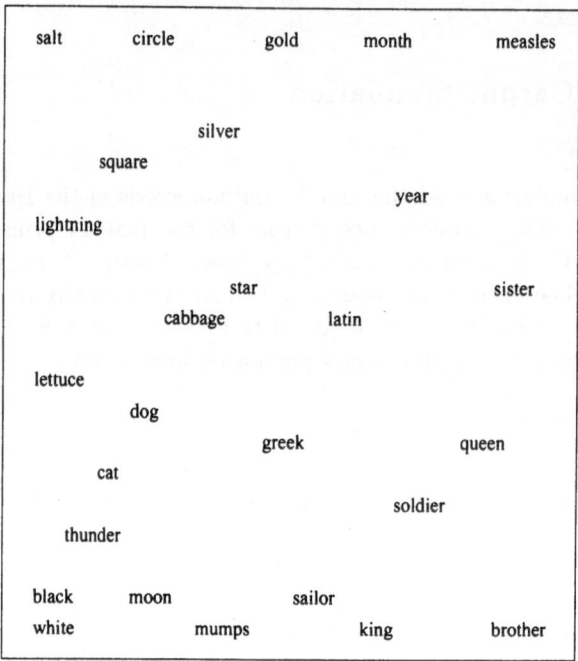

Figure 5: Most active units for semantically and associatively related category coordinate stimuli

the prime confers to each word. The more activation the prime gives to a particular target word, the quicker the target word will be responded to. Therefore, in a priming experiment if the amount of activation the prime confers on a 'related' target exceeds the amount of activation it gives to an unrelated word, then the related word is responded to faster, and priming occurs. In the simulation below, a baseline activation level is calculated as the average amount of activation that each prime gives to all other words besides the target. Priming occurs when the target is significantly more activated than the baseline.

When priming is simulated in this way the activations for each related target are significantly greater than their respective baselines (Baseline mean 0.351, standard deviation 0.129. Related mean 0.576, standard deviation 0.225. $t(26) = 21.292\ p < 0.001$). Priming effects found in the experiment are also found in the network.

5 Conclusion

This paper has presented a model of the mental lexicon and its formation based on the self-organizing map. It also presented an explanation of semantic priming based on co-occurrence statistics and topographic representation.

Two simulations were presented in an attempt to show how a lexical semantic network can be created using only information available from raw text. In the first simulation, a lexical-semantic network was created using co-occurrence information successively re-estimated from an artificial text corpus. In the second simulation, the model was trained with co-occurrence vectors derived from the British National corpus and tested on stimuli taken from a semantic priming experiment.

Acknowledgments

I would like to thank my supervisors, Richard Shillcock and Mark Ellison, and Joanna Bryson. I also grateful to John Bullinaria and two anonymous reviewers for many helpful comments and suggestions. This work was done while supported by studentship from the Medical Research Council.

References

[1] J. R. Anderson. *The Architecture of Cognition*. Harvard University Press, 1983.

[2] C. M. Bishop. *Neural Networks for Pattern Recognition*. Oxford University Press, 1995.

[3] J. A. Bullinaria and C. C. Huckle. Modelling lexical decision using corpus derived semantic representations in a connectionist network. In *Proceedings of the Fourth Neural Computation and Psychology Workshop*, 1997.

[4] G. Burnage and D. Dunlop. Enoding the British National Corpus. In *Papers from the Thirteenth International Conference on English Language Research on Computerized Corpora*, 1992.

[5] K. W. Church and P. Hanks. Word association, mutual information,and lexicography. *Computational Linguistics*, 1989.

[6] K. W. Church and R. L. Mercer. Introduction to the special issue on computational linguistics using large corpora. *Computational Linguistics*, 19:1–24, 1993.

[7] A. M. Collins and E. F. Loftus. A spreading activation theory of semantic processing. *Psychological Review*, 82:407–428, 1975.

[8] T. Dunning. Robust statistics for surprise and coincidence. *Computational Linguistics*, 1993.

[9] J. L. Elman. Finding structure in time. *Cognitive Science*, 14:179–211, 1990.

[10] S. Finch. *Finding Structure in Language*. PhD thesis, Centre for Cognitive Science, Edinburgh University, 1993.

[11] C. C. Huckle. *Unsupervised Categorization of Word Meanings Using Statistical and Neural Network Methods.* PhD thesis, Centre for Cognitive Science, Edinburgh University, 1995.

[12] E. I. Knudsen, S. du Lac, and S. D. Esterly. Computational maps in the brain. *Annual Review of Neuroscience*, 10:41–65, 1988.

[13] T. Kohonen. Self-organized formation of topologically correct feature maps. *Biological Cybernetics*, 43:59–69, 1982.

[14] T. Kohonen. *Self-organization and associative memory.* Springer Verlag, 1984.

[15] T. Kohonen. Physiological interpretation of the self-organizing map algorithm. *Neural Computation*, 6:895–905, 1993.

[16] T. Kohonen. *Self-organizing maps.* Springer Verlag, 1995.

[17] T. K. Landauer and S. T. Dumais. A solution to Plato's problem: the latent semantic analysis theory of induction and representation of knowledge. *Psychological Review*, 104:211–240, 1997.

[18] Will Lowe. Meaning and the mental lexicon. In *Proceeding of the 15th International Joint Conference on Artificial Intelligence*, 1997.

[19] K. Lund, C. Burgess, and R. A. Atchley. Semantic and associative priming in high-dimensional semantic space. In *Proceedings of the 17th Annual Conference of the Cognitive Science Society*, pages 660–665, 1995.

[20] M. E. Masson. A distributed memory model of context effects in word identification. In D. Besner and G. W. Humphreys, editors, *Basic Processes in Reading: Visual Word Recognition*. Lawrence Erlbaum Associates, 1991.

[21] J. McClelland and D. Rumelhart. *Parallel Distributed Processing: Explorations in the Microstructure of Cognition*, volume 1. MIT Press, 1988.

[22] S. McDonald. A context-based model of semantic similarity. Unpublished.

[23] S. Monsell. The nature and locus of word frequency effects in reading. In D. Besner and G. W. Humphreys, editors, *Basic Processes in Reading: Visual Word Recognition*. Lawrence Erlbaum Associates, 1991.

[24] J. Morton. Word recognition. In J. Morton and J. C. Marshall, editors, *Psycholinguistics Series 2: Structures and Processes*. Elek, 1979.

[25] H. E. Moss, R. K. Ostrin, L. K. Tyler, and W. D. Marslen-Wilson. Accessing different types of lexical semantic information: Evidence from priming. *Journal of Experimental Psychology: Learning, Memory and Cognition*, pages 863–883, 1995.

[26] J. H. Neely. Semantic priming effects in visual word recognition: A selective review of current findings and theories. In D. Besner and G. W. Humphreys, editors, *Basic Processes in Reading: Visual Word Recognition*. Lawrence Erlbaum Associates, 1991.

[27] D. I. Perrett. View-dependent coding in the ventral stream and its consequences for recognition. In R. Caminiti, K-P Hoffmann, F. Lacquaniti, and J. Altman, editors, *Vision and Movement: Mechanisms in the Cerebral Cortex*, volume 2 of *HFSP*, pages 142–151. Publisher, Strasbourg, 1996.

[28] D. C. Plaut. Semantic and associative priming in a distributed attractor network. In *Proceedings of the Seventeenth Annual Conference of the Cognitive Science Society*, 1995.

[29] F. Pulvermüller and H. Preissl. A cell assembly model of language. *Network: Computation in Neural Systems*, pages 455–468, 1991.

[30] H. Schütze. Word space. In S. J. Hanson, J. D. Cowan, and C. L. Giles, editors, *Advances in Neural Information Processing Systems*, volume 5, pages 895–902. Morgan Kaufmann, 1993.

[31] M. S. Seidenberg. Visual word recognition and pronunciation: A computational model and its implications. In W. Marslen-Wilson, editor, *Lexical Representation and Process*, chapter 2. MIT Press, 1989.

[32] J. R. Shelton and R. C. Martin. How semantic is automatic semantic priming? *Journal of Experimental Psychology: Learning, Memory and Cognition*, 18:1191–1210, 1992.

[33] J. Sirosh and R. Miikkulainen. How lateral interaction develops a self-organizing feature map. In *Proceedings of the IEEE International Conference on Neural Networks*, 1993.

[34] D. P. Spence and K. C. Owens. Lexical co-occurrence and association strength. *Journal of Psycholinguistic Research*, 19:317–330, 1990.

[35] M. Taft. *Reading and the Mental Lexicon*. Lawrence Erlbaum Associates, 1991.

[36] K. Tanaka. Inferotemporal cortex and object recognition. In R. Caminiti, K-P Hoffmann, F. Lacquaniti, and J. Altman, editors, *Vision and Movement: Mechanisms in the Cerebral Cortex*, volume 2 of *HFSP*, pages 126–133. Publisher, Strasbourg, 1996.

Distributed representations and the bilingual lexicon: One store or two?

Michael S. C. Thomas,
Department of Psychology, King Alfred's College,
Winchester, UK

Abstract

Several researchers have put forward models of bilingual lexical representation based on extensions to traditional monolingual models, such as those using serial search and interactive activation paradigms. In this paper we examine the implications of employing a distributed notion of lexical representation in a model of the bilingual lexicon. A model is presented that stores knowledge about the words in two languages in a single connectionist network. The model simulates both empirical evidence taken to indicate independent lexical representations, as well as evidence of between language similarity effects. The latter type of evidence is problematic for models which employ strictly independent lexical representations for each language. The implications of evidence from bilingual language development and from second language acquisition are discussed.

1 Introduction

There has been a good deal of interest in how the bilingual's language system relates to that of the monolingual. At one extreme is the view that we must postulate a separate language system for the bilingual's second language [1]. At the other extreme is the view that the two languages may merely serve as subdivisions within a single system, perhaps only differentiated on the basis that words of different languages often sound or look different [2]. In this paper, we will focus on the bilingual lexicon. Here the question becomes, 'does the bilingual have two mental dictionaries to recognise the words in each language, or a single combined dictionary?'.

One of the principal tools that researchers have used to investigate this question is the lexical decision task, usually for visually presented words. Two types of evidence are often used. The first is priming, whereby researchers examine whether word recognition in one language affects later recognition in the other language. Priming paradigms show that short term semantic priming occurs between as well as within languages (e.g. [3]). However long term lexical priming between the first and second presentations of a word is only found for repetitions within a language, not between translation equivalents in different languages [4].

The second sort of evidence relies on the fact that for many pairs of languages, there are word forms that exist in both languages. Here researchers examine whether such words (referred to as *homographs*) behave differently from matched words existing in only one of the languages (henceforth referred to as *Singles*). *Non-cognate homographs* are words that have the same form but a different meaning in each language (e.g. MAIN and FIN in English mean 'hand' and 'end' in French). Since they have a different meaning, these words often have a different frequency of occurrence in each language. Results have shown that the same word form is recognised quickly in the language context where it is high frequency, and slowly in the language context where it is low frequency [5]. The fact that these words show the same frequency response as Singles suggests that their behaviour is unaffected by the presence of the same word form in the other language, and in turn, that the lexical representations are therefore independent. In support of this view, presentation of a non-cognate homograph in one language context does not facilitate later recognition of the word form in the other language context [6].

On the basis of the above findings, researchers have tended to conclude that the bilingual has independent representations for a word and its translation equivalent at the lexical level, but a common representation at the semantic level [7].

There is a caveat to this story however. While the general picture is that lexical representations are independent, nevertheless under some circumstances, between language similarity effects are found. That is, words in one language show a differential behaviour because of their status in the other language. Thus Klein and Doctor [8] found that non-cognate homographs were recognised more slowly than matched *cognate homographs* (words which have the same form and meaning in each language, such as TRAIN in English and French). Cristoffanini, Kirsner, and Milech [9] and Gerard and Scarborough [5] found that cognate homographs in a bilingual's weaker language were recognised more quickly than Singles of matched frequency, as if the stronger language were helping the weaker language on words they had in common. And Beauvillain [10] found that when operating in just one language, bilingual subjects recognised words with orthographic patterns specific to that language more quickly than words with orthographic patterns common to both languages.

Several researchers have put forward models of bilingual lexical representation based on extensions to traditional monolingual models, such as the serial search and interactive activation models [11, 12, 13]. Given the apparent independence of the lexical representations, models have promoted language as playing a key role in structuring the representations, so that there might be a separate word list for each language in the serial model, or a separate network of word units for each language in the interactive activation model. The problem for models of this type is that they then have difficulty in accounting for between language similarity effects.

In this paper we consider an extension of the distributed word recognition framework to the bilingual case. We will specifically consider the hypothesis that the presence of between language similarity effects is a marker that both languages are stored in a single distributed connectionist network.

2 Modelling the bilingual lexicon

We will follow Plaut [14, 15] in modelling performance in the visual lexical decision task via a connectionist network mapping between the orthographic codes and semantic codes of the words in the lexicon. This network is taken to be part of the wider processing framework involved in reading [26]. Several simplifying assumptions will be made in constructing the initial model. Firstly, we will employ two artificially created 'languages' (see below), which capture a number of features of interest but do not have the complexity (or vagaries) of natural languages. Secondly, the model will employ a strictly feedforward architecture, although this should be seen as an approximation to an interactive system developing attractors (see Plaut, [15]). Thirdly, our aim will be to compare simulation results with empirical data on normal performance and priming effects in the lexical decision task. However, we will use the accuracy of the network's semantic output to match to subjects' response time data. It has been shown that network error scores do not precisely map to reaction times [16]. The accuracy of the network's responses (as measured by the error between the target semantic code and the network's output) is intended to give an indication of the characteristics of processing in a network computing the meanings from the words in two languages. If the predicted base rate differences and similarity effects do not appear in the accuracy measure, it is hard to see where they will come from in generating the final response times. The use of error scores allows us to temporarily side-step the complexity of implementing cascaded activation and response mechanisms in the model, and to focus on the implications of representing two languages in a single network.

2.1 Designing two artificial word sets

Two artificial languages, A and B, were created for the model to learn. These each comprised approximately 100 three letter words, constructed from an alphabet of 10 letters. Words were randomly generated around consonant / vowel templates. These are shown in Table 1. The languages each shared two templates, and had two unique templates. The words were represented over 30 orthographic input units. Meanings for the words were generated at random across a semantic vector of 120 features. For a given meaning, each feature had a probability of 0.1 of being active [14]. Words were defined as high or low frequency, whereby low frequency words were trained at 0.3 of the rate of high frequency words (corresponding roughly to the logarithmic difference between high and low frequency words in English).

Words could have three types of relation between the two languages. (1) Singles were word forms which existed in only one language. These words were assigned a translation equivalent in the other language which shared its meaning and frequency, but which possessed a different word form. For English and French, examples of Singles in English would be RAIN (shared template) and COUGH (unique template), in French BAIN (shared template) and OEUF (unique template). (2) Cognate homographs were word forms which existed in both of the languages, and which shared the same meaning and frequency in each language (e.g. TRAIN).

(3) Non-cognate homographs were word forms which existed in both of the languages but which had a different meaning and frequency in each language (e.g. MAIN).

Three letter words employing a 10 letter alphabet.		
(C)onsonants:	$b, f, g, s, t.$	
(V)owels:	$a, e, i, o, u.$	
	Language A Templates	Language B Templates
Shared	CVV and CVC	CVV and CVC
Unique	VCV and VVC	CCV and VCC
Illegal in both	VVV and CCC	VVV and CCC

Procedure.

1 20 of each template are selected at random.
2 10 of each set of 20 are assigned to be high frequency, 10 to be low frequency.
3 Low frequency words are trained at 30% of the rate of High Frequency words.
4 8 Cognate Homographs and 8 Non-cognate Homographs are chosen at random, 4 of each 8 from CVV, 4 from CVC (the two shared templates).
5 Meanings are generated over a bank of 120 semantic feature units. Meanings are randomly generated binary vectors, where each unit has a probability of 10% of being active in a given meaning (and at least 2 features must be active).
6 Words are paired between languages at random, to be translation equivalents, with the constraint that a meaning has to be the same frequency in each language.
7 Cognate homographs are assigned the same meaning in each language.
8 Non-cognate homographs are assigned a different meaning for the same letter string in the two languages.
9 4 of the non-cognate homographs are assigned to be high frequency in A, low frequency in B, and the other 4 to be low frequency in A, high frequency in B.

Table 1: Construction Scheme for the 2 languages, A and B.

2.2 Language context information

Both the orthographic and semantic vectors for each word were associated with a language context vector. This was 8 units long, of which 4 units were turned on for words in Language A, and 4 were turned on for words in Language B. This allowed language membership information to be at least as salient to the network as the orthographic identity of the word (see Thomas and Plunkett for the implications of varying the size of the language vector [17]). This vector is best thought of as tagging the language membership of a word on the basis of language specific features available to the language learner. These features may be implicitly represented in the languages or be drawn out explicitly as representational primitives by the language system. The notion of language tagging is consistent with the majority of previous models of bilingual lexical representation (see e.g. [13]).

2.3 Network architecture

The network architecture is shown in Figure 1. The network initially used 60 hidden units, although variations between 40 and 80 units did not significantly affect the pattern of results. The network was trained on both languages simultaneously for 600 epochs, at a learning rate of 0.5 and momentum of 0, using the cross-entropy algorithm. At this stage, 99.99% of the semantic features were within 0.5 of their target values. A balanced and an unbalanced condition of the network were run. In the balanced condition, both languages were trained equally. In the unbalanced condition, L2 was trained at a third of the rate of L1. There were six replications of each network using different randomised initial weights.

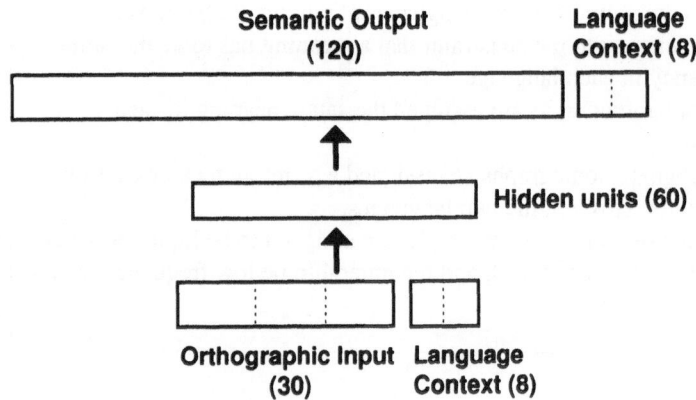

Figure 1. Architecture of the Bilingual Single Network model.

2.4 The simulation of priming

Long term repetition priming was simulated in the model by further training the network for 12 additional cycles on the prime, using the same learning rate (see [18], [19]) and then recording the accuracy of the output for the target. Thomas [6] has shown that priming by additional training on a single mapping does not cause significant interference to other mappings stored in the network, and is a plausible way to model long term repetition priming effects.

3 Results implying independence

Figure 2 shows a principal components analysis of the hidden unit activations of a representative balanced network after training. This analysis shows that the network has formed distinguishable representations for the two languages over the single hidden layer. Figure 3 shows the accuracy with which the semantic vectors are produced for the three types of word. Singles showed the expected frequency effect (analysis of variance, $F(1,3)=907.95$, $p<0.001$). Importantly, non-cognate homographs showed the *same* frequency effect as Singles (non-significant interaction of word type and frequency effect, $F(1,2)=0.13$, $p=0.724$). Here the same word form shows a different frequency response in each language context, even when both word forms are stored in the same network. Empirical evidence to this effect has been taken to imply independent lexical representations [5].

For the priming results, we will concentrate on the results for Singles and non-cognate homographs. Figure 4 shows a comparison of the network's performance (lower panel) with data from two empirical studies using English and French (upper panel). Data are averaged over the two languages. The empirical data for Singles and non-cognate homographs are from separate studies. The within and between language priming effects for Singles are from Kirsner et al [4]. The empirical data for non-cognate homographs are from Thomas [6]. Since these data are from separate studies, the similarity in base rate responses between the two studies is co-incidental. These graphs show normal performance for words in their unprimed state, the within language repetition priming effect (dashed line), and the between language repetition priming effect (solid line). For Singles, the between language priming effect represents priming gained from previous presentation of the word's translation equivalent in the other language. For non-cognate homographs, the between language priming effect represents priming gained from previous presentation of the same *word form* in the other language.

With regard to Singles, in contrast to the empirical data, the model shows a between language priming effect, albeit only 19% of the size of the within language repetition effect. Here we find a residue of the representations occupying the same network. Between language priming is caused by the common semantic output. Two points are of note here. Firstly, this simulation result might well be reduced for natural languages, since their orthographic spaces are far more sparsely populated. Real words can be far more different than the 3-letter words used in this simulation. A greater difference in similarity at input would reduce the between language priming effect. Secondly, the model makes the empirical prediction that if restricted word sets were chosen from a pair of natural languages which increased the orthographic similarity between translation equivalents in line with the artificial languages, cross language repetition effects should be found. Cristoffanini, Kirsner, and Milech [9] examined cross language priming patterns between translation equivalents with greater or lesser degrees of orthographic relation, and indeed found data consistent with the view that greater orthographic similarity produces greater cross language priming.

With regard to non-cognate homographs, the model shows no between language facilitation at all, indeed there is an inhibition effect 13% of the size of the within language effect. Again this effect is not shown in the empirical data. However, under certain network conditions the effect was eliminated (when the language coding vector was 16 units, and when the network was trained for 3000 epochs). An effect much smaller than this might be hard to find in the data in any event.

In sum, the network shows an approximate fit to the empirical data, data which has been taken to imply independent representations. However, the presence of the between language effects shows some residue of the fact that these two sets of language representations are distributed over the same multidimensional space. There are grounds to believe that under certain conditions, the network results will approximate the empirical data even more closely, when the artificial languages more closely resemble natural languages, or when subsets of natural languages are chosen that increase the orthographic similarity of translation equivalents towards that of the artificial languages. The model produces additional between language effects, but in the following cases, we will see that they fit with empirical data.

4 Results demonstrating similarity effects

The balanced network showed a disadvantage for non-cognate homographs compared to cognate homographs ($F(1,2)=8.66$, $p=0.003$). Klein and Doctor [8] found this effect for bilinguals in the lexical decision task. In the unbalanced condition, cognate homographs in L2 were advantaged compared to frequency matched Singles ($F(1,3)=9.49$, $p=0.002$), an empirical result found in a number of studies (see [5]). Beauvillain [10] found that words with language specific orthographic patterns were advantaged compared to those with patterns common to both languages. Recall that in the model, languages have both shared and unique templates. Similar although noisy results were found when testing the balanced network across a range of parameter conditions. Words from unique templates produced more accurate responses than those from shared templates. However, this effect was more prevalent in Language A which showed this advantage over all conditions, than Language B, which showed it only intermittently. Orthographic effects were compromised by the fact that 3-letter words with language specific and language non-specific orthographic patterns could nevertheless have very similar orthographic forms (for instance the word ITO was a legal string only in A, the word STO was a legal string only in B). The effect of language specific orthography is currently the subject of further work.

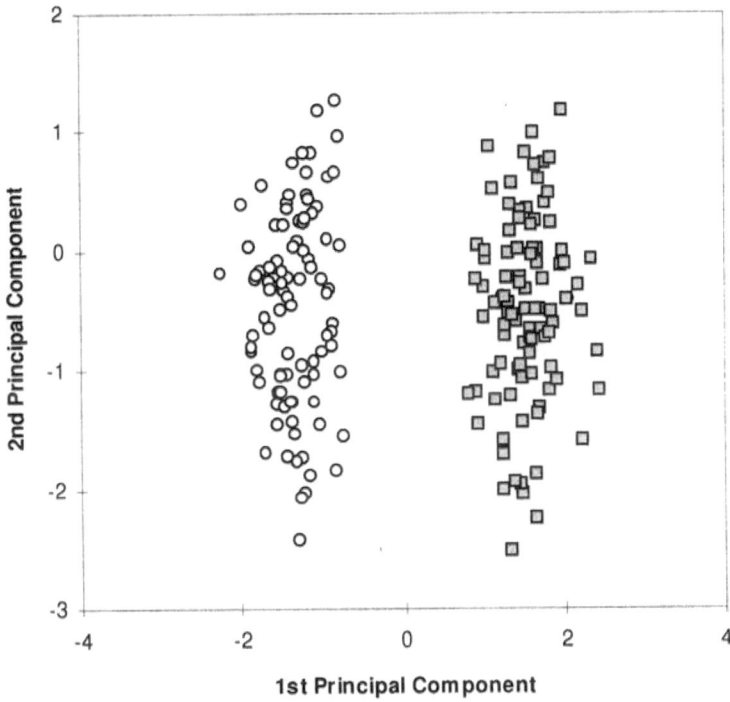

Figure 2. Principal components analysis of the hidden unit activations for the balanced bilingual network. Lang. A = White Circles, Lang. B = Grey Squares.

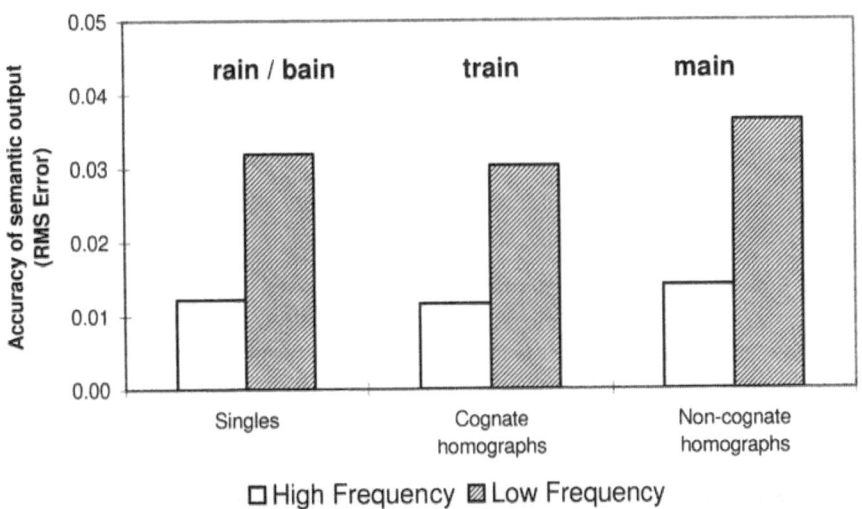

Figure 3. Base rate response of the balanced network for each word type. Examples of each word type from English and French are shown.

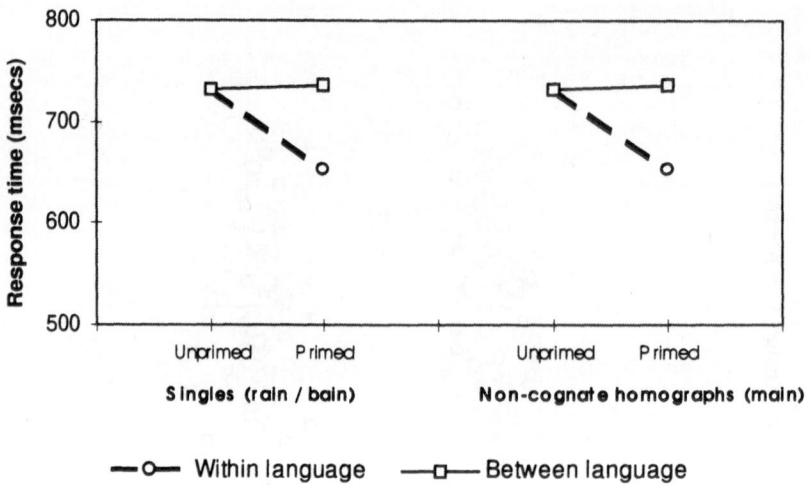

Figure 4. Patterns of within and between language priming.
a) Empirical data.
  Data for Singles and for non-cognate homographs are from separate studies. For
  Singles, the data are from Kirsner et al [4]. For non-cognate homographs, data are
  from Thomas [6]. In each study, data are averaged over both languages.

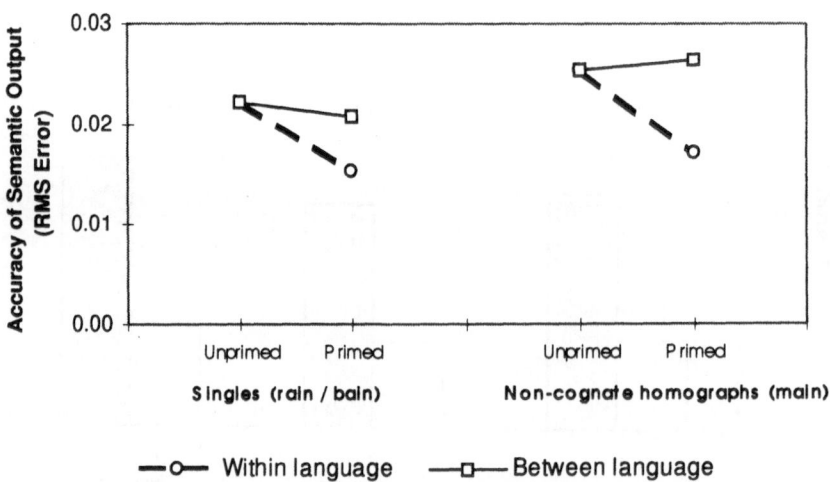

b) Simulation data from the Bilingual Single Network model.
  For Singles / translation equivalents, similarity at output causes a small between
  language facilitatory priming effect. For non-cognate homographs, similarity at
  input causes a small between language inhibitory priming effect.

5 Evaluation

The Bilingual Single Network model shows both effects taken to imply separate mental dictionaries, as well as a number of between language similarity effects which are problematic for the independent lexicons view.

Why would one want to include both languages in a single network? This approach has the advantage of parsimony: It does not require that we assume any special structures for the bilingual language system. The Single Network model is consistent with the notion of a distributed lexicon, where many constraints determine the representations developed by the system. In the bilingual case, language membership serves as an additional constraint in performing the computations necessary in word recognition. In principle, we could think of it as similar to the constraint of tagging the meaning of ambiguous words by semantic context or grammatical class. Thus where bilingual research shows that non-cognate homographs are recognised according to within language frequency [5], monolingual research shows that ambiguous words with a noun and a verb meaning (such as BOX) are recognised according to the noun frequency or verb frequency, depending on the sort of word subjects are expecting to see [20]. Thus BOX seen as a verb is recognised as if it were low frequency, but as a noun, as if it were high frequency. And where bilingual research shows that non-cognate homographs show no repetition priming from one language to the same word form in the other language, monolingual research shows that an ambiguous word will only experience repetition priming if semantic context causes the same meaning to be accessed on both the first and second presentations [21].

On the other hand, models of bilingual word recognition that postulate entirely independent representations must generate a separate account of the between language similarity effects. Such an account might be based on competition and co-operation effects between the lexicons. It would revolve around the way that bilinguals control their lexicons. Normally, bilinguals generate responses according to a single language. Effects originating from the context-irrelevant language would then need to be sub-threshold. A control based account of similarity effects has yet to be clearly formulated, since there is limited knowledge about the control processes that operate over internal representations in general (e.g. see [22]).

6 The constraints of acquisition

Evidence from language acquisition has implications for both approaches. The Single Network model detailed here assumes simultaneous acquisition of both languages. However, in the case of second language acquisition, a single network runs up against the problem of catastrophic interference. In catastrophic interference, training on a new set of knowledge can damage the network's performance on the knowledge it already has [27, 28]. There is little overt evidence of impairments to L1 during L2 acquisition [23], although it is not clear that anyone has specifically looked for such effects (under, say, conditions of intense L2 acquisition). Yet empirical data suggest that after two years of learning a second language, the functional structure of the bilingual's lexicon is little different from that produced by simultaneous acquisition [29, 30, 31], albeit a structure that exhibits a number of asymmetries between the languages (such as in translation and in cross-language priming effects). The question of catastrophic interference has yet to be resolved for connectionist models of cognitive processes in general, although some suggestions have been offered (e.g. see [32]). For example, it is not clear that in principle, the acquisition of a new language is any different from expanding one's existing vocabulary in a single language. While there is a difference in scale, both involve sequential acquisition. Since in the Single Network model, the late arrival of a second language at least necessitates the addition of language context units, some recruitment of resources is implied. Thus an account based on a generative algorithm might be an appropriate way to proceed. Note that the Single Network model is not committed to a particular learning algorithm, simply to the idea that there are no architectural partitions in the lexicon and that soft constraints allow both independence and similarity effects to emerge.

A model that postulates independent representations for each language can account straightforwardly for second language acquisition ("new language? new network!"). However, this model has trouble in justifying its architecture during simultaneous acquisition. Developmental evidence suggests that children show differential use of their two languages from a very early age, as young as 2 years [24, 25]. Their *bilingual* language development appears primarily to involve working out when it is appropriate to use each language. This would imply a very early commitment to separate representations, if indeed such a commitment is made. Early commitment is of course risky: it wouldn't do for a child to choose separate representations if his or her parents merely turned out to have different regional accents.

7 Conclusion

In conclusion, both the Single Network account and Independent representations account have to be extended in order to meet the constraints of acquisitional data. However, as we have seen here, the Single Network account is not only parsimonious in its assumptions, it also accounts for more of the data on adult bilingual word recognition than previous models based on independent representations. Specifically, a distributed model can capture both evidence for the independence of lexical representations and evidence of between language similarity effects. The mappings for each language are distinguished in the coding scheme. However, the network's behaviour is a result of the internal representations it develops to solve the computational task of producing the meanings for the words in two languages. This contrasts with the a priori specification of the representations that occurs in serial access and interactive activation models.

Further work remains to be done. For example, much of the relevant empirical data on bilingual lexical processing derives from the visual lexical decision task, yet a definitive account of monolingual lexical decision based on distributed representation remains to be formulated [6, 15, 16]. Moreover, a network that maps between orthography and semantics is only part of a processing framework that contributes to performance in the lexical decision task. Other information sources may be used, such as the orthographic familiarity of the input string, and the familiarity of the pronunciation it produces. Sources of information must be combined somehow to drive a response mechanism. At present, such considerations are beyond the scope of the bilingual model. The aim of this paper has been to explore the implications of distributed representations for bilingual lexical processing. Some of these implications will inevitably change as distributed models of monolingual lexical processing evolve. Here we have suggested that distributed networks have much to offer the study of bilingual word recognition.

References

1. Lambert WE. Psychological studies of the interdependencies of the bilingual's two languages. In Puhvel J (Ed.), Substance and structure of language. Los Angeles: University of California Press, 1969.
2. Kirsner K, Lalor E, and Hird K. The bilingual lexicon: Exercise, meaning, and morphology. In Schreuder R and Weltens B (Eds.) The Bilingual Lexicon. Amsterdam/ Philadelphia: John Benjamins, 1993. Pp. 215-248.
3. Chen H-C and Ng ML. Semantic facilitation and translation priming effects in Chinese-English bilinguals. Memory and Cognition 1989, 17, 454-462.
4. Kirsner K, Smith MC, Lockhart RLS, King ML, and Jain M. The bilingual lexicon: Language-specific units in an integrated network. Journal of Verbal Learning and Verbal Behaviour 1984, 23, 519-539.
5. Gerard LD and Scarborough DL. Language-specific lexical access of homographs by bilinguals. Journal of Experimental Psychology: Learning, Memory, and Cognition 1989, 15, 305-315.
6. Thomas MSC. Connectionist networks and knowledge representation: The case of bilingual lexical representation. Unpublished D.Phil. Thesis. Oxford University, 1997
7. Smith MC. On the recruitment of semantic information for word fragment completion: Evidence from bilingual priming. Journal of Verbal Learning and Verbal Behaviour 1991, 17, 234-244.
8. Klein D and Doctor EA. Homography and polysemy as factors in bilingual word recognition. South African Journal of Psychology 1992, 22(1), 10-16.
9. Cristoffanini P, Kirsner K, and Milech D. Bilingual lexical representation: The status of Spanish-English cognates. The Quarterly Journal of Experimental Psychology 1986, 38A, 367-393.
10. Beauvillain C. Orthographic and lexical constraints in bilingual word recognition. In R. J. Harris (Ed.) Cognitive Processing in Bilinguals. Elsevier Science Publishers, 1992.
11. Grainger J. Visual word recognition in bilinguals. In Schreuder R and Weltens B (Eds.) The Bilingual Lexicon. Amsterdam/Philadelphia: John Benjamins, 1993. Pp. 11-25.

12. French RM and Ohnesorge C. Using orthographic neighbourhoods of interlexical nonwords to support an interactive-activation model of bilingual memory. Proceedings of the 18th Annual Conference of the Cognitive Science Society. Lawrence Erlbaum Associates, 1996. Pp. 318-323

13. Grainger J and Dijkstra T. On the representation and use of language information in bilinguals. In Harris RJ (Ed.) Cognitive Processing in Bilinguals. Elsevier Science Publishers, 1992. Pp. 207-220.

14. Plaut DC. Semantic and Associative Priming in a Distributed Attractor Network. In Proceedings of the Seventeenth Annual Conference of the Cognitive Science Society. Lawrence Erlbaum Associates, 1995. Pp. 37-42.

15. Plaut DC. Structure and function in the lexical system: Insights from distributed models of word reading and lexical decision. Language and Cognitive Processes. In press.

16. Bullinaria JA. Modelling reaction times. In Smith LS and Hancock PJB (Eds.) Neural Computation and Psychology, Proceedings of the 3rd Neural Computation and Psychology Workshop. Springer, 1995. Pp. 34-48.

17. Thomas MSC and Plunkett K. Representing the bilingual's two lexicons. In Proceedings of the 17th Annual Cognitive Science Society Conference. Hillsdale, NJ: Lawrence Erlbaum, 1995. Pp. 760-765.

18. Becker S, Behrmann M, and Moscovitch M. Word priming in attractor networks. In Proceedings of the 15th Annual Meeting of the Cognitive Science Society, Erlbaum, 1993. Pp. 231-236.

19. McClelland JL and Rumelhart DE. A Distributed Model of Human Learning and Memory. In McClelland JL, Rumelhart DE, and the PDP Research Group, Parallel Distributed Processing: Explorations in the Microstructure of Cognition. Volume 2: Psychological and Biological Models. MIT Press, 1986.

20. Roydes RL and Osgood CE. Effect of grammatical form-class set upon perception of grammatically ambiguous English words. Journal of Psycholinguistic Research 1972, 1, 165-174.

21. Masson MEJ and Freedman L. Fluent identification of repeated words. Journal of Experimental Psychology: Learning, Memory, and Cognition 1990, 16, 355-373.

22. Monsell S. Control of mental processes. In Bruce V (Ed.) Unsolved mysteries of the mind: Tutorial essays in cognition. Erlbaum, 1996. Pp. 93-148.

23. Ellis R. The study of second language acquisition. Oxford University Press, 1994.

24. Genesee F. Early bilingual development: one language or two? Journal of Child Language 1989, 6, 161-179.

25. Lanza E. Can a bilingual two-year-old code-switch? Journal of Child Language 1992, 19, 633-658.

26. Seidenberg MS and McClelland JL. A distributed, developmental model of word recognition and naming. Psychological Review 1989, 96, 523-568.

27. Ratcliff R. Connectionist models of recognition memory: Constraints imposed by learning and forgetting functions. Psychological Review 1990, 97, 285-308.

28. McCloskey M and Cohen NJ. Catastrophic interference in connectionist networks: The sequential learning problem. In GH Bower (Ed.) The

psychology of learning and motivation, vol. 24, 1989. New York: Academic Press.

29. Magiste E. Stroop tasks and dichotic translation: The development of interference patterns in bilinguals. Journal of Experimental Psychology: Learning, Memory, and Cognition 1984, 10(2), 304-315.

30. Potter MC, So K-F, von Eckhardt B, and Feldman LB. Lexical and conceptual representation in beginning and more proficient bilinguals. Journal of Verbal Learning and Verbal Behaviour 1984, 23, 23-38.

31. Kroll JF and Curley J. Lexical memory in novice bilinguals: The role of concepts in retrieving second language words. In M. Gruneberg, P. Morris, and R. Sykes (Eds.), Practical Aspects of Memory, Vol. 2. 1988. London: John Wiley and Sons.

32. McClelland JL, McNaughton BL, and O'Reilly RG. Why there are complementary learning systems in the hippocampus and neocortex: Insights from the successes and failures of connectionist models of learning and memory. Psychological Review 1995, 102, 419-457.

Recognising Embedded Words in Connected Speech: Context and Competition

Matt H. Davis, M. Gareth Gaskell and William Marslen-Wilson
Centre for Speech and Language
Birkbeck College, London

Abstract

Onset-embedded words (e.g. *cap* in *captain*) present a problem for accounts of spoken word recognition since information coming after the offset of the embedded word may be required for identification. We demonstrate that training a simple recurrent network to activate a representation of all the words in a sequence allows the network to learn to recognise onset-embedded words without requiring a training set that is already lexically segmented. We discuss the relationship between our model and other accounts of lexical segmentation and word recognition, and compare the model's performance to psycholinguistic data on the recognition of onset-embedded words.

1 Introduction

A significant problem for both human and machine speech recognition is how to determine the location of boundaries between lexical items or words. Connected speech does not contain gaps between words analogous to the spaces in written text [1], nor are there any explicit cues that reliably mark the position of boundaries between words [2]. Accounts of how listeners segment the speech stream during spoken word recognition can be divided into two broad classes. The first is based on the use of sub-lexical cues that can identify word boundaries prior to, or in the absence of, lexical access to words in the speech stream. Examples of cues that have been suggested in the literature include, prosodic [3], metrical [4] or phonotactic [5] regularities, or some combination of these [6,7]. However, since these cues are unable (either singly or in combination) to reliably identify all word boundaries, a second class of account has also been proposed suggesting that for adult listeners, the recognition of individual words contributes to lexical segmentation. We will focus on this second class of account here.

In theories of lexical access, most notably the cohort model [8], the recognition of connected speech is argued to proceed in a maximally efficient manner, i.e. words are identified as soon as they become uniquely specified in the speech stream. By this account, many words can be recognised before their offset, and word boundaries can be predicted for the offset of the current word. However, the presence of large numbers of words which are not unique at their offset [9] presents a challenge to lexical accounts of segmentation. At the offset of a word such as *cap*, the recognition system may be unable to distinguish this word from longer competitors (such as *captain* or *captive*) and may therefore be unable to reliably locate a word boundary. This seems to require that the recognition of onset-embedded words be delayed until after a word boundary, when longer competitors can be ruled out. This is supported by experiments showing that monosyllables are commonly not recognised until after their acoustic offset [10,11]. Such results have been taken as evidence that no sequential recognition system is capable of recognising onset-embedded words.

1.1 Connectionist accounts of spoken word recognition

Connectionist models of spoken word recognition illustrate many of the problems associated with different accounts of lexical segmentation. Simple recurrent networks [12], trained to map sequences of phonetically coded segments to a lexical representation of the current word [13, 14], show maximally efficient recognition of words in connected speech. During recognition, the network produces parallel activation of lexical representations for all the words that match the current input. So for the input sequence /kæptɪ/ (matching both *captain* and *captive*), a network trained to represent the lexical identity of words in the input will activate a blend of the representations of both words. In producing this parallel activation, the network activates the arithmetic mean of the output representations of all the words that match the speech input. Consequently, the network only fully activates a single lexical representation when the speech stream uniquely identifies a word.

However, since these networks are trained to activate a representation of the current word in a sequence, they are unable to correctly identify onset-embedded words such as *cap*. For these items, the speech stream only uniquely identifies such words after a lexical boundary, by which point the network will be activating a representation of the following word. Therefore at no point in the speech stream will the network fully activate the lexical representation of an onset-embedded word.

An alternative account of the time course of lexical activation in spoken word recognition is used in interactive activation models such as TRACE [15]. In these models, mutually inhibitory connections between lexical units that share segments produce partial activation of multiple candidates that match the speech input. Since these inhibitory connections cross potential word boundaries, the network can use following contexts (that rule out longer competitors) to account for the delayed recognition of onset-embedded words.

However, the architecture used in TRACE is computationally inefficient since it relies on duplicating units and connections to code for different time slices. Consequently Shortlist [16] combines the bottom-up activation of lexical candidates in a recurrent network with a competition network 're-wired on the fly' to account for the recognition of onset embedded words. Effective as this hybrid model may be [17], it remains of interest whether the approach used in the recurrent network simulations (where effects of competition are a result of the network evaluating the conditional probability of different words at each point in the speech stream) can also be used to account for the delayed recognition of onset embedded words.

Content and Sternon [18] show that adding a set of output units representing the previous word in a sequence (as well as the current word) allows a simple recurrent network to recognise onset-embedded words. The additional output task ensures that the network continues to represent hypotheses regarding the identity of previous words in the speech stream, and is therefore able to revise its output using following context. This allows the network to display appropriately delayed recognition of onset embedded words. However as in previous SRN simulations, the target vector is changed at each word boundary. Thus the training regime requires specification of the location of word boundaries in the speech stream, as well as the identity and order of occurrence of the lexical items divided by these boundaries. This is unrealistic since it assumes that the language learner has access to a lexically segmented corpus in which correspondences between the speech stream and lexical items are already known. The goal of the work that we shall be reporting here is to investigate whether simple recurrent networks can be trained to lexically segment speech and recognise onset-embedded words *without* requiring a pre-segmented training set. We assume that in the early stages of vocabulary acquisition children are mapping whole utterances onto their interpretation of the world.

2   Learning to segment connected speech

The simple recurrent networks [12] investigated here were given the task of mapping sequences of phonemes to a representation of all the words contained in those sequences [19]. To allow easier interpretation of the network's output, this representation is composed of localist lexical units, each representing a word in the network's vocabulary. However, in contrast to previous simulations, the training set does not contain any explicit information about which segments in the speech stream map onto lexical items (i.e. the locations of word boundaries is not given). Nor is there any information about the order in which words occur in the training sequences. The target activation for the network remains static throughout an sequence; the network being trained to activate the lexical units for all the words in the input. A psychological account of this mapping is that the network is building an interpretation of each sequence of lexical items. By this account, the network must preserve a representation of words that have already been identified, as well as activating lexical representations for words as they occur in the input.

Since the network is unable to activate units representing the final words in a sequence until those words have been presented in the input, we cannot expect the network to learn the training set to perfection. However, as in networks learning to predict the next segment in an utterance, distinctions between the task on which the network is trained, and the performance of the network when tested may help provide a fully elaborated psychological account [6]. In the case of the networks investigated here, the immediate task for the network is to associate strings of phonemically coded segments with a representation of the lexical items contained in that sequence. During testing however, we will be interested in comparing the time-course of activation of individual lexical items with available psycholinguistic data on the recognition of words in connected speech. The architecture of the network and the training regime are illustrated in Figure 1.

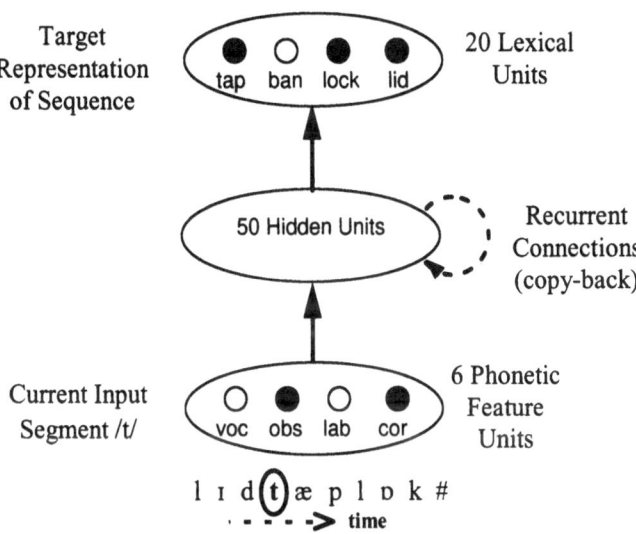

Figure 1: Simple recurrent network architecture used for these simulations showing a snapshot of training activations during the segment /t/ in the sequence "*lid tap lock*". Throughout each training sequence, the target for the network is to activate a representation of all the words in that sequence, not just the current word.

An important issue in justifying any psychological model involving supervised learning is to elaborate where the training information comes from. As in other models of word learning [20] we assume that vocabulary acquisition involves learning a mapping from form to meaning. However, in contrast to these accounts (and previous models of spoken word recognition [13,14]) we do not assume that correspondences between the speech stream and lexical or semantic representations are available to the learner on a one to one basis. The assumption made in this model is that a substantial part of the problem of vocabulary acquisition is to extract these correspondences from experience of spoken words and the meanings of sequences of those words [21]. The specific implementation of this assumption - that all words in a sequence have lexical representations as targets during training - is less theoretically vital. It is likely that only a subset of the words in any utterance have an obvious interpretation during acquisition. Nonetheless the idea that correspondences between the speech stream and lexical/semantic representations are learnt from experience of sequences of words where meanings must be assigned to lexical items (instead of being pre-specified) is an important part of this model.

2.1 Training sets

For all the simulations reported here, the training set was constructed from an artificial language containing 7 consonants and 3 vowels coded over a set of 6 phonetic features [22]. These segments were placed in a CVC syllable template used to create a vocabulary of 20 lexical items. Of these 20 words, 14 were monosyllables and 6 bisyllables. To allow investigation of the time course of recognition, lexical items varied in the point at which they became unique from all other words in the networks vocabulary. The simulations included 'cohort' pairs such as *lick* and *lid*, that share the same onset and become unique on their final segment, as well as two pairs of onset-embedded words (e.g. *cap* and *captain*) where the monosyllable is not uniquely identifiable until following context rules out longer competitors. There were also two pairs of offset-embedded words (*lock* and *padlock*) to allow comparison of the network's sensitivity to preceding and following context in the recognition of embedded words. These vocabulary items are shown in Table 1.

Type	Word	Phonology	Word	Phonology
Onset-Embedded Bi.	captain	/kæptɪn/	bandit	/bændɪt/
Offset-Embedded Bi.	topknot	/topnot/	padlock	/pædlok/
Non-Embedded Bi.	landed	/lændɪd/	picnic	/pɪknɪk/
Onset-Embedded Mono.	cap	/kæp/	ban	/bæn/
Offset-Embedded Mono.	knot	/not/	lock	/lok/
Cohort Monosyllable	dot	/dot/	dock	/dok/
	lick	/lɪk/	lid	/lɪd/
Non-Embedded Mono.	tap	/tæp/	bat	/bæt/
	knit	/nɪt/	cat	/kæt/
	pot	/pot/	bid	/bɪd/

Table 1: Vocabulary items used in these simulations

These 20 words were randomly selected without replacement to create sequences of between 2 and 4 words in length, separated by a boundary marker (zero input and output vectors). No attempt was made to capture higher-order distributional regularities such as syntactic or constituent structure, however a subset of word pairs were held back during training to allow testing of the networks generalisation performance. These sequences of were presented to a simple recurrent network (6 inputs, 50 hidden units with copy-back connections, 20 outputs) trained to activate lexical units for all the words in the current utterance. Weights were updated by the standard back-propagation algorithm following the presentation of every input segment (learning rate = 0.02, no momentum, cross-entropy error).

In preliminary simulations we found that changes to the bias weights on the output units were considerably larger than those to weights connecting the output and hidden units. This is caused by repeated weight updates with the same target pattern. To allow larger learning rates in these simulations, bias weights were disconnected from the output units in subsequent simulations[*]. Training time apart, results were comparable to simulations that included bias weights to the output units.

---

[*] Thanks to Gary Cottrell for suggesting this

2.2 Results

Ten simulations were carried out using the network architecture and training regime described above. Each network was trained on 500 000 sequences using small, random initial weights and different seeds for generating the training sequences. Figure 2 shows the activation of target words for an example sequence averaged over 10 fully trained networks. As can be seen in the graph, the network partially activates words as segments are presented at the input. Words become fully activated when they are uniquely specified in the speech stream, and once identified remain active until the end of the sequence. Such behaviour indicates that the network has learnt to lexically segment the speech stream by associating sections of the speech with the corresponding lexical units. During training, the network was not provided with explicit cues to the location of word boundaries or with information about which segments make up individual lexical items. However, by generalising its experience of different sequences, the network has learnt correspondences between the speech stream and lexical items. This is illustrated by the network's identical pattern of performance on sequences that were held back during training.

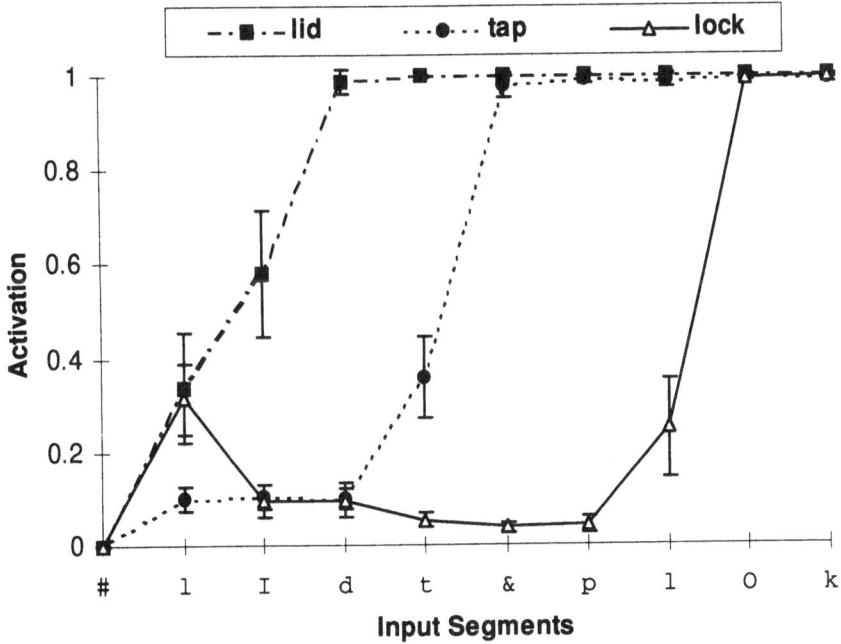

Figure 2: Activation of target words during the sequence *"lid tap lock"*.
The network activates words as they are presented in the input and preserves their activation until the end of the sequence. Error bars are 1 standard deviation.

2.2.1. Onset-embedded words

A systematic comparison of the partial activation observed for lexical items with different competitor environments is shown in Figure 3. The left hand chart shows the pattern of activation observed for items with cohort competitors (in this case *lick* and *lid*). As can be seen, output activations in the network approximate the conditional probabilities of partially matching lexical candidates [23]. Thus at the onset of *lid* (where three candidates match the input) each competing word is activated to just over 0.3. On presentation of the second segment, when two candidates match, each item is activated to approximately 0.5. It is only at the offset of *lid* that full activation is obtained at the appropriate lexical unit. Recent work using cross-modal semantic priming [24] is consistent with this account since the magnitude of priming observed for ambiguous word fragments is proportional to the conditional probability of the prime word in that cohort environment.

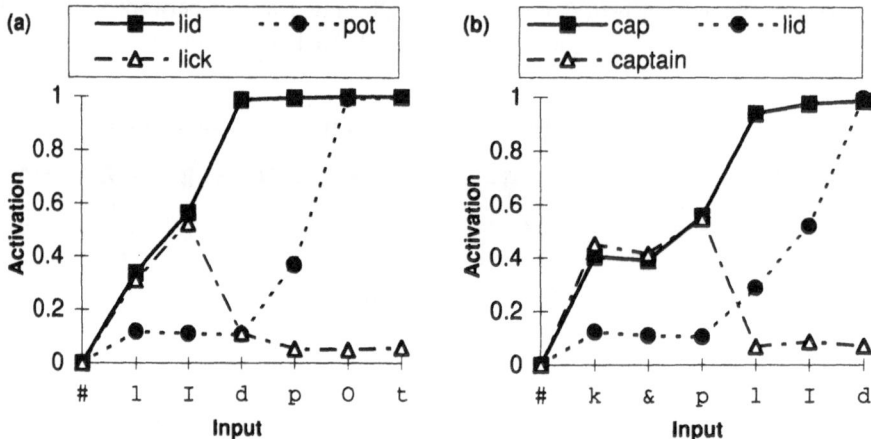

Figure 3: Activation of targets and competitors
(a) Cohort competitors (*lid/lick*) during the sequence *"lid pot"*
(b) Embedded words (*cap/captain*) during the sequence *"cap lid"*

The pattern of activation for cohort members is repeated almost identically in Figure 3(b) for onset-embedded words. At the offset of the monosyllable, the matching lexical items (*cap* and *captain*) are equally activated. It is only at the onset of the following word (*lid*) that the network receives disambiguating input (since the input mismatches with *captain*) and fully activates the target word *cap*. The network displays the optimal pattern of activation for ambiguous inputs, regardless of whether the ambiguity is resolved within a lexical item or following a word boundary. Such behaviour is comparable to experimental results from gating [10] since the network predicts that the identification of onset-embedded words requires post-offset information. Efficient recognition of embedded words like *cap* therefore does not require mutually inhibitory connections between competing lexical items.

These simulations support an account of segmentation in which post-offset mismatch with longer competitors plays an important role in the recognition of embedded words. But what is the pattern of activation displayed by the network when such mismatch is absent? Figure 4 shows the network's response in two such cases. The first example (4a) is where the network is presented with an item that contains a word embedded at the onset (for example *captain*). In this case the network strongly activates the longer competitor following the offset of the embedded word. However, in the 'lexical garden path' case in Figure 4(b), where the onset of the continuation matches the longer competitor, (e.g. *cap tap*) the network is still able to revise its lexical hypotheses in response to mismatch between the speech stream and the longer competitor. Further simulations showed that the network retained the ability to correctly resolve these lexical garden paths even when such sequences were not presented to the network during training. The disruption produced at the onset of the second word (*tap*) has also been confirmed in gating and cross-modal priming experiments using similar stimuli [25].

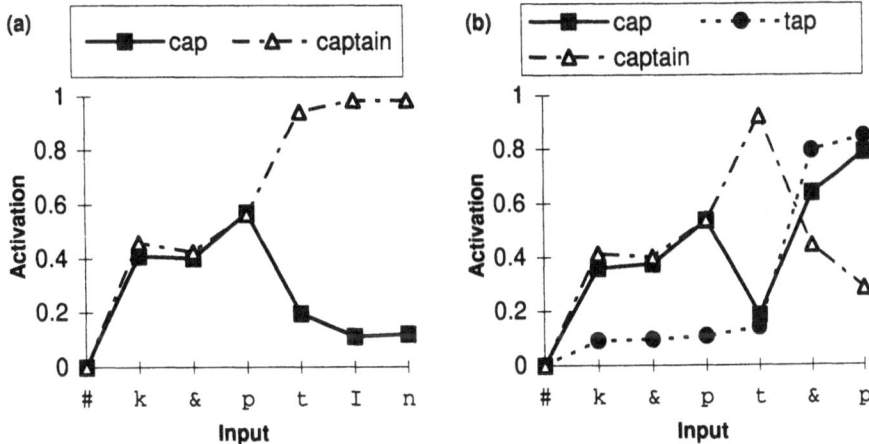

Figure 4: Activation of targets and competitors during sequences containing
(a) Bisyllables with embeddings (*captain/cap*) during *"captain"*
(b) Lexical 'garden paths' (*cap/captain*) during *"cap tap"*

2.2.2. Offset embedded words

The final set of results shown for these networks concern the identification of offset embedded words. By the account proposed in the original cohort theory [8] (where only words sharing the same onset are jointly activated) it would be predicted that the network would not activate offset-embedded words (e.g. *lock* in *padlock*) during recognition. Such a pattern of performance is illustrated in Figure 5. In contrast to the networks performance for onset-embedded words, the network is clearly capable of rejecting offset-embedded words during recognition.

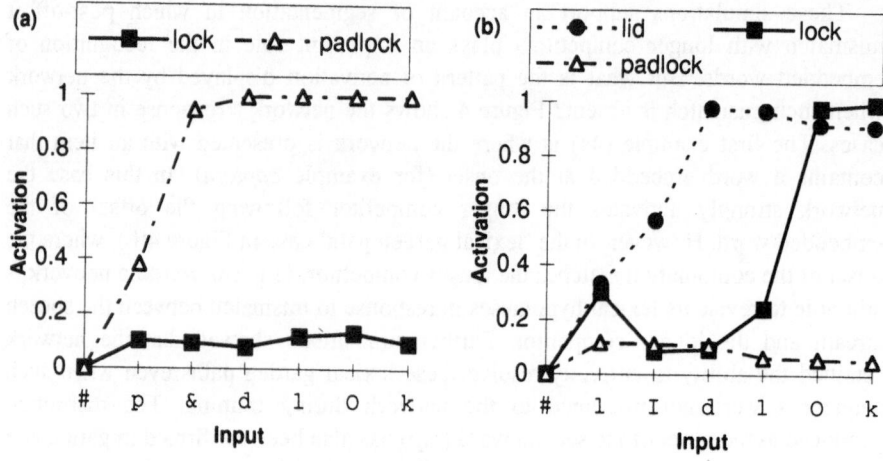

Figure 5: Activation of targets and competitors during sequences containing (a) Bisyllables with offset embeddings (*padlock/lock*) during *"padlock"* (b) Offset embedded words (*lock/padlock*) during *"lid lock"*

Empirical evidence on the activation of offset embedded words is unfortunately less clear. Several studies [26,27] report obtaining significant priming from offset-embedded words to an associatively related target (e.g. *trombone* primes RIB, via *bone*) though other experiments have failed to replicate this finding [28,29]. However, no results reported so far are inconsistent with the pattern shown in this network (and in models such as TRACE), where offset-embedded words receive substantially less activation that the longer words in which they are embedded.

3 Conclusions

The network described here learns to implement the maximal efficiency assumption in recognising words in sequences. Unlike previous accounts using simple recurrent networks [13,14], the network is able to deal with temporally ambiguous input not only where the ambiguity is resolved within a word, but also where post-offset information is required for recognition (as is the case for onset-embedded words). In recognising onset-embedded words the network displays an optimal compromise between partial activation of words for which the input is still ambiguous and full activation for unambiguous input. This holds even in cases where the network is presented with lexical garden-path sequences, where segments after the offset of an embedded word continue to match the longer competitor.

Furthermore, unlike previous simulations [18] the network is trained on input that does not contain any information about the location of word boundaries. We are therefore justified in claiming that the system is 'learning' lexical segmentation. At least for this limited training set, correspondences between form and meaning do provide a means by which a network could learn to identify individual words in connected speech. Further simulations are required to investigate whether this method remains effective for more realistic vocabularies.

In making this claim we do not wish to suggest that this is the only means by which segmentation can be learnt. The results obtained by self-supervised and unsupervised methods [6,7] suggests that distributional analysis plays an important role in discovering lexical units in connected speech. Indeed, empirical evidence suggests that infants are capable of rapidly extracting distributional information from artificial speech *before* they have any knowledge of individual words [30]. However distributional analysis may operate more effectively in conjunction with mappings that identify meaningful units in connected speech. Further simulations, not reported here suggest that the architecture investigated here provides an ideal environment in which to explore the relationship between distributional analysis and lexical identification in the learning of segmentation. We show that adding a temporal auto-encoder mapping (an output trained to predict the next segment in the input) significantly speeds the network's acquisition of the recognition task. Further investigation of these networks' training profiles may therefore help to clarify the role of distributional analysis and pre-lexical segmentation cues in vocabulary acquisition.

3.1 Representational assumptions

The ability of these networks to recognise onset-embedded words is a direct consequence of using a target representation which preserves information about previous words in the speech stream. Instead of this representation changing with each word onset as in prior simulations [18], the target activation remains constant throughout each sequence of words. By using a representation that is static with respect to the speech stream, the network learns to segment speech into lexical units through extracting correspondences between form and meaning across different sequences. It is these correspondences that we consider to be the essence of lexical representation.

In constructing the output representations for these simulations we have used localist lexical units. Although the use of localist representations have considerable benefits in terms of ease of interpretation, they also introduce the unrealistic assumption that a word's lexical representation is categorical and invariant. Distributed output representations would allow the network to extract invariant representations from noisy and contextually variable meanings.

However, it is no straightforward matter to re-implement networks of this type using a distributed output representation. The useful property of localist lexical representations is that they provide a simple solution to the problem of how to activate multiple representations (of all the words in a sequence) whilst preserving similarity between the representation of the same lexical item in different positions. In a distributed scheme where lexical representations are non-orthogonal, multiple activation produces blend states with accompanying limitations on representational capacity [31]. To be able to use distributed representations we require some means of reducing the overlap between the lexical representation of different words, while at the same time preserving the similarity between the representation of the same lexical item occurring in different positions. One such method would be to use a role/filler 'sentence gestalt' output [19] or a tensor product representation [32]. Such representations would also permit the incorporation of syntactic and constituent structures into these networks.

3.2 Comparing competing accounts

Having demonstrated the success of our model in learning to recognise onset-embedded words, it would be of interest to compare this model with previous accounts of spoken word recognition that incorporate lexical level competition [15,16]. This is made more difficult by the additional free parameters available in interactive activation models. However, one prediction made by both TRACE and Shortlist is that in recognising onset-embedded words greater competition between units representing long words (e.g. competition between *captain* and *captive*) would produce a short word advantage for input that was ambiguous between a short and a long word[*]. As can be seen in Figure 3, the networks investigated here produce lexical activations that approximate the conditional probabilities of all words that match the input, regardless of length. So for onset-embedded words such as *cap* and *captain* that occur with equal frequency in the training set, the network predicts equal activation of both candidates at the offset of *cap*.

Empirical evidence on this issue is inconclusive at present, particularly given the presence of acoustic cues such as vowel duration that distinguish the syllables of short and long words [25]. Indeed it may be that providing a psychologically realistic account of subjects sensitivity to duration differences in the speech stream presents a substantial challenge to accounts both with and without lexical competition. However the clear prediction made by recurrent network accounts (that responses to ambiguous input represent conditional probabilities) suggests that these models will reward future investigation. Further simulations are therefore required to investigate whether recurrent network models are able to account for the range of experimental data proposed as evidence for lexical competition.

Acknowledgements

We wish to thank John Bullinaria, Gary Cottrell, Joe Levy, Tom Loucas, Billi Randall and members of the Birkbeck Centre for Speech and Language for valuable discussions on this work. We are grateful to Morten Christiansen for comments and suggestions on an earlier draft of this manuscript. This work was supported by EPSRC research studentship number 94700590.

---

[*] see for example Figure 3 on page 213 of Norris, 1994 [15]

References

[1] Lehiste, I. The timing of utterances and linguistic boundaries. Journal of the Acoustical Society of America 1972; 51 (6): 2018-2024

[2] Nakatani, LH., Dukes, KD. Locus of segmental cues for word juncture. Journal of the Acoustical Society of America 1977; 62 (3): 715-719

[3] Nakatani, LH., Schaffer, JA. Hearing words without words: Prosodic cues for word perception. Journal of the Acoustical Society of America 1978; 63 (1): 234-245

[4] Cutler, A., Norris, D. The role of strong syllables in segmentation for lexical access. Journal of Experimental Psychology: Human Perception and Performance 1988; 14 (1): 113-121

[5] Cairns, P., Shillcock R., Chater N., Levy J. Bootstrapping word boundaries: a bottom-up corpus based approach to speech segmentation. In: Levy, J., Bairaktaris, J., Bullinaria, J., Cairns, P. (eds), Connectionist models of memory and language (289-310). UCL Press, London, (1995)

[6] Christiansen, MH., Allen J., Seidenberg, MS. Learning to segment speech using multiple cues: a connectionist model. Language and Cognitive Processes (in press)

[7] Brent, MR., Cartwright, TA. Distributional regularity and phonotactic constraints are useful for segmentation. Cognition 1996; 61: 93-125

[8] Marslen-Wilson, WD., Welsh A., Processing interactions and lexical access during word recognition in continuous speech. Cognitive Psychology 1978; 10: 29-63

[9] Luce, PA. A computational analysis of uniqueness points in auditory word recognition. Perception and Psychophysics 1986; 39: 155-158

[10] Grosjean, F. The recognition of words after their acoustic offset: Evidence and implications. Perception and Psychophysics 1985; 38 (4): 299-310

[11] Bard, EG., Shillcock RC., Altmann GT. The recognition of words after their acoustic offsets in spontaneous speech: Effects of subsequent context. Perception and Psychophysics 1988; 44: 395-408

[12] Elman, J. Finding structure in time. Cognitive Science 1990; 14: 179-211.

[13] Norris, D. A dynamic-net model of human speech recognition. In: Altmann, G. (ed) Cognitive Models of Speech Processing, MIT Press, Cambridge, MA, 1990

[14] Gaskell, MG., Marslen-Wilson, WD. Integrating form and meaning: A distributed model of speech perception. Language and Cognitive Processes, in press

[15] McClelland, JL., Elman, JL. The TRACE model of speech perception. Cognitive Psychology 1986; 18: 1-86

[16] Norris, D. Shortlist: a connectionist model of continuous speech recognition. Cognition 1994; 52: 189-234

[17] Norris, D., McQueen JM., Cutler, A., Butterfield, S. The possible-word constraint in the segmentation of continuous speech. (submitted).

[18] Content, A., Sternon, P. Modelling retroactive context effects in spoken word recognition with a simple recurrent network. In: Ram, A., Eiselt, K. (eds) Proceedings of the Sixteenth Annual Conference of the Cognitive Science Society, Lawrence Erlbaum, Hillsdale, NJ, 1994

[19] St. John, MF., McClelland, JL. Learning and applying contextual constraints in sentence comprehension. Artificial Intelligence 1990; 46: 217-257

[20] Plunkett, K., Sinha C., Møller MF., Strandsby, O. Symbol grounding or the emergence of symbols? Vocabulary growth in children and a connectionist net. Connection Science 1992; 4 (3/4): 293-312

[21] de Sa, VR. Unsupervised classification learning from cross-modal environmental structure. PhD Thesis, University of Rochester, New York, 1994

[22] Ladefoged, P. A course in phonetics. Second Edition Harcourt Bruce, New York, 1982

[23] Servan-Schreiber, DA. Cleeremans A., McClelland, JL. Graded-state machines: The representation of temporal contingencies in simple recurrent networks. Machine Leaning 1991; 7: 161-193

[24] Gaskell, MG., Marslen-Wilson, WD. Measuring lexical competition in speech perception. submitted

[25] Davis, MH., Marslen-Wilson, WD., Gaskell, MG. Ambiguity and competition in lexical segmentation. In: Proceedings of the Nineteenth Annual Conference of the Cognitive Science Society (in press)

[26] Shillcock, RC. Lexical hypotheses in continuous speech. In: Altmann, G. Cognitive Models of Speech Processing, MIT Press, Cambridge, MA, 1990

[27] Vroomen, J., de Gelder, B. Activation of embedded words in spoken word recognition. Journal of Experimental Psychology: Human Perception and Performance 1997; 23(3): 710-720

[28] Marslen-Wilson, WD., Tyler LK., Waksler R., Older L. Morphology and meaning in the English mental lexicon. Psychological Review 1994; 101(1): 3-33

[29] Gow DJ., Gordon PC. Lexical and pre-lexical influences on word segmentation. Journal of Experimental Psychology: Human Perception and Performance 1995; 21(2): 344-359

[30] Saffran, JR., Aslin, RN., Newport, EL. Statistical language learning by 8 month-old infants. Science 1996; 274(5294): 1926-1928

[31] Gaskell, MG. Parallel activation of distributed concepts: Who put the P in the PDP? In: Cottrell, GW. (ed) Proceedings of the Eighteenth Annual Conference of the Cognitive Science Society, Lawrence Erlbaum, Mahwah, NJ, 1996

[32] Smolensky, P. Tensor product variable binding and the representation of symbolic structures in connectionist systems. Artificial Intelligence 1990; 46: 159-216

The Representation of Serial Order

Dynamic Representation of Structural Constraints in Models of Serial Behaviour

David W. Glasspool and George Houghton

Department of Psychology, University College London, England

Abstract

The Competitive Queuing (CQ) approach to the generation of serial order views sequential behaviour as the result of competition between a set of alternative responses all activated in parallel. This type of model can show a general error pattern when damaged which is very like that of psychological subjects in several different modalities and paradigms. However, many forms of serial behaviour are subject to tight, domain-specific constraints on just which sequences can be produced. Such constraints are revealed in the fine structure of the errors which subjects make. This paper identifies two general strategies for the representation of such domain-specific sequential constraints within the overall framework of CQ. These approaches are discussed in the context of a number of different models in the domains of speech generation and spelling.

1 Introduction

Neural networks are parallel machines. When used to generate behaviour, rather than as perceptual systems, they lend themselves naturally to the generation of complex patterns of activation patterns which appear simultaneously over a parallel field of output units. The majority of human and animal behaviour, by contrast, is characterised by patterns which unfold over time [1]. A set of actions have to be made in the correct order if the desired goal is to be achieved. This is as true of a behaviour as simple as putting one foot in front of the other as it is of one as complex as driving a car.

At first sight this incompatibility between parallel connectionist systems and the seriality required for useful behaviour in the world seems to place connectionists at a disadvantage compared with computational modellers in the symbolic tradition, who have all the serial structures and processes offered by the "von Neumann" style of processing to hand. However, the ease of generating serial behaviour in traditional programming languages has tended to give the impression that the psychological problem of serial order has been solved or is trivial. One of the benefits of the recent rise of connectionist models has been to highlight this assumption by forcing modellers to address the problem of serial behaviour from first principles.

This paper briefly describes a class of mechanisms for the generation of serially ordered behaviour within a connectionist framework - the Competitive Queuing

(CQ) framework – which we believe offers a good model of the way in which sequential behaviour is generated by a basically parallel substrate in a number of areas in human and animal cognition. While the CQ framework represents a general approach to seriality, it is clear that many forms of serial behaviour are mediated by neural systems which are specialised for the domain in which they operate. We take the view that such domain-specific systems, although they may differ in aspects of their low-level operation, are nonetheless amenable to a description at some level of abstraction by which they all operate according to a common dynamic process - a process which is well modelled by CQ. The result is a sequential behaviour which has the general characteristics of the Competitive Queuing approach but which shows specific constraints on the classes of error which may occur in sequences, depending on the behavioural domain. This paper addresses the question: How should such domain-specific sequential constraints be represented in connectionist models?

2 Competitive Queuing

In experimental studies of serial tasks, it is striking that several characteristics are common to many different types of serial behaviour. Many studies in linguistic and motor areas such as speaking, typing, spelling and short-term memory for verbal, spatial and movement sequences (all of which involve producing many different orderings of a small set of elements) share some or all of the following characteristics:

- The longer the sequence, the less likely correct recall.

- There is generally no evidence that any form of associative chaining is taking place between one response in a sequence and the next - in fact, in some cases there is clear evidence that chaining is not present [2].

- Most errors occur towards the middle of the sequence. The familiar primacy and recency effects of verbal short-term memory are a well-known example [3], but "inverted-U" serial error curves also occur in spelling [4, 5, 6], "tip-of-the-tongue" (TOT) experiments [7], and short-term memory for spatial information and sequences of movements [8].

- Most errors involve the ordering of items. That is, most errors involve the correct items but produced in the wrong order, rather than items which do not appear in the target sequence.

- In many types of serial behaviour errors in which two items exchange places are common. These are interesting because they are particularly difficult for some accounts of serial processes to explain.

Many "common sense" approaches to the generation of serial behaviour which are often assumed to be plausible for example, associative chaining of one response to the next [9, 10], or placing responses in notional "boxes" [11], simply do not explain the types of error people make [12].

Competitive Queuing (CQ) [13] is an approach which views sequential behaviour as the result of competition for output between a set of alternative responses which are all activated in parallel. The system repeatedly makes the most salient response, and then inhibits it. This type of model can show error behaviour when disrupted which has many of the general characteristics of human serial behaviour as outlined above - for example, most errors involve the order in which responses are generated, and most occur towards the middle of the sequence. [12, 13, 14]. The basic strategy is that the items to be produced in a sequence are activated in parallel, and the order of production is determined by their relative activation levels. More concretely, CQ models comprise at heart three main elements:

1. A set of nodes representing items to be produced, with a gradient of activations such that the first item to be produced is the most active.

2. A mechanism which (i) Selects the most active node for output and (ii) then inhibits that node.

3. A "control signal", with which the item nodes are associated and which establishes the activation gradient across the item nodes. This signal may vary over time during the production of the sequence. This allows the activation gradient to change with time, enabling the system to produce repeated responses, and allows winning items to be evenly activated which increases the robustness of sequencing.

Sequencing in a CQ system is a dynamic process. The sequence is constructed on-line through competition between alternative responses. Figure 1 shows the typical activity profile of such a system during the production of a sequence, the letters of the word "cinema". Notice that the closer two letters are in the word the closer their activation levels are at any point during production (up until the point at which one of them is selected for output, when it is inhibited and subsequently recovers only slowly). It may easily be seen that if the competition between items is made noisy by small random fluctuations in activation levels errors will occur which mainly affect the order of responses.

The CQ paradigm has a number of attractions as a basis for models of serial behaviour [12]. It does not involve associative chaining, it very naturally gives rise to the expected effect of sequence length, and it gives a clear and simple account for the high incidence of ordering errors in general and exchange errors in particular in serial tasks. Finally, simple versions of the model have given a good account for the higher incidence of errors in medial positions of sequences. Not surprisingly, given these advantages, CQ models have been successful in a range of psychological domains - for example, short-term memory [15, 16, 17, 18, 19, 20], typing [21], spelling [22, 23, 24], and speech production [25, 13, 26, 27].

We would claim, on the basis of the striking commonalties between serial processing in each of these different domains (as well as some others not yet modelled by CQ systems, such as finger tapping experiments [28] and piano playing [29]) and the good performance of the CQ models listed above, that the

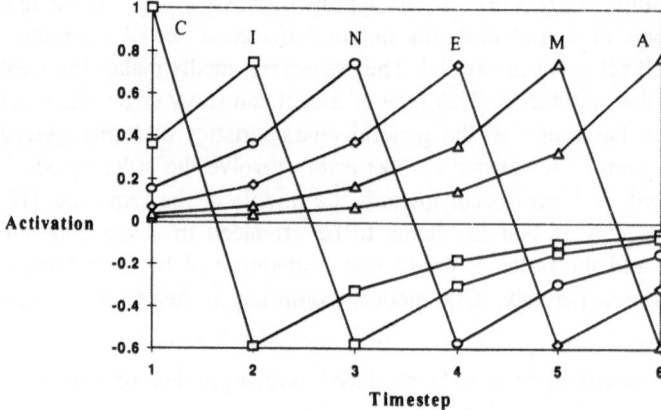

Figure 1. CQ activation dynamics of nodes representing letters during production of the word "CINEMA". The activation level of each letter is shown at each timestep during production of the word. The trace for each letter is labelled at the point where it wins the competition for output.

same type of dynamic process is at work in each of these domains. This is not to say, however, that there is necessarily any overlap in the brain mechanisms utilised in these different tasks. Indeed it seems likely to us that different mechanisms are involved, but that they each operate on similar principles - principles well modelled by the CQ architecture.

3 Domain-specific sequential constraints

Since the basic CQ dynamics operating in each domain are embedded in domain specific machinery, we should expect that the errors made are of fundamentally the same type in each domain but vary in detailed form between domains. In fact this is exactly what is found on a close examination of the data - the basic error types predicted by CQ dynamics are present, but they are modulated or constrained by the domain within which the mechanisms are operating. For example, in the domain of speech production a fairly tight set of constraints governs which phonemes may legally be present at which stage of syllable production [26]. Thus in English the syllable "flunt" is legal, but "lfunt" is not. When errors occur on individual phonemes within a word, the erroneous phoneme is virtually always one which is legal in the syllable position. The constraint on errors is even more striking in the case of exchange errors, when a phoneme will only exchange with another phoneme originating in the same position within another syllable. Thus the exchange error BARN DOOR → DARN BORE, where two onset phonemes have exchanged, is quite possible, whereas the exchange of an onset phoneme with a coda phoneme: BARN DOOR → OORARN DB is extremely unlikely. (Notice that the former error involves both the anticipation of an up-coming phoneme, which implies that at some level different phonemes in the same word are active in parallel, and the apparent inhibition of the D once produced. This is exactly what one would expect of the CQ framework). Similar constraints operate at different structural levels in speech production. For example, syntactic class is generally preserved when errors involve the movement of entire words.

The same phenomenon is shown by the errors of neurological patients with the acquired dysgraphia "Graphemic Buffer disorder" (GBD) [5, 6]. These patients make errors in spelling which show no significant influence of phonology, but nonetheless show a striking preservation of consonant/vowel (CV) letter identity. Thus the exchange error CINEMA → CENIMA is considerably more likely than CINEMA → CIENMA, despite the fact that the exchanged letters in the latter are closer together than those in the former - usually a factor which makes exchanges more likely in CQ models. However, in the former the CV status of the erroneous letters is preserved, whereas it is violated in the latter error. In each case the sequencing system is operating within the wider context of the domain involved, which appears to be constraining the sequential output which may be produced.

Houghton & Hartley [12] develop a framework for models of serial order based on the CQ paradigm. The framework is based on insights from the work of numerous authors (e.g., Burgess & Hitch [15], Dell [25], Estes [30], Glasspool [17], Grossberg [31], Hartley & Houghton [26], Houghton [13], Norman & Shallice [32], Rumelhart & Norman [21]), and organises models into three types, of increasing levels of complexity. Models of type 1 are the most basic (eg. [32, 31, 21]). They incorporate items which compete for output on the basis of activation level, but their sequential operation relies entirely on the inhibition of "used" responses allowing later items to win the competition. Models of type 2 and 3 incorporate all or most of the features of the simpler types, but add new characteristics. Type 2 models incorporate a dynamic "context" signal which provides an endogenous cue to the state of sequencing (eg. [13, 15, 22]). Such models overcome many limitations of type 1 models (see [22] for discussion), including the ability to repeat responses. Type 3 models add domain-specific constraints of the type discussed above, and it is to the means by which this may be achieved that we now turn.

The operation of serial constraints can be well characterised by a simple model - the operation of multiple queues (see Figure 2). In the case of the CV constraint in GBD patients, it is as though in positions where a consonant appears in the target word, only the consonants compete for output during spelling, and only the vowels compete for output in vowel positions. The CINEMA → CENIMA error would then be predicted, since in the second letter position only vowels compete, the most active being the target I, with E and then A at lower activations. The most likely error in this position is thus I → E. In the fourth position, with E still partially inhibited following its earlier selection, the most likely substitutes will be I or A, since again this is a vowel position and the closer consonant letters are excluded from the competition.

There are two problems with the simple idea of separate queues. Firstly, it implies that the switch between alternative queues is absolute - there is no chance, for example, of a consonant appearing in a vowel position since only vowels compete for that position. While this may be true of some domains, such as speech

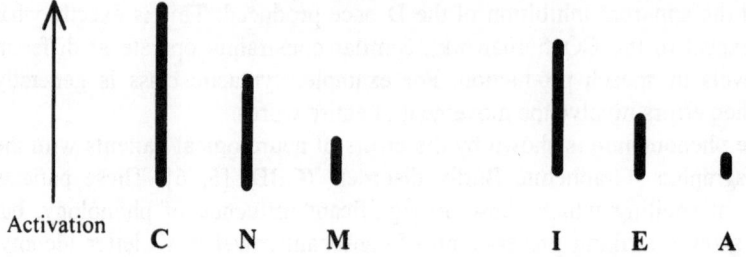

Activation

C   N   M   I   E   A

Figure 2. Serial constraints implemented by multiple parallel queues. Vowels only compete with vowels, consonants only compete with consonants.

production, it is certainly not true of GBD spelling [5, 6]. The data simply show an advantage for vowels in vowel positions- consonants do appear in vowel positions, albeit with a significantly lower probability. The second problem is the extra complexity required of a model which has to maintain multiple simultaneous queues and switch between them during production.

It is however straightforward to achieve a similar effect without resorting to structurally independent queues by dynamically biasing the competition within a single queue. Consider the production of the word CINEMA in a system with a single queue, but with a small constant bias added to the activation of all consonant letters when a consonant should be produced and to all vowel letters when a vowel should be produced (Figure 3).

C   I   N   E   M   A   C   I   N   E   M   A

Activation

Figure 3. A CV implemented by adding a dynamic bias, which raises the activity of all vowel letters in vowel positions (left) and all consonant letters in consonant positions (right).

The effect is similar to that of separate queues - the main competitors in vowel positions are other vowels, which have been boosted above the level of nearby consonants by the bias. However, the constraint is not absolute like that imposed by separate queues. The degree to which the consonant and vowel queues separate can be varied smoothly and continuously by varying the bias: a large bias gives a complete separation, with no chance at all of a consonant appearing in a vowel position. A small bias gives only a slightly higher chance of a vowel than a consonant appearing in a vowel position. (There is of course no need for the bias to be in the positive direction; the approach would work just as well if items which should not compete for the current position are depressed). Only a single competitive queue is required whatever the number of categories which must be differentiated, and the machinery required to switch the categories being biased is likely to be greatly simplified by comparison with that required to switch between queues.

One problem remains: Where might the bias originate? There are many ways in which such a bias could arise, but we believe they fall into two major classes which we term *internal* and *external* constraint systems. External constraint systems are those in which the bias originates in an explicit representation of the response category structure of the target sequences. This has the effect of reinforcing the sequencing process by boosting the activity of a subset of items in each sequential position. In an internal constraint system the bias results from increased competition between items which share properties, and is thus a consequence of the representation of the competing items themselves.

4 External constraint systems

External constraint systems share two characteristics: The sequential constraints are applied by an externally generated abstract or idealised framework into which the generated sequence must fit, and the bias operates by enhancing the activation of those items which fit the template, or inhibiting those which do not, and thus operates so as to reduce the chance of error in sequence generation by removing some of the possible competitor items from the output competition.

The template may be highly stereotyped, limiting the possible responses in each position to a strict subset in a framework into which all possible sequences must fit. Hartley & Houghton [26] present a model of speech production which incorporates a general template for syllable structure in English. Spoken syllables have a highly regular internal structure, consisting of a (possibly empty) onset consonant, followed by a vowel, and a consonantal coda. Phonological speech errors have been universally found to conform to such constraints so that, for instance, when phonemic transposition errors occur, underlying syllable structure and phonotactic regularity is preserved. Vowels swap with vowels, onset consonants with onsets and so on. Hartley and Houghton [26] add a syllable template to a model of speech production which uses the parallel, competitive dynamics of the CQ framework. The template (see Figure 4) is cyclic and comprises five nodes, each corresponding to a phase in the production of a syllable and each connected by permanent excitatory connections to a subset of phoneme nodes in the CQ sequencing system. During syllable production each template node is activated in turn, cyclically biasing the associated phoneme nodes. Phonemes also receive top-down activation from syllable nodes (specifying which phonemes are in the syllable), and the combination of top-down and template activation is required for the model to articulate a phoneme. When the syllable template is in the "vowel" state, the competition is between the target vowel and the partially activated vowels of upcoming words, rather than between the vowel and the following consonant. The Hartley and Houghton model thus implements a highly stereotyped form of serial

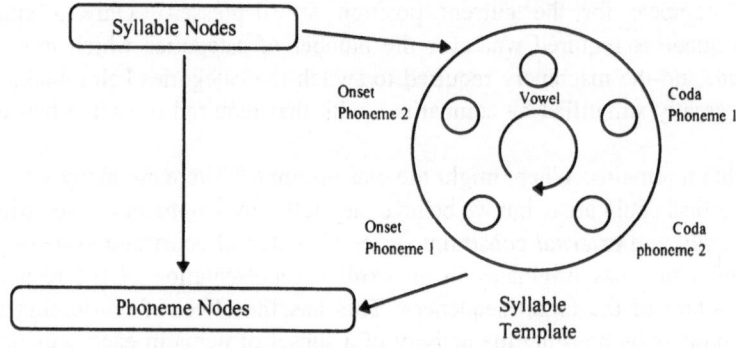

Figure 4. Outline of the Hartley and Houghton speech production model.

constraint, the syllable template always providing the same pattern of biases regardless of the particular syllable being articulated. Another possibility is that the external constraint may comprise one of a set of alternative possible "frameworks", each specifying a different possible abstract structure into which sequences may be fitted, the particular structure being specified somehow along with the identity of the sequence to be generated. In the field of spelling, Glasspool and Houghton [24] describe a model which adds a template specifying the consonant/vowel (CV) structure of the target word to an underlying sequencing system which takes the CQ approach. While the model makes no claims concerning the origin of this template information, it is shown that its incorporation not only causes the model to make a high proportion of errors in which the CV status of the target letter is preserved (for example, CINEMA → CENIMA), in good agreement with the experimental data on the spelling of Graphemic Buffer Disorder patients, but also significantly improves the model's performance in the face of disrupting noise. This improvement in performance is a clear prediction of the external template approach, since the number of responses competing in any serial position is effectively reduced by the introduction of additional information from the template.

5 Internal constraint systems

Internal constraints are the result of similarities between the internal representations of similar items. A good example of this type of constraint is the explanation for the effect of phonological similarity in CQ-based models of verbal short-term memory. The Articulatory Loop (AL) is perhaps the most studied element of Baddeley and Hitch's "Working Memory" framework for short-term memory [33]. The AL is a theoretical component dedicated to the short-term storage and retrieval of verbal information. Burgess and Hitch [15] use a serial recall mechanism based on Houghton's CQ architecture in a network model of the articulatory loop, subsequently extended by Glasspool [34, 17] and Burgess & Hitch [35]. Many of the details of these models are not pertinent to the present discussion. However, all share a common core consisting of a basic CQ sequencing system of

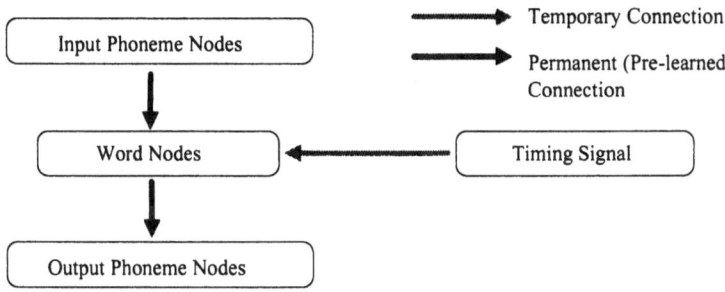

Figure 5. A generalised articulatory loop model, based on [15, 17, 35].

the type shown in Figure 5. The input to the model is a sequence of words, represented by the parallel activation of sets of phoneme nodes. These nodes give rise to the activation of word nodes which become associated with a stereotyped changing context signal. During recall the same changing context signal is recreated, leading to activation of the associated word nodes which compete via a competitive layer for control of the output phoneme nodes. Given the assumption of decay in the context-to-word weights, and a small amount of random noise in word node activations, the models perform well on a variety of data traditionally associated with the articulatory loop.

Of particular interest here is the effect of phonemic similarity. It is well known that memory for lists of words is impaired when the words are phonemically similar [36, 37]. Conrad [38] demonstrated that when subjects make errors in the order of recall of a list of words, the substituted items are significantly more likely to be phonemically similar to the correct items than dissimilar. On the model, these effects are due to the fact that similar words share phonemes. Thus when a stimulus word arrives at the input the pattern of activated phoneme nodes not only fully activates the associated word node but also partially activates those of any phonemically similar words, which then become weakly associated with the current state of the context signal. During recall any words in the list which are phonemically similar compete more strongly with each other than would otherwise be the case due to the additional activation they receive via their weak association with each other's context signals. This leads to a higher rate of errors in lists containing similar words, and more specifically a high rate of errors involving pairs of similar words. In this case the constraints observed on errors from the model are not explained by postulating the extraction of an explicit abstract template for the target sequence, which biases response competition at particular locations towards particular subsets of responses, but emerge instead from interaction between the items themselves.

Most CQ models to date have employed a fully localist architecture with direct associations between the timing signal and the competing output items, and Hebbian learning of sequences. Glasspool [39] shows how a model based on a multi-layer perceptron architecture and trained with an algorithm based on standard backpropagation can generate sequential responses using the dynamic process of

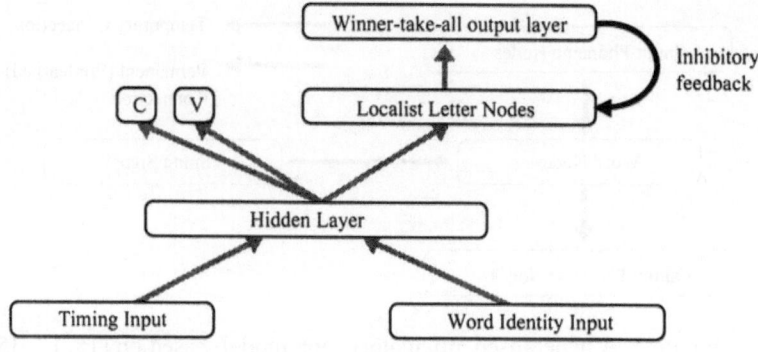

Figure 6. A multi-layer version of the CQ architecture, shown here in a version suited to the modelling of spelling from semantics.

competitive queuing. The general arrangement is shown in Figure 6.

The model retains a localist output representation with a single unit for each output item and uses a standard arrangement to produce the select-inhibit sequencing dynamic, comprising a competitive "winner-take-all" final output layer with inhibitory feedback connections to the item nodes. A localist rather than distributed output representation is preferable since the representations of particular items must be locally inhibited without affecting other competing items. However this architecture allows a distributed representation to be developed on the hidden layer in response to an input comprising (i) a distributed pattern representing the identity of the sequence required, and (ii) a timing signal. The sequence identity input is a binary vector which remains constant throughout the duration of the sequence. The timing signal is similar to that used by Burgess and Hitch [15], and changes at every time-step during sequence production. The timing signal changes slowly - consecutive states are similar, and the more distant two states are the more they differ. The input thus provides both sequence identification and a stereotyped measure of current position in the sequence. Noise is added to the output layer to render the output competition error-prone, but this architecture offers the additional possibility of lesioning sets of connections as an alternative means of eliciting errors.

The architecture is currently being applied to the problem of spelling a word from memory in an attempt to model the same body of data as the fully localist spelling model of Glasspool and Houghton [24] discussed above. Again, the effect of interest here is the preservation of consonant/vowel status in spelling errors. This is shown by the model when the representation developed on the hidden layer differentiates between consonants and vowels. The hidden representation of up-coming letters with the same C/V status as the current letter may then be more active in advance of production than those of intervening letters with the opposite C/V status. One way to force the internal representations to differentiate CV status is to add two extra nodes to the output to represent consonant or vowel status, as shown in Figure 6. The network is trained to activate the appropriate node for each letter during training - the nodes may be ignored during recall. The hidden representations thus learned lead to a strong tendency to preserve CV status in spelling errors. While work is still in progress on this network, there are indications that C/V differentiation in internal representations can also result if a representation of the phonology of the target word forms part of the static sequence identity pattern, which may be a more realistic means of addressing the issue.

6 Discussion

There are clearly differences between the types of domain which favour the use of internal or external constraint systems. An obvious difference is that external systems require the addition of special-purpose mechanisms to the underlying model, whereas internal constraints take advantage of internal representational regularities and require no additional machinery.

The improvement in performance afforded by the extra information which is available from an external template provides a principled justification for the inclusion of the additional mechanism required. There will obviously be a trade off between the degree of flexibility required in the template and the advantages which accrue from an external as opposed to an internal constraint system. In the extreme case, there would be no point in externally constraining the phonemic content of random lists of words in the articulatory loop. On the other hand, in highly constrained domains like that of speech production the benefits of a single stereotyped template may well outweigh the cost of implementing it.

External constraint systems are able to embody highly stereotyped sequential templates. Such an arrangement represents the first step towards a true "dynamic grammar", and the success of models such as Hartley and Houghton [26] encourages us to speculate that it may be possible with this approach to incorporate many more complex grammatical aspects of language production into models of serial behaviour.

By contrast, an internal constraint system imposes no such stereotyped template on the sequence - the abstract template for the sequence, such as it is, is formed by the target sequence itself and is thus not limited by any form of underlying grammar. The idea of a bias added to certain competing items still holds good, but in this case all items similar to the target item receive a bias, while the target itself does not.

The dynamic model underlying the CQ approach to serial order has proved remarkably successful in explaining the basic forms of error which subjects make on serial tasks. All too often in such cases the devil proves to be in the detail: It is one thing for a theory to explain the general pattern of results, but quite another to extend it to encompass a finer level of accuracy. The various pieces of work we have summarised here have set out to do just that, and the picture which has emerged is encouraging. Firstly, the data in a variety of areas can be interpreted as showing the same pattern, viz.: The underlying error pattern is that predicted by the basic CQ architecture, but constraints operate on the errors so produced such that some forms are more likely than others. Secondly, as we have shown, adding such constraints to the basic CQ architecture does not involve a major rethink of the theory, but is a simple and natural extension. "Biasing the competition" is very much in the spirit of the CQ approach. Sequencing is achieved in the first place by manipulating the salience of internally represented items according to the specific sequence required, and similarly serial constraints operate by biasing saliences, but in a more general, less sequence-specific fashion. Approaching the regularities in errors on serial tasks from the point of view of constraints acting on a CQ sequencing system has already influenced experimental work [40] and we hope that this will prove to be a very productive framework for understanding the operation of low-level serial systems in the future.

Acknowledgements

The application of the multi-layer variant of the CQ architecture described in this paper to spelling is work being carried out in collaboration with Tim Shallice at University College London.

References

1. Lashley KS. The problem of serial order in behaviour. In Jefress LA. (ed) Cerebral mechanisms in behaviour. Wiley, New York, 1951. pp 112-136.
2. Henson RNA, Norris DG, Page MPA & Baddeley AD. Unchained memory: Error patterns rule out chaining models of immediate serial recall. Quarterly Journal of Experimental Psychology 49A, 1996. pp 80-115.
3. Crowder RG. Visual and auditory memory. In Kavanagh JF & Mattingley IG (eds) Language by Ear and by Eye. Cambridge, Mass.: The MIT Press. 1972.
4. Wing AM & Baddeley AD. Spelling errors in handwriting: A corpus and a distributional analysis. In Frith U. (ed), Cognitive processes in spelling. London: Academic Press. 1980.
5. Jonsdottir M, Shallice T & Wise R. Language-specific differences in graphemic buffer disorder. Cognition 59. 1996. pp 169-197.
6. Caramazza A & Miceli G. The structure of graphemic representations. Cognition, 37. 1990. pp 243-297.
7. Tweney RD, Tkacz S & Zaruba S. Slips of the tongue and lexical storage. Language and Speech, 18. 1975. pp 388-396.
8. Wilberg RB. The retention and free recall of multiple movements. Human Movement Science, 9. 1990. pp 437-479.
9. Jordan M. Attractor dynamics and parallelism in a connectionist sequential machine. Proc. of the 8th Annual Conference of the Cognitive Science Society. pp. 10-17. Hillsdale, NJ: Lawrence Erlbaum Associates. 1986.
10. Elman JL. Finding structure in time. Cognitive Science, 14. 1990. pp 179-211.
11. Conrad R. Order error in immediate recall of sequences. Journal of Verbal Learning and Verbal Behaviour 4. 1965. pp 161-169.
12. Houghton G and Hartley T. Parallel models of serial behaviour: Lashley revisited. Psyche. psyche-95-2-25-lashley-1-houghton. 1996.

13. Houghton G. The problem of serial order: A neural network model of sequence learning and recall. In Dale R, Mellish C & Zock M. (eds) Current Research in Natural Language Generation. London: Academic Press. 1990.

14. Shallice T, Glasspool DW & Houghton G. Can neuropsychological evidence inform connectionist modelling? Analyses of spelling. Language and Cognitive Processes 10. 1995. pp 195-225.

15. Burgess N & Hitch JG. Towards a network model of the articulatory loop. Journal of Memory and Language, 31. 1992. pp 429-460.

16. Milner PM. A neural mechanism for the immediate recall of sequences. Kybernetic 1. 1961. pp 76-81.

17. Glasspool DW. Competitive queuing and the articulatory loop: An extended network model. In Levy JP, Bairaktaris D, Bullinaria JA & Cairns P (eds), Connectionist Models of Memory and Language. London: UCL Press. 1995.

18. Page MPA & Norris DG. The primacy model: A new model of immediate serial recall. (submitted).

19. Henson RNA. Short-term memory for serial order: The Start-End model. (submitted).

20. Brown GDA, Preece T & Hulme C. Oscillator-based memory for serial order. (Submitted).

21. Rumelhart DE & Norman DA. Simulating a skilled typist: a study of skilled cognitive-motor performance. Cognitive Science, 6. 1982. pp 1-36.

22. Houghton G, Glasspool DW & Shallice T. Spelling and serial recall: Insights from a competitive queueing model. In Brown GDA & Ellis NC (eds), Handbook of Spelling: Theory, Process and Intervention. pp. 365-404. Chichester: John Wiley and Sons. 1994.

23. Glasspool DW, Houghton G & Shallice T. Interactions between knowledge sources in a dual-route connectionist model of spelling. In Smith LS and Hancock PJB (eds) Neural Computation and Psychology. Springer-Verlag. 1995.

24. Glasspool DW. & Houghton G. Response category constraints in serial behaviour: Consonant-vowel structure in a model of graphemic buffer disorder. (Submitted).

25. Dell GS. The retrieval of phonological forms in production: Tests of predictions from a connectionist model. Journal of Memory and Language, 27. 1988. pp 124-142.

26. Hartley T & Houghton G. A linguistically constrained model of short-term memory for nonwords. Journal of Memory and Language 35. 1996. 1-31.

27. Vousden JI & Brown GDA. To repeat or not to repeat: The time course of response suppression in sequential behaviour. In Bullinaria JA, Glasspool DW & Houghton G (eds) Proceedings of the fourth Neural Computation and Psychology Workshop. Springer-Verlag, 1997.

28. Rosenbaum DA, Kenny SB & Derr MA. Hierarchical control of rapid movement sequences. Journal of Experimental Psychology: Human Perception and Performance, 9. 1983. pp 86-102.

29. Shaffer LH. Intention and performance. Psychological Review, 83. 1976. pp 375-393.
30. Estes WK. An associative basis for coding and organization in memory. In Melton AW and Martin E (eds) Coding Processes in Human Memory. Washington DC: V. H. Winston & sons. 1972.
31. Grossberg S. A theory of human memory: Self-organisation and performance of sensory-motor codes, maps and plans. Progress in theoretical biology 5. 1978. pp 233-302.
32. Norman DA & Shallice T. Attention to action: Willed and automatic control of behaviour. Center for Human Information Processing (Technical Report No. 99) 1980. Reprinted in revised form in Davidson RJ, Schwartz GE & Shapiro D (eds) Consciousness and self-regulation (Vol. 4). New York: Plenum Press. 1986.
33. Baddeley AD & Hitch GL. Working Memory. In Bower GH (ed) Recent Advances in the Psychology of Learning and Motivation, Vol. VIII, 47-90. New York: Academic Press. 1974.
34. Glasspool DW. Competitive queuing and the articulatory loop: an extended network model. MSc. thesis. Department of Psychology. University of Manchester. 1991.
35. Burgess N & Hitch GJ. A connectionist model of STM for serial order. In Gathercole SE (ed.) Models of Short-Term Memory. Hove: Psychology Press. 1996.
36. Conrad R & Hull AJ. Information, acoustic confusion and memory span. British Journal of Psychology, 5. 1964. pp 429-432.
37. Baddeley AD. Short-term memory for word sequences as a function of acoustic, semantic and formal similarity. Quarterly Journal of Experimental Psychology, 18. 1966. 362-365.
38. Conrad R. Acoustic confusions in immediate memory. British Journal of Psychology, 55, 1. 1964. pp 75-84.
39. Glasspool DW. Competitive Queueing dynamics in a multi-layer network. Internal Technical Report, UCL-PSY-CQ2. Dept. of Psychology, University College London. 1997.
40. Sevald C, Dell G & Cole J. Syllable structure in speech production - are syllables chunks or schemas? Journal of Memory and Language 34. 1995. pp 807-820.

Representations of Serial Order

R. N. A. Henson

Department of Psychology, University College London, UK

N. Burgess

Department of Anatomy, University College London, UK

Abstract

Three means of representing serial order in connectionist models are identified: interitem associations (e.g., the recurrent network of Jordan [1]), ordinal representations (e.g., the activation gradient of Grossberg [2]), and positional representations (e.g., the control signal of Houghton [3]). Error data from studies of human short-term memory favour positional representations. Three types of positional representations are possible: those of temporal position (e.g., the OSCAR model of Brown et al. [4]), absolute position (e.g., the Articulatory Loop model of Burgess & Hitch [5]) and relative position (e.g., the Start-End Model of Henson [6]). Recent data [7] favour representations of relative position. A connectionist implementation of relative position is discussed.

1   Introduction

The problem of serial order is to explain how people store and retrieve a sequence of items in the correct order. This problem pervades many aspects of cognition, from the ordering of digits in a telephone number to the ordering of phonemes in a spoken word. However, since the importance of the problem was raised by Lashley [8], an agreed solution has proved surprisingly elusive.

This chapter begins by reviewing three main approaches to the problem. These approaches have their roots in psychological theories and are exemplified in several recent connectionist models. When tested within the domain of short-term memory (STM) however, only one of these approaches appears viable. This approach assumes that each item is coded for its position within a sequence. The question then becomes whether that position is represented temporally, absolutely or relatively. Connectionist models of STM tend to assume representations of temporal or absolute position, whereas recent psychological data [7] favour representations that code position relative to the start and end of a sequence. The chapter concludes with a new connectionist model that accommodates these data by assuming an array of oscillators of different frequencies that compete to best represent the input.

2   Three Approaches to Serial Order

Existing approaches to the problem of serial order can be categorised as interitem associations, ordinal representations or positional representations.

2.1 Interitem associations

This approach assumes that a sequence is stored by the formation of associations between representations of successive items. The order of items is retrieved by stepping along the chain of associations, such that each item becomes (part of) the cue for recall of its successor (also known as *chaining theory* [9]). Interitem associations are probably the oldest approach to serial order [10], being a simple extension of stimulus-response theory in which each response can become the stimulus for the next [8].

The simplest chaining theories assume only pairwise associations between representations of adjacent items [11] and cues that consist entirely of the preceding response. However, these theories face problems with a) repeated items, because the items following a repetition will share the same cue, and b) erroneous responses, because the cue for subsequent responses will be incorrect. More sophisticated theories overcome these problems by assuming remote associations as well as adjacent ones [12]. In such *compound chaining theories* (Figure 1A), the cue consists of a number of preceding items, providing additional context with which to disambiguate repeated items and to cater for occasional errors in recall.[1] Connectionist implementations of compound chaining theories include the recurrent neural networks of Jordan [1], Elman [13] and Taylor [14], which have successfully modelled some aspects of sequence production and recognition. Nonetheless, there are general arguments against chaining theory [8, 15] and it is argued later (Section 3.1) that there is no empirical support for interitem associations underlying STM for serial order.

2.2 Ordinal representations

Ordinal representations assume a single dimension along which order is defined, such as the relative strengths of item representations in memory. The connectionist models of Grossberg [2] for example assume that order is stored in a primacy gradient of strengths, such that the representation of each item is stronger than that of its successor. The order of items is retrieved by an iterative process of selecting the strongest item representation, and then suppressing it so that it is not selected again (Figure 1B). Other ordinal representations include the cyclic reactivations of Estes [16] and activation gradient in the Primacy Model of Page and Norris [17] (see Norris & Page, this volume).

Ordinal representations generally require token representations in order to handle repeated items: The order of sequences with repeated items can not be represented over type representations, each with a single strength. Because order is defined relationally, ordinal models also imply that errors will cooccur: If, for example, the representation of an item becomes stronger than that of its predecessor in the Primacy Model, owing to random noise, then the two items will transpose [17]. This is an attractive property, because such paired transpositions of adjacent items are common in people too (Section 2.2).

Unlike chaining models, models like the Primacy Model do not require feedback of responses, and a process like suppression can operate independently of errors occurring at later stages of output. Moreover, the processes of selection and suppression are simple to implement in connectionist models as winner-take-all networks (e.g., the competitive filter of Houghton [3]). Nonetheless, it is argued below (Section 3.2) that ordinal representations are not sufficient to

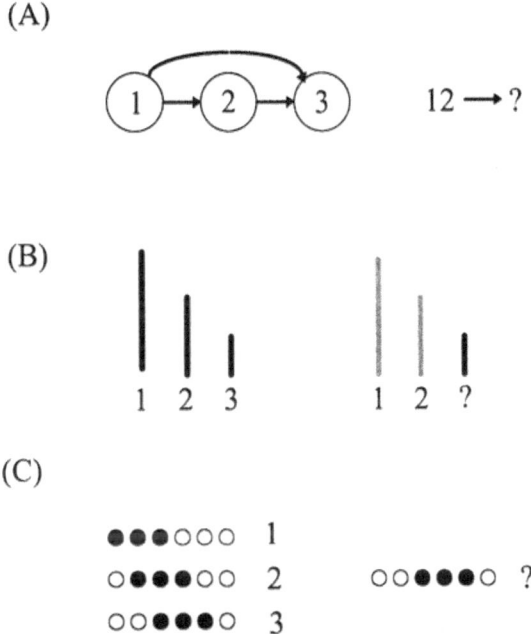

(A)

1 → 2 → 3   12 → ?

(B)

1 2 3   1 2 ?

(C)

● ● ● ○ ○ ○   1
○ ● ● ● ○ ○   2   ○ ○ ● ● ● ○   ?
○ ○ ● ● ● ○   3

Figure 1: (A) Remote interitem associations (e.g., Jordan [1]); (B) an ordinal representation (e.g., Grossberg [2], suppression indicated by lighter lines); (C) a positional representation (e.g., Burgess & Hitch [5], filled circles represent active nodes in a connectionist network, unfilled nodes represent inactive nodes).

account for the errors people make in recall from STM.

2.3 Positional representations

This approach assumes that order is stored by associating each item with its position in a sequence, and that the order is retrieved by reinstating each positional code and cueing the associated item.

The extreme case of a positional representation is Conrad's "box" model [18]. Conrad suggested that people possess a number of boxes in STM in which item representations can be stored. The items can be retrieved in order by stepping through the boxes according to a predetermined routine. This model does not have a problem with repeated items, because they are stored in separate boxes, nor with erroneous responses, because the retrieval mechanism can continue to the next box irrespective of whether the contents of the previous box were retrieved correctly. This is of course the method by which conventional Von Neumann computers store and retrieve order, through routines accessing separate addresses in memory.

As a psychological theory, this approach is elaborated in the Perturbation Model of Lee and Estes [19, 20], in which of the positions of items are initially coded perfectly, but get perturbed over time such that nearby items are likely to exchange. An alternative proposal is that positional codes are not perfect, but overlap, in that the code for one position is similar to the codes for nearby positions. This is the approach taken in the connectionist model of Burgess and Hitch [5, 21, 22]. A "window" of activity moves from left to right across an array of nodes for each position in a sequence (Figure 2C), and is associated with other nodes (not shown) representing each item. However, because there is some overlap in the set of active nodes for nearby positions, items at these positions can be confused during retrieval.

The main question facing positional models is how the positional codes themselves are reinstated in the correct order. One suggestion is that the codes are derived from temporal oscillators in the brain [4, 21, 23]. Item representations can be associated with successive states of the oscillators, and these states reinstated simply by resetting the oscillators and letting them evolve under their own dynamics. However, though there is good evidence for positional representations in STM (Section 3.2), one goal of the present chapter is to argue for a modified interpretation of the oscillators assumed to underlie positional codes.

3 Evidence from Short-Term Memory

In spite of the strengths and weaknesses of the specific connectionist models mentioned above, important differences remain between the three general approaches to serial order. The difference between interitem associations and positional representations is obvious: The retrieval cue in the former is the previous item; the retrieval cue in the latter is some (abstract) positional code. The difference between positional and ordinal representations is less obvious, but relates to whether the position of an item can be defined independently of surrounding items. In positional representations, it can; in ordinal representations, it cannot. The consequence is that, with ordinal representations like that in the Primacy Model [17], the middle item in a sequence can only be retrieved after retrieval of its predecessors. With positional representations however, it is possible in principle to retrieve the middle item without retrieving its neighbours, by reinstating the appropriate positional code.

These differences can be tested empirically within the domain of STM by using the memory span task, in which subjects must recall a novel list of items in the correct order. It is particularly fruitful to examine the errors people make when they misrecall a list. It will be argued that these errors necessitate some type of positional representation in STM.

3.1 Evidence against interitem associations

The main prediction of chaining models is that recall of an item will depend on the properties of its predecessor. In particular, "...errors are more likely when discriminations must be made between similar states..." (Jordan, p.37 [1]). For example, it is well-established that lists of similar-sounding items (e.g., BTGPDV) are harder to recall in order than lists of dissimilar items (e.g., HRMQJY), even when presented visually (e.g., [24, 25]). This suggests that items are represented in STM in a phonological form. If so, chaining models predict that (part of) the difficulty people face with lists of phonologically similar items stems from the similarity between the cues for each item. However, using lists in which similar and dissimilar items alternated in order (e.g., BRGQDY), Henson et al. [25] found no effect of whether or not the previous item was phonologically similar to other items in the list. This is problematic for any model that chains along associations between phonological representations. Furthermore, Henson et al. found that the probability of recalling a dissimilar item appeared independent of whether or not the previous similar item was recalled correctly. This is troublesome for any closed-loop chaining model that assumes responses are fed back to cue subsequent items.

An extreme case of similarity is of course identity. Even compound chaining models with remote associations predict that there should be a greater probability of errors following repeated items (assuming they employ type representations of items). For example, in a list $HRMRJY$, there should be more errors in recalling the items following the repeated item (i.e., M and J) than for items at corresponding positions in control lists with no repeated items. In fact, chaining theory predicts that these errors are likely to be exchanges between the following items themselves (e.g., $HRMRJY$ recalled as $HRJRMY$), given that they share the same cue. Preliminary support for this hypothesis was reported by Wickelgren [26]. However, several recent experiments [9] found only a small effect of repetition on recall of subsequent items, which failed to reach significance. Furthermore, any small difference that is found may well have alternative explanations, given that the sheer presence of repeated items has several effects on recall of a list [27]. For example, because there are fewer different items to guess from in a list with a repeated item than one without, a simple guessing hypothesis also predicts a higher incidence of exchanges following repeated items when compared with control lists. Thus there does not appear to be any conclusive evidence for an effect of repetition on cueing either.

The failure to find reliable evidence for an effect of phonological similarity, errors or repetition on cueing is problematic for chaining models. It may be possible to construct a specific chaining model that is consistent with the above data (such a model might chain along associations between nonphonological, token representations for example, independently of response feedback). However, given that there is not, as yet, any positive evidence for chaining, and that there is positive evidence for positional representations (below), it seems reasonable to argue against interitem associations on the grounds of parsimony.

3.2 Evidence for positional representations

The most common errors in serial recall from STM are order errors, or *transpositions*. The most striking aspect of these errors is their distribution: Erroneous items are clustered around their correct position, rather than being randomly distributed (e.g., [16, 25]). This finding is often taken as evidence for positional representations, by suggesting that there is some generalisation across positional codes that occasionally causes errors between items at nearby positions. However, the finding does not force this conclusion, because similar distributions of transpositions can be produced by models with ordinal representations (see [17]): Errors in the relative order of nearby items also produce the appropriate clustering of transpositions, without any coding of the position of those items. In fact, the same pattern can even be produced by compound chaining theories [28].

However, there are two types of error that do imply the presence of positional representations. The first of these occurs when lists are grouped. Grouping items by their rhythm of presentation, as common with telephone numbers for example, is well known to improve recall (e.g., [29]). Though grouping reduces the overall incidence of errors, one type of error actually increases [30]. These *interpositions* [9] are transpositions between groups that maintain their position within groups (and are not simply the result of whole groups swapping [9, 20]). These errors imply that items can be coded for their position within a group independently of surrounding items.

The second type of positional error is found between recall of lists on successive trials. Conrad [31] showed that an erroneous item in one trial is more likely than chance to have occurred at the same position in the previous trial. Henson [9] called the errors caused by such proactive interference of positional information *protrusions*. These errors imply that items can be coded for their position within a trial.

Protrusions and interpositions are examples of a general tendency for errors between sequences to maintain their position within a sequence. Such errors cannot be attributed to errors of relative order within a sequence, and are therefore inexplicable by ordinal representations. Nor can they be explained by interitem associations. Positional errors can only be explained if STM for serial order utilises positional representations.

4   Positional Representations

Three types of positional representations can be distinguished: representations of temporal position, absolute position and relative position.

4.1   Temporal Position

In models that code temporal position, items are associated with a representation of their time of occurrence (often relative to the start of a sequence). Such representations have been proposed by both Burgess and Hitch [21, 22] and Brown et al. [4]. In particular, the OSCAR model [4] (see also Vousden & Brown, this volume) is a connectionist model that assumes an array of free-running oscillators of different frequencies, the phases of which can be combined to form a smooth "timing signal". Items are associated with the states of this signal at their time of presentation, and recalled in order simply by resetting the oscillators to their states at the start of presentation.

A simple formalisation of such a timing signal uses an array of harmonically-related sinusoidal oscillators $s = 1..N$, such that the phase of oscillator s at time t, $\phi_s(t)$, is:

$$\phi_s(t) = sin(\frac{2\pi t}{2^{s-1}B} + \Phi_s)$$

where B is the period of the *base* (fastest) oscillator $s = 1$ and Φ_s is a random starting phase for oscillator s at $t = 0$. The timing signal can then be represented by a dynamic vector $\mathbf{v}(t)$ generated from a weighted combination of the oscillator phases, with more weight given to slower oscillators, such that:

$$v_s(t) = W^{N-s}\phi_s(t)$$

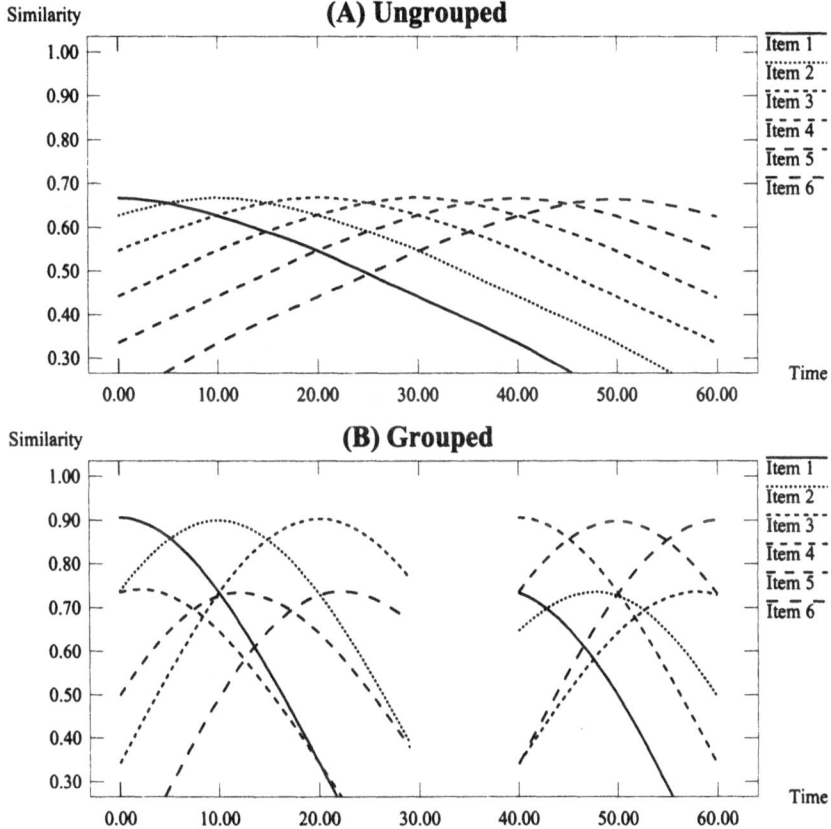

Figure 2: Similarity gradients for six items presented every 10 time units (A) and for six items presented as two groups of three (B) via an extra 10 time units between the third and fourth item ($B=10$, $N=6$, $W=0.5$, weighting of oscillator $s=4$ increased to 1.0 for the grouped list). Gradients are averaged over 10,000 runs with random initial phases for each oscillator.

where $W < 1$ is a weighting parameter. Providing there are sufficient oscillators, the period of the slowest oscillator can be made long enough to ensure that the timing signal does not repeat within the timescale of interest.

Assuming the initial state of the timing signal during presentation can be reinstated at recall, the similarity (inner product) between the state of the timing signal for each position in a list of six items and its state at each time point during recall is shown in Figure 2A (averaging over random initial phases, Φ_s; equivalent to the combination of multiple timing signals in OSCAR). These similarity gradients indicate the degree of temporal generalisation across positions. In a model where items were output when this similarity exceeded a threshold, any noise in the temporal codes or in the thresholding process would produce the clustered pattern of transposition errors seen in the data (the greater similarity between Positions 1 and 2 than between Positions 1 and 3 making Item 1 more likely to transpose with Item 2 than with Item 3).

Temporal grouping can be simulated by giving more weight to the oscillator whose half-period is closest to the group period. This might arise for example if the rhythm of presentation caused people to focus attention on the timescale of groups. The further assumption that this group oscillator can be reset between groups (so that all oscillators are reset at the start of recall, but only the group oscillator is reset at the start of each group) produces the similarity gradients shown for two groups of three in Figure 2B. In this example, the oscillator $s = 4$ with a half-period equal to the group period (40 time units) had its weighting increased from 0.25 to 1.00 (and the weightings of other oscillators were normalised so that the sum total of weightings remained constant). The effect of this resetting and increased relative weighting is to improve the temporal resolution of positions within groups, by producing taller and sharper similarity gradients, but impair the resolution of positions between groups, by increasing the similarity between the same positions within groups (e.g., increasing the similarity between the Positions 1 and 4). Both these properties are true of the data [9], the latter accounting for the interpositions between groups that support a positional representation of serial order (Section 3.2).

If it is also assumed that the oscillators are yoked such that an increase in the frequency of the base oscillator produces a proportionate increase the frequency of the other oscillators, then the recall rate can be uncoupled from the presentation rate. A tonic signal to increase the frequency of the base oscillator prior to recall for example would allow the items to be recalled faster than they were presented. However, unless this tonic signal can also vary *during* presentation and recall, a model using temporal representations always predicts that the relative timing of recall of each item will match that of presentation of each item. As discussed later (Section 5.1), this property proves problematic.

4.2   Absolute Position

Rather than coding each item with its temporal position, items can be coded with their absolute (ordinal) position (e.g., first, second, third, etc.). This is the positional representation adopted by event-driven models, such as the original connectionist model of Burgess and Hitch [5]. In this model, the context signal (Figure 1C) only changes as each item occurs, irrespective of the temporal spacing between items. Thus the positional codes for a list of items presented slowly are identical to those for the same list presented rapidly. However, it will be argued later (Section 5.2) that even this level of abstraction is not sufficient to explain the pattern of errors in recall from STM.

4.3   Relative Position

The most abstract representation of position is a relative one, in which items are coded for their position relative to the start and end of a sequence. This is the representation chosen in the computational model of Henson [6, 9] and in the connectionist model of Houghton [3]. These models assume a start marker, which is strongest at the start of a sequence but decreases in strength with each subsequent item, and an end marker, which increases in strength with each item towards its maximum strength at the end of a sequence. The relative strengths of the start and end markers therefore provide an approximate two-dimensional code for each position within a sequence.

One problem facing these models is to specify how items are coded relative to the end of the sequence when the end of the sequence has not yet occurred. Henson [7] suggested that the strength of the end marker might correspond to the degree of expectation for the end of a sequence. Houghton [3] assumed that the end marker was only triggered at the very end of presentation, upon which it was associated with a recency gradient of decaying activations of item representations. By growing in strength more gradually during recall, these associations allowed the end marker to exert an influence backwards in time. Both these models are consistent with the evidence for relative position discussed below (Section 5.2). Nonetheless, Section 6 describes a new model that codes relative position without the problems associated with an end marker.

5 Evidence from Short-Term Memory

There is also evidence from STM experiments concerning the three types of positional representation. Though the evidence is not clear cut, the pattern of positional errors between sequences certainly favours a representation of relative position over representations of purely temporal or absolute position.

5.1 Evidence for and against temporal position

One clear prediction of representations of temporal position is that the positions of items closer in time will be harder to discriminate. In STM experiments, this implies that slower presentation rates should produce better recall. However, one problem with this prediction is that subjects will often rehearse items subjectively, at a rate that may differ to the objective presentation rate. Faced with a slow presentation rate for example, rehearsal rate is likely to exceed presentation rate. When covert rehearsal was prevented by concurrent articulatory suppression, Baddeley and Lewis [32] found that serial recall was worse for slow presentation rates, contrary to the prediction of temporal position. Likewise, when covert rehearsal was minimised by articulation of distractors between presentation of each item, Neath and Crowder [33] found that overall performance decreased as the number of interitem distractors increased, in spite of the greater temporal separation entailed.[2]

One objection to the above evidence is that slower presentation rates and greater numbers of interitem distractors also entail a greater delay between presentation and recall of each item. Given the transient nature of information in STM, longer delays are likely to produce a greater loss of information, which may override any advantage from more distinctive temporal coding. What is required is a comparison of performance when the temporal spacing between items is varied but the temporal spacing between presentation and recall of the first item is kept constant (and rehearsal is prevented). The authors are not aware any such STM experiment to date.[3]

Some evidence that supports a role for temporal factors comes from other findings by Neath and Crowder [33]. When comparing presentation schedules in which the temporal spacing between items either increased or decreased over successive positions (with the total presentation time equated at six seconds), free recall was better with the decreasing schedule than the increasing schedule. This is explicable if subjects adopted a backward temporal perspective, for

(A) Different Group Rates

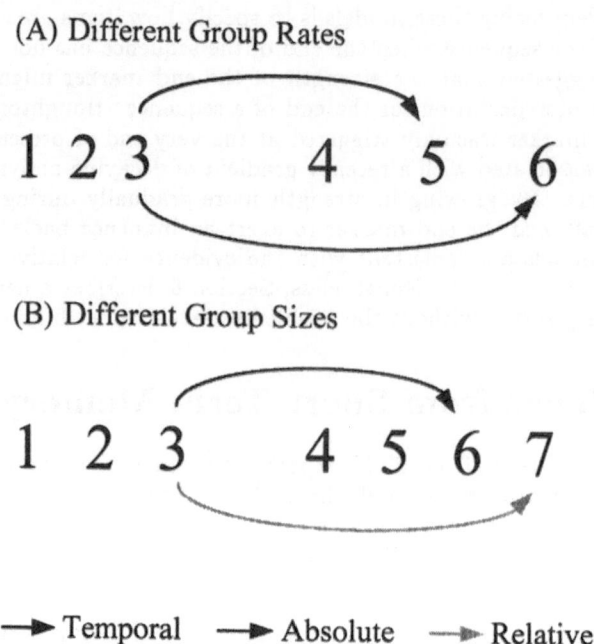

(B) Different Group Sizes

→ Temporal   → Absolute   ⇢ Relative

Figure 3: Examples of groupings used by (A) Ng [35] and (B) Henson [7] and the corresponding transposition errors predicted by representations of temporal, absolute and relative position.

which a greater separation of early items is more advantageous than a greater separation of late items (so-called *temporal distinctiveness theory*, cf. a line of telegraph poles receding from the observer). However, in experiments with a total presentation time closer to one second, Neath and Crowder [34] found that performance was better with the increasing schedule. The authors suggest that with such fast presentation rates (and a tendency to recall serially), subjects adopt a forward perspective, in which case it is more advantageous for later items to be widely separated. These data are returned to in Section 6, in relation to a connectionist model that incorporates some influence of temporal factors in the coding of relative position.

Perhaps more difficult for representations of purely temporal position are the error data from an experiment by Ng [35]. Ng used nine items grouped as three groups of three, such that the middle group was presented either faster or slower relative to the first and last groups (a two-group example is shown in Figure 3A). The interest was in whether transpositions between groups were more likely between the same temporal positions within groups (e.g., Positions 3 and 5) or the same absolute positions within groups (e.g., Positions 3 and 6). Ng found that transpositions were more likely between the same absolute position within groups, and argued in favour of an absolute or event-driven coding of position.

5.2 Evidence against absolute position

Because Ng's groups were of equal size however, her data are equally well compatible with a representation of relative position. To contrast the predictions of absolute and relative position, Henson [7] examined the transpositions between groups of different size, such as a group of three followed by a group of four (Figure 3B). Transpositions were more likely between the ends of groups (Positions 3 and 7) than between the same absolute position within groups (Positions 3 and 6). In a second experiment, Henson [7] also found that protrusions between trials of different length were more likely between the ends of trials than the same absolute position within trials. These data favour the representation of relative position over the representation of absolute position.

One caveat with the experiments of Ng [35] and Henson [7] is that neither controlled for covert rehearsal. In Ng's experiment for example, subjects may have rehearsed the groups at the same rate, in spite of the differences in their presentation rates. If so, the predictions of temporal and absolute position would be confounded. However, this possibility seems less likely for Henson's experiments, because there is no apparent reason why subjects should rehearse longer sequences faster than shorter ones, such that their total rehearsal time is equated. Thus the conclusion that positional representations in STM are relative rather than absolute will be maintained.

6 A Connectionist Model of Relative Position

The model of relative position described by Henson [6, 9] is a psychological-level model that is useful in allowing quantitative fits to data and making predictions for future experiments. However, it is not a connectionist model and makes no attempt to offer a neural-level implementation of relative position. Below we sketch such an implementation in terms of temporal oscillators, given the considerable evidence for such oscillators in the brain [36]. This implementation offers a novel positional representation that combines aspects of both temporal and relative position.

The basic idea behind the model is that many oscillators of different frequencies compete to best represent the input.[4] The winning oscillators are those with a half-period closest to the temporal duration of a sequence. Thus groups of different temporal duration (by virtue of different presentation rates or different numbers of items) are represented by different oscillators. During recall however, oscillators of a single frequency are selected (depending on the recall rate), and items are cued to the extent that the phases of these oscillators match the phases of the oscillators that won the competition to represent the sequence. The model is therefore able to adapt to different presentation and recall rates. Moreover, by having all oscillators compete in parallel, but only selecting those with a half-period close to the sequence duration (apparent as soon as no more items occur; see below), the model finesses the problem of predicting the end of a sequence that plagues models with an end marker.

More specifically, an array of oscillator pairs $p = 1..N$ with half-periods $H_p = 1..N$ time units is assumed, such that the phases $\phi(t)$ and $\phi'(t)$ of the oscillators in pair p are:

$$\phi_p(t) = sin(\frac{\pi t}{H_p}) \qquad \phi'_p(t) = sin(\frac{\pi t}{H_p} + \frac{\pi}{2})$$

In other words, the two oscillators are phase-lagged by 90 degrees [37].

During presentation, the occurrence of the first item in a sequence causes all oscillators to be reset such that $t = 0$. The oscillators then run at their different speeds, each item being associated with the phases of all oscillators at its time of occurrence, until no further items occur. The winning oscillator pair then selected to represent the sequence is the pair $p = w$, where H_w is the total duration of the sequence. The positional code for the item presented at time t_1 after the start of the sequence is the two-dimensional vector $< \phi_w(t_1)\ \phi'_w(t_1) >$. Assuming that oscillator pair $p = r$ is chosen for recall (and reset at the start of recall), then the strength with which the item presented at time t_1 is cued at time t_2 relative to the start of recall is given by the inner product of the positional codes for presentation and recall, equal to:

$$sin(\frac{\pi t_1}{H_w})sin(\frac{\pi t_2}{H_r}) + sin(\frac{\pi t_1}{H_w} + \frac{\pi}{2})sin(\frac{\pi t_2}{H_r} + \frac{\pi}{2}) = cos(\frac{\pi t_1}{H_w} - \frac{\pi t_2}{H_r})$$

In other words, the similarity gradient for the item occurring at time t_1 during presentation is a cosine function of the angle between the phase of the first oscillator in the pair selected at presentation and the phase of the first oscillator in the pair chosen for recall at time t_2 (without needing to average over oscillators with different initial phases).

The ability of this representation to capture the appropriate similarity gradients for grouped lists is shown in Figure 4. For these simulations, a number of further assumptions were made about grouping. Firstly, a group was assumed to end when no item occurred in a given interval after the most recent item, where that interval was equal to the time between the presentation of the previous two items. In other words, prior rhythmic parsing of the input was assumed, such that a group boundary was located whenever an item failed to occur before or in time with the beat defined by the last two items. Secondly, two sets of oscillator pairs were assumed: one in which all oscillators were reset at the start of a new group, and one in which oscillators were only reset at the start of a list. The winning oscillator pair(s) in the first set represented the relative position of items within groups, whereas the winning oscillator pair in the second set (those with a half-period equal to the length of the whole list) represented the position of groups within the list. Positional codes therefore consisted of two vectors, one comprising the phases of the winning group oscillator pair at the time each item was presented, and one comprising the phases of the winning list oscillator pair at the time the first item in each group was presented. During recall, the inner products between these vectors and those derived from the group oscillator pair and list oscillator pair chosen for output were combined by simple addition (and halved to normalise similarity to the range -1 to 1). Finally, it was assumed that reset of the group oscillator pair during recall was triggered when the phases of the list oscillator pair chosen for output matched those possessed at the start of presentation of each group by the list oscillator pair chosen for input (these phases perhaps being stored in temporary associations between the two sets of oscillators).

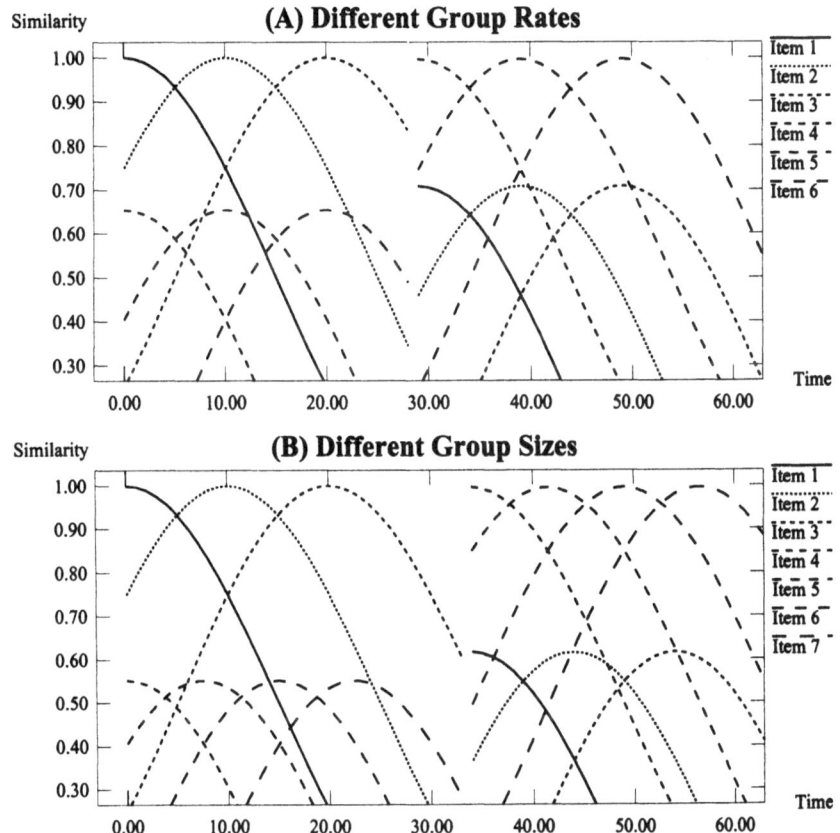

Figure 4: Similarity gradients for two groups of three items, the first presented every 10 time units and the second presented every 20 time units (A), and for a group of three items followed by a group of four items, presented every 10 time units (B), with an extra 10 time units between each group (half-periods of group and list oscillator pairs used for recall were 30 and 80 time units respectively).

Figure 4A shows the similarity gradients for two groups, the second of which was presented twice as slowly as the first (as in Figure 3A); Figure 4B shows the gradients for a group of three items followed by a group of four (as in Figure 3B). In both cases, the similarity between items in different groups is greatest for items at the same relative position within a group. Thus, in the case of groups presented at different rates, Item 3 is more likely to transpose with Item 6 than with Item 5, and in the case of groups of different size, Item 3 is more likely to transpose with Item 7 than with Item 6.

As well as being compatible with the error patterns in STM, it is interesting to note that such a representation also shows some influence of temporal factors. With the increasing or decreasing presentation schedules of Neath and Crowder [33, 34] for example, the parser will not identify any rhythm or grouping during presentation, and will therefore code the whole list with a single oscillator pair. Because the increasing and decreasing schedules will result in successive positions being represented with increasing and decreasing phase differences respectively, the model predictions coincide with those of temporal distinctiveness theory. In other words, the representation coded by a single oscillator pair is of relative, temporal position. Where the model might differ to temporal distinctiveness theory is with rhythmic presentation schedules that allow hierarchical representations of position. In these cases, the present model predicts that errors between sequences will respect relative rather than temporal position within sequences (because different-duration sequences are coded by different-frequency oscillators), consistent with the above data, whereas the predictions of temporal distinctiveness theory are unclear. Future work will hopefully clarify the similarities and differences between the two approaches.

6.1 Future Work

Several questions remain of the model outlined above. Foremost is the problem of synchronising the phases of the group and list oscillators used in recall. If such synchronisation is not achieved, the relative phases of the group and list oscillators selected after presentation will not match the relative phases of the group and list oscillators chosen for recall, and appropriate similarity gradients are not guaranteed. This problem was overcome above by coding items for the position of their group in the list (rather than directly for their position in the list), and by resetting the group oscillator pair during recall whenever the appropriate phases of the list oscillator pair were reached. There is still a problem in choosing the frequency of the group oscillator pair relative to that of the list oscillator pair at recall: If the group oscillator pair is too slow relative to the list oscillator pair, the group oscillators may be reset before they have completed one half-period. Alternative solutions to the problem of synchronisation might be worth considering. Finally, the assumptions behind the rhythmic parser need to be examined. For example, the current parser predicts that an input of *1 2 3* would be parsed as a group of two followed by a group of one, whereas an input of *1 2 3* would be parsed as a single group of three. This would be simple to test empirically, yet surprisingly, we know of no data on the effects of such temporal presentation schedules on grouping.

7 Summary

The problem of serial order illustrates both the importance of representations in psychological theorising and connectionist modelling, and the valuable interplay between these two fields. Since their inception as psychological theories, all three approaches to the problem, interitem associations, ordinal representations and positional representations, have subsequently been instantiated in various connectionist models. Though the data from STM experiments favour positional representations, it is only through the precision required of connectionist instantiations that the nature of positional representations, whether they are temporal, absolute or relative, has been questioned. These connectionist models are therefore now feeding back into psychological theorising to make predictions that can be tested empirically. As such, the problem of serial order exemplifies both the theme of this year's Workshop, and the rationale behind the Neural Computation and Psychology Series as a whole.

Acknowledgements

Rik Henson was supported by BBSRC Grant Number SO5000. Neil Burgess was supported by a Royal Society University Research Fellowship. The authors can be emailed via r.henson@ucl.ac.uk and n.burgess@ucl.ac.uk.

Notes

1. There are other possible solutions of course. With respect to repeated items, one can appeal to the type/token distinction, so that two occurrences of the same type have nonidentical token representations [38]. With respect to errors in recall, open-loop chaining models like TODAM [39] can cue with previous items whether or not they are recalled correctly (as opposed to closed-loop chaining models in which responses feedback to cue subsequent items [9]).

2. Neath and Crowder [34] found that slower presentation rates did aid recall when much faster rates were used (around five items per second, in comparison with the maximum of two items per second in the study of Baddeley & Lewis [32]). However, under such rapid presentation of items, there is a danger that faster presentation rates do not allow as effective encoding.

3. Numerous experiments have shown that measures of recency are positively correlated with the ratio of interitem interval to retention interval [40, 41], in support of temporal distinctiveness theories [42, 43]. However, these experiments have tested mainly recognition, or free recall, rather than memory for serial order (apart from those discussed in Section 5.1). Moreover, recency is not necessarily the best index of temporal distinctiveness because it is a relative measure, comparing performance on the last position with that on penultimate positions, and is therefore likely to depend on other factors, including overall performance level. Indeed, when overall performance levels are compared, greater temporal spacing does not always aid free recall [40] (though see [42]).

4. We thank Tom Hartley for this idea.

References

[1] Jordan M I, Serial order: a parallel distributed approach (ICS Report 8604), San Diego: University of California, Institute for Cognitive Science, 1986.

[2] Grossberg S, Behavioral contrast in short-term memory: serial binary memory models or parallel continuous memory models? Journal of Mathematical Psychology, 17, 1978, pp 199-219.

[3] Houghton G, The problem of serial order: A neural network model of sequence learning and recall, in Dale R, Mellish, C & Zock M (Eds.), Current Research in Natural Language Generation, London: Academic Press, 1990, pp 287-319.

[4] Brown G D A, Preece T, & Hulme C, Oscillator-based memory for serial order, manuscript submitted for publication.

[5] Burgess N, & Hitch G, Toward a network model of the articulatory loop, Journal of Memory and Language, 31, 1992, pp 429-460.

[6] Henson R N A, Short-term memory for serial order: The Start-End Model, manuscript submitted for publication.

[7] Henson R N A, Positional information in short-term memory: relative or absolute?, manuscript submitted for publication.

[8] Lashley K S, The problem of serial order in behavior, in Jeffress L A (Ed.), Cerebral Mechanisms in Behavior: The Hixon Symposium, NY: John Wiley & Sons, Inc., 1951, pp 112-136.

[9] Henson R N A, Short-term memory for serial order, unpublished doctoral dissertation, University of Cambridge, England, 1996.

[10] Ebbinghaus H, Memory: a contribution to experimental psychology, New York: Dover, 1885/1964.

[11] Wickelgren W A, Short-term memory for phonemically similar lists, American Journal of Psychology, 78, 1965, pp 567-574.

[12] Slamecka N, Ebbinghaus: some associations, Journal of Experimental Psychology: Learning, Memory and Cognition, 11, 1985, pp 414-435.

[13] Elman J L, Finding structure in time, Cognitive Science, 14, 1990, pp 179-211.

[14] Taylor J G, Neural network capacity for temporal sequence storage, International Journal of Neural Systems, 2, 1991, pp 47-54.

[15] Houghton G & Hartley T, Parallel models of serial behaviour: Lashley revisited, PSYCHE, 95-2-25, 1996.

[16] Estes W K, An associative basis for coding and organisation in memory, in Melton A W & Martin E (Eds.), Coding Processes in Human Memory, Washington DC: V. H. Winston & Sons, 1972, pp 161-190.

[17] Page M P A & Norris D G, The primacy model: a new model of immediate serial recall, manuscript submitted for publication.

[18] Conrad R, Order error in immediate recall of sequences, Journal of Verbal Learning and Verbal Behavior, 4, 1965, pp 161-169.

[19] Lee C L & Estes W K, Order and position in primary memory for letter strings, Journal of Verbal Learning and Verbal Memory, 16, 1977, pp 395-418.

[20] Lee C L & Estes W K, Item and order information in short-term memory: evidence for multilevel perturbation processes, Journal of Experimental Psychology: Human Learning and Memory, 7, 1981, pp 149-169.

[21] Burgess N & Hitch G, Memory for serial order: a network model of the phonological loop and its timing, manuscript submitted for publication.

[22] Burgess N & Hitch G, A connectionist model of STM for serial order, in Gathercole S (Ed.), Models of short-term memory, UK: Psychology Press, 1996, pp 51-71.

[23] Hitch G H, Burgess N, Towse J N & Culpin V, Temporal grouping effects in immediate recall: a working memory analysis, Quarterly Journal of Experimental Psychology, 49A, 1996, pp 116-139.

[24] Conrad R & Hull A J, Information, acoustic confusion and memory span, British Journal of Psychology, 55, 1964, pp 429-432.

[25] Henson R N A, Norris D G, Page M P A & Baddeley A D, Unchained memory: error patterns rule out chaining models of immediate serial recall, Quarterly Journal of Experimental Psychology, 49A, 1996, pp 80-115.

[26] Wickelgren W A, Associative intrusions in short-term recall, Journal of Experimental Psychology, 72, 1966, pp 853-858.

[27] Henson R N A, Item repetition in short-term memory: Ranschburg repeated, manuscript submitted for publication.

[28] Henson R N A, Mathematical analysis of a linear compound chaining model, unpublished manuscript.

[29] Ryan J, Grouping and short-term memory: different means and patterns of grouping, Quarterly Journal of Experimental Psychology, 21, 1969, pp 137-147.

[30] Wickelgren W A, Rehearsal grouping and hierarchical organization of serial position cues in short-term memory, Quarterly Journal of Experimental Psychology, 19, 1967, pp 97-102.

[31] Conrad R, Serial order intrusions in immediate memory, British Journal of Psychology, 51, 1960, pp 45-48.

[32] Baddeley A D & Lewis V J, When does rapid presentation enhance digit span?, Bulletin of the Psychonomic Society, 22, 1984, pp 403-405.

[33] Neath I & Crowder R G, Schedules of presentation and temporal distinctiveness in human memory, Journal of Experimental Psychology: Learning, Memory and Cognition, 16, 1990, pp 316-327.

[34] Neath I & Crowder R G, Distinctiveness and very short-term serial position effects, Memory, 4, 1996, pp 225-242.

[35] Ng L H H, Are time-dependent oscillators responsible for temporal grouping effects in short-term memory?, unpublished Honours Thesis, University of Western Australia, 1996.

[36] Treisman M, Cook N, Naish P L N & McCrone J K, The internal clock: electroencephalographic evidence for oscillatory processes underlying time perception, Quarterly Journal of Experimental Psychology, 47A, 1994, pp 241-289.

[37] Hartley T, Syllabic phase: bottom-up representations of the structural properties of speech, manuscript in preparation.

[38] Wickelgren W A, Context-sensitive coding, associative memory, and serial order in (speech) behavior, Psychological Review, 76, 1969, pp 1-15.

[39] Lewandowsky S & Murdock B B Jr, Memory for serial order, Psychological Review, 96, 1989, pp 25-57.

[40] Bjork R A & Whitten W B, Recency-sensitive retrieval processes in long-term free recall, Cognitive Psychology, 6, 1974, pp 173-189.

[41] Neath I, Distinctiveness and serial position effects in recognition, Memory & Cognition, 21, 1993, pp 689-698.

[42] Glenberg A M & Swanson N G, A temporal distinctiveness theory of recency and modality effects, Journal of Experimental Psychology: Learning, Memory and Cognition, 12, 1986, pp 3-15.

[43] Marks A R & Crowder R G, Temporal distinctiveness and modality, Journal of Experimental Psychology: Learning, Memory & Cognition, 23, 1997, pp 164-180.

To Repeat or Not to Repeat: The Time Course of Response Suppression in Sequential Behaviour

Janet I. Vousden   Gordon D. A. Brown
University of Warwick
Coventry, CV4 7AL, United Kingdom

Abstract

Data from the study of human speech, spelling, and short-term memory for serial order are often taken to reflect the operation of post-output response suppression mechanisms. This inhibitory processing forms a central component of many models of human sequential behaviour. In this paper an oscillator-based model of sequential behaviour is used to show that varying the time-course of response suppression, in accordance with task demands, can explain differences in the error patterns produced in different sequential cognitive tasks. More specifically, we show that increasing the response suppression in a model of speech production causes the model's error patterns to change and become similar to those observed in human short-term memory for serial order.

1 Introduction

As Lashley emphasised nearly half a century ago, much of human cognitive behaviour is sequential in nature [1]. In the present paper we focus on the computational mechanisms underlying speech production and short-term memory for serial order. In particular, we show that characteristic differences in the patterns of errors produced in these different sequential tasks can be explained on the assumptions that (a) similar basic mechanisms are involved in the control of different types of sequential behaviour, and (b) the time course of post-output response suppression varies adaptively according to the nature of the task demands. It is concluded that the interplay between the dynamic activation and suppression of representations is central to understanding the role such representations play in sequential behaviour.

In the first part of the paper we attempt to motivate some intuitions concerning the importance of inhibitory processes in sequential behaviour, and we go on to consider differences between the task requirements involved in speech production and short-term memory for serial order. We then use a model of the control of sequential behaviour (OSCAR, for OSCillator-based Associative Recall) to illustrate, by simulation, that varying the time-course of post-output response suppression can account for the qualitatively different error patterns observed in speech production and short-term memory for serial order.

2 The importance of inhibition

Inhibitory processing appears to play a central role in many types of psychological processing, and response inhibition mechanisms have an important function in many recent models of sequential processing [2,3,4,5,6,7,8,9]. Many neural network models invoke lateral inhibition networks to implement competitive "winner take all" behaviour, in which many units compete to activate themselves and simultaneously inhibit all other units in an interconnected network (e.g. [5,6,10]).

However, the lateral-inhibitory mechanisms in conventional winner-take-all networks can cause problems when more than one response must be made, as in sequential output (see [6]). As several researchers have noted, the self-excitatory mechanisms that are involved in such processes can potentially lead to unstable states. Furthermore, once a unit has won a winner-take-all competition and suppressed its competitors, it becomes ever harder for any other unit to become active and take over the control of behaviour. This is because even with the help of external input a suppressed unit will find it difficult to bootstrap its activation up to the point where it can inhibit the self-sustaining activation of the currently most activated unit. This can lead to particular problems in producing sequential behaviour, in which units that win the competition to control behaviour at one point in time must give way to other units if progression through the target sequence is to be possible.

To counteract such undesirable outcomes, a "switch-off" mechanism can be included to suppress or inhibit the most active unit after a time delay or after the response output controlled by the unit has completed (see [6] for extensive discussion). This serves to restore equilibrium to the organism and prevent repetitive and perseverative behaviour [6]. It is this latter type of inhibition that is so important for the control of sequential behaviour — once an action has been performed, it can be suppressed, allowing the next action in the sequence to be output and suppressed, until the sequence of actions is complete. However, complete response suppression may lead to errors in the frequent cases (repeated letters in spelling; repeated phonemes in speech) when it *is* necessary to produce a response repeatedly within a short period of time. The systems responsible for controlling sequential behaviour must therefore achieve an appropriate compromise between the need to avoid inappropriate repetition of outputs and the need to repeat items where necessary. The main claim of the present paper is that differences in observed performance on different sequential tasks (such as short memory for serial order and speech production) can be explained on the assumption that different solutions to this trade-off problem are appropriate in the light of differing task demands. We begin with an examination of some relevant psychological data.

3 Data

The most relevant experimental data are sequence production errors that either involve producing a repeated item, or mistakenly repeating an item. A failure to recall a repeated item correctly will be termed a *repetition omission* (e.g. target **A B C B D** being produced as **A B C D**), and production of a repeated action in error will be termed a *repetition insertion* (e.g. **A B C D** being produced as **A B C B** or as **A B C B D**). Both types of error give an insight into the form and duration of response suppression in behaviour.

In one extreme case, if inhibition were complete and permanent, we would never be able to repeat the same actions twice, however far apart they should occur. This would lead to many repetition omissions, and no repetition insertions. Conversely, in the absence of any inhibition at all, we would expect many repetition insertions and no repetition omissions.

However we can conduct more subtle examination of the data than simple examination of the two types of repetition errors. Many models [2,3,5,9,11,12] make the computationally plausible assumption that response suppression is high immediately after a response is produced (to prevent immediate repetition insertions) and gradually diminishes over time (to avoid omissions of appropriate repetitions later in the sequence). We can therefore gain insight into the time course of response suppression in a given task by examining the probability of repetition insertion and omission errors as a function of the separation of the related items in the presented input (for repetition omissions) or the recalled output (for repetition insertions).

Repetition omission errors, and their time-course, have been extensively studied by others in the domains of spelling [9,12], speech production [9], and short-term memory for serial order (e.g. [11,13,14]). In the current section we therefore examine repetition *insertion* errors in speech production and short-term memory for serial order, with a view to showing that differences in the observed error patterns can be explained in terms of differences in the time-course of response suppression in the different tasks of speech production and short-term memory for serial order.

3.1 Repetition insertion errors in speech production

Words and streams of speech often contain repeated phonemes. However repetition insertions occur frequently, comprising about 60% of all speech errors [15]. Repetition insertions can be divided up into *anticipations* and *perseverations*. An anticipation occurs when a phoneme is spoken too early as well as in the correct position, as in the error *Do fries have brains* for *Do flies have brains*. A perseveration, in contrast, occurs when a phoneme is repeated after it has already been spoken in the correct position, as in *atomic wopons* for *atomic weapons*. In normal speech, anticipation errors generally outnumber perseveration errors. In a corpus of spontaneously occurring speech errors [16], there were a total of 805 anticipation errors compared to 603 perseveration errors (full details of the corpus and categorisation are given in [15]). In other words, we are more likely to repeat a phoneme if we accidentally say it too soon than we are to repeat phonemes

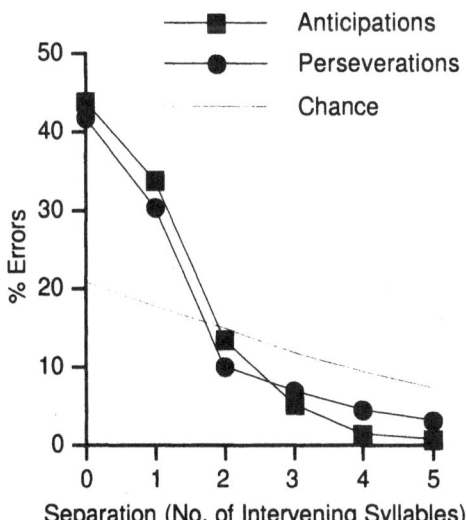

Figure 1. *The proportion of anticipation and perseveration errors in speech that occur over different separations*

after they have been spoken in their correct place.

The distance (or separation) between repeated phonemes is measured here by the number of intervening syllables. The separation between repeated phonemes in adjacent syllables is said to be zero; if there is one whole syllable between the repeated phoneme the separation is one, and so on. Figure 1 shows the proportions of anticipation and perseveration errors that occur over different separations. The proportion of errors that could have occurred by chance is also shown (this reflects the fact that for a sequence of any fixed length there will be more opportunities for repetitions to occur over short distances rather than long distances), averaged over many sequences of different lengths to reflect the variation in utterance length in the naturalistic speech error corpus.

It can be seen that the majority of repetition intrusions in speech production — and substantially more than would be expected by chance alone — occur over short distances. In other words, an intruded repetition error is likely to occur close to the first occurrence of the repeated phoneme. In intuitive terms, this suggests that response suppression is relatively weak in speech production, for if there was a large amount of response suppression immediately after a phoneme was output, and/or if the suppression only gradually reduced over time, then a below-chance proportion of close repetition intrusions would be expected.

A relatively small amount of inhibition might, in terms of the discussion above, be expected to result from the demands of fluent speech production. There are many repeated phonemes in English, and the repetition often occurs after a short duration (whether duration is measured in terms of absolute time or in terms of the number of intervening syllables or phonemes). Therefore, a high degree of response suppression would be likely to lead to a large number of repetition omissions, and the level of response suppression must therefore be kept low, even at the cost of an increased number of repetition intrusions.

To assess this account further, we examined repetition intrusions in a rather different sequential task: short-term memory for serial order.

3.2 Repetition insertions in short term memory for serial order

In a typical short-term serial recall task, participants are presented with a list of 6 or 7 letters and are subsequently required to recall the letters in the correct serial order. Here we consider the standard case where each list to be recalled contain no repeated letters. Because participants are aware that the lists contain no repeated items, it will be adaptive for them to avoid repeating items in recall, and this suggests that a relatively high level of response suppression might be adopted by participants. Indeed, many models of short-term memory for serial order incorporate the assumption that participants will not repeat items at all during short-term serial recall of lists that contain no repeated items.

If a higher level of response suppression is adopted in short-term memory for serial order tasks, as compared with speech production, it would be expected that (a) repetition intrusions would form a smaller proportion of the total number of errors produced, and (b) there would be a relatively small number of repetition intrusions occurring over short distances. We examined both of these possibilities using unpublished data from our own laboratory.

First of all, we have found in a number of studies that repetition intrusion errors (which can be separated into anticipations and perseverations, just as in the speech error data), form only about 5% of the total number of errors produced in serial recall of six-item lists (cf. 70% in the case of speech production above). The relatively low number of repetition insertions is consistent with the results of other studies that have examined serial recall of lists that contain no repeated items (cf. [11], who also found a smaller number of repetition insertions than would be expected if participants were guessing randomly from the set of list items on incorrect trials).

Secondly, Figure 2 shows the proportions of anticipation and perseveration errors that occur over different separations during serial recall from short-term memory. It can be seen that the observed pattern is very different from that seen in the analysis of speech errors. In short-term memory there are very few repetition intrusion errors occurring over short distances, with the majority of such errors occurring over intermediate separations. As Figure 2 shows, the modal separation is 3 for anticipations and 4 for perseverations (although the precise number will be determined partly by the length of the list).

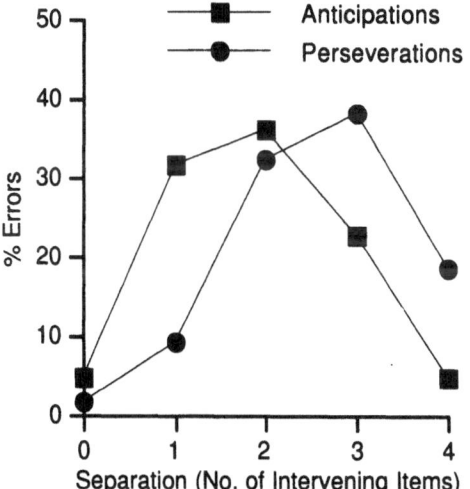

Figure 2. *The proportion of anticipation and perseveration errors in STM for serial order that occur over different separations*

In intuitive terms this appears to be consistent with the assumption that participants engaged in short-term serial recall of lists of non-repeated items do indeed use a greater degree of response suppression (explaining the small number of immediate repetition intrusions), and with the assumption that this response suppression wears off over time (explaining the larger number of repetition intrusions occurring over intermediate separations). This appears to confirm the suggestion that the time-course of response suppression may vary according to task demands. In the next section, we use a computational model to investigate the effects of varying the time-course of response suppression on anticipations and perseverations.

4 Aim of study

The aim of the modelling we describe here is to examine, in the context of an implemented model, the effects on repetition intrusion errors (anticipations and perseverations) of varying the time-course of response suppression. The methodology is as follows. We begin with an existing model of speech production [15,17], which has already been shown to be capable of accounting for a wide range of empirical data from the study of speech errors. The basic sequencing mechanism that this model uses is similar to one used in a model of short-term memory for serial order [18], and many of the model's resulting properties are also similar. We then examine the effects of increasing the extent of response suppression in the model of speech production, and show that this leads to a similar pattern of anticipation and perseveration errors to that observed in short-term serial recall and described above.

Thus we follow other researchers (e.g. [19]) in emphasising the similarities between the sequential cognitive tasks of speech production and maintaining short-term memory for serial order (because the same basic sequential ordering mechanism underpins the models of speech production and short-term memory for serial order). However we also extend the approach by showing that observed *differences* between the tasks can also be explained in the context of a single computational framework.

5 OSCAR

In this section we provide an intuitive description of the OSCAR model of speech production. A more detailed description of the model can be found in [15] and [17], while a description of the model applied to STM paradigms can be found in [18]; see also [20]. Here we provide a relatively informal account of the model; full technical and implementational details can be found in the above references.

The central mechanism underpinning OSCAR's speech production behaviour is a *dynamic lexical-context signal*. In the model, successive phoneme representations (representing the combination of syllable programs for the current sequence) are associated with successive states of this dynamic signal. We note that these are "type" representations — a given phoneme is assigned the same representation however often it occurs (although a small amount of random noise is added to the representations on each occasion). This principle is similar to that adopted in a number of other models of serial order (e.g. [2,3,5]). There are however important differences between these models, arising mainly from the formation of the lexical-context signal.

5.1 Model architecture

The basic architecture of the model can be seen in Figure 3. The left part of the diagram shows the lexical-context as a vector, and the right part shows the phoneme vector representations that become associated to successive states of the lexical-context vector.

The lexical-context vector is constructed from the outputs of an array of internal oscillators, whose frequencies are scaled such that there is a range of slow and fast oscillators. In the model, the oscillators are represented by the ovals, whose output is modelled as a sinusoidal signal, as depicted in Figure 3. The lexical-context vector is represented by the sigma-pi units directly to the right of the oscillators. There are 32 elements in the lexical-context vector, each of which consists of the product of the output of 5 oscillators, indicated by the lines connecting the oscillators and the lexical-context elements. Phonemes are represented in the model as a set of articulatory features according to place and manner of articulation, voicing, and nasality [21]. Finally, each element of the lexical-context vector is connected to each articulatory feature node, and the lexical-context vector is associated with a phoneme representation via a Hebbian weight matrix.

The lexical-context *signal* (or just the lexical-context), is actually composed of many lexical-context *vectors*, which are assumed to operate in parallel. The phoneme output from the lexical-context signal is the averaged output from the set of individual vectors.

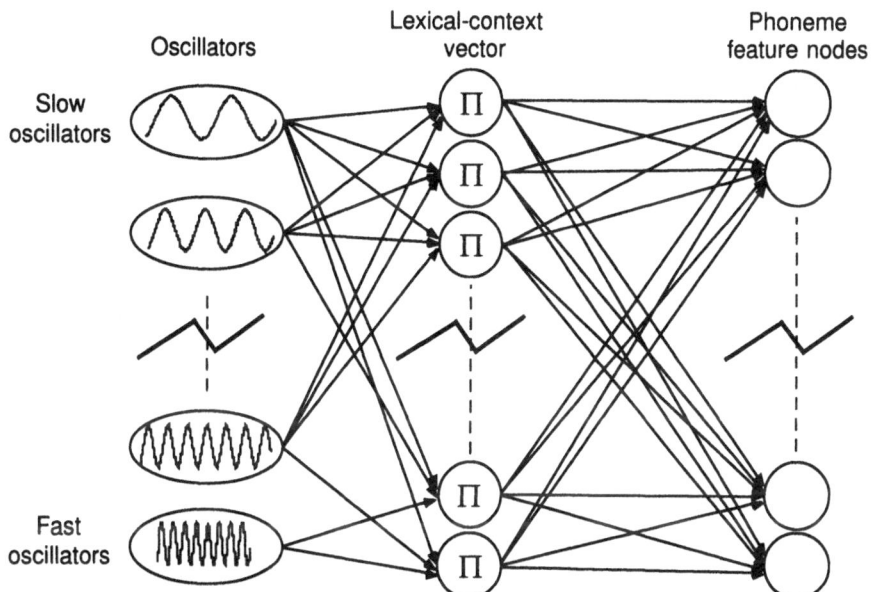

Figure 3. *The architecture of the OSCAR speech model; not all connections are shown, see text for details*

It is parsimonious to think of the set of individual lexical-context vectors as a single reinstateable lexical-context signal that drives production. Throughout the rest of this paper we refer to the lexical-context as a single signal.

5.2 The properties of the lexical-context signal

Each element of the lexical-context is constructed by multiplying together the output of a subset (in this case, 5) of the 31 oscillators. The oscillators are arranged such that slower-frequency oscillators contribute to more elements of the lexical-context signal than do faster oscillators. Put another way, each element of the lexical-context signal is constructed mainly from slower oscillators (for details of the full implementation, see [15,17]). A helpful analogy in understanding the dynamics of the lexical-context signal is the operation of an analogue clockface. The lexical-context signal is analogous to the representation of the clockface as a whole, and the oscillators are analogous to the hands. So the lexical-context signal as a whole can be thought of as a clock with many hands, some moving fast (like the second hand), and some moving more slowly (like the hour hand). Different states of the lexical-context signal are generated through time as the oscillators change state dynamically. The contribution made by the slower oscillators (at each state in time) serves to distinguish states of the lexical-context signal far apart in time, while the contribution of the faster oscillators distinguishes the nearby states of the lexical-context signal, again analogously to the hands on the clockface.

The advantage of a signal constructed in this way is that states of the lexical context signal that are nearby in time are more similar than are states that are further apart in time. This is illustrated in Figure 4, which shows the similarity between states of the signal (again, averaged over the set of individual vectors) generated through time.

As the separation between temporal states of the lexical-context signal increases, their similarity decreases. This is analogous to the observation that the state of the clockface at 5 o'clock is more similar to the 5.05 face than it is to the clockface at 5.10. An important point to note is that a lexical-context generated as described will not repeat itself, i.e., the decrease in similarity between states of the signal as their temporal separation increases is approximately monotonic.

The lexical-context signal can be modified such that it does partially repeat itself at controlled intervals; this is particularly useful in incorporating effects of syllabic structure. In the present account we ignore this aspect of the model's architecture, although it is important for providing a complete account of effects of syllabic structure (see [15] for details).

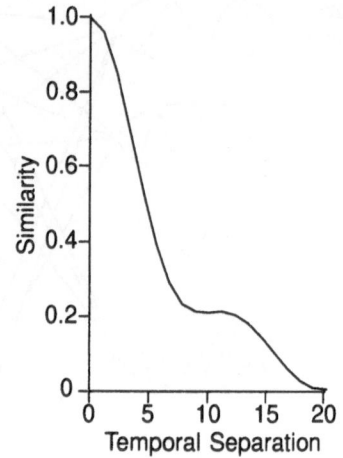

Figure 4. *A self-similarity function of states of the lexical-context signal*

5.3 Storing and retrieving syllable programs

So far we have described how sequences of phonemes are associated with successive states of a lexical-context signal generated through time. To explain in more detail how phoneme sequences are stored and then retrieved by the model, we refer back to the clockface analogy, where the hands represent the individual oscillators and the clockface represents the lexical-context signal as a whole. As the hands on the clock move, so the face of the clock will change, and storing a phoneme sequence is analogous to associating each phoneme with the clockface each time one or more of the hands moves (e.g. every second, or every minute). This is shown in Figure 5.

In the left-hand panel of Figure 5, the clockface at 5 o'clock represents the state of the lexical-context signal at the beginning of the phoneme sequence. This clockface becomes associated with the first phoneme in the sequence. After some time, the minute hand has changed (i.e. the oscillators have moved on) and the next phoneme becomes associated with the 5.05 clockface (the new state of the lexical-context signal). This continues until all the phonemes have been associated with different clockface representations.

During production, the initial state of the lexical-context signal must be reinstated. This is analogous to resetting the clockface to 5 o'clock, as in the right-hand panel of Figure 5. The phoneme that was associated with the 5 o'clock clockface will now be activated, and output. The lexical-context changes state under its own dynamics, just as the clockface changes state each time the hands move. Continuing with the analogy, when the clockface reaches 5.05, the next phoneme in the sequence will become activated, and be output. This continues for the rest of the sequence.

The output process is a simple winner-take-all mechanism, implemented by comparing the output of the model to the vocabulary of all phonemes, and outputting the phoneme with the best match to the model output. We also assume that this process is noisy, and a small amount of normally distributed noise is added to the match to each phoneme before the winner is chosen, and output.

Note that to the extent that states of the clockface are similar, phonemes associated with similar states will tend to be partially co-activated. The clockface at 5 o'clock is more similar to the 5.05 and 5.10 clockface than it is to the 5.15 clockface and hence the /r/ phoneme is partially activated by the 5 o'clock cue to a greater extent than is either the /l/ or /p/ phoneme. Indeed, at all serial positions in the output, the state of the learning-context signal at that position will act as a partial retrieval cue for neighbouring phonemes in the sequence. This is an important feature of the model because it allows adjacent phonemes to be partially co-activated, as occurs with co-articulation in human speech. If, as we assume, the output process is noisy, phoneme confusions are more likely to occur between nearby phonemes. To summarise, only the initial state of the lexical-context signal is necessary to recall the sequence — the rest of the states are generated by the intrinsic dynamics of the lexical-context signal, analogous to the changing state of the clockface. There is therefore no need for the system to maintain a separate memory for the successive states of the signal.

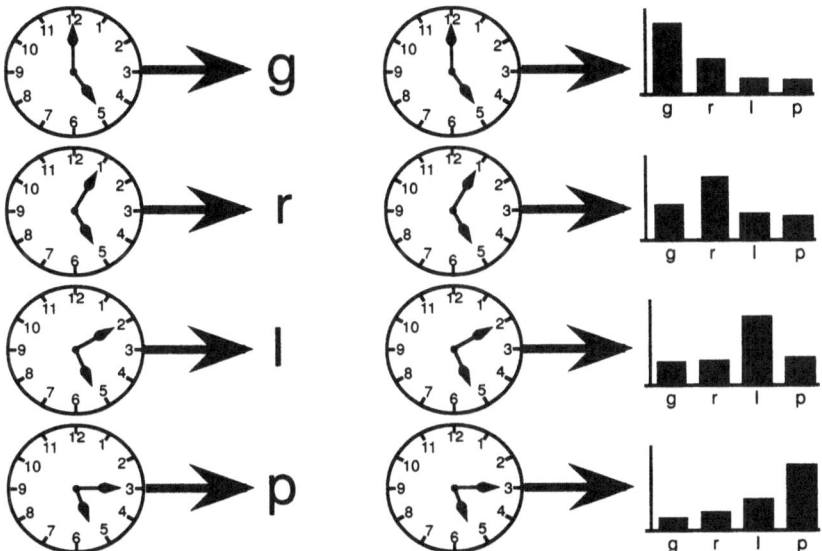

Figure 5. *Storing a phoneme sequence is analogous to associating each phoneme with successive states of the clockface, at 5 o'clock, 5.05, 5.10, and 5.15, as shown in the left-hand panel. The same sequence is retrieved by reinstating the 5 o'clock clockface, and outputting each phoneme as the clockface subsequently changes over time. Retrieval is illustrated in the right-hand panel*

5.4 The inhibition process

As described so far, the model contains no post-output response suppression mechanism. There is therefore nothing to prevent a phoneme being perseverated or anticipated and, because of the gradually-changing self-similarity of the lexical-context signal, such errors would frequently occur over short distances.

Post-output response suppression is implemented in the model as follows. When a phoneme has been output, it becomes less likely to be output in subsequent positions because its activation in subsequent output positions is inhibited. The amount of inhibition after s syllables have elapsed since the phoneme was last output is given by:

$$I_s = I_0 * (1-d)^s$$

where I_s is the amount of inhibition after s syllables have passed, I_0 is the amount of inhibition applied initially (i.e., during pronunciation of the syllable immediately following that in which the phoneme was first produced), and d is a decay rate parameter ($d <= 1$). The amount of inhibition is simply subtracted from the level of activation that the previously-output phoneme would have had if no response suppression took place. (This is a relatively simple form of response suppression; other mechanisms, in which the inhibition is driven directly by the activity of a winning phoneme itself [e.g. 5,6], have generally similar effects).

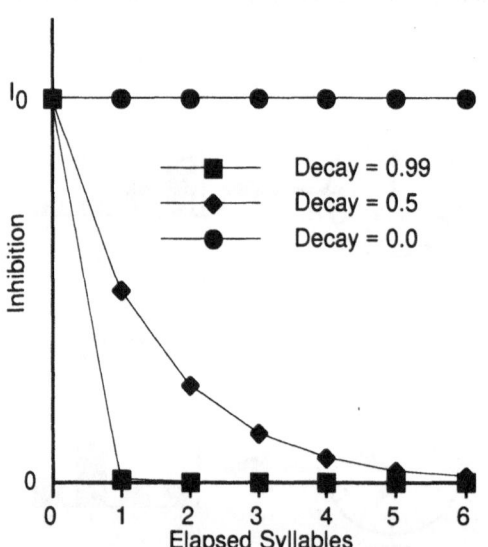

Figure 6. *The effects of different values of inhibition decay on the time-course of inhibition*

The inhibition parameter for a given phoneme changes over time such that the inhibition gradually wears off as more syllables are spoken. The time course of the inhibition is controlled by the decay rate parameter, as illustrated in Figure 6.

When the inhibition decay rate parameter d is set to a very high value, for example 0.99, then only the adjacent syllable receives significant inhibition, (given by the initial inhibition parameter, I_0) after which it decays rapidly towards zero. At the other extreme, when d is set to 0, then all subsequent syllables receive the same amount of inhibition, which does not wear off. In between d values of 0.99 and 0, inhibition decays at less extreme rates (see Figure 6). With appropriate values chosen for the two parameters, the model gives a good fit to the anticipation and perseveration gradients observed in speech production and illustrated above in Figure 1 [15,17]. Next, we examine the effects on errors of varying the inhibition parameters.

6 Demonstration

We have chosen to model the production of polysyllabic utterances, each containing 6 simple CV syllables. Each phoneme sequence is created by drawing, without replacement, alternate consonants and vowels at random from the set of English phonemes. Each phoneme sequence is then associated with a different lexical-context signal. Phoneme sequences are produced by reinstating the initial state of the lexical-context signal for the sequence. The phonemes associated with each state of the signal as it dynamically changes state make up the output sequence.

This enabled us to explore the effects of varying the time course of post-output response suppression during speech production by manipulating the inhibition parameters. Here we make the simplifying assumption that the syllable represents the basic "unit" underlying the time-course of suppression (see [17] for details). The effects are seen by the change in the number and form of repetition errors made. For example, in the case where there is no response suppression at all, it might be expected that (a) there would be a relatively large number of repetition intrusion errors (perseverations and anticipations); (b) the number of anticipations and perseverations would be approximately the same, and (c) their distance functions would be monotonic and quite steep, reflecting the fact that phonemes are more likely to be produced in a syllable close to the correct syllable than they are to be produced in one further away, because of the gradually-changing nature of the lexical-context signal.

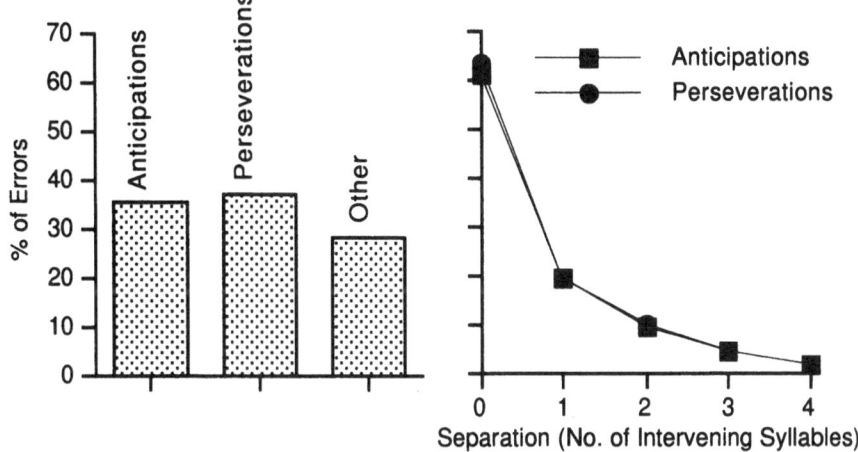

Figure 7. *Errors produced by the model when no response suppression occurs. The left-hand panel shows repetition intrusion errors (anticipations and perseverations) as a proportion of all phoneme errors. The right-hand panel shows the proportion of anticipation and perseveration errors that occur at different separations*

The behaviour of the model without response suppression is shown in Figure 7. It can be seen that, as predicted, there are many repetition intrusions (accounting for about 70% of all the errors produced), and that most of them occur in syllables adjacent to the syllable in which the phoneme is correctly pronounced (i.e. with a separation = 0). Furthermore, as expected, there is no difference between the anticipation and perseveration gradients (Figure 7). Note that there are many more repetition intrusion errors, and with a shorter mean separation, than is observed in the data (Figure 1), confirming that some degree of response suppression is necessary to account for the pattern of errors empirically observed.

An alternative possibility is that phonemes are completely inhibited for just the duration of the next syllable after they were spoken, but that the inhibition wears off

312

very quickly so that there is effectively no suppression after the first post-production syllable. The model's behaviour in this case is shown in Figure 8, where the inhibition function is such that there is a large inhibition for the first syllable after the current one, but almost no inhibition thereafter. This is achieved by setting the inhibition parameter to 0.5, and the inhibition decay rate parameter to 0.99.

In this case it can be seen that, as expected, there are no one-apart repetition intrusions, but several over longer distances (because of the large but short-lived inhibition). The proportion of errors that are repetition intrusions is reduced to around 40%. Comparison with the data in Figure 1 now suggests that weaker response suppression is appropriate to account for the observed data.

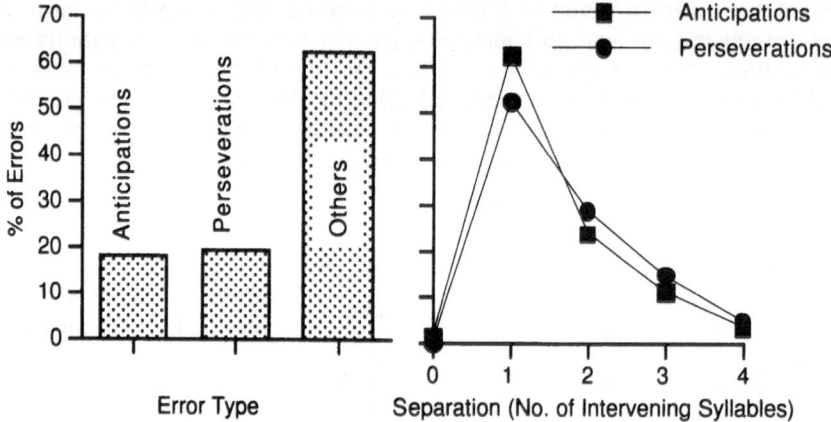

Figure 8. *The effects of strong inhibition for one syllable only. The left-hand panel shows repetition errors (anticipations and perseverations) as a proportion of all phoneme errors. The right-hand panel shows the proportion of anticipations and perseverations that occur at different separations*

Finally, we examined the effect of varying the amount of initial inhibition, I_0, while holding d constant at 0.5. Values of 0.05, 0.2 and 0.5 were used for I_0. The results are illustrated in Figure 9. A small amount of inhibition reduces the proportion of repeat errors that are perseverations, as shown in the top leftmost panel of Figure 9. This is because a phoneme that has been output too early, although inhibited, will receive additional activation from the lexical-context signal once the correct position for that phoneme's output is reached. Perseveration errors are less likely to occur because once the phoneme has been output and suppressed, it is less likely to be output again as it will not receive extra activation from the lexical-context signal in the same way an anticipated phoneme does. This can also be seen in the bottom leftmost panel of the Figure, as a slight flattening of the distance function for the perseveration errors. As the inhibition increases, the overall proportion of repetition intrusions decreases, as expected. This can be seen in the graphs in the top three panels of Figure 9. The distance functions also change as the inhibition increases: the effects are seen first of all in the perseveration errors, where progressively few perseverations occur at short distances. The distance functions of the anticipation errors follow the same pattern, although not until the inhibition is larger. This is seen in the graphs in the bottom panel of Figure 9.

The results of varying the amount of inhibition are striking. In particular, it can be seen that increasing the amount of response suppression transforms the anticipation and perseveration gradients from a pattern similar to that observed in human speech errors (Figure 1) to a pattern qualitatively very similar to that observed in human short-term memory for serial order (Figure 2). We take this as support for the suggestion that the different patterns of repetition intrusion errors in the two tasks can be captured in terms of the extent and time-course of post-output response suppression.

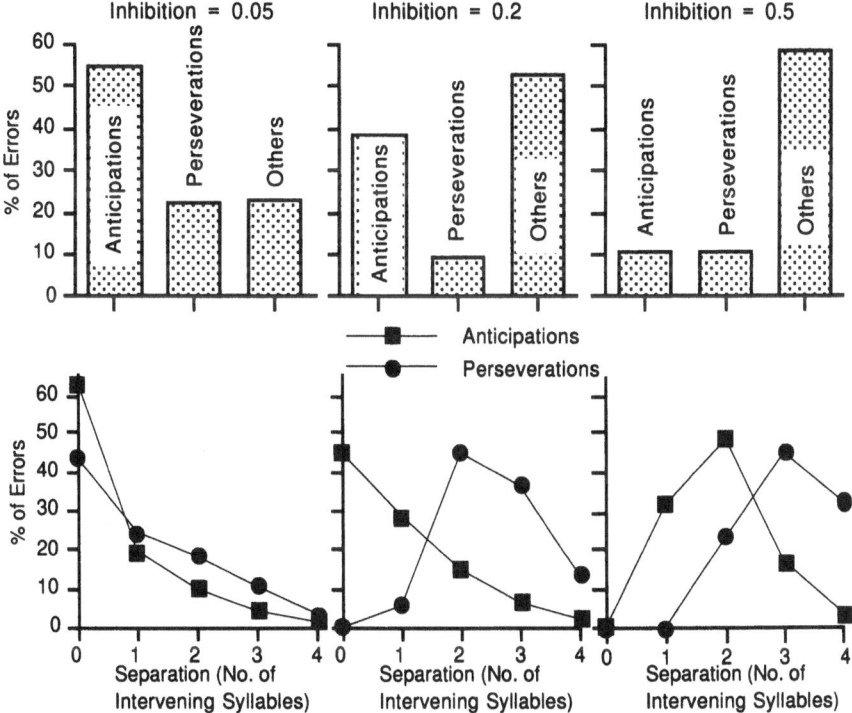

Figure 9. *The effects of varying the amount of inhibition while holding the time-course parameter constant. The top three panels show repetition errors (anticipations and perseverations) as a proportion of all phoneme errors. The corresponding lower panel shows the proportion of anticipations and perseverations that occur at different separations*

7 Conclusion

The modelling work that we have described was motivated by the suggestion that the time-course of response suppression might vary adaptively in response to differences in the demands of different types of sequential cognitive behaviour (such as speech production, spelling, and short-term memory for serial order). More specifically, it was suggested that in tasks such as speech production, where the same phoneme must often be produced twice within a fairly short duration, response suppression must be relatively weak and short-lived. When short-term memory for serially ordered lists of non-repeating items is required, in contrast, response suppression was expected to be stronger and/or longer lasting. We have shown, with the aid of a model, that qualitative differences in the detailed patterns of repetition intrusion errors observed in speech production and short-term memory for serial order can indeed be explained in terms of the time-course of post-output response suppression. Thus it is possible that speech production and short-term memory for serial order involve similar basic mechanisms for the sequencing of behaviour, coupled with differently-configured response suppression mechanisms. We can also make the prediction that the movement gradients in short-term memory would change to be more similar to those observed in speech production if the lists used in short-term memory studies always contained repeated items.

In the present paper we have focused on repetition intrusion errors. Earlier studies have, in contrast, emphasised repetition omission errors in short-term memory for serial order [11,13,14]; speech production [9] and spelling [6,9,22]. These data are largely consistent with the idea that repetition omissions do occur to the greatest extent in short-term memory for serial order, and to a lesser extent in spelling and speech production, consistent with the suggestion that a reduced level of post-output response suppression is used in these latter tasks. ([11] notes that some but not all of the effect in short-term memory for serial order may be due to a guessing bias of some kind.) In the case of both spelling and short-term memory, however, it seems clear that a special "repetition tagging" mechanism exists to enable production of list items or letters in immediate succession. Thus the spelling of words with immediately repeated letters, or the recall of lists with immediately repeated items, can be superior to that of control words or lists containing non-repeated items, even though words or lists with more widely spaced elements suffer from reduced performance due to repetition omissions (see [11,12] for discussion).

In summary, there is extensive converging evidence that the differences, as well as the similarities, in different sequential tasks can be captured within a single basic serial ordering mechanism.

Author Notes

Janet I. Vousden, Department of Psychology, University of Warwick, Coventry, England; Gordon D. A. Brown, Department of Psychology, University of Warwick, Coventry, England. The research was supported by a grant from the Economic and Social Research Council (U.K.), ref. R000236216. Correspondence concerning this article should be addressed to Janet I. Vousden, Department of Psychology, University of Warwick, Coventry, CV4 7AL, U.K. Electronic mail may be sent via Internet to J.I.Vousden@warwick.ac.uk

References

1. Lashley KS. The problem of serial order in behavior. In Jeffress LA (ed), Cerebral mechanisms in behavior. Wiley, New York, 1951
2. Burgess N, Hitch, GJ. Towards a network model of the articulatory loop. Journal of Memory and Language 1992; 31:429-460
3. Burgess N, Hitch GJ. (1996). A connectionist model of STM for serial order. In Gathercole SE (ed), Models of short-term memory. Psychology Press, Hove, England, 1996 (pp. 51-72)
4. Hartley T, Houghton G. A linguistically constrained model of short-term memory for nonwords. Journal of Memory and Language 1996; 35:1-31
5. Houghton G. The problem of serial order: A neural network model of sequence

learning and recall. In Dale R, Mellish C, Zock M (eds), Current research in natural language generation. Academic Press, London, 1990 (pp. 287-319)

6. Houghton G. Inhibitory control of neurodynamics: Opponent mechanisms in sequencing and selective attention. In Oaksford M, Brown GDA (eds), Neurodynamics and psychology. Academic Press, London, 1994 (pp. 107-155)

7. Lewandowsky S, Murdock BB. Memory for serial order. Psychological Review 1989; 96:25-57

8. Lewandowsky S, Li S-C. Memory for serial order revisited. Psychological Review 1994; 101:539-543

9. MacKay DG. The organization of perception and action. Springer-Verlag, New York, 1987

10. Kohonen T. Self-organization and associative memory. Springer-Verlag, Berlin, 1984

11. Henson RNA. Short-term memory for serial order. Unpublished doctoral dissertation, University of Cambridge, Cambridge, England, 1996

12. Houghton G, Glasspool GW, Shallice T. (1994). Spelling and serial recall: Insights from a competitive queueing model. In Brown GDA, Ellis NC (eds), Handbook of spelling. Wiley, Chichester, England, 1994 (pp. 365-404)

13. Crowder RG. Intraserial repetition effects in immediate memory. Journal of Verbal Learning and Verbal Behavior 1968; 7:446-451

14. Jahnke JC. The Ranschburg effect. Psychological Review 1969; 76:592-605

15. Vousden JI. Serial control of phonology in speech production. Unpublished doctoral dissertation, University of Warwick, Coventry, England, 1996

16. Harley TA, MacAndrew SBG. Interactive models of lexicalisation: Some constraints from speech error, picture naming, and neuropsychological data. In Levy J, Bairaktaris D, Bullinaria J, Cairns D (eds), Connectionist models of memory and language. UCL Press, London, 1995

17. Vousden JI, Brown GDA, Harley TA. An oscillator-based model of speech production. Manuscript in preparation, 1997

18. Brown GDA, Preece T, Hulme C. Oscillator-based memory for serial order. Manuscript submitted for publication, 1996

19. Ellis AW. Errors in speech and short-term memory: The effects of phonemic similarity and syllable position. Journal of Verbal Learning and Verbal Behavior 1980; 19:624-634

20. Brown GDA, Vousden JI. Adaptive sequential behaviour: Oscillators as rational mechanisms. To appear in Oaksford M, Chater N (eds), Rational models of cognition. Oxford University Press, Oxford, England (in press)

21. Wickelgren WA. Distinctive features and errors in short-term memory for English consonants. Journal of the Acoustical Society of America 1966; 39:388-398

22. MacKay DG. The repeated letter effect in the misspellings of dysgraphics and normals. Perception and Psychophysics 1969; 5:103-104

A Localist Implementation of the Primacy Model of Immediate Serial Recall

Dennis Norris and Mike Page

Medical Research Council Applied Psychology Unit

Cambridge, U.K.

Abstract

We present a localist, connectionist implementation of the Primacy model of immediate serial recall. We demonstrate a connectionist ordering mechanism which is localist and activation-based rather than based on association and illustrate the parallels between the Primacy model and current connectionist models of speech production. This enables us to give an integrated explanation both of phonological errors in short-term memory and of errors in speech production.

1   Introduction

In earlier papers we have described the Primacy model of immediate serial recall [24, 25, 28] and shown how the model can simulate data from a wide range of experiments on serial recall from short-term memory. The model can account for phenomena such as primacy and recency effects, the effects of word and list length, and phonological similarity. In all cases the model gives very accurate quantitative fits to the experiental data. However, even though the model is computational, and we have described its operation in terms of 'nodes', 'activation' and 'supression', we have not offered any specific connectionist implementation of the model. Largely this is because we felt that it would be possible to construct a number of different connectionist implementations of the theory, and that the details of any of these implementations would be a distraction from the more important psychological and computational principles which are the true source of the theory's explanatory power. In what follows we develop a localist, connectionist implementation of our model and suggest some overlap with existing models of speech production.

2   The Primacy Model

Previous models of immediate serial recall have concentrated on two principal approaches, namely item-item chaining and position-item association. The former approach (e.g. [22]) suggests that lists of items are stored via a chain of associations between consecutive items, with a contextual association to the first item to allow recall to commence. The latter approach (e.g. [4]) suggests that list items are associated, in turn, with a series of pre-ordered positional codes: at recall the positional codes are sequentially reinstated and their associates are recalled. By contrast, the primacy model [28] assumes that order is stored more directly by the graded activation of representations of list items. More particularly, we assumed that the stimulus list ABCD would lead to a situation in which $x_A > x_B > x_C > x_D$, where x_i represents the activation of a node that responds to item i. Given such activations, ordered recall can proceed by choosing the node with the largest activation, outputting the corresponding item, and suppressing the node so that it is not chosen again, this sequence of actions being repeated for each item to be recalled. To the extent that the process of choosing the node with the largest activation is subject to noise, there will be errors in recall.

In our earlier description of the primacy model, we suggested that the graded activations required by the model might be thought of being derived from associations of each item with a context signal representing the start of the list: items later in the list would be more weakly associated with the start-of-list context, so that, at recall, cuing with that context would lead to a *primacy gradient* of activations (cf. the start-end nodes in [16] and [14]). This associative mechanism was suggested so as to provide some continuity with the item-item chaining and position-item association theories, in as much as both classes of theory require at least one item to be associated with a start-of-list context. Nonetheless, the primacy model was influenced by ideas in, for instance, Grossberg [12, 13], later developed by Nigrin [23] and Page [26, 27], which generated a primacy gradient of activations without postulating any context-item associations. (Similar ideas were suggested by Estes,[11], though Estes chose to retain the idea of contextual associations.) In the following section, therefore, we will give an example of an implementation of the primacy model which not only serves to contrast ordinal models with chaining and position-item associative models, but also dispenses with the associative framework, in favour of one based directly on node activations.

Because we are providing a connectionist implementation of the primacy model, our account of the theory is necessarily rather more complex than in earlier work. However, although we are supplying a new connectionist mechanism to explain the low-level details of the primacy model, the higher-level explanation offered by the earlier formulation still holds in its entirety. One of the many attractions of the localist approach is that we can add a new level of explanation without undermining a previous, higher-level account.

2.1 Specific Implementation

The following description will be based on the lower part of the simple network depicted in Figure 1, specifically the two layers of nodes labelled L_1 and L_2. In the lower layer, L_1, are nodes each of which activates in response to presentation of a particular item. For simplicity, we assume that, in response to the corresponding item, the node activates to a given level, K, remains at that level for a short time, and then resets to zero. (In fact, it is not necessary to define precisely the trajectory which the activation of these cells takes and K can be set arbitrarily, providing it exceeds a given lower bound.) The nodes in the second layer, L_2, are connected in a one-to-one fashion to the corresponding nodes in L_1, and their activations, x_i, vary such that:

$$\frac{dx_i}{dt} = -Dx_i + (A - x_i).y_i \qquad (1)$$

where D is a decay parameter, y_i is the activation of the corresponding L_1 cell and A is given by

$$A = s.(1 - \frac{n}{P}) \qquad (2)$$

where P is a parameter of the model, representing, as will become clear, the peak value of the primacy gradient, and n is the number of nodes active in the upper layer, L_2, at the time of the item's onset. Finally, s is the activation of a node which activates to a given level at the onset of a to-be-remembered list, and decays thereafter with exponent D as above. The level to which this cell activates at list-onset is arbitrary, and can be set to P for definiteness. The use of the value A in equation 1 simply ensures that the upper limit towards which activation grows in response to the occurrence of a given item is modulated by the activation s, and is reduced to the extent that other nodes at the same level are already active.

Whenever recall of the next item is required, the node activations at L_2 are forwarded to a competitive layer (see Figure 1), where the node with the largest activation is chosen, subject to that node not being suppressed as a result of having been chosen previously (cf. [4] [3][12][16][22]). This choice process is subject to noise, either in the L_2 activations themselves, or introduced during the competition. The presence of noise is modelled by adding zero-mean, Gaussian noise, with standard deviation N to each of the activations forwarded to the competitive layer, before the node with the largest resulting activation is chosen (cf. [30]). N is the model's third parameter, after D and P. Finally, the activation of the chosen node is further forwarded to an output stage, where it is compared with an output threshold, T (cf. [4]). This threshold comparison process is also deemed to be noisy, and zero-mean Gaussian noise, with standard deviation M, is added to the threshold before the comparison is effected. T and M are the fourth and fifth model parameters. If the activation falls below the threshold an omission results, otherwise the item is recalled. Note that the output stages depicted in Figure 1 will be described in the latter part of this paper and should, for the moment be assumed to implement the thresholding function described here.

To give an idea how the network described above functions, assume that it is presented with the sequence ABCDEF, with each item being presented at a rate of one item per second. Let us assume, arbitrarily, that L_1 cells latch on for 200 milliseconds after their corresponding item is presented, and that K is set

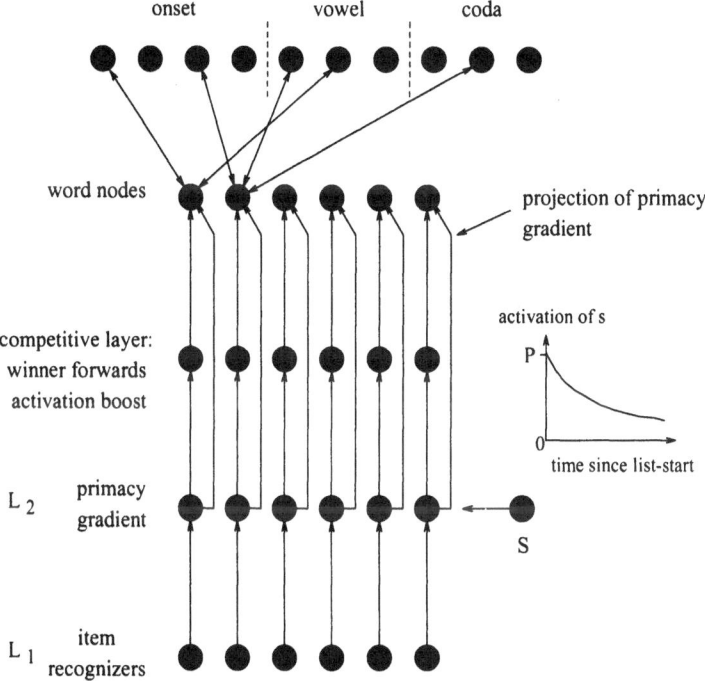

Figure 1: A schematic diagram of the network.

to 50. Essentially, as each L_1 node activates, the corresponding L_2 node grows in activation reaching an equilibrium value very close to $\frac{(P-n)s}{P}$ some time before its L_1 node turns off, decaying with exponent D thereafter. If the decay exponent, D, were equal to zero, thus keeping the activation, s, equal to P throughout list presentation, the L_2 activations measured at any time after the offset of the L_1 node corresponding to the last item (i.e. after list presentation is complete) would be $x_A = P, x_B = (P - 1), x_C = (P - 2) \ldots x_F = (P - 5)$. If, as is assumed to be the case, $D > 0$, all these activations will be multiplied by a factor equal to e^{-Dt_d}, where t_d is the time between the onset of the first list-item and the point at which the activations are measured (the subscript can be thought of as indicating the delay between presentation and recall). Correspondingly, the difference in activation between any node and the node corresponding to its predecessor or successor will be e^{-Dt_d} (i.e., equal to one when $D = 0$, as above).

It should be noted that, in the absence of (covert) rehearsal, it is easy to calculate the value of t_d, if the time at which recall is attempted, t_r, is known. The value of t_d is simply $t_r - t_p$, where t_p is the time at which the first item of the list was presented. In the case in which covert rehearsal is possible, each rehearsal can be thought of as a (more recent) presentation of the list (cf. [2]). In other words, at each rehearsal, the part of the list that has so far been presented is read out of memory in order, and re-presented to the network afresh

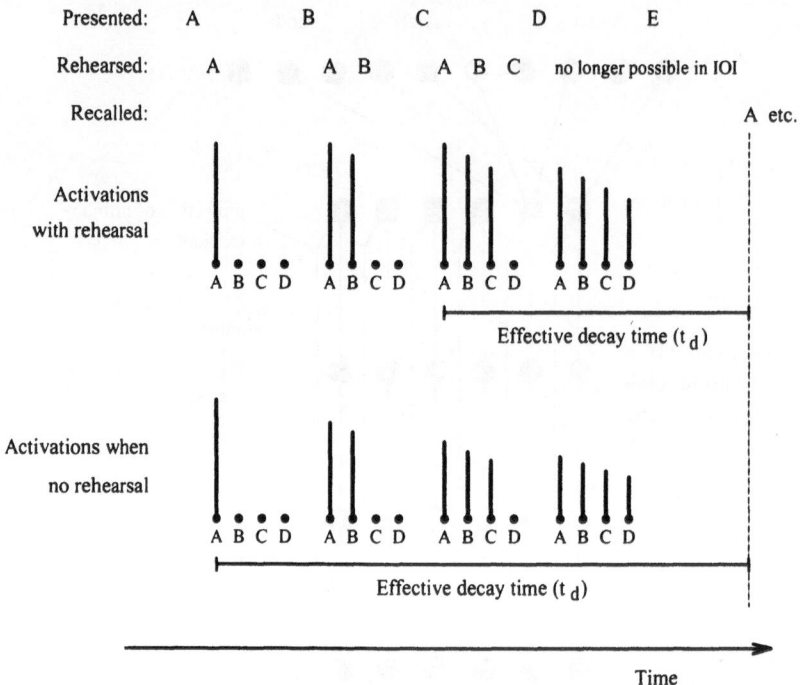

Figure 2: The evolution of primacy gradient activations with and without rehearsal. IOI is the stimulus inter-onset-interval

(i.e., with activation s being reinitialized to P). The consequences of rehearsal, in particular the effect it has in offsetting decay, can be seen in Figure 2. We assume that rehearsal is perfect in the sense that the items so far presented are rehearsed in the correct order. We make this assumption because it is rarely possible, in typical experimental contexts, to perform more than four cumulative rehearsals for a given trial, and lists of length four are invariably recalled correctly.

2.2 Model Performance

Before showing how the primacy model accounts for more general phonological-loop phenomena, we will first show how it can account for the form of the serial-position curve. More extensive simulations demonstrating effects of word-length, list-length, and the relation between span and articulation rate are given in [28] which also gives a fuller explanation of the model's behaviour.

Briefly, the primacy model accounts for the recency effect and part of the primacy effect as a result of end-effects (cf.[11][17]). Items in terminal positions can only exchange position with items to one side of them. Items in the middle of a list can exchange position with items on either side and therefore have more opportunity to be recalled out of position. The overall decrease in performance throught the list is attributable to the effect of decay. As recall procedes the difference in activation levels between adjacent items decreases and there is a greater chance that this activation difference will be bridged by noise, leading to and order error.

In the first simulation reported here the model was run for the equivalent of $10,000$ trials, which was more than sufficient to ensure a stable pattern of results. For all of the simulations reported here and in [29] four of the five parameters of the model remained fixed: $P = 11.5, D = 0.27, T = 0.49, M = 0.74$. These of parameters were selected by trial-and-error to give a good account of the basic serial-position data (see Figure. 3). The only parameter which was changed to achieve a good fit to different data sets was the noise parameter N which varied from 0.16 to 0.23. Variation in the noise level can be taken as representing variation in overall level of performance of different subjects groups used in different experiments.

It should be noted that, in order to calculate plausible values for t_p, and thus t_d (see above), we have to make some approximations of the covert rehearsal rates and output times for the materials used in the various experiments. For the simulations reported here we assume a rehearsal rate of 4 items/sec and an output rate of 2 items/sec.

Given these rates, the number of cumulative rehearsals, C, performed by subjects was estimated as $C = R(I-0.2)$, where I represents the stimulus interonset-interval used in the experiment, measured in seconds, and R denotes the covert rehearsal rate. The constant 0.2 represents an approximation to the time needed to recognize the list item. Therefore, the delay time, t_d is given by

$$t_d = I. \max(1, L - C) \tag{3}$$

where L is the number of items in the stimulus list and C and I are given above. Given approximations of the recognition time and rehearsal rates, t_d can be calculated for any given experiment.

2.3   The Phonological Similarity Effect

The *phonological similarity effect* refers to the finding that lists consisting of items which are phonologically similar to each other are recalled worse than lists comprising phonologically distinct items. The data on which this section concentrates are those from [1] which further constrain models of this effect by showing that, in lists containing some phonologically nonconfusable items and some confusable items, the level of recall of nonconfusable items is independent of the degree of confusability between other list items. This observation was confirmed in a near replication reported in [15].

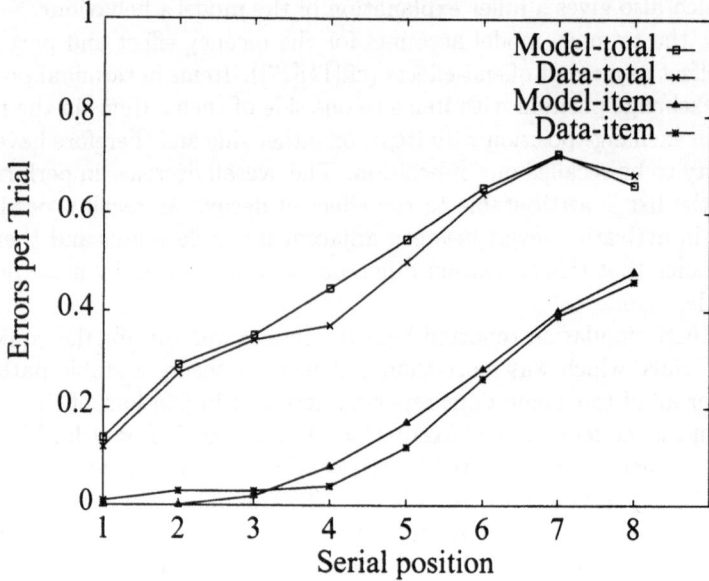

Figure 3: Simulations of serial-position curves for visually-presented lists of eight, nonconfusable, letters, using the five-parameter model. The parameter values are given in the text.

Previously [24, 25, 28] we have demonstrated that such a pattern of errors can be simulated using a two-stage model of recall. The first stage of recall can be thought of as comprising the ordering mechanism described above. The primacy gradient stores order information across nodes in such a way that the node activations are independent of the phonological content of the corresponding list-items. In other words, the primacy gradient will look the same for a list of confusable items as it will for a list of nonconfusable items: at this level, phonological content has been factored out. During recall, items are forwarded from the first stage, one at a time, as each wins the competition amongst unsuppressed nodes to "pick the biggest". At the second stage, which we loosely term an output stage, localist representations of items which are phonologically similar to the single item most recently forwarded from the first stage are activated, together with the representation of the forwarded item itself. The extent to which the "similars" are activated is determined by the product of a value representing their similarity to the forwarded item and the degree to which their corresponding representation is active at the level of the primacy gradient. The latter assumption is to account for the fact that the "additional" transpositions that result from phonological confusability between list items are, like first-stage transpositions, distance related, that is, nearby items are more likely to transpose with each other than items further apart in the list. It is also consistent with the observation that those phonologically similar items that are erroneously recalled tend to originate from within the list, that is they are transpositions rather than intrusions.

Once the forwarded item, and the list items with which it is phonological confusable, are activated at the second stage, a further noisy-choice operation takes place to determine the item that will be recalled. Since the model already incorporates a noisy output-stage, at which the activation of the forwarded item, distorted by zero-mean Gaussian noise with standard deviation M, is compared with the output-threshold, T, all that is required is one additional parameter, S, which represents the level of similarity between the phonologically confusable list-items. It is this value which, when multiplied by the corresponding primacy gradient activation, gives the activation of a given item at the second stage. We emphasize that similarity is determined with relation to the item forwarded from the first stage. The item itself, as represented at the second stage, is deemed to have a similarity value of 1 and items nonconfusable with it deemed to have a similarity value of 0, with S being set somewhere in between these limits. In our previous work, a value of $S = 0.8$ afforded extremely good fits to the experimental data. More importantly, the pattern of errors found in the data is successfully simulated: nonconfusable items forwarded from the first stage "pass through" the second-stage unhindered, since there are no list-items sufficiently similar to activate and compete at the second stage; it is only items confusable with other list-items that suffer from such additional competition, and hence additional error. The mechanism ensures that, at the second stage, the confusable items compete with, and therefore transpose with, each other. This is the pattern of errors found in the data.

While the two-stage process described above enables accurate simulation of the data, one might wonder whether it would be possible to construct a simpler, one-stage model. In fact we have made various attempts to model the detail of the phonological similarity effect using a simpler, single-stage model. For reasons given in [28] none of these attempts has met with success. We believe that the experimental data place such strong constraints on potential models to render it unlikely (though not impossible) that a very much simpler alternative to the two-stage model will emerge. While the data alone appear to force us to accept a two-stage model, further support for such a mechanism comes from parallels with models of speech production, in which speech errors are held to occur at a late stage, after the ordering of intended utterances has, to a large extent, been decided (e.g. [8][9][21]). In what follows, we will develop the view that the additional (second-stage) errors found in immediate serial recall tasks are essentially speech errors, and we will suggest a connectionist architecture, similar to that found in [8][9], within which such errors might be held to occur. We will show how such a model can provide accurate simulations of the data reported in [1].

In suggesting that the additional errors due to phonological similarity result from speech errors localized at an output process, we are reiterating a hypothesis previously developed by [10]. The hypothesis is particularly pertinent with reference to experiments which, like those in [1], employ the rhyming letter-names (B, C, D, etc.): for this particular set of stimuli it is not possible to distinguish between the misordering of items in a report as opposed to the misordering of syllable onsets (i.e. Spoonerisms).

2.4 A Specific Implementation of the Phonological Output Stage

Our network implementation of the phonological output stage is shown in the upper part of Figure 1. It is similar to Dell's simplified model [9] in that it comprises two interconnected layers: one layer contains word nodes; the other layer contains phoneme nodes (or possibly phoneme-cluster nodes), where a given onset phoneme is represented separately from the same phoneme in a coda (e.g. the word "bib" would be represented by activation of three separate nodes). Word nodes are connected to the nodes representing their constituent phonemes, and vice versa, by connections of strength set arbitrarily to 1. (Note that reciprocal connections in this model exist mainly to produce effects of phonological similarity; similar effects could be achieved in a feed-forward system by other means.) The word nodes are also connected, in a one-to-one fashion, to the L_2 nodes across which the primacy gradient is instated as above. All word and phoneme nodes start with zero activity. When the recall of a word is required, the noisy pick-the-biggest process at the competitive layer identifies the unsuppressed L_2 node with the largest primacy-gradient activation. The corresponding word node then receives an activation boost equal to a multiple, B, of the relevant primacy gradient activation. This is akin to the activation boost hypothesized in Dell's model, though here the ordering mechanism that determines which word-node should receive this boost has been made explicit. To the extent to which the pick-the-biggest process is subject to noise, there is a potential for order errors at this stage — these are the serial recall errors described in the first parts of this chapter.

After one of the word-layer nodes has received a boost, the activations of the word nodes, w_i, evolve such that

$$\frac{dw_i}{dt} = -Qw_i + t(u_i) + f(t(u_i)).x_i + \text{noise} \tag{4}$$

where Q is a decay parameter (cf. [8][9]), x_i represents, as above, the activation of the ith node in the primacy-gradient layer, L_2, t and f are threshold functions, described below, and u_i is the phoneme-to-word input to the ith word node, given by

$$u_i = \sum_{c_{ji}=1} p_j \tag{5}$$

where p_j indicates the activation of the jth phoneme node and the delimiter on the sum term simply restricts the sum to those phoneme nodes which are connected to the ith word node, that is those for which the connection strength $c_{ji} = 1$. The activations of the phoneme nodes, p_j, change in an almost identical fashion, but without the direct influence from the primacy-gradient activations, such that

$$\frac{dp_j}{dt} = -Qp_j + t(d_j) + \text{noise} \tag{6}$$

where d_j is the input from the word nodes, given by

$$d_j = \sum_{c_{ji}=1} w_i \tag{7}$$

The threshold functions, t and f, play an important rôle in the operation of the output stage. They are defined as

$$t(x) \;\; = \;\; \begin{cases} 0 & \text{if } x < \theta \\ x & \text{otherwise} \end{cases} \tag{8}$$

$$f(x) \;\; = \;\; \begin{cases} 0 & \text{if } x < \theta \\ F & \text{otherwise} \end{cases} \tag{9}$$

$$\tag{10}$$

where F is a constant.

The function t is simply to prevent phoneme-node and word-node activations resulting from activation noise alone from being passed between layers. This is desirable because the the two layers are connected in a positive feedback loop, notwithstanding the decay term which, in general, prevents activation levels from growing without bound. The function f prevents word-layer nodes from activating in response to primacy-gradient activations alone. This assumption is similar to that embodied in the "$\frac{2}{3}$-rule" first adopted by [5], which implements the notion that nodes should not be able to activate in response to "top-down" (priming) support alone. In our formulation, the priming effect of the primacy gradient activations, x_i, is only manifested at word-layer nodes which are simultaneously receiving phonemic support. For simplicity, we have chosen to implement this constraint using a binary threshold function.

The second stage functions as follows. A single word-node receives an activation boost from the first stage. That word node sends activation to the nodes representing its constituent phonemes, which begin to activate. Activation from these phoneme-nodes can project back to any word-nodes to which they are connected. In the event that the item chosen at the first stage was a nonconfusable item, the only word-node which will receive such activation will be that corresponding to the chosen item itself. By contrast, in the event that the item chosen at the first stage was confusable, word-nodes corresponding to the list-items to which it is similar will also receive activation from the phoneme layer. (In fact, in both cases other nonlist items will receive phonemic activation but these will not subsequently benefit from any priming and can therefore be ignored for simplicity.) As stated earlier, word-nodes receiving phoneme-to-word activation, albeit "inadvertently", can benefit from the support afforded by activation in the primacy-gradient layer. All such nodes begin to grow in activation, towards an equilibrium activation which is approximately proportional to the corresponding primacy-gradient activation. The chosen item will be further advanced towards this equilibrium point by virtue of the activation boost it has previously received, and the fact that all its constituent phonemes are active, from the start, at the phoneme layer. At some point, typically before the equilibrium point is reached, a decision is made to output a word. As in Dell's network, this consists of activating the appropriate "word-shape" (e.g. onset-consonant, vowel, coda-consonant) and "filling" this structure by choosing the most activated phoneme (or phoneme cluster) of each type. This process of choice is assumed to be subject to noise. To the extent to which multiple word-nodes corresponding to confusable items are active at the word layer, and their constituent phonemes, including their onset consonants, are thereby activated at the phoneme layer, there is the potential for the incorrect consonant to be selected. Because the word-node activations are approximately proportional to the primacy-gradient activations, potential consonant errors will be distance-related, as required.

In our model, a single word-node is given an activation boost and thereafter word-nodes which are supported from the primacy gradient and the phoneme layer, will begin to *grow* in activation, towards some equilibrium value. To the extent that the final decision to output a word can be delayed, the activations will become larger and the probability of a speech error will decrease. However, such an option will not be helpful in immediate serial recall tasks as any delay in responding will lead to increased decay of the primacy gradient activations.

As described above, we assume that the only word nodes (other than the selected word) that can take advantage of any lexical priming, in this case from the primacy gradient, are those which receive some phoneme-to-word activation. This assumption places our model somewhere between that position taken by Levelt and his colleagues (e.g. [18][20][19]) and that taken by Dell and colleagues (e.g. [6, 7]), on the subject of interaction between the processes of lexical selection and word-form retrieval. In what follows we treat the primacy-gradient layer, L_2, as being equivalent to a lemma-level layer in Levelt's terminology. Like Levelt we assume that a single lemma is selected for forwarding to the word-form retrieval process. In the case where no other activated lemma has a corresponding word-form that shares phonemic content with the word corresponding to the selected lemma, there will be no semantic neighbours activated at the lexeme level, since none will receive phoneme-to-word support. In the case where there is shared phonemic content, however, alternative lexemes, semantically related to the selected word, may activate — we are in agreement with Dell, therefore, in as much as this might be the origin of mixed semantic and phonological errors.

The model, with the output stage described above, was fitted to data from [1]. The model requires additional parameters similar to those proposed in Dell's models. Many of the parameters can be set reasonably arbitrarily and do not need to be varied thereafter. As noted above, the connection strengths between word-nodes and the nodes representing their constituent phonemes are set to 1; the decay parameter Q is set to 2; the threshold θ is set to 0.025; the constants B and F are set to 0.13 and 2.5 respectively; the noise in equations 4 and 6 is zero-mean Gaussian noise with standard deviation 0.1, and the noise in the phoneme selection process is of the same form, with a standard deviation of 0.12. The primacy gradient parameters are exactly the same as before. The omission threshold now acts as a threshold on the process that supplies the activation boost at the second stage: if the activation of the item forwarded

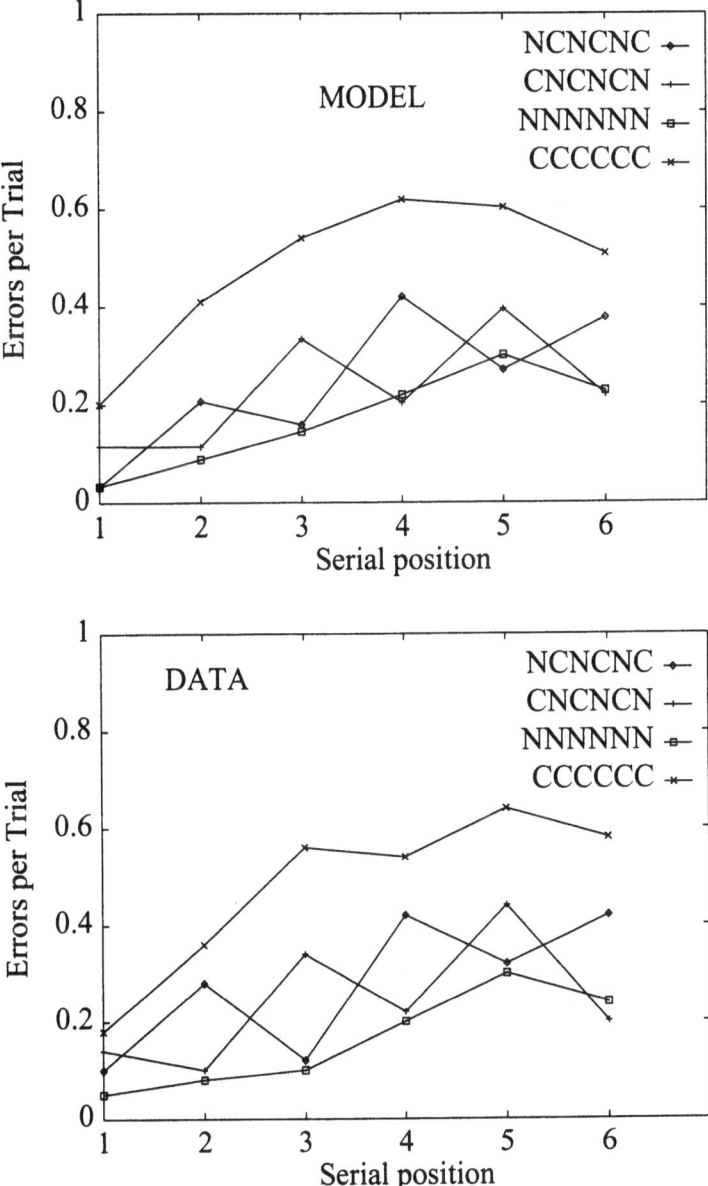

Figure 4: Simulations of four conditions from Baddeley (1968, Exp.V). The data are shown in the lower panel, the results of simulations are shown in the upper panel. The simulation parameters are given in the text. The key indicates stimulus-list composition, where N refers to a nonconfusable item, C refers to a confusable item.

from.the first stage is below this noisy threshold, then no boost is supplied to the second stage, and no phonemes activate sufficiently at the second stage to fill the syllable slots which we assume are still activated (cf. tip-of-the-tongue states).

The results of simulations (1000 pseudotrials) are shown in Figure 4. As is evident, the simulations provide a very good fit to the experimental data, the overall r.m.s. error being 0.048 for Figure 4.

3 Summary

The paper has shown how the primacy model of immediate serial recall can be implemented within a localist connectionist framework. Moreover, we have demonstrated how it is possible to construct a model of the immediate serial recall task that is activation-based, rather than being association-based. We have noted how the highly constraining data found in [1] and [15] can be simulated by postulating a two-stage process and have sought, like others, to identify the second stage with the locus of speech errors in everyday speech, and of blend errors found in the immediate recall of lists of nonwords and, less commonly, in the recall of lists of familiar words. We have suggested a possible implementation of this output stage, and have shown how this provides good fits to the relevant data. Our implementation is necessarily directed towards producing good quantitative fits to the data on the phonological similarity effect — further work is necessary to ensure that our suggested implementation can simultaneously provide a good quantitative fit to data from experiments in which speech errors have been elicited.

Author Notes

We would like to thank Rik Henson and Alan Baddeley for their considerable help in the preparation of the work presented here.

All correspondence and requests for reprints should be sent to the authors at M.R.C. Applied Psychology Unit, 15, Chaucer Rd., Cambridge, CB2 2EF, U.K. (dennis.norris@mrc-apu.cam.ac.uk, mike.page@mrc-apu.cam.ac.uk)

References

[1] Baddeley A. D. How does acoustic similarity influence short-term memory? Quarterly Journal of Experimental Psychology, 1968, 20:249–263.

[2] Baddeley A. D. and Lewis V. When does rapid presentation enhance digit span? Bulletin of the Psychonomic Society, 1984, 22(5):403–405.

[3] Burgess N. A solvable connectionist model of immediate recall of ordered lists. In Tesauro G., Touretzky D., and Keen T. K., editors, Advances in Neural Information Processing Systems, 7, 1995, pages 51–58, Cambridge, MA. MIT Press.

[4] Burgess N. and Hitch G. J. Towards a network model of the articulatory loop. Journal of Memory and Language, 1992, 31:429–460.

[5] Carpenter G. A. and Grossberg S. A massively parallel architecture for a self-organizing neural pattern recognition machine. Computer Vision, Graphics and Image Processing, 1987, 37:54–115.

[6] Dell G. S. and O'Seaghdha P. G. Mediated and convergent lexical priming in language production: A comment on levelt et al. (1991). Psychological Review, 1991, 98(4):604–614.

[7] Dell G. S. and O'Seaghdha P. G. Stages of lexical access in language production. Cognition, 1992, 42(1–3):287–314.

[8] Dell G. S. A spreading-activation theory of retrieval in sentence production. Psychological Review, 1986, 93(3):283–321.

[9] Dell G. S. The retrieval of phonological forms in production: Tests of predictions from a connectionist model. Journal of Memory and Language, 1988, 27:124–142.

[10] Ellis A. Errors in speech and short-term memory: The effects of phonemic similarity and syllable position. Journal of Verbal Learning and Verbal Behaviour, 1980, 19:624–634.

[11] Estes W. K. An associative basis for coding and organization in memory. In Melton A. W. and Martin E., editors, Coding Processes in Human Memory, 1972. V. H. Winston, Washington, D.C.

[12] Grossberg S. A theory of human memory: Self organization and performance of sensory-motor codes, maps and plans. In Roden R. and Snell F., editors, Progress in theoretical biology, 1977. Academic Press, New York.

[13] Grossberg S. Behavioral contrast in short term memory: Serial binary memory models or parallel continuous memory models? Journal of Mathematical Psychology, 1978, 17:199–219.

[14] Henson R. N. A. Short-term memory for serial order. PhD thesis, University of Cambridge, UK, 1996.

[15] Henson R. N. A., Norris D. G., Page M. P. A., and Baddeley A. D. Unchained memory: Error patterns rule out chaining models of immediate serial recall. Quarterly Journal of Experimental Psychology, 1996, 49A:80–115.

[16] Houghton G. The problem of serial order: A neural network memory of sequence learning and recall. In Dale R., Mellish C., and Zock M., editors, Current Research in Natural Language Generation, 1990. Academic Press, London.

[17] Lee C. L. and Estes W. K. Item and order information in short-term memory: Evidence for multilevel perturbation processes. Journal of Experimental Psychology: Human Learning and Memory, 1981, 7:149–169.

[18] Levelt W. J. M. Accessing words in speech production: Stages, processes and representations. Cognition, 1992, 42:1–22.

[19] Levelt W. J. M., Schriefers H., Vorberg D., Meyer A. S., Pechmann T., and Havinga J. Normal and deviant lexical processing: Reply to Dell and O'Seaghdha (1991). Psychological Review, 1991, 98(4):615–618.

[20] Levelt W. J. M., Schriefers H., Vorberg D., Meyer A. S., Pechmann T., and Havinga J. The time course of lexical access in speech production: A study of picture naming. Psychological Review, 1991, 98(4):122–142.

[21] Levelt W. J. M. Speaking: from Intention to Articulation, 1989. MIT Press, Cambridge, MA.

[22] Lewandowsky S. and Murdock Jnr. B. B. Memory for serial order. Psychological Review, 1989, 96:25–57.

[23] Nigrin A. L. Neural Networks for Pattern Recognition, 1993. MIT Press, Cambridge, MA.

[24] Norris D., Page M. P. A., and Baddeley A. D. Serial recall: It's all in the representations, July 1994. Paper presented at the International Conference on Working Memory, Cambridge, UK.

[25] Norris D., Page M. P. A., and Baddeley A. D. Connectionist modelling of short-term memory. Language and Cognitive Processes, 1995, 10:407–409.

[26] Page M. P. A. Modelling Aspects of Music Perception using Self-Organizing Neural Networks. PhD thesis, University of Wales College of Cardiff, Cardiff, UK, November 1993.

[27] Page M. P. A. Modelling the perception of musical sequences with self-organizing neural networks. Connection Science, 1994, 6(2/3):223–246.

[28] Page M. P. A. and Norris D. The primacy model: A new model of immediate serial recall. submitted to Psychological Review, 1995.

[29] Page M. P. A. and Norris D. A localist implementation of the primacy model of immediate serial recall. In Jacobs A. M. and Grainger J., editors, Symbolic Connectionism, 1997. Lawrence Erlbaum Associates, Hillsdale, NJ.

[30] Thurstone L. L. Psychophysical analysis. American Journal of Psychology, 1927, 38:368–389.

Connectionist Symbol Processing with Causal Representations

Roman Pozarlik

Institute for Engineering Cybernetics, Wroclaw University of Technology
Janiszewskiego Str. 11-17, PL 50-372 Wroclaw, Poland
E-mail: rpoz@pwr.wroc.pl

Abstract

In this paper representation in connectionist symbol processing is addressed. There is a putative view that symbol processing requires structural representations and sensitive-to-structure procedures. Here it is proposed that symbolic information processing is based on causal nonstructural representations when computation is massively-parallel. Such representations are formed causally and need not be structural in the sense of constituent symbolic structures. A method of causal representation construction is presented along with a simple example. An implementation of the method in Simple Recurrent Network is shown.

1 Introduction

The processing of symbolic information (henceforth called *symbolic information processing* or SIP) can be defined as a process of symbol handling according to a given set of rules. However, such a definition raises a number of questions. Most important of all, the concept of a set of symbol handling rules needs further specification. A description of rules is created and it is based on structural representations of a symbolic nature. So, using a given information medium, the human uses symbols he understands along with a given order of their notation on the medium to create such a description. So it is obvious that SIP must be understood as processing of symbolic data structures. Specifically, the modelling of a symbol handling process is also described by another symbol handling process (symbolic computation). Alan Turing's works are so significant primarily because he managed, in a brilliant way, to break down the process to as simple a form as possible. In effect, every formally defined process of symbolic computation can be expressed by a sequence of universal Turing machine's computations. However, must SIP have the character of algorithmic computations on structural representations?

Even if there is an alternative to symbolic computations based on structural representations, the symbol handling process can still be described by sensitive-to-structure rules of processing such representations. It is the only reasonable (i.e. feasible on the symbolic level) description, and it must in fact be identified with the level of structural representations. There are, however, situations where such a description cannot fully characterize the process of symbol handling that ensues from this alternative process of computations. Natural language may be one of the examples of such a situation. Humans learn to use the language before they know, and can consciously make use of, the formal rules for sentence construction in this language. We must keep in mind, however, that such rules are developed as a result of attempts to describe the language on symbolic level. We can only conjecture that during learning the language a human develops a description similar to the above-mentioned one. It is difficult to give such a description — no entirely satisfactory results have so far been obtained in this matter because the computation processes which constitute the foundation of language performance resist full formalization on the symbolic level. Therefore we have to consider the rules of symbolic information handling again, and find a possible alternative to the symbolic approach.

Connectionist models are the most obvious alternative to symbolic models, for their construction and operation resemble the human brain. In spite of the clear differences between the connectionist and symbolic models, connectionist symbol processing is not presently deemed to be fundamentally different in its nature from the symbolic computation processes [1, 2]. The connectionist approach is now treated as one of the possible solutions to the symbolic data structure processing problem, due to the ability of connectionist models to acquire holistic rules of processing such structures [3]. This paper presents a different opinion, namely that the nature of symbolic information handling is qualitatively different from the processing based on structural representations. The basis for this opinion is the following theorem: *If the computations are performed in the massively-parallel way, then they are based on nonstructural representations.* Such representations are causally created during a computation course (see also [4]) but it is not necessary for such a causal construction to be based on a process of handling those symbolic data structures. Massively-parallel computations can be implemented using the associative memory mechanism used for these nonstructural representations. Connectionist models seem to be the ideal form of implementation of such a mechanism.

The definition of SIP given at the beginning of this section indicates that the structural approach does not arise from the problem definition itself. This subject will be discussed more thoroughly in section two. We shall also explain informally the concept of a nonstructural representation. Section three is an attempt to formalize the problem of SIP. Next we shall present the idea of causal computations on nonstructural representations. The fourth section discusses a possibility of implementation of the earlier-introduced mechanism of causal computations.

2 Representations

We propose in the idea of causal computations that the fundamental difference between the symbolic and connectionist computations lies in the representations on which the computations are performed. Causal computations are based on nonstructural representations whilst symbolic computations require structural representations. We shall now discuss this distinction in an informal way.

2.1 Structural representations

We can say that symbolic computations are fundamentally characterized by the structurality of data representations together with the sensitive-to-structure procedures for processing the data. Below we try to prove that structurality of representation arises from the serial character of the computations. A model of Turing machine will be used. Our task is to derive the list (B C) from the list (A (B C) D).

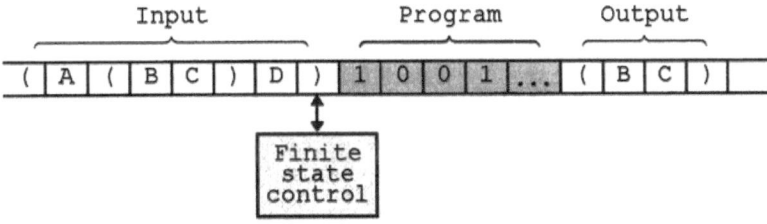

Figure 1. The Turing machine to compute the list (B C) from the list (A (B C) D).

The model has 2 basic elements: a tape divided into the input, output and program segments, and the finite-state control (later called the *finite-control*). The finite control reads and writes symbols on the tape using the read-write head. Our task is to isolate the internal list in the symbol list at the input segment, and to write it at the output segment. The program (a symbol sequence written on the tape) is a solution of the task, and it defines the instruction sequence for the finite control to perform. Computing (B C) from the list (A (B C) D) <u>must</u> be decomposed into a sequence of symbol-read and -write instructions, the result of which is the appropriate modification of the output tape segment. For such computations to be feasible both the data (i.e. the input tape segment) and program must be represented by a sequence of symbols written on the tape in a <u>specific order</u>. Only then will it be possible to formulate an algorithm of transforming the symbol sequence in the input tape segment into the symbol sequence required at the output tape segment. Taking into account the necessary order of symbols on the tape we can speak of the necessary structurality of representation. This requirement ensues from the serial character of computations with the computation sequentiality engaging more than one computation instruction to achieve the result. Making the computations parallel by using many control devices does not remove this requirement. We still have to perform more than one instruction to achieve the result, which implies both the necessity of establishing the order of operation (i.e. the order of performing the instructions) and the structurality of representations the computations are based on. It is only the massively-parallel processing that can change the situation.

2.2 Causal nonstructural representations

Representation structurality is implied by the serial nature of computations, because the representation is used only partially in each computation step. Moreover, it is necessary to establish the order of performing the particular computation steps. It turns out that if the computations are entirely distributed and parallel, then the structurality of representation is not necessary. In such a case the computation can be based on a nonstructural representation.

When we analyse the task to be achieved using the Turing machine model shown in Figure 1 we see that another solution of the task can be proposed. Figure 2 shows two tape segments, the input and output ones, which contain the input and output patterns of a two-layer feed-forward neural network.

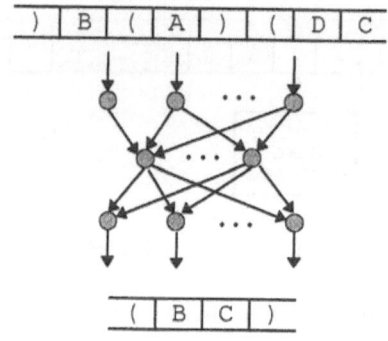

Figure 2. Computations based on the pattern association mechanism.
The input symbol sequence need not constitute any specific order.

The appropriate selection of connection weights in the network enables us to achieve an association between the input and output patterns, the association being the solution to the posed task. The sequence of symbols constituting the input pattern does not have, in this case, to be built according to any particular order. Now the representation structurality is not needed.

Figure 2 shows a solution that is not general in the sense of a program written for a Turing machine. Other instances of that same problem may require a modification of the connection weights. The general solution is possible due to the ability of neural networks to generalize for new data. Such an operation can exactly express the precisely defined rules used to build the examples for network training (although achieving it may be difficult). This operation, however, is a rather regular one, and is not involved by network-interpreted rules having been defined on the symbolic level. This property of computations based on the pattern association allows modelling computations that are difficult to be formally described on the symbolic level. On the other hand, there is no theoretical obstacle for a network similar the one shown in Figure 2 to compute any mapping. In this case the form of representation of the input and output patterns does influence the possibility of achieving the desired mapping. However, it is not necessary that the representations should be identical to those used in Turing machine computations (concatenative structural representations).

The above discussion does not, however, already entitle us to maintain that massively-parallel processing of information is fundamentally different from symbolic computations. To prove that the nonstructural approach (and so the connectionist processing of information) is different, we have to discuss the computation mechanism concerned with the symbol handling process.

3 Symbolic processing

The definition of the causal computation model must be preceded by defining what is understood by the problem of SIP. How can the problem be formulated in a way other than that of processing of symbolic data structures?

To answer this question, the Turing machine should again be addressed and a general description of its operation introduced. At a given time instant the state of the Turing machine is defined by the sequence of symbols written on the tape and by the current state of the finite control. Such a state can therefore be expressed as a sequence $w_1 q w_2$, where w_1 is a sequence of symbols written to the left of the read-write head, w_2 is a sequence of symbols which starts at the read-write head and continues onward in the right-side direction, and q is the current state of the finite control. A state so defined is an instantaneous description of Turing machine computations. We now have to make the assumption that the tape is finite although it can be a very long tape. This assumption practically does not impose any limitations on Turing machine's operation (and it always appears in practice). Computations involved by SIP are described by a given sequence of states; this sequence is concerned with: 1) appropriate modification of the output tape segment and/or 2) reading the input tape segment. The same computation process can be modelled in the nonstructural approach. In this case, the network input is presented with an input vector that represents the state at the current instant, and the network computes an output vector that represents the state at the next instant [5]. When we assume that the network works by pattern association which can correspond to any possible mapping, the representation structurality necessary for the Turing machine operation is no longer necessary. Moreover, is it still necessary to simulate Turing machine operation in such a case?

If the model of parallel computations (i.e. neural network) fulfils the proposed property of being able to acquire (and perform) any possible mapping, the obvious response to the above question is *no*. Even if computations are based on a representation identical to that used for the Turing machine operation, one association is enough to obtain the same result when the input data causally determine this output result. In our discussion we focus on the way the computations are performed, not on the computation speed. The proposed mechanism of parallel computations requires no structural representations and, what follows, no algorithms for processing such representations.

As the causality of computations is the only necessary condition for the above-proposed model to operate, it should not be assumed that SIP is based on symbolic data structure processing. The computations do not even need to be deterministic. The assumption that computations have a structural nature would exclude some of the possible solutions. That's why we think it is useful to give such a definition of the SIP problem for which no assumptions are made regarding the intra-model information processing, and which comprises symbol handling both involved by the conscious application of formally defined rules (e.g. the rules of logic) and handling for which it is only attempted to define such a set of rules (natural language).

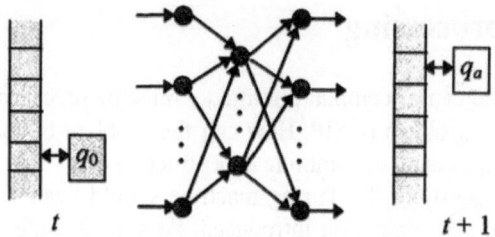

Figure 3. In this model the neural network need not simulate Turing machine's operation to compute the final state.

Let's consider a behaviour of a discrete dynamical system (DDS) that is described by an input vector u_n, an output vector y_n, and a state vector x_n. If the input and output vectors represent symbols, SIP can be defined as the *sequence mapping problem* (SMP). Let the processing domain be the alphabet $\Sigma = \{\sigma_1, \sigma_2, ..., \sigma_M\}$. The definition of SMP can then be the following: *for a given input symbol sequence $\sigma_i\,\sigma_j\,...\,\sigma_k$ an output symbol sequence $\sigma_l\,\sigma_m\,...\,\sigma_n$ should be generated so that the output sequence fulfils the assumed criteria.* The method of defining such criteria need not be exactly specified. In addition, the criteria themselves may not be fully formally definable[1]. The SMP is equivalent to a mapping realized by the DDS: $(\sigma_l\,\sigma_m\,...\,\sigma_n) = h(\sigma_i\,\sigma_j\,...\,\sigma_k)$. Special properties of the mapping (limitations) may ensue from a specified model of computations. However, we do not discuss this problem in this paper.

The main objective of introducing the SMP definition is to distinguish the SIP problem from that of symbolic data structure processing. The premise for the lack of equivalence between the two problems is the above suggested method for obtaining an SMP solution in the massively-parallel computation model. The implications of a possible course of such computations suggest the following form of this solution. First the input symbol sequence is read in successive steps. Then the required output symbol sequence is generated, also in successive steps. Such a solution cannot be obtained using the Turing machine, and it is necessary to apply the distributed massively-parallel processing to achieve it. In this case, algorithmic processing of data structures is not involved in the computations. It would be completely unjustified to postulate for parallel performing of the algorithms (holistic processing of symbolic data structures [3]). Certainly, however, the computation process should be causal — the causality assumption is the base for the idea of causal computation.

---

[1] The requirement to give such a definition for any possible case would lead us to the limitation of SMP to solutions achieved in the symbolic domain only.

3.1 Causal computations

In order to define the model of causal computations it is necessary to analyse sequential behaviour of the DDS. Its operation can be described using the following pair of equations:

$$x_n = f(u_n, x_{n-1}),\qquad(1)$$

$$y_n = g(x_n),\qquad(2)$$

where, as above, u_n is an input vector, y_n is an output vector, and x_n is a state vector. Let's assume that the input and output vectors represent symbols from a finite set $\Sigma = \{\sigma_1, \sigma_2, ..., \sigma_M\}$. Let's also assume that the state vector is an N-dimensional binary vector: $x_n \in \{0, 1\}^N$. From (1) it follows that x_n can be determined if x_0 and the input symbol sequence up till $n \geq 1$ are known. Equation (2) gives the relationship between the output symbol at instant n and the whole sequence of input symbols. Equation (1) is fundamental for the model description given below for it determines the form of the (2) equation. If the model state is determined unequivocally and uniquely for each finite symbol sequence incurred by a given SMP, it is possible to define the (2) equation in a form required for this specific SMP. This requirement determines the course of causal computations[2]. With the nonstructural approach a state vector is represented by a set of parameters called features and denoted as f_i. The finite set of features is denoted as F. To construct the state x_n causally one has to specify how u_n and x_{n-1} determines x_n. Having analysed a possible form of such a construction in the model of massively-parallel computations we propose the following solution [6]

$$x_n = \alpha(u_n) \cup \beta(u_n) \cap [\gamma(x_{n-1}) \cup x_{n-1}].\qquad(3)$$

Equation (3) contains three functions, $\alpha(.)$, $\beta(.)$ and $\gamma(.)$. The functions $\alpha(.)$ and $\beta(.)$ determine how the input influences x_n. $\alpha(.)$ defines the direct influence of u_n on x_n. $\beta(.)$ defines the indirect influence on that state, for it depicts how x_{n-1} influences x_n. It is possible to say that x_n depends on u_n in the context of x_{n-1}. Therefore the features of x_n following from x_{n-1} are called the *context* features. $\beta(.)$ influences the set of context features in x_n, the features having their origin in one of the two mechanism. Namely, they can arise directly from x_n (passive propagation of features) or they can be constituted by the function $\gamma(.)$. As the propagation of features itself is not sufficient for a unique construction of causal representation in the general case, the function $\gamma(.)$ appears in equation (3).

Equation (3) expresses a causal construction of states which participate in the computations. The computations are most often defined by a transition relation,

---

[2] Turing machine computations also fulfil this requirement but this is not the only requirement which determines the course of such computations.

338

which is fulfilled by the $g(.)$ function in this approach[3]. This function is a deterministic version of the relation $g' \subseteq 2^F \times 2^\Sigma$, which is a set of pairs of the form $g_i = (A_i, B_i)$. Such pairs are called *associations* with A_i being the input, and B_i being the output, of the association. The output at instant n is determined by the association that matches x_n best with the matching criterion defined as follows:

$$A_i \subseteq x_n \quad \text{and} \quad \underset{A_k \subseteq x_n}{\forall} |A_i| \geq |A_k|, \tag{4}$$

where $|.|$ denotes power of a set. If no association fulfils equation (4), then the output symbol is undefined. The computation definition has a non-deterministic nature (since many associations can fulfil equation (4)). For the computation process to have the deterministic course, additional criteria to choose the association are needed which originate outside the SMP definition. The associations depend causally on the sequence of computation steps. In this case the computations can be called as sensitive-to-content, not sensitive-to-structure, because the criterion for association choice is the presence/absence of features in a feature set that represents a state. To define computations for a given SMP it is necessary to determine the following: $\alpha(u_n)$ and $\beta(u_n)$ for each $u_n \in \Sigma$, $\gamma(x_{n-1})$ for each possible x_{n-1}, and finally g' for that SMP. All the mappings can be implemented by multi-layer feed-forward neural networks.

For a better explanation of the idea of causal computations, let's use the following illustration of the relation between structural and nonstructural level of computations.

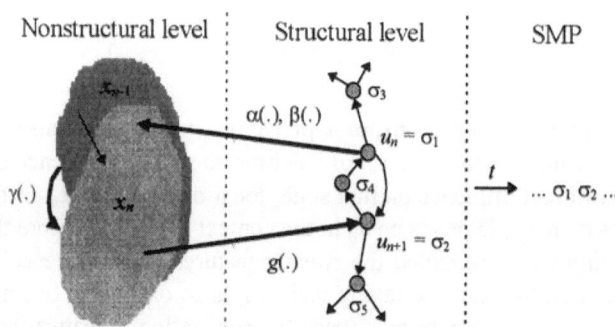

Figure 4. A relation between structural and nonstructural level of computations.

Figure 4 shows the structural computation level as a graph representing the structure of associations between symbols, which results from a given SMP. In the SMP context, moving over this graph is equivalent to sequential reading or generating of

---

[3] Obviously, a state-transition relation can be defined, but as a state always has a symbolic interpretation, it is required to determine the interpretation to determine the state (see [5]).

symbols. Such a process, however, is not feasible without an appropriate algorithm. As a result, the graph is only an illustration of the real problem, i.e. the construction of such an algorithm (the SMP definition does not help us at all to solve the problem). On the nonstructural level, symbols are represented in a distributed manner (the reciprocally overlapping areas in Figure 4), simultaneously by all state variables, and a sequence of the states reflects handling the symbols. The symbolic level and the nonstructural level intertwine in causal computations. First a symbol implies a state in the context of the previous state of computations. Next, the function $g(.)$ determines a prediction of a possible symbol at the next instant. The next state is constructed at the next instant for the symbol, and so on. Symbol reading and generating is an expression of the same process of state sequence construction. The appropriate causal construction of states is a basis for this process.

3.2 Simple example of causal computations

Let's consider an example of how causal computations are performed for a simple task of SMP, i.e. transforming of sentence templates of natural language. In our example three sentence templates (called later templates) for the active voice are to be transformed to the corresponding sentence templates for the passive voice.

Table 1. A list of sentence templates for active and passive voice, separated by '–'.

Active templates:	separator	Passive templates:
⟨ noun verb noun	–	noun be verb by noun ⟩
⟨ det noun verb det noun	–	det noun be verb by det noun ⟩
⟨ det noun verb det adj noun	–	det adj noun be verb by det noun ⟩

The above templates are constructed using the following symbols: *det* for determiner, *adj* for adjective, *noun*, *verb*, *be* for the appropriate verb form of the verb *to be*, and *by* for the preposition. Additionally, the characters '<' and '>' denote the start and end of the whole symbol sequence respectively, whilst the character '–' is a separator between an active voice template and the corresponding passive voice template.

The objective of causal computation model is the task of generation at output of a symbol sequence corresponding to the passive voice template for a template represented by an input symbol sequence. So the task is divided into two stages. At the first stage one of the three sequences of symbols defining an active voice template is read. At the second stage, when the character '–' has been found, the symbol sequence for the appropriate passive voice template is generated.

The alphabet in the above task is the set $\Sigma = \{\langle, \rangle, det, adj, noun, verb, be, by, -\}$. One of the possible definitions of the functions $\alpha(.)$ i $\beta(.)$ is given below:

$$\beta = \{ \; (\langle \, , \{ \} \,),$$
$$(\rangle \,), \{ \} \,),$$
$$(\, det \, , \{ f_9, f_{10}, f_{11}, f_{12} \} \,),$$
$$(\, adj \, , \{ f_9, f_{10} \} \,),$$
$$(\, noun \, , \{ f_8, f_9, f_{10}, f_{11}, f_{12} \} \,),$$
$$(\, verb \, , \{ f_8, f_{11}, f_{22} \} \,),$$
$$(\, be \, , \{ f_8 \} \,),$$
$$(\, by \, , \{ f_8, f_{11} \} \,),$$
$$(\, - \, , \{ f_8, f_{12} \} \,) \; \}.$$

$$\alpha = \{ \; (\langle \, , \{ f_3, f_4, f_8, f_{20} \} \,),$$
$$(\rangle \,), \{ f_{21} \} \,),$$
$$(\, det \, , \{ f_2, f_4, f_{13} \} \,),$$
$$(\, adj \, , \{ f_4, f_{12}, f_{14} \} \,),$$
$$(\, noun \, , \{ f_5, f_6, f_{15} \} \,),$$
$$(\, verb \, , \{ f_1, f_3, f_7, f_9, f_{16} \} \,),$$
$$(\, be \, , \{ f_6, f_{11}, f_{17}, f_{22} \} \,),$$
$$(\, by \, , \{ f_1, f_3, f_{18} \} \,),$$
$$(\, - \, , \{ f_1, f_3, f_{10}, f_{19} \} \,) \; \}.$$

The presented SMP example is not very simple because the sequences of symbols are not constructed very regularly. Although a greater and more regular set of sequences could perhaps have required simpler definitions of the functions, its discussion might have made it more difficult to explain the mechanism of causal computations. Moreover, the example does not necessitate the definition of $\gamma(.)$ $(\gamma(.) = \{ \})$. For $\alpha(.)$ and $\beta(.)$ defined above the definition of the mapping g' is as follows:

$$g' = \{ \; (\, \{ f_7, f_{11}, f_{22} \} \, , \{ \, by \, \} \,), \qquad (\, \{ f_1, f_8 \} \, , \{ \, noun \, \} \,),$$
$$(\, \{ f_2, f_{10}, f_{12} \} \, , \{ \, adj \, \} \,), \qquad (\, \{ f_2, f_9 \} \, , \{ \, noun, adj \, \} \,),$$
$$(\, \{ f_5, f_9 \} \, , \{ \, - \, \} \,), \qquad\qquad (\, \{ f_3 \} \, , \{ \, det \, \} \,),$$
$$(\, \{ f_5, f_{10} \} \, , \{ \, be \, \} \,), \qquad\quad (\, \{ f_4 \} \, , \{ \, noun \, \} \,),$$
$$(\, \{ f_5, f_{11} \} \, , \{ \rangle \} \,) \,), \qquad\quad (\, \{ f_6 \} \, , \{ \, verb \, \} \,) \; \}.$$

Let's consider now the model operation during translation of the sequence *noun verb noun* into the sequence *noun be verb by noun*. Table 2 shows model input, output and state at the successive computation steps.

Table 2. Performance of the model for transforming active to passive templates (# indicates the successive time steps).

#	Inputs	States	Outputs
1	$\langle$	$\{ f_3, f_4, \mathbf{f_8}, f_{20} \}$	$\{ \, det, noun \, \}$
2	*noun*	$\{ f_5, f_6, \mathbf{f_8}, f_{15} \}$	*verb*
3	*verb*	$\{ f_1, f_3, f_7, \mathbf{f_8}, f_9, f_{16} \}$	*noun*
4	*noun*	$\{ f_5, f_6, \mathbf{f_8}, f_9, f_{15} \}$	$-$
5	$-$	$\{ f_1, f_3, \mathbf{f_8}, f_{10}, f_{19} \}$	*noun*
6	*noun*	$\{ f_5, f_6, \mathbf{f_8}, \mathbf{f_{10}}, f_{15} \}$	*be*
7	*be*	$\{ f_6, \mathbf{f_8}, \mathbf{f_{11}}, f_{17}, f_{22} \}$	*verb*
8	*verb*	$\{ f_1, f_3, f_7, \mathbf{f_8}, f_9, \mathbf{f_{11}}, f_{16}, \mathbf{f_{22}} \}$	*by*
9	*by*	$\{ f_1, f_3, \mathbf{f_8}, \mathbf{f_{11}}, f_{18} \}$	*noun*
10	*noun*	$\{ f_5, f_6, \mathbf{f_8}, \mathbf{f_{11}}, f_{15} \}$	$\rangle$
11	$\rangle$	$\{ f_{21} \}$	$\{ \}$

Features written in boldface in Table 2 ensue from the context in which a given state is formed. At instant $n = 1$ the symbol '$<$' is read and state $x_1 = \{f_3, f_4, f_8, f_{20}\}$ formed which represents the symbol just read according to the $\alpha(.)$ function definition (we assume that $x_0 = \{\}$). Based on this state the model performs the prediction of a possible input symbol at instant $n = 2$. From the definition of the g' mapping and equation (4) it follows that the next input symbol can be either *det* or *noun*. As *noun* turns out to be the next input symbol, the state $x_2 = \{f_5, f_6, f_8, f_{15}\}$ is formed. The process repeats until the character '-' is read which distinguishes the reading stage from the response generation stage. From this time on the symbols generated at output become also the input symbols for the next computation step. The generated output symbol sequence is causally determined by the representation of state $x_5 = \{f_1, f_3, f_8, f_{19}\}$ which depends on the symbol sequence that has been read.

4 Causal neurocomputing

The proposed mechanism for causal computations is not based on any specific neural network model. Neural networks are the most natural, though perhaps not the only possible implementation for this mechanism of computations.

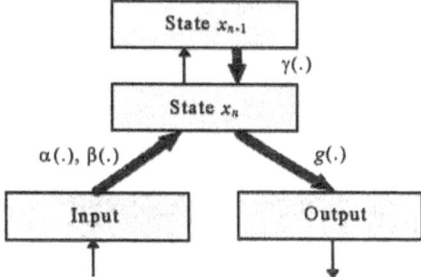

Figure 5. An interpretation of SRN in terms of causal computations.

Figure 5 shows the SRN network [7], drawn so as to emphasize that the feedback loop plays the fundamental role in causal construction of network states. Bold arrows represent the modifiable connections. When we compare Figure 4 and Figure 5 we will see the role of particular connection layers for modelling the particular elements of the mechanism of causal computations. Based on the representation constituted by the $\alpha(.)$, $\beta(.)$ and $\gamma(.)$ functions and by the g' mapping one can design a network of the above mentioned kind [6]. In this case the PCA diagrams show vector representations for the network's hidden layer which are very similar to the representations obtained as a result of the network training [7]. In some cases, such as our example, the network construction gets simplified if $\gamma(.) = \{\}$ (the feedback connections need not be modifiable).

5 Conclusions

This paper presents a causal computation model offering a solution to the SMP problem which is a formal way of expressing the SIP problem but is, at the same time, more general than the problem of symbolic data structure processing. This distinction is essential in the proposed model of computations on causal representations. Both the distributed form of these representations and the massively-parallel nature of processing them make causal computation model the base for construction of connectionist models of SIP.

The presented model of causal computations is based on an analysis of a computation course if massively-parallel information processing is possible to be achieved through the pattern association mechanism. We have emphasised the solution to the problem of reconciling the global sequentiality of the model's behaviour with the massively-parallel course of computations. We have solved the problem using nonstructural causal representations for which no computation algorithmization is required. The solution has fundamental importance even if the nonstructural level were formally equivalent to symbolic computations (which cannot be assumed when we take into account possible complexity of a DDS's operation).

The idea of a nonstructural level of computations can also be developed from a wider perspective as a solution to a problem of computing a response to a stimulus in time that is short enough for the model of computations to survive [8]. Such an approach involves many possible processing levels between the structural and entirely nonstructural level of computations.

References

1. Honavar V. Symbolic artificial intelligence and numeric artificial neural networks: towards a resolution of the dichotomy. In Sun R, Bookman LA. (Eds.) Computational architectures integrating neural and symbolic processes. Kluwer Academic Publisher 1995; 351-388
2. Special issue on connectionist symbol processing. Artificial Intelligence 1990; 46(1-2)
3. Chrisman L. Learning Recursive Distributed Representations for Holistic Computation. Connection Science 1991; 3(4):345-366
4. Butler K. Towards a Connectionist Cognitive Architecture. Mind & Language 1991; 6(3):252-272
5. Pozarlik R. An unstructured representation for subsymbolic computation. Proc. of the Third World Congress of Neural Networks. Lawrence Erlbaum Associates, Hillsdale NJ 1995; 2:309-312
6. Pozarlik R. An unstructural approach to natural language processing in neural networks. Tech. Rep. ICT-48-95, Doctoral dissertation, Institute of Engineering Cybernetics, Wroclaw University of Technology, 1995
7. Elman JL. Distributed Representations, Simple Recurrent Networks, and Grammatical Structure. Machine Learning 1991; 7:195-225
8. Langloh N, Cottam R, Vounckx R, Cornelis J. Towards distributed statistical processing - aquarium: a query and reflection interaction using magic: mathematical algorithms generating interdependent confidences. In Smith S, Neale RF. (Eds.) ESPRIT Basic Research Series, Optical Information Technology, Springer-Verlag, Berlin 1993; 303-319

Author Index